A WORLD HISTORY OF ANCIENT
POLITICAL THOUGHT

A World History of Ancient Political Thought

Antony Black

OXFORD
UNIVERSITY PRESS

OXFORD
UNIVERSITY PRESS

Great Clarendon Street, Oxford OX2 6DP

Oxford University Press is a department of the University of Oxford.
It furthers the University's objective of excellence in research, scholarship,
and education by publishing worldwide in

Oxford New York

Auckland Cape Town Dar es Salaam Hong Kong Karachi
Kuala Lumpur Madrid Melbourne Mexico City Nairobi
New Delhi Shanghai Taipei Toronto

With offices in

Argentina Austria Brazil Chile Czech Republic France Greece
Guatemala Hungary Italy Japan Poland Portugal Singapore
South Korea Switzerland Thailand Turkey Ukraine Vietnam

Oxford is a registered trade mark of Oxford University Press
in the UK and in certain other countries

Published in the United States
by Oxford University Press Inc., New York

© Antony Black 2009

British Library Cataloguing in Publication Data

Data available

Library of Congress Cataloging in Publication Data

Library of Congress Control Number: 2009921238

Typeset by SPI Publisher Services, Pondicherry, India
Printed in Great Britain
on acid-free paper by
the MPG Books Group

ISBN 978-0-19-928169-5

1 3 5 7 9 10 8 6 4 2

To
The Venerable Gelong Karma Jiga
teacher of meditation

Preface and Acknowledgements

Few things are as unexpected as the past. There were astonishing intellectual achievements in the ancient world. Ancient thinkers speak to us even now, and we can learn from what has been said in many cultures. All the political ideas of the modern world had their origins in the ancient world.

The poet Rilke said, 'Is it possible that the whole of world history has been misunderstood? Yes, it is possible'. The argument of this book is that this is indeed true for the world history of ancient political thought; and that, to understand it, we need to look at all the phenomena side by side, in Egypt, Mesopotamia, Iran, Israel, India, China, Greece, Rome, and early Christianity. For some reason this has not previously been done.

This book begins with the earliest written records, which were in third-millenium Egypt, and it ends with the decline of the first imperial dynasty in China, and of the Roman empire in the West. By this time, the political development and intellectual creativity of the last millenium BCE[1] had everywhere run their course.

Humans started together, and today we all interact with one another in a single global society, whether we like it or not. Between these two points lie very diverse histories. Nowadays it is not nations or faiths, but humanity that is in need of a story. A complete world history of political thought, coming up to our own period of 'globalization', including the spread of liberal, socialist, and democratic ideas to the Middle East, China, and India, is urgently needed.[2]

I have been conscious while writing this book that we will probably not be around for much longer. No words can express this; alas, none will be needed. As if that were not enough, two rich religious hooligans have tried to take the world to war in the name of false faiths. Where nowadays is the compassion of Islam, where is the humanism of the West? But one still feels that justice must be done, especially to the dead, of whom one will soon be one. It is worthwhile to try to remind ourselves of the only political value capable of saving us: the priority of the common over the private good. Our remoter ancestors seem to have had a greater awareness of this than we have, and they lasted a lot longer than we probably will.

---

[1] Hereafter all dates are BCE unless stated.

[2] See Nederman and Shogimen (2009). The *Cambridge History of Twentieth-Century Political Thought*, ed. T. Ball and R. Bellamy (Cambridge: Cambridge University Press, 2003), does not provide this.

This work would have been unthinkable without significant help from scholars in different fields. I am deeply grateful to Kevin Laland for putting me on the right path in prehistory; to Julian Reade for helping me with Egypt and Mesopotamia; to Nathan Macdonald for guidance on Israel; to Anthony Parel for helping me with India; to Christopher Smith for many suggestions on Rome. I would like above all to thank Yuri Pines for the care with which he set me right about China. He was generous enough to show me his 2009 book a while before it was published. Without him, I could not have dealt at all adequately with this most difficult topic. I am also grateful to Ron Terchek, Lisa Raphals, Melissa Lane, Jill Harries, and Stefan Manz for their suggestions. None of these scholars are responsible for the many errors that remain.

Brian Baxter, head of the Politics Programme in the Faculty of Humanities at the University of Dundee, has been unfailingly supportive. Susan Malloch has helped me with secretarial and technical matters. The inter-library loans staff of the Dundee University Library have been unfailingly efficient. The Nuffield Foundation awarded me two small grants which enabled me to travel to various libraries in Britain. The university libraries of St Andrews and Cambridge have been courteous and helpful. I am grateful to Oxford University Press, in particular Dominic Byatt, the Politics editor, and to Jeff New, the copy-editor, for their support and approach.

It is difficult to know where to begin acknowledging more personal help on a work which I have been at for so long, and one which I intend to be my last book of this kind. I was taught at the Craig School, Windermere, under Edward Hewetson, a rare man. I was taught at Shrewsbury by two outstanding geniuses in their profession: Jimmy Street, who made me love Greek and Latin poetry; and Anthony Chevenix-Trench, who introduced me to Aeschylus (whose words have strengthened me in some terrible moments).

On a more intimate level, I owe to my mother's parents, Joseph and Mary Wood, the haven of my childhood. I am indebted to Tony, Jack, Steve, Neil, David, and Graham for inspiring weekly symposia. My children Steve, Tommy and his wife Emma and my grandsons Oisin and Fergus, Esther, Matthew and his partner Tessa, and Christopher are in my thoughts every day. My greatest debt is to my wife, Aileen, without whom all my work would be as dust.

This book is dedicated to the one who set up Rokpa ('helping where help is needed') in Dundee in 1997, and taught me and many others the Buddhist tradition of meditation.

Contents

Abbreviations   xii

Time Chart   xiii

Introduction   1

1. Early Communities and States   6
   Human groups   6
   Social behaviour and intelligence   7
   Small groups and reciprocal altruism   8
   Symbolic systems   9
   Democracy?   11
   Tribes   11
   Hierarchy and ownership   12
   Them and us   14
   Sacred monarchy   15

2. Egypt   22
   Morality: justice   25
   Equality   28
   Individuals   29
   Spin   29
   Conclusion   30

3. Mesopotamia, Assyria, Babylon   33
   The functions of monarchy   38
   Justice   40
   City assemblies   42

4. Iran   47

5. Israel   50
   The covenant   52
   The people of Israel   55
   Nation   56
   The elders and the people   57
   Monarchy   60
   The Messiah   63

 6. India   69
    Castes   72
    Kingship   74
    Morality and pragmatism   79
    Kautilya's Arthashastra: *approach and method*   80
    Kautilya on political economy and foreign policy   82
    Buddhism   84

 7. China   92
    The Mandate and the people   95
    Status and meritocracy: 'advance the worthy'   100
    Public service   102
    Confucius on li *(ritual conduct) and* ren *(humaneness)*   103
    Persuasion, not coercion   105
    Mozi   107
    The origins of the state   108
    Shang Yang and Han Feizi: coercion and Realpolitik   110
    A new kind of monarchy: the Laozi *and Han Feizi*   115
    The First Emperor   120
    Han Confucianism   122
    Conclusion   125

 8. The Greeks   130
    The polis   130
    Athens and demokratia   138
    Plato   148
    Aristotle   158
    Conclusions   168

 9. Rome   175
    Cicero and the Roman republic   175
    Stoicism and the principate   191
    Power and philosophy in Rome and China   197

10. Graeco-Roman Humanism   203
    Globalization   205
    Pax romana   205
    Cosmopolis   207
    Natural law   210

11. The Kingdom of Heaven and the Church of Christ   215
    After Jesus   219
    How do we know?   220
    Ritual   222

The church 222

The state 224

12. Themes: Similarities and Differences Between Cultures 227

Sacred monarchy 227

The state 228

Justice 229

The origins of kingship 230

The people 231

Social categories 232

Genres 233

Theory and practice; ethics and expediency 234

13. General Conclusion 237

Bibliography 240

Index 255

Abbreviations

Full references to books listed below will be found in the Bibliography.

ANE	Pritchard, *Ancient Near Eastern Texts Relating to the Old Testament*
B&B	Confucius, *The Original Analects*, trans. Brooks and Brooks
CA	Confucius, *The Analects* (or *Sayings*)
CAH	*Cambridge Ancient History*
CCRR	*The Cambridge Companion to the Roman Republic*
CHAC	*The Cambridge History of Ancient China*
CHC	*The Cambridge History of China*
CGR	*The Cambridge History of Greek and Roman Political Thought*
CHI	*The Cambridge History of Iran*
CHMPT	*The Cambridge History of Medieval Political Thought*
CHP	*The Cambridge History of Hellenistic Philosophy*
EB	Ernest Barker, *From Alexander to Constantine*
ECF	*The Early Christian Fathers*
ECW	*Early Christian Writings*
EG	*Early Greek Political Thought*
EI	*Encyclopaedia of Islam*
HCPT	Kung-chuan Hsiao, *A History of Chinese Political Thought*
HPT	Coleman, *A History of Political Thought*
KA	*The Kautiliya Arthashastra*
KR	Kulke and Rothermund, *History of India*
KRS	Kirk, Raven, and Schofield, *The Presocratic Philosophers*
Lichtheim	Lichtheim, *Ancient Egyptian Literature*
NE	Stevenson, *A New Eusebius*
OCCL	*The Oxford Companion to Classical Literature*
OHAE	*The Oxford History of Ancient Egypt*
OHG	*The Oxford History of Greece and the Hellenistic World*
OHR	*The Oxford History of the Roman World*
ST	*Sources of Chinese Tradition*
VAE	Parkinson, *Voices from Ancient Egypt*

Time Chart

	Egypt	Mesopotamia	Israel	India	China	Greece
Before 2000	Old Kingdom, 2686*–2125* Middle Kingdom, 2055*–1650* Instructions of Ptahhotep; autobiographies; Instructions to Merikare	First dynasties of Sumer, 2450**–2200** Akkad, 2200**–2059**				
2000–1000	New Kingdom, 1550*–1069* Amenhotep IV (Amarna), 1352*–1336*	Old Babylonia, 1798*–1499* Hammurabi, 1792–50* Assyria, 1750*–612	Israelites in Canaan, 1300/1200** Joshua and Judges, 1200**–1025** Kingdom of Israel, 1025*–950*	Early *Rig Veda*, 1300**	Shang dynasty, 1600**–1046 Zhou dynasty, 1046–771	
1000–700			First biblical texts, 1000/900** Division into Northern and Southern Kingdoms, 930* First prophetic texts, 800/700* Israel conquered by Assyria, 722	*Mahabharata*, 800**–200 CE**	Spring and Autumn period, 771–453	Homer and Hesiod, 750–700*

Note: Dates marked ** are very imprecise; dates marked * are fairly imprecise.

B. From *c.* 700 to *c.* 200 BCE

	Iran	Israel	India	China	Greece	Rome
700–500	New Babylonia, 626–539 Cyrus (r. 559*–530) founds Achaemenid empire, captures Babylon, 539	Deuteronomist texts, 622* Reforms of Josiah, 621* Exile in Babylon, 587–538 Biblical texts composed or edited, 550*–450*	Buddha active, 550**–500**	Confucius, 551*–479*	Solon's reforms at Athens, 594 Thales, first Greek scientist, active 585 Cleisthenes' reforms, 508	Republic founded, 509*
500–400				Mozi, 460*–390* Warring States period, 453–221	Ionian poleis revolt against Persia, 499 Persians defeated, 490, 480–79 *Dēmokratia* at Athens, 461–338 Aeschylus' *Oresteia*, 458 War between Athens and Sparta, 431–404 Execution of Socrates, 399 Philip of Macedon conquers Greek poleis, 338 Alexander (336–323) conquers Persia	'Struggle of the orders', 494*–440*

400–200	Ashoka king of India, 268–233	Shang Yang's reforms in Qin, 356–48 Mengzi, 379*–304*	Plato founds Academy, 387; Aristotle founds Lyceum, 335 Zeno founds Stoic school, 310	Defeat of Carthage, 202
		Daodejing, 350*–250* Xunzi, 310*–218* Han Feizi, 280*–233 Unification, 221		

C. c. 200 BCE to c. 200 CE

	Israel	India	China	Rome	Christianity
200–100	Last prophetic texts	*Kautilya's Arthashatra*, from 200 BCE* *Laws of Manu*, 200 BCE*–200 CE	Han dynasty, 209 BCE–220 CE	Defeats Greek states, 196–148 Polybius at Rome, 167–118* T. Gracchus tribune, 133 Marius consul six times, 107–100	
100–0				Cicero active, 81–43 Disintegration of republic, 60–49 Caesar dictator, 47–44 Augustus princeps, 31 BCE–14 CE	
0–200 CE	Defeat of Jewish revolts, 66–73, 132–5			Epictetus teaches, 97*–140 CE Marcus Aurelius' *Meditations*, 174–80 CE Toleration of Christianity, 312 CE	Death of Jesus, 33 CE** First New Testament texts, 50 CE* Nero's persecution, 64 CE Letter of Clement, Bishop of Rome, 93 CE Cyprian martyred, 258 CE

Introduction

Why a world history of ancient political thought? People study history either out of curiosity, or to acquire a better understanding of themselves, their society, or even their species. I suggest that we cannot achieve these latter objectives by looking at one culture alone. People study the history of ideas partly to find out how and why we today have come to think as we do. Human society is constantly being remade; it is not a matter of a generation or two. It comes to us from the past, much of it from the remote past. This study has led me to the conclusion that virtually all the political ideas we hold today originated in the ancient world.

Today all societies interact and affect one another. It is, therefore, necessary to understand how other societies function, and how the people in them think, by looking at the different cultures into which humankind has been thrust, and divided, in the course of history.

Comparative political thought and a comparative history of political thought are, furthermore, necessary for sensible decision-making in the world today. The findings which historians and philosophers arrive at are now more than ever relevant to policy-makers. We need informed knowledge of where different ways of thinking are coming from. The present tendency to focus on Europe or the West, in teaching as well as research, is a barrier to mutual understanding between different cultures. It privileges one tradition above all the rest.

I have also to confess that one reason why I have studied political thought in different ancient cultures is that I find it intrinsically fascinating. It is a privilege to be in contact with great minds through their writings. We should seek out ancient understandings from all civilizations for their own sake.

Sociology has long been inter-cultural. World history is at last coming into its own.[1] But in the history of ideas, globalization still has some way to go. While histories of Western political thought, usually starting with the ancient Greeks, abound, there are few histories of political thought in other civilizations. And there is none of the ancient world taken as a whole. This is astounding, when one considers that the period covered in this book was the most eventful in the whole history of political thought: it was then that political philosophy was invented (independently) in China and Greece; political science was invented in Greece; statecraft in China and India. Democracy and liberty (as every schoolboy or -girl perhaps knows) began in ancient Greece. Israel led directly to Judaism, indirectly to Christianity and Islam.

This present imbalance in scholarship is all the more surprising in an age of globalization, mass migration, and disputes about multiculturalism. Today, perhaps more than ever before, men and women from different cultures live in the same neighbourhoods. Some non-Western cultures have revived, both among thinkers and among whole populations. Non-Western political cultures play a major role in regional politics in Muslim-majority countries, in South-East Asia, India, China, and Japan (to mention a few): in approximately three-quarters of the world's population, in other words.

Understanding different traditions of thought is thus necessary for civic and international harmony. This has always been so, but today it is a more obvious and pressing need than ever before. In order for people of different philosophical and religious backgrounds to understand one another and to live peacefully together, there has to be dialogue.[2] Heraclitus said that: 'Reason is common to all but most people live as if each had their own private understanding'. There have been dialogues between cultures in the past, and ideas have been transmitted from one culture to another. Moreover, apparently lost pasts have been rediscovered. We can learn from one another; even, I would venture to say, the West can learn from other cultures.[3]

In international policy a too West-centred approach has already had appalling results. Worldwide enquiry will help to unearth the modes of thought which often underlie global conflicts; in which bands of men undertake to fight to the death (probably someone else's) on behalf of interests or creeds which their adversary may not understand, may not care about, and may despise. One hopes that this study will promote mutual understanding and increased harmony. (This is of course rather optimistic.)

Many have doubted whether we can learn from thinkers in other cultures, or from thinkers in the remote past even in our own culture. I would suggest that, if men and women of different races and cultures can fall in love, if we share enough human experience to be able to appreciate the art and poetry of other peoples, then there is no reason to presuppose that we cannot understand their philosophies of state and society. We should at least try. If we can empathize with Homer, we can empathize with Confucius.

We can, similarly, learn from thinkers of the remote past, despite the fact that our material circumstances and the means of communication have changed in so many ways. Quentin Skinner is right to remind us that what has been said in the past cannot mean the same to us as it did then.[4] But one must not exaggerate historical relativity. People of all epochs and all cultures love, fight, and compete. Early thinkers encapsulate millenia of pre-literate thought. What they have to say has been highly selected out over generations of human experience and communication.

We may, for example, learn new ways of viewing the relationship between the individual and the community, how to balance the private and the public good, and the duties of the present to future generations. If intellectual history teaches one thing, it is that views about social relationships and the state, as well as views about the universe, change considerably from one time and place to another. It is possible that they will change again. The study of radically different ideas from other times and places opens up the mind. That anyone ever believed that the problems of political philosophy had been solved[5] reveals the capacity of faith to triumph over history.

We can learn both from what they said, and from the spirit in which they said it, the courage with which they confronted their crises. One example is the different ways in which ancient thinkers tried to come to terms with the problem of large-scale political power. Every generation makes some contribution to the understanding of human relationships. Our own generation is no more intelligent than previous ones; it is tragic to lose their insights.[6] (Biological evolution seems sometimes more economical than cultural evolution.) As T. S. Eliot put it: 'How much wisdom have we lost with knowledge?'

Lastly, one can only fully understand and appreciate Western political thought itself by comparing it with other traditions. Otherwise, how can one know what its distinctive features are? Other societies are the nearest thing a historian has to a repeatable experiment. One indispensable way of explaining sequences of phenomena is by comparing them with other sequences. Max Weber (1864–1920) perceived more clearly than anyone, before or since, the role of comparison in historical explanation. He formulated a method for comparing (among other things) the political ideas of different cultures from all over the world. His comparative method has been enormously influential in the history and sociology of ideas.[7] But no one since has attempted an enquiry on the same scale. Worldwide comparison is forbidding; it requires mastery of different languages and specialisms. Institutional and career pressures discourage scholars from working outside their own 'field', especially today when scholarship is so routinized.[8]

I have presented the political thought of each civilization separately and in chronological sequence. I start with pre-history (Chapter 1). Next, I examine the earliest literate civilizations of Egypt (Chapter 2) and Mesopotamia (Chapter 3); then, the adjacent cultures of Iran (Chapter 4) and Israel (Chapter 5); then India (Chapter 6) and China (Chapter 7). Only then do

I come to Greece (Chapter 8), Rome (Chapter 9), and early Christianity (Chapter 11). All of these civilizations left records of what people thought about social relationships and the state, about the purpose and scope of political authority, about social justice, rights, and duties. I conclude by considering the similarities and differences between their ideas (Chapter 12). For example, ethics and expediency, right and might, were related to one another in a variety of ways.

I could have planned this book to be primarily comparative throughout,[9] rather than first treating each civilization separately. But this would have meant wrenching ideas out of their cultural contexts. The overall character of each culture would have been obscured, the voices of individuals muted.

'Political thought' is used here to embrace political philosophy and ethics, constitutional theory, and political culture. In using modern Western terms to describe what people in other cultures were talking about, I have tried to indicate what exactly it was that 'monarchy', 'law', 'the state', 'the people', and so on meant in their different contexts.[10]

Our sources include philosophical and religious texts, codes of law, epic poetry, inscriptions, royal proclamations, and so on. One can infer much of what people believed from institutions and the way they were run, the behaviour of rulers, and the relics of popular culture. Power then as now was justified, guided, and sanctified by ideology, spin, and myth.

NOTES

1. See e.g. Felipe Fernandez-Armesto, *Civilization* (New York: Free Press, 2001). There is a *Journal of World History*.
2. Fred R. Dallmayr, *Alternative Visions: Paths in the Global Village* (Lanham, Md.: Rowman and Littlefield, 1998).
3. See Antony Black, 'Towards a Global History of Political Thought', in Nederman and Shogimen (2009: 25–42.)
4. Quentin Skinner, 'Meaning and Understanding in the History of Ideas', *History and Theory*, 8 (1969), 3–53.
5. Francis Fukuyama, *The End of History and the Last Man* (London: Penguin, 1992). Consider also Daniel Bell, *The End of Ideology and the Exhaustion of Political Ideas in the Fifties*, 2nd edn. (New York: Free Press, 1965).
6. Consider, on the other hand, Geertz: 'The essential vocation of interpretive anthropology is not to answer our deepest questions, but to make available to us answers that others, guarding other sheep in other valleys, have given, and thus to include them in the consultable record of what man has said' (1973: 30).

7. See Michael Mann, *The Sources of Social Power*, vol. 1: *A History of Power from the Beginning to A.D. 1760* (Cambridge: Cambridge University Press, 1986).

8. 'Social and institutional resistance...results at the present time in the great isolation of each worker, in the great difficulty of communication and agreement among them...The major obstacles do not lie in the object of study but in the subjects who study it' (Dumont 1975: 170).

9. I adopted a comparative approach in dealing with Western, Islamic, and Byzantine political thought in the medieval and early modern periods in *The West and Islam: Religion and Political Thought in World History* (Oxford: Oxford University Press, 2008).

10. Dumont has suggested that we should draw elements of 'a comparative language' from every civilization: 'in the present state of knowledge, each civilization... should deliver some conclusions of general use, should, that is, provide some elements of a comparative language' (1975: 159). See Antony Black,'Decolonization of Concepts', *Journal of Early Modern History: Contacts, Comparisons, Contrasts*, 1 (1997), 55–69.

1

Early Communities and States

It is impossible to know when social reflection, criticism, and idealism began. But it seems that humans possessed codes of behaviour and social values from the very start. In order to investigate the beginnings of political thought, therefore, we have to take some account of prehistory. We need to look at human groups before there were states. This is an essential introduction to a study of ancient political thought. It will indicate the background to the first written records of political thought, and where the first political thinkers were coming from.

HUMAN GROUPS

Archaeology can tell us something about the structures and behaviour patterns of early societies (Hodder 1982; Braithwaite 1984). We may compare this with what anthropologists have discovered about the structures and ideas of tribal societies today. Moreover, great advances have been made in social biology over the last fifty years. If some 'sociobiologists' have been too quick to identify parallels and continuities between animal, hominid, and human behaviour, many of those in the social and human sciences have, out of prejudice or ignorance, unreasonably rejected them. (Aristotle observed that all human conduct involves 'nature, custom, and mind (*phusis, ethos, logos*)'; *Politics* 1332a40.) Eating and excreting require forethought. How we think is patterned by how we live.

When humans first left archaeological traces of their social organization, let alone of their ideas, they had already passed through many thousands of generations.[1] Considering the changes in political life and outlook which have occurred over the 5,000 years (approximately 130 generations) of recorded history, and which nowadays take place within two or three generations, one can only wonder how many fundamental changes occurred before records began. Here social biology may throw a glimmer of light.

The way social behaviour has evolved may, first, influence political thought and practice due to *continuities* between strategies evolved by natural selection and strategies found later in human societies. It may also, secondly, do so due to *predispositions* among humans for thinking and behaving in certain ways. In other words, some cultural phenomena may have their roots in social biology: we may be psychologically predisposed, through biological evolution, to find certain relationships, social patterns, and types of leadership satisfying or difficult because of what happened to our remote ancestors long ago. For example, both kinship and personal acquaintance remain dominant factors in all human life. Most moral systems take account of these. We know only too well how much they affect politics today. None of this means, of course, that what we like is necessarily either good or useful today; nor that what we dislike is necessarily wrong or harmful.

Thirdly, humans have *modified* patterns which developed through natural selection, for example the regulation of sex by social customs, or the functions ascribed to the old because of their experience. In modern tribal societies, elders often play a critical role in settling disputes.[2] Humans may, fourthly, *accentuate* factors rooted in biological predispositions, for example by specifying and enforcing rules about ownership and about the inheritance of status, wealth, and power. On the other hand, hunter-gatherer societies may have bequeathed a contrary predisposition to equality among males, which may find expression in, for example, Islam, anarchy, or communism.

SOCIAL BEHAVIOUR AND INTELLIGENCE

'In primates intelligence has evolved as an adaptation to life in societies.'[3] Brains evolved side by side with social relationships and their subtleties; not surprisingly, we seem to value social relationships more highly than anything else. But what differentiates humans from other species is the development of culture. This is made possible by, and is dependent upon, language.[4] Significant modifications in behaviour were made possible by the brain and mouth capable of speech—the final products of human biological evolution. The ability to use language is one undisputed human universal,[5] and it is a faculty in which women and men are more or less equal. 'Talking rather than grooming' enabled early humans to interact on a very much wider scale.[6]

Human minds were capable of engineering some of their own adaptations for survival. Learning increasingly replaced natural selection as a way of benefiting from experiences without having lived (or died) through them. Hence, variations in behaviour, culture, and thought emerged within the single human species. 'Human nature consists not of some one fixed pattern of behaviour, but of the capacity to develop a variety of different patterns of behaviours in different circumstances' (Smith 1975: 312). This interdependence of brains, life in society, and culture may also help explain why most of us humans set so much store by our own social system, its norms, and myths.

SMALL GROUPS AND RECIPROCAL ALTRUISM

Early humans lived in small groups of between twenty and 100 persons; today among Yanomamo Indians, 'communities range in size from about 40 individuals to about 300', usually fissioning when they reach 125–150.[7] In both early human groups and today, 'the composition of local groups... is heavily dominated by related individuals' (Chagnon 1982: 292); all or most are kin. According to the theory of inclusive fitness, or kin selection, 'natural selection favors not the individual that maximizes her reproductive success but the individual that maximizes her personal reproductive success plus effects on relatives, devalued by the appropriate degree of relatedness' (Trivers 1985: 65, summarizing Hamilton). The 'selfish gene' syndrome means that in such groups people are prepared to look after one another and sacrifice themselves for the group; for in that way they will be increasing the spread of genes which they share with others in that group.[8]

Small groups have been around long enough to have influenced human behaviour-patterns and mindsets through natural selection. Reciprocal altruism appears to be one case of this. It has evolved among several species as the most effective means of maximizing benefits for members of a group within which there is continuous interaction, and therefore a likelihood of occasions for ongoing reciprocity.[9] It resembles 'tit-for-tat', which game theorists have identified as the most robust strategy: 'never be the first to defect; retaliate only after the partner has defected; be forgiving after just one act of retaliation' (Axelrod 1981). Among chimpanzees, the 'tremendous need for reconciliation with their opponents probably reflects the importance of alliances, since each individual is both friend and foe, depending on context' (Trivers 1985: 376). In groups of up to ten, evolved reciprocal behaviour allows members to behave altruistically towards others without expecting reciprocation *from the same individual* ('indirect reciprocity') (Krebs and Davies 1984: 83–4).

This is obviously where size matters. Relationships have to be quite different in larger human societies. Here, altruistic behaviour cannot be an evolved strategy; it can come only from moral education and/or a Hobbesian threat of coercive sanctions against defaulters. The latter *can*, presumably, make it rational for humans to practise repicrocal altruism in larger groups. So too could education *if* it is reliably inculcated and widespread, so as to affect behaviour, and so increase the expectation of reciprocity from others, throughout that society. Reciprocal altruism has featured, as we shall see, in the ethical doctrines of several mature cultures (first, and most obviously, in Confucius) (below, p. 104). Social biology seems to suggest that coercive power was only part of a more complex scenario.

Trivers has also suggested that 'a sense of fairness has evolved in human beings as the standard against which to measure the behaviour of other people, so as to guard against cheating in reciprocal relationships . . . Since small inequities repeated many times over a lifetime may exact a heavy toll in inclusive fitness, selection may favour a strong show of aggression when the cheating tendency is discovered.'[10] The priority of *justice* as a social and political norm is indeed found in all cultures (Rappaport 1999: 323; below, p. 229). Humans seem to have evolved a particular sensitivity to 'violations of conditional rules that express social contracts' (Laland and Brown 2002: 169); Rappaport suggests that breach of contract is 'the only act that is always and everywhere held to be immoral' (1999: 132). This could also be a reaction to the highly developed ability of humans to mind-read, manipulate, and deceive (Krebs and Davies 1984: 389).

Both morality and law are peculiar to humans, and they are human universals (Brown 1991): only humans make moral choices, and all humans make moral choices. Morality constitutes, as it were, the grammar of behaviour for speaking, intelligent beings; the capacity to take part in morality seems, like ordinary grammar, to be hard-wired. Again, only human societies have laws; and every human society has laws (whether formal or informal).[11]

SYMBOLIC SYSTEMS

Alongside this, there developed symbolic systems of meaning: carved objects, beads, body-paint, ritual, and dancing were additional means of communicating both facts (people with a certain appearance and wearing certain objects belong to such-and-such a clan, have such-and-such status) and sentiments or opinions ('I esteem you', 'I love you'). Symbolism may be defined as 'external storage of information, in jewelry, art, language or tools' (Wong 2006: 77). It is found in all early societies, and in tribal societies today. Humans interpreted the world through poetry and song, stories and myth.

Our brains had developed in a context where it was advantageous to understand, and be skilled in, social relationships; to be able to identify plants and animals (the 'natural-history' brain); and to make tools and weapons (Mithen 1996). These aptitudes appear to have influenced our first understanding of larger issues. Patterns of belief and myth provided ways for people to understand their lives and the world around them, as well as managing their social relationships (Lévi-Strauss 1963: 21, 37). The first attempts to explain natural phenomena posited various kinds of agency. Yet it may be that almost at once thought-processes and the imagination took on a life of their own.

Religious beliefs, especially about the afterlife, were probably, among other things, a means of seeing and coming to terms with the world in such a way as to make life bearable for creatures with an enormously enhanced awareness of themselves and of other human persons. 'There are ultimate situations which everyone encounters, such as suffering, death...to which every mythology must give a response in order to assure the internal equilibrium of societies, their psycho-affective cohesion and thereby their very survival.'[12]

Symbolic systems were part of our equipment for survival and successful reproduction. They would also have become increasingly important as clans fissioned or coalesced into larger, 'tribal' groupings. They could facilitate social integration, and law and order, among people who did not know each other personally. Symbolic systems supplement kinship as a means of defining a group, of giving group members their identity, and of setting them off from non-members (Trigger 2003: 48, 409). In African societies today, attachment to symbols 'more than anything else gives [societies] cohesion and persistence. In the form of myths, fictions, dogmas, rituals, sacred places and persons, these symbols represent the unity and exclusiveness of the group', signifying their 'ultimate group values'. The social system is 'as it were, removed to a mystical plane, where it figures as a system of sacred values beyond criticism or revision'.[13] Here—as we find in the first known ideologies of Egypt, Mesopotamia, and China—society, nature, kingship, and the supernatural all tend to be seen as interacting parts of a whole.

Diversity of languages and of symbolic systems, however, also made communication *between* cultures difficult, though not impossible.[14] If everything which gives meaning to us humans were as culture-specific as some suggest, how come that we can understand the first written evidences of humans' mental products in diverse cultures at all? In fact, they show concerns and feelings fairly like our own: lists of goods, love and loss, fairness and good behaviour. Early China and Greece produced poetry which we can instantly relate to; indeed, can anything since compare with it? People from different cultures fall in love.

DEMOCRACY?

In the small face-to-face groups of very early human society many decisions were probably made by consensus. In village communities in modern Africa disputes may be 'talked out in the presence of the headman and elders, and the nearest approach to a verdict is the consensus of opinion reached in this public discussion' (Mair 1962: 49, 71). There may be a reference to this in Mesopotamian mythology (below, p. 42–3). Relics of such a system may have survived in the Greek poleis (below, pp. 30–1). But in tribal societies today, even the band tends to recognize a leader or headman who may 'have authority to take communal decisions' (Mair 1962: 17).

It does not seem helpful to call this 'democracy'; [15] the differences between this and what is called 'democracy' today are all too obvious, and have been at the root of many recent tragedies. As Barbara Kingsolver puts it, in a novel set in Congo around 1960:

to the Congolese it seems odd that if one man gets fifty votes and the other gets forty-nine, the first one wins altogether and the second one plumb loses. That means almost half the people will be unhappy, and . . . in a village that's left halfway unhappy you haven't heard the end of it. The way it seems to work here is that you need one hundred per cent. It takes a good while to get there. They talk and make deals and argue until they are pretty much all in agreement on what ought to be done.[16]

Group size is an important factor today. Important decisions tend to be taken in groups of between two and seven, in government and business (Verba 1961: 4–19), not to mention clubs, gangs, and terrorist cells. Only in small groups are we capable of cooperating *voluntarily* to achieve collective goals, without having to rely on coercion. In larger groups, people cannot so easily be persuaded that it may be to their benefit to subordinate their interest to the whole: coercion is needed.[17] These limitations on humans' ability to cooperate—in stark contrast with some social insects—have momentous consequences for politics.

TRIBES

Bands grouped together in—or fissioned into—tribes with the same language, symbolic system, religion, and common rules for the settlement of disputes. The whole tribe tends to be conceived as a single descent group (Crone 1986: 55–6) (as was Israel, a confederacy of tribes: below, p. 50–1).

Within the tribe, family-clans and villages may remain semi-autonomous. Tribes continued as important social units much longer in some regions than others.

HIERARCHY AND OWNERSHIP

Hunter-gatherer societies tended to be egalitarian. In bands and tribal society, differences in status appear to have been relatively small and to have depended on age, gender, and personal qualities, including less tangible ones such as the ability to make and keep friends, good sense, and what the army calls 'leadership qualities'. This does not rule out an element of hierarchy. Among primates, hierarchy is based on various factors, including in some cases who your parents were. Among some species of baboon, 'the group is ruled by a "central hierarchy" of dominant males who cooperate in defense and the control of subordinates'.[18] Intra-group alliances, and the social skills required to construct these, are important, as they surely were among early humans. Among non-human species, superior status means above all access to females. It is reasonable to infer that among humans it has the same meaning, although other meanings come to be attached to it.

Social stratification appears to have developed long before there were centralized monarchies. Inequality seems to have become accepted as the norm.[19] At a time of population growth, 'beads [and] body paint...may have functioned as indicators of an individual's membership and status within a clan, which would have been especially important when laying claim to resources in short supply' (Wong 2006: 82). In the 'rich individual burials' common in prehistoric societies, social differentiation was presented as 'natural and immutable' (Shennan 1982). By the time centralized states appeared, class distinctions were universal. States introduced new forms of hierarchy through differential access to 'the top administrative, military and religious posts' (Trigger 2003: 145, 153). In general, it seems that here culture reinforced and accentuated a biological tendency.

Among humans, social distinctions were accentuated by differential *ownership* of resources, and by the ability to inherit these (as Marx so clearly perceived). The acquisition and possession of objects takes on a whole new dimension among humans; it becomes the general category of *wealth*. Most striking of all is the capacity of individuals and families to pass on wealth, along with the status that goes with it, to later generations. Class distinctions also enable groups within the larger societies to retain the intimacy of the small group.

The correlation between wealth, power, and sexual acquisition (plus successful reproduction) has been found in all types of human society today, from tribes to the 'advanced' West.[20] Wealth makes the male more desirable so that he can corner desirable females: *cupido* abets *libido.* So does power over others (aptly called *libido dominandi* by Augustine). Status differentiation and the qualities which produce it form a basis for political power in states (Trigger 2003: 677–9).

Inequalities in power and wealth have of course remained in advanced human societies, including (but not only) 'liberal democracies', despite proclamations about equality by moralists and political theorists. Indeed inequality of wealth has increased, and is increasing. Wealth in modern industrial societies appears to be distributed in roughly the same proportions as copulations among elephant seals.[21] In Islamic societies, differential access to females is legitimized by law.[22] In the West, no amount of moral idealism has removed economic inequalities, which have, rather, increased dramatically.

The inheritance of wealth, status, and power is more extensive in human than in other animal societies; and it also lasts much longer—longer than the qualities (genetic and other) by which it was acquired. This is partly due to law and its codification. Here one may say that social norms exceed genetics. This maintenance of status across generations may help reduce conflict. Social mobility, on the other hand, widens the gene pool, increases the talent available for leading roles, and is a major reason for the competitive success of 'open' societies.

Ownership is an area in which humans have accentuated a pre-existing tendency, and also specified new patterns of behaviour. In other species, ownership, whether by individuals/pairs or groups, is usually about territory.[23] Among humans, it becomes vastly more complicated, as people come to possess their own food supplies, implements, clothing, shelter, and land. The specifically human praxis of *property* derives from an enhanced ability to distinguish what belongs to one person from what belongs to others, and also, thanks to money and law, to transmit belongings from one generation to the next. Differences in status become enshrined in law.

With the exception of India, hierarchy and inequality were not built into ancient world-views to anything like the same extent as was monarchy. On the other hand, they were no less present in republican Greece than in monarchical Egypt or China. Social ranking was generally taken for granted (Trigger 2003: 490, 671). A frequent theme was that the upper and lower classes ('rich' and 'poor') ought to treat each other with respect: the rich should be generous and just, the poor dutiful and obedient; such behaviour would benefit both groups.

Classes were more often discussed in Greece than anywhere else; and it was the reconciliation of rich and poor (below, p. 139) that enabled Greek states like Athens—and also Rome—to thrive, and also set some of them on the path to *dēmokratia*. In several societies, most of all China, people argued that hierarchy was necessary for the well-being of society as a whole. Thus a practice with roots in natural selection became an *institution*. Israelite monotheism, on the other hand, was an ideological leveller, at least within the chosen people.

THEM AND US

Humans, like other primates and many species, make a sharp distinction between insiders—kin or allies whose cooperation is necessary for survival—and outsiders, those who are in competition for resources. In all such cases, there tends to be 'altruistic behaviour towards in-group members and hostility to outsiders'.[24] Among the Nuer of the upper Nile, men of one village would join forces against a neighbouring village; but then join forces with *them*, if threatened by a remoter group; and so on (Mair 1962: 40). In human societies, we may call this 'tribalism'; or, in some larger societies, nationalism. A shared cultural world may enhance communication, and the prospects of mutual attraction, *within* the group; but they also build up the boundaries, and make communication harder, *between* groups.

Group aggression and genetic usurpation are common among primates. Archaeological evidence suggests that some early humans may have systematically killed outsiders (this is also recorded in Homer), using their intelligence to 'dispose of a neighbouring band, appropriate its territory, and increase [their] own genetic representation in the metapopulation, retaining the tribal memory of this successful episode, repeating it... and quickly spreading [their] influence still further in the metapopulation'. Such 'genocide or genosorption strongly favoring the aggressor need take place only once every few generations to direct evolution'.[25]

Humans have a *predisposition* to collective enmities. The us–them attitude, far from being eliminated by the absorption of clan and band into larger groups, was projected onto the larger human group, first the tribe, and then the state. It has been a powerful psychological force to be reckoned with in all civilizations, ancient and modern. Hostility towards outsiders has tended to be reinforced by belief in one's own unique, perhaps divine, perhaps universal, *authority* over outsiders; by ideologies of racial or religious superiority, uniqueness, exclusiveness. We find this in most ancient political cultures, though it is much stronger in some (Israel, for example) than in others (the Greeks and Romans, for example).

Throughout history, aggression towards outsiders has beeen used by rulers to increase internal solidarity and their own authority. Sometimes, if no obvious 'other' exists, one has to be invented (for example, Jews and heretics in medieval Europe). The idea that 'all men are brothers' is extremely rare (see below, Ch. 10). One does, however, find it in Mozi and the Stoics.

One modifying factor has been long-distance trade with outsiders and across state borders. Acquiring resources from outsiders through mutually agreed exchange seems to be a human invention, and it cuts across the us–them distinction. Commercial relationships, and also the division of labour based on craft specialization, have throughout history contributed to ethnic, cultural, and religious mixing, coexistence, and toleration. Hence 'civil society', in which groups, including nations and states themselves, may coexist peacefully (see Hayek 1982: i. 35 ff.).

SACRED MONARCHY

The first states with a single centre of government developed from around 3000 BCE in Egypt and Mesopotamia, somewhat later in China and India, and much later in central America and parts of Africa. Many were large territorial states, some relatively small city-states.[26] In the ancient world, states developed independently of one another in Egypt, Mesopotamia, and China; and in later times among the Inkas, and in regions of city-states: the Valley of Mexico, the Classic Maya, the Yoruba and Benin in West Africa (Trigger 2003: 28, 94). Centralized political authority may have been a response to rising population, the need to organize agriculture (by irrigation, for example), and new military techniques. It was accompanied by expansion of trade, growth of cities, and of course administrative regulation.

For the first time, the family-clan and the tribe ceased to be the primary focus of allegiance. Major decisions, on which life depended, were now taken elsewhere. From now on, we begin to encounter nuclear families. People seem to have become more conscious of themselves as individuals.[27] Villages continued to manage local affairs; craft guilds developed. Written laws, formal procedures, and royal courts superseded informal oral rules interpreted by tribal elders. This may also have been the stage at which women, in all cultures, became excluded from public life.

The sentiments attached to clan and tribe were transferred to these larger groups and their rulers.[28] It was surely symbolic systems, and especially ritual and religion, which made it possible for humans thus to aggregate their forces while retaining stability, allegiance, and a sense of membership. Dramatic changes in symbolic systems and religious ideas certainly now took place;[29] there were more systematic beliefs about gods, the afterlife, the nature and origin of the world, human society, and physical processes, especially fertility. Shared beliefs and rituals enabled people who did not know one another to relate to a collective identity and feel themselves part of it. They reinforced social discipline and the transmission of codes of behaviour from one generation to the next. Temples and their rituals were another means of mass communication, presenting the images and character of power and perceived reality to the people. The early monarchical states, such as Egypt, China, Iran, India, and Israel, were also religious communities, defined in part by their shared beliefs—prototypes in fact of the modern nation (Thapar 1984). Some of them still exist: for example, Egypt, China, Iran, Israel. There were doubtless costs in 'freedom'. Until representation was invented, popular opinion could be channelled upwards to the centre only by spies or rebellion.

Religion seems also to have facilitated altruistic behaviour in large anonymous associations. The expectation of reciprocity now rested on cultural factors, both in oneself and in others. The anticipation of rewards and punishments after death made sacrificing oneself for a political community composed largely of non-kinsfolk and complete strangers at least *seem* rational. You don't need someone else watching if god sees it all. 'The invention of heaven and hell contributed a more powerful prime mover to human society than the wheel' (de Borhegyi, in Flannery 1972: 407). This may give people more common ground, a basis for trust, a point of intersection among individuals and among interests: a domain of peaceful interaction like spires in a modern cityscape. It is hardly surprising that 'religion' plays such a large part in 'politics'. They are out of the same stable.

Religious and political ideologies became more articulate, more systematic, and, to varying degrees, controlled and supervised by the centre. Sometimes they were managed by ritual and religious specialists, shamans and priests, funded by the state and under the supervision of the court. Only in India and Israel was religion independent of kings.

Then there was the question of how to *make decisions* in large groups. Humans have the ability to consider many different possible courses of action, weigh them against one another, and choose that course which is most likely to promote their interest. One of the most dynamic capacities of our brains and language is to imagine a very wide variety of possible courses of action and their likely outcomes. This, combined with the ability to undertake complex calculations, increases the survival and reproductive strategies available to us by enabling us to respond more flexibly than any other animal (see Krebs and Davies 1984: 136–7). But it brings with it (as every human knows) individual anxiety, social disagreement, and now the whole issue of decision-making by, or on behalf of, a very large group: politics. Episodes in Homer indicate uncertainty and ambiguity in the decision-making process in an early society. People don't know the best course to take; therefore, they resort to whatever devices will give a result which all can accept.

In the first states, decision-making was often a partly religious procedure. Major decisions were typically taken after consulting oracles—or other conveyors of numinous information—perhaps under the guidance of priests. Kings tended to be credited with unique abilities in these fields, having recourse to obscure, even secret, decision-making rituals, partly perhaps so that everyone could accept the outcome. This was also a way of sharing any blame later incurred.

Leadership and decision-making in large complex societies differs in kind from that in small groups. There is a greater concentration of coercive power, and there has to be a new kind of trust—in the unknown qualities of others. Monarchy appears to come to the rescue. In the new political societies, the king and his officials took over decision-making functions from elders and clan chiefs. Kingship became by far the most common form of leadership. It may have developed out of chieftainship as found in some modern African tribal societies.[30] (The seafaring Greeks never got beyond this stage, for which we may be thankful.) There may have been kings with limited powers before there were centralized states; but there were no centralized states without kings (Gledhill et al. 1988: 10–13). In both ancient states and modern tribal societies, kingship was hereditary.[31]

In nearly all early civilizations, monarchy was both sacred and patrimonial.[32] It related to the king's perceived relationship with divinity; he was a father figure, and ruled his domain as a household. The first cultures to have left written records relied heavily on religions which authorized sacred monarchy. These literate monarchical states based their authority on the king's relationship to the divine. Flannery notes how, in both early and modern tribal societies, chiefs 'are not merely of noble birth, but usually divine'; their 'special relationships with the gods... legitimize their right to demand community support and tribute'.[33] This resembles the view of kingship in ancient Egypt, Mesopotamia, and China. The shared ancestor was a common myth in ancient societies. In modern tribal societies, too, 'genealogies often serve... as "charters" of present social institutions' (Goody and Watt 1968: 33).

The symbolisms of lineage and tribe were transferred to the new extended form of political community. The ruler was portrayed as a shepherd, father, or even god, who protects and nurtures his people. He was also their role model. They owed him loyalty and reverence. People 'symboliz[ed] the unity of the state through a single person who was believed to be responsible for the functioning of all aspects of society [and] the principal intermediary with the supernatural'.[34] The same occurred later in religious communities: Moses, Jesus, Muhammad, and, despite himself, the Buddha.

The state was represented as an artificial family, bound together by adherence to a supreme patriarch. Ruler and ruled should love one other (Johnson 1987). This was a useful political symbolism for large societies not based on kinship or face-to-face acquaintance. Sacred monarchy in turn reinforced the symbolic system by giving it an earthly counterpart; kingship was supposed to bestow tangible benefits, the king was beneficent and the source of society's well-being. Projection of the social order, partly as it is, partly as one might like it to be, onto the cosmos was a means of affirming its legitimacy. There was thus continuity between early monarchical political ideas in Egypt and China and the ideology of tribal society, in which certain peoples 'believed and acted as if they lived in a society whose form and order were laid down virtually at creation... [S]ocial life reflects the working of the universe and, conversely, the world order depends on the proper ordering of society' (Gluckman 1965: 269).

The first recorded attempts to justify the state and kingship stressed that without them there would be anarchy (below, p. 24). Some African peoples in recent times have believed 'that a time when there is no king is a time of lawlessness' (Mair 1962: 208). This idea was further elaborated by Augustine, Irano-Islamic philosophers, and Thomas Hobbes. Parallels can thus be found between the monarchical political thought of ancient states as it appears in the first written records, and that of modern societies, both tribal and sophisticated.

Sacred monarchy arose after the development of agriculture. Just as, on a practical level, it facilitated the development of irrigation, transport, and trade, so it functioned as a magical means of ensuring the right environmental, and especially climatic, conditions. In Egypt, Mesopotamia, and China the king was the link between nature and human society. Spiritual and material well-being depended upon him performing certain tasks for the deities, and upon his subjects performing certain tasks for him. One of the functions of a king which set him apart from others was to give deities the human support, food, and so on, that they needed (Trigger 2003: 680, 684). In modern tribal society, as in ancient states, the king tends to be held directly responsible for the satisfactory functioning of nature. He must therefore be of unblemished character, be kept in good health, and perform the necessary rituals and sacrifices.[35] Natural disasters can discredit the king.

From earliest recorded history, kings were ascribed a role in society as embodiments of justice and benevolence. Again, there are parallels with tribal kingdoms in recent times, where kings are 'expected to epitomise the qualities that their subjects most admire, justice in particular'; the king being viewed 'as the ultimate source of order and justice' (Mair 1962: 143, 205). A twentieth-century Ugandan king (in his own words) 'must equally love his subjects, however poor they may be, he must look after orphans, and he must justly [decide disputes]' (Gluckman 1965: 16–17; Claessen 1978: 563). This could have come straight from ancient Egypt or Mesopotamia. Kings, and in Mesopotamia temples, also played a role in the redistribution of resources.

To vest authority in an individual whom people could recognize as no ordinary mortal was an immense imaginative leap. In a sense, the idea of the state originated in Egypt and Sumer: rulership is conceived as an 'office' which 'exists apart from the man who occupies it' (see below, p. 38).[36] Hobbes's description of the state as 'artificial' is perfectly accurate: humans are not biologically ('by nature') attuned to the state; artifice alone has made possible a wider (though not yet a worldwide) peace. It is, as Hobbes implied, precisely this artificiality, together with the much greater size of population, that necessitates a degree of coercion over members of one's own species which has no parallel elsewhere in nature. It also requires the constant management of consensus by, among other things, political theory. Later, and especially in modern times, attention turned to how this central state power can be regulated.

To all of this the Greeks, Phoenicians, Etruscans, and Romans were exceptions. The Greek poleis were the only face-to-face *states* in human history. This was an alternative way of organizing societies not based on kinship; and, unlike monarchy, it eliminated kinship at the top of the political system. And the Greeks were the least religious ancient people.

These early religious monarchies may be seen as a cultural equivalent of an 'evolutionarily stable strategy': a behaviour pattern which maximizes benefits for a group, whether bees, chimpanzees, or humans (Parker 1984). This goes some way towards explaining the nature of early political thought.

NOTES

1. 'The traits that differentiate us from chimpanzees have passed through at least 200,000 generations of selection. Most of the rapid increase in brain size took less than 100,000 generations. The development of religion and art has probably experienced about 10,000 generations of selection' (Trivers 1985: 29).
2. Mair 1962: 54–7, 62–3, 76, 91.
3. Smith 1975: 323, summarizing Chance. He goes on: 'intelligence first evolved to cope with living in society and was later applied to the control of the material world through the use of tools...the intelligence we use today in theoretical physics first evolved to help us live in society'.

4. Barrett, Dunbar, and Lycett 2002: ch. 13.

5. 'The basic design of language is innate'; the human brain is hard-wired not only to create complex voice modulations but to communicate in grammatical sentences (Chomsky 1957; Pinker 1997: 32, 34, 111).

6. Aiello and Dunbar 1993. See also Pinker 1994: 68, 73; Pinker 1997: 25.

7. Chagnon 1982: 292, 305. See also Fortes and Evans-Pritchard 1940: p. xix; Clark 1970: 184; Mann 1986: 42–3. Hawkes gives a figure of between six and thirty for early human groups (Hawkes and Woolley 1963: 121). Gluckman observes of bands today that, when they exceed 200, 'the social organization tends to become much more complicated' (1965: 87).

8. Barrett, Dunbar, and Lycett 2002. 'Kin selection has been invoked to explain a great deal of altruistic behaviour in humans, with some success' (Krebs and Davies 1984: 76, 79).

9. Trivers 1985: 47–9, 361–94; Krebs and Davies 1984: 328–9; Smith 1975: 184–5.

10. 1971: 388. He goes on: 'The emotion of guilt' may have 'been selected for in humans partly in order to motivate the cheater to compensate for misdeeds and to behave reciprocally in future, thus preventing the rupture of reciprocal relationships'.

11. Hawkes and Woolley 1963: 484–97; Gluckman 1965: 178 ff.; Trigger 2003: 221–39.

12. Cauvin 2000: 67–9, 122; Rappaport 1999; Laland and Brown 2002: 217–19, 230, 239.

13. Fortes and Evans-Pritchard 1940: 16–19; Gluckman 1965: 91, 245–6, 254, and (citing Malinowski) 284; Mair 1962: 15, 47.

14. See Laland and Brown 2002: 249; Smith 1975: 312; Trigger 2003: 687.

15. *Pace* Jean Baechler, who suggests that, because for millenia humans lived in bands, we are 'democratic by nature', 1985: 305 ff.

16. *The Poisonwood Bible* (Faber & Faber 1998), 298–9.

17. Mancur Olson, *The Logic of Collective Action: Public Goods and the Theory of Groups* (Cambridge, Mass.: Harvard University Press, 1965); Verba 1961: 2, 33–4, 62.

18. Wilson 1975: 264. Among monkeys, 'the greater the brain size and the more flexible the behavior, the more numerous are the determinants of rank' (ibid. 143).

19. As it was until recently in Rwanda: J. J. Macquet, *The Premise of Inequality in Rwanda* (Oxford: Oxford University Press, 1969). (I am grateful to my late colleague Philip Whitaker for this reference.)

20. Laland and Brown 2002: 125–8, 170–1; Trivers 1971: 297. See also Steve Jones's Reith Lecture, as reported in the *Observer*, 19 Mar. 1989: 'often the most successful [human] males are the ones who have the most worldly wealth and social position'; among the Yanomano, 'in one village, four of the men had more than 40 grandchildren, while 28 had only one and many had none'.

21. 'In one study of elephant seals, 4% of the males accounted for 88% of all the copulations observed' (Dawkins 1976: 154; Wilson 1975: 264).

22. The bin Laden patriarch sired 54 children from 22 wives (*Economist*, 12 Apr. 2008, p. 92).
23. Krebs and Davies 1984: 43, 148: a commonly evolved social rule is 'owner returns to the territory, intruder retreats' (known as the 'bourgeois' strategy).
24. Laland and Brown 2002: 266, 282, summarizing Richerson and Boyd. One of the tasks of the 'guardians' in Plato's Republic was to distinguish between members and outsiders; their ability to do so was one basis of their 'wisdom' (below, p. 150).
25. Wilson 1975: 298–9; Krebs and Davies 1984: 60.
26. Mair 1962: 13, 125, 166; Cohen 1978; N. Yoffee, *Myths of the Archaic State* (Cambridge: Cambridge University Press, 2005).
27. This can be seen from funerary monuments and inscriptions. Some of the earliest records of human self-expression in Egypt, China, and Mesopotamia were love-poems.
28. See Ibn Khaldun, *Muqaddima*, a helpful complement to modern anthropology on state origins, written by a person in direct contact with both tribe and state (Black 2001: 165 ff.).
29. Cauvin 2000: 70–1, 120, 208–9. He argues that 'an impulse of the religious imagination' drove the agricultural revolution, rather than vice versa.
30. Mair observes how one individual 'becomes predominant in a neighbourhood and is known as its "spokesman"; he is not deliberately chosen, but rather is found to be in this position' due to the support he commands and his wealth. 'Essentially [he] is a persuasive talker whose views have been proved wise by experience', so that 'he can speak with authority' (1962: 97). On the other hand, the powers of chiefs and kings in modern Africa are seldom as absolute as they were in ancient monarchies (Fortes and Evans-Pritchard 1940: 12–13).
31. Trigger 2003: 75; Mair 1962: 108. The relationship of clientage, so important in recent tribal kingship (Mair 1962: 166–70), does not appear in the literature of early monarchies.
32. Trigger 2003; Francis Oakley, *Kingship: The Politics of Enchantment* (Oxford: Blackwell, 2006).
33. 1972: 411; Mair 1962: 69; Gluckman 1965: 154–6.
34. Trigger 2003: 672, 680; Skalnik 1978: 607.
35. For example the Inka (Trigger 2003: 79–81) and the Nilotic Shilluk (Mair 1962: 69).
36. Elaborate royal regalia in early states symbolize 'the continuation of the state over and above any single incumbent's lifetime' (Cohen 1978: 64); compare Flannery 1972: 411, on several American Indian tribes today.

2

Egypt

The first surviving records of political thought are from Egypt under the Old Kingdom (2686–2125 BCE).[1] The moral and emotional language of ancient Egypt is immediate, accessible, indeed familiar. Their political language is comprehensible but certainly not familiar. Egyptian religion promoted the earliest-known example of transcendent divinity: deities were seen as all-powerful, all-pervading powers; they dominated the imagined universe and the mental life of Egyptians, perhaps more than of any other people. The people themselves were thought to have been created, and the state founded, by the god.[2]

In Egypt the king was more closely identified with the gods than in any other culture. He was the incarnation of Horus and Osiris, the son of the supreme god Ra himself (Frankfort et al. 1946: 71). He was the supreme representative of the religious as well as the political order. The king's relationship to his subjects was thus also a spiritual relationship; the great god Ptah was in all living beings, so that the king was connected to the life-force (*ka*) of every individual (Frankfort 1948: 29, 69, 78). The king was revered as 'greatest god', the 'perfect god'; he was said to have been conceived when Amun desired a royal wife, 'the god's wife'. The pharaoh ruled even over the netherworld as Osiris and 'deceased father'. He was credited with the power of divine 'utterance', his word 'became a reality immediately'.[3]

Egyptian political thought was based on this relationship between religion and the state (Assmann 2001: 19, 124). Partly as a consequence, it was the most extreme theory of *absolute* monarchy. While others could be brought to justice, there was no indication that the pharaoh could be judged even after death, presumably on the hypothesis that a deity could commit no wrong. The priests, who conducted the religious cult in the temples, represented the pharaoh, and they were appointed by him. The temples' enormous wealth was part of the royal domain.

Royal authority was identified with the person of the king as an individual. 'I was the beginning and the end of mankind, since nobody like myself existed nor will he exist', said a pharaoh of the twenty-second century BCE (*OHAE* 128–9). 'I am king by virtue of my being, a sovereign to whom [the office] is not given', said Senusret I (1956–1911 BCE) (*VAE* 41). The pharaoh's title 'nesu-bit' meant both the individual ruler and 'the unchanging divine king' (*OHAE* 9).[4]

Ancient Egyptians were enthralled by the sun (and why not?). The intensity of their political theology owed much to the apparently arbitrary forces of nature on which they, more obviously than most people, depended for their livelihood. And it was the pharaoh who, through his relationship with the gods, managed nature for the welfare of his people. Amenemhat I (1985–1952 BCE) claimed that: 'I was one who produced barley and loved the corn-god. The Nile respected me at every defile. None hungered in my years, nor thirsted in them'.

The pharaoh's correct moral and ritual conduct kept the cosmos running, the sun rising, the Nile flooding. One of his functions was to promote good relations between the gods and the people of Egypt. He did so by making offerings from the people's labour to secure their well-being and prosperity. He had to keep the gods happy and give them a home on earth by building temples (Assmann 2001: 159). The king's relationship to the gods was one of 'systematic mutual aid' based on strict reciprocity ('reimbursement'; Posener 1956: 40–1).[5]

It was the Egyptians who introduced the metaphor of the king as shepherd into political thought. What they meant was that, just as a landowner entrusts his sheep to a shepherd, the god transmitted his authority and responsibility to the king. Senusret I said, '[the god] appointed me shepherd of this land, knowing him who would herd it best for him . . . He destined me to rule the people, made me to be before mankind' (Lichtheim: i. 116). '[The god] made me the herdsman of this land, for he discerned that I would keep it in order for him; he entrusted to me that which he protected' (in Frankfort et al. 1946: 78). 'Humankind [are] the cattle of the god . . . It is for them he rises in the sky, for them he makes plants and animals . . . when they weep, he hears' (2100–1800 BCE; in Assmann 2001: 57).

The pharaoh was conceived as all-powerful among mortals. 'Mine is the land, I am its lord, my power reaches to heaven's height. I excel by acting for my maker, pleasing the god with what he gave ' (Senusret I, in Lichtheim: i. 117). The pharaoh was 'theoretical owner of all resources' with 'practically absolute' powers over, among other things, taxation and compulsory labour (*OHAE* 102, 172–3).

According to Egyptian religious and political belief the pharaoh had the right to rule the whole earth (Posener 1956: 14). It was his divine prerogative not only to suppress rebellion and to defend Egypt, but also to expand the state's boundaries. 'Asiatics will fall to his sword, Libyans will fall to his flame, rebels to his wrath' (said about Amenemhat I, r. 1985–1956 BCE). Senusret III

(1870–1831 BCE) extolled the 'good god who massacres the Nubians'. This ideology was further developed under the New Kingdom (1550–1069 BCE), when the empire was extended to northern Sudan, Palestine, and Syria (Kemp 1989: 223). Amun was made to proclaim: 'I bestowed on you the earth, its length and breadth, Westerners and Easterners are under your command... [Amun] himself made [the king] rule what his eye encircles, what the disc of Ra illuminates.' The king was therefore commanded by the god 'to conquer all lands without fail'.[6]

This is the earliest record of nationalist religious imperialism and divinely mandated universal empire. 'What are these Asiatics to you, O Amun, the wretches ignorant of god?'[7] Foreigners were regarded as neither 'men' nor 'people'. The oldest religious monarchy was global and racist.

A pharaoh is beneficent towards his subjects, ruthless towards his enemies: 'a smasher of foreheads... he fights without end, he spares not... He is a master of graciousness, rich in sweetness, and he conquers by love.'[8] Pharaohs were credited with special qualities as warrior kings, particularly under the New Kingdom. Rameses II (r. 1279–1213 BCE) described how at the battle of Kadesh, all by himself, with the god's help, he had turned the tide: 'no officer was with me, no charioteer... I raised my shout to my army: "Steady your hearts... For Amun is my helper, his hand is with me"' (Lichtheim: ii. 65–7).

It was the special task of the pharaoh to uphold justice (*maat*): this referred to right order and justice in nature, in ethics, in law, and in ritual (Assmann 2001: 4). '[The sun-god] Ra has placed the king in the land of the living... judging humankind and satisfying the gods, realizing Maat and destroying [lack of it]' (in Assmann 2001: 3).

The highest praise was reserved for those pharaohs who had rescued their country from disaster, disunity, or disorder, when 'each man's heart is for himself... The land is shrunk—its rulers are many. It is bare—its taxes are great.'[9] It was then that the pharaoh's virtues of justice and beneficence were most of all on display. The pharaoh is presented as a saviour 'announced in the most ancient prophecies' (Posener 1956: 29, 77): 'then a king will come from the south... then order will return to its seat' (Lichtheim: i. 143). Amenemhat I (r. 1985–1956 BCE) was said to have come 'to root out disorder, having raised himself up like Atum in person; he has re-established what had been found wanting, and what one town had taken from another... So great was his love of justice' (in Posener 1956: 130). A full list of good works was ascribed to Rameses IV (r. 1153–1147 BCE) at his coronation: 'those who had fled have returned to their cities... Those who hungered are satisfied and happy, those who thirsted are drunk, those who were naked are clothed in fine linen... Those who were imprisoned are set free... A high Nile has sprung from its source, to refresh the hearts of the people' (in Assmann 2001: 142).

The idea of religious monarchy in Egypt was brought to a strange climax in an attempted religious revolution by Amenhotep IV (r. 1352–1336 BCE). He proclaimed the Aten (sun-disc) as sole god, and proclaimed himself the son of the Aten. He abolished the festivals and processions of all other gods, including the supreme Amun, systematically destroying their images, monuments, and inscriptions. The capital was transferred to a new city, Amarna.

The Aten was supposed to be a god 'without any other except for himself'.[10] The pharaoh was elevated to be 'sole king like Aten; there is no other great one except for him' (in Hornung 1983: 246). This has been seen as the first monotheism (ibid.). But, unlike all later versions, only the king could worship the god; everyone else had to worship the king (*OHAE* 311).

This was also the first documented attempt to impose belief on a population by force (Assmann 2001: 199, cf. 222). It did not outlast Amenhotep himself; the traditional religion was promptly restored. The memory of Amarna was so hated, and all traces of it so effectively obliterated, that the whole episode has only recently come to light. The priests eventually exercised their own kind of theocracy, with the high-priest acting on behalf of Amun.[11] The god was now regarded as the real king (*OHAE* 313, 332). This was related to a growing belief that the god communicated important political decisions through oracles. By the time of Alexander's conquest of Egypt in 332 BCE, 'the Egyptian kingship faded into mere theory' (Assmann 2001: 150).

To be successful as a metaphor of royal legitimacy (and of a large-scale unified society), religion must, it seems, be kept at one remove from institutions. Kings may use religion but they cannot invent it.[12]

MORALITY: JUSTICE

The *Instruction of Ptahhotep*, written during the Old Kingdom, is the oldest treatise on ethics.[13] It urged unselfishness, generosity, and trustworthiness. The *Instruction to Merikare*, written between 2100 and 1800 BCE, is the oldest political treatise.[14] It is also the first example of the 'advice to kings' genre; this developed in fourth-century Greece (below, p. 165) and became widespread under Islam (Black 2001: 108–14). It contained advice on bureaucratic ethics and management, religious buildings and observances, and the defence of Egypt.

Both these works exhorted people to behave morally both on principle and for the rewards which will follow (in today's language, they were at once moral and prudential, Kantian and utilitarian). For example, 'follow your heart as long as you live . . . that man endures whose rule is rightness' (*Ptah-hotep*, in Lichtheim: i. 66, 69). Religious motives are presented in a similar (and rather modest) vein: 'work for god, he will work also for you'.

The central values stipulated for both rulers and people in general, for both private and political conduct, were justice (*maat*) and benevolence. These are especially incumbent upon all who hold power. They are two sides of the same coin. 'I judged two trial partners so as to content them. I saved the weak from one stronger than he as best I could; I gave bread to the hungry, clothes to the naked.'[15]

Appeals are made to the rewards and punishments of the afterlife as inducements to justice and social discipline. The afterlife was thus explicitly seen as one foundation of morality and the state. Only belief in the afterlife could enable one to be sure that good would be rewarded and evil punished: it was the ultimate basis for reciprocity in a very large society. So the dead man pleads his good works: 'I did not begin my day by exacting more than my due . . . I have not robbed the poor . . . I have not caused pain, I have not caused tears, I have not killed, I have not ordered to kill, I have not made anyone suffer . . . I have not held back the water in its season'. Rather: 'I have given bread to the hungry, water to the thirsty, clothes to the naked'.

But justice will also earn you a good name *on earth* after death. 'Make firm your station in the graveyard by being upright, by doing justice' (*Merikare*, in Lichtheim: i. 106). 'Justice [lasts] for ever and goes down into the necropolis with him who renders it. When he is buried . . . his name is not wiped out from the earth, but he is remembered for his goodness. That is a principle of the divine order'.[16] Justice pays in the long run ('do justice, then you endure on earth . . . Do not kill, it does not serve you'; Lichtheim: i. 100).

It was also argued that justice pays off even during one's own lifetime: 'the riches of the unjust cannot stay . . . There are no heirs for the violent-hearted . . . The merciful—the cow bears for him; the evil shepherd—his herd is small' (*VAE* 71–2). Acting justly makes you happy here and now: 'better is a measure that the god gives thee than five thousand [taken] illegally . . . Better is poverty in the hand of the god than riches in a storehouse; Better is bread, when the heart is happy, than riches with sorrow' (*ANE* 422b: cf. Proverbs 15: 17). It was in the ruler's own interest to treat cultivators decently, not overtaxing them: 'when free men are given land, they work for you like a single team' (Lichtheim: i. 103). 'Do not make the labourer wretched with taxes; enrich him and he will be there for you next year' (*VAE* 71). There are similar arguments in Hebrew literature.

The wealthy and powerful have an obligation to provide for the poor and vulnerable. This was a central principle of the patrimonial state. The point was that no one should go hungry, not equal distribution (*OHAE* 113).

Professions of good deeds appear in inscriptions of all periods: 'I gave bread to the hungry and clothing to the naked...I gave sandals to the barefooted; I gave a wife to him who had no wife' (from the 2100s, in *OHAE* 129); 'Calm the weeper, don't oppress the widow' (*Merikare,* in Lichtheim: i. 99–107); 'I was a father to them. I judged the wretched and the mighty, the powerful like the weak...I gave burial to the heirless...I looked after the orphan, I took care of the widow...I extended my hand to the needy, I provided for the have-not' (high-priest of Amun, 13th century BCE); 'Guard thyself against robbing the oppressed and against overbearing the disabled. Stretch not forth thy hand against the approach of an old man, nor steal away the speech of the aged' (Advice Book, 10th–6th century BCE). Beethoven kept a copy of one such list on his desk.

A similar list of good works would appear many centuries later in the Gospel of St Matthew, where Jesus uses it as the criterion for distinguishing between those destined for heaven and hell (Matt. 25: 35–43). This is in the same spirit as the Egyptian texts, except, crucially, that the obligation to benevolence (Christian charity) is now laid on all people.

The administration of justice in the courts was also an expression of benevolence. The duty to treat all people equally—procedural justice—was especially urged upon those with judicial powers. The *Instructions of Ptah-hotep* advised people in positions of command to observe justice and 'listen calmly to the speech of one who pleads'; it advised the litigant not to 'vent yourself against your opponent'. The obligation to ignore personal acquaintance in hearing lawsuits was made especially clear in instructions to a vizier in the fifteenth century: 'Thou shalt look upon him whom thou knowest like him whom thou knowest not, upon him who has access to [thy person] like him who is far [from thy household]' (in Frankfort et al. 1946: 89); 'When I judged the petitioner, I was not partial. I did not turn my brow for the sake of reward...I rescued the timid from the violent' (*ANE* 213a).

The judicial role of the monarch was part of his general duty to uphold *maat,* also an aspect of his benevolence. Justice revealed the king's closeness to divinity. During the early second millenium there was a new emphasis on the moral duties of kingship (Posener 1956: 9, 14). The king is and should be like Ra, the 'lord of *maat*', who 'listens to the entreaty of one in distress...saves the timorous from the hand of the violent, pronounces justice between the poor and the rich' (in Assmann 2001: 196). Similarly, Amun 'hears the prayer of him who is in capitivity, gracious of heart in the face of an appeal to him, saving the fearful from the terrible of heart, judging the weak and the injured' (*ANE* 366a). He is 'lord of the silent, who comes at the call of the poor. I called to you when I was in sorrow, and you came to save me. You gave breath to the one who was imprisoned' (*c.*1330 BCE, cit. Assmann 2001: 223–5). Procedural justice is one aspect of this: the ruler and his vizier are urged to 'administer equal justice to all' regardless of wealth, status, or affinity to the judge (in Engnell 1967: 12). The principle of equality before the law was as emphatically upheld as it was later in the Greek poleis (below, p. 142).

The pharaoh's closeness to god was thought to make a code of law unnecessary. A gift of divine 'perception' gave a king perfect knowledge in his heart (Assmann 2001: 4, 65–8, 71): 'there is nothing at all which he does not know' (in Frankfort et al. 1946: 76). The vizier and other officials, on the other hand, should act according to 'the precedent', 'the regulations' (*ANE* 213; Boorn 1988: 321).

EQUALITY

There were no castes, fixed classes, or other fundamental differences among the pharoah's subjects. Amun says, 'I made the four winds that every man might breathe thereof like his fellow...I made the great inundation that the poor man might have rights therein like the great man...I made every man like his fellow' (*c.* 2000 BCE: *ANE* 7–8). Appointments should be made on the basis of merit, not status ('do not prefer the wellborn to the commoner, choose a man on account of his skills') (*Merikare*, in Lichtheim: i. 101). Male and female were on the same moral plane. Was this related to the wide gulf between pharaoh and *all* subjects? Was there a connection between social equality and a strong sense of overarching deity?[17]

The *Instruction of Ptahhotep* was addressed to all kinds of people in all kinds of situations: the farmer, the poor man, the man of substance, officials. It explained how to behave as a guest, how to deliver messages, how to conduct relationships with neighbours, friends, children, and wife ('fill her belly, clothe her back, ointment soothes her body, gladden her heart as long as you live'); and other social skills (Lichtheim: i. 69). The author took social mobility for granted ('If you are great after having been humble, have gained wealth after having been poor...'). Another work, perhaps from the twentieth century BCE, emphasized the role of manual labourers: 'it is men who create that which exists; one lives on what comes from their hands...The provider of provisions is the professions...They are a flock, excellent for their lord' (*VAE* 70–2). The *Protest of the Eloquent Peasant* (2000–1800 BCE) shows an ordinary cultivator pleading his case so eloquently that the judge feigns indifference to keep him talking (*VAE* 63–4).

INDIVIDUALS

The Egyptians had a sense of the individual and of a personal life after death.[18] During the transition from the Old to the Middle Kingdom (*c.* 2160–2055 BCE), there was a religious 'levelling': people developed a direct personal relationship with deities, without royal or priestly mediation (*OHAE* 181). There was also a 'democratization of the afterlife' (*OHAE* 180, 153): it was thought that every individual person became Osiris after death. During the New Kingdom (1550–1069 BCE), religious individualism was taken further; it was said that the god 'knows your innermost feelings', and that he 'comes at the voice of him who calls on him' (in Vernus 1995: 85). Direct communication between god and the individual involved the use of oracles, which led to an increase in the power of temples and priests at the expense of the pharaoh.[19]

Two remarkably personal writings from the early second millenium deal with the plight of the ordinary poor peasant in the face of officialdom and fate: the *Protest of the Eloquent Peasant* and *A Dispute Over Suicide*. The latter examined the feelings of a man for whom everything has gone wrong: 'to whom can I speak today? Hearts are rapacious'. His life-force assures the man that, whether he decides to live or die, it will remain with him, and after death 'we shall make a home together' (*ANE* 405–7).

SPIN

The art of writing always had 'a royal context, and was an innovation of great importance to [the Egyptian] state',[20] both for propaganda and for management purposes. It seems to have been recognized that political stability—and hence people's livelihoods—depended upon belief in the legitimacy of the pharaoh and his office. It was after the breakdown of the Old Kingdom and during the subsequent period of disorder that social and political doctrines were first articulated, at a time when the absence of a strong pharaoh most obviously led to social disaster. Rhetoric and writing now became increasingly important in shaping public opinion.[21] They were used to 'restore the prestige of the pharoah and inculcate obedience in the people' (Posener 1956: 16). Inscriptions ('placarding') were used as a means of mass communication to explain and justify kingship (ibid. 18).

Words were seen as the pharaoh's strongest weapon. The pharaohs were served by professional scribes. Writing—then as now—was also seen as a way of achieving immortality: ancient authors (it was said) 'made heirs for themselves in writings...Books of wisdom were their pyramids, the pen was their child' (in Frankfort et al. 1946: 118). Through one's writings one will benefit posterity (Posener 1960: 73).

The importance of inscriptions and texts was enhanced by the nature of Egyptian religious ritual. This consisted in performative utterances: what pharaoh or priest enacted or intoned was believed to become reality in the divine realm (Assmann 2001: 51). People were probably predisposed to believe (even more than today) that because something was published it was true, and that kings actually possessed the attributes ascribed to them in inscriptions and texts (Frankfort 1948: 58; Posener 1960: 12). These developments in political communication may have been effective: there was no police force, yet there was never a popular uprising (Frankfort et al. 1946: 52; *OHAE* 100–1).

CONCLUSION

Egypt's was the first expression of sacred monarchy. It was effective for an enormous stretch of time because it was tied in to the current view of the way things were. Somewhat similar political systems, also based on sacred monarchy, arose independently, somewhat later, in other parts of the world. The ideas underpinning these varied more than the institutions themselves; this is particularly obvious in the case of China.

The idea of an absolute monarchy authorized by god, of the king as god's representative on earth, was taken up by the Hellenistic and Roman and Muslim monarchies which succeeded the pharaohs. Aspects of Egyptian monarchical theory were either shared with, or passed on to, other cultures: for example, the idea of the king as shepherd. Some of the characteristics of the pharaoh were later ascribed to the god of Israel (below, p. 62).[22]

The most long-lived, and at times the most powerful, state of the ancient world was founded on ideas which to us seem fantasy. But this may not put them in a very different league from ourselves in relation to future generations. They had experience on their side: the king performed his rituals, and the sun did keep on rising, the Nile did keep on flooding. Does our belief in 'the market' bear any resemblance to theirs in the sun god?[23]

NOTES

1. It is not known whether Egypt or Mesopotamia is the older civilization.
2. *ANE* 366. 'The founding of the state amounted to the same thing as the founding of the cult'; Assmann 2001: 18, 46.
3. By the 26th century BCE the king 'was sublimated into a manifestation of the sun-god' (Kemp 1989: 62; cf. Frankfort et al. 1946: 65, 85).
4. Old Kingdom: Hornung 1983: 141; *OHAE* 99, 109; Assmann 2001: 4, 116–17, 146, 185; Kemp 1989: 198–200.
5. 'How joyful are thy lands; thou hast fixed their boundaries. How joyful are thy ancestors; thou has increased their portion... How joyful are the people in thy government; thy mighty power hath suppressed usurpation' (in Engnell 1967: 13, hymn to Senusret III, 1870–1831 BCE).
6. Lichtheim: ii. 33, 36, 40: *Annals of Thutmose III*, r. 1492–1479 BCE. See also Vernus 1995: 92; Assmann 2001: 205.
7. Rameses II (r. 1279–1213 BCE), inscription in Lichtheim: ii. 65.
8. *Tale of Sinuhe*, in Frankfort et al. 1946: 71; cf. *VAE* 43; Posener 1956: 135 (mid-19th cent. BCE or earlier).
9. 19th cent. BCE, in Lichtheim: i. 142; see Posener 1956: 17, 40–60.
10. The hymn to the Aten began: 'Praise of Re... the living great Aten... and praise of the King of Upper and Lower Egypt who lives on truth... and praise of the Chief Wife of the King, his beloved, the Lady of the Two lands...' (*ANE* 370a). The queen Nefertiti was also a close associate of the Aten. The holy royal family was worshipped by the Amarna elite in their homes (*OHAE* 284).
11. In the period after the fall of the New Kingdom (Third Intermediate Period, 1069–664 BCE), the high-priests of Amun became hereditary and gained control of Upper Egypt, assuming the royal title of 'first prophet' (*OHAE* 305–7, 331–3, 346; Vernus 1995: 91–4).
12. The closest, but not very close, parallel was Akbar, who tried to found a new religion, supposedly based on Akbar's personal religious experiences, in 16th-century India. He too used this, among other things, as a way of securing devotion from officials (Black 2001: 239–46).
13. Lichtheim: i. 62–75. Ptahhotep was an ancient sage.
14. Ibid. 99–107; Assmann 2001: 57, 171–4.
15. *The Book of the Dead*, final form 664–332 BCE; Lichtheim: ii. 125–9. Cf. the Christian version, Matt. 25: 35–43.
16. Written *c.* 1850: in Frankfort et al. 1946: 84; Lichtheim: i. 64.
17. See the *New York Review of Books*, 25 Sept. 2001, p. 23.
18. Each individual has his own *ka* (life-force: Frankfort et al. 1946: 97). The Egyptians had a stronger sense of life after death than any other ancient people. 'Most examples of early writing are associated with the funerary cult' (*OHAE* 81).
19. Vernus 1995: 84, 88–9; Assmann 2001: 166.
20. *OHAE* 78; see also Assmann 2001: 51, 91–2.

21. Posener 1956: 17; Assmann 2001: 164–5.
22. Jan Assmann has argued for a direct transference: Israelite monotheism was a 'theologization' of Egyptian royal ideology; *Politische Theologie zwischen Aegypten und Israel* (Munich: Carl Friedrich von Siemens Stiftung, 1995). This view has not been widely accepted.
23. I wrote this before summer 2008.

3

Mesopotamia, Assyria, Babylon

The political thought of ancient Mesopotamia has to be gleaned from hymns, myths, inscriptions, and political practices. A few prologues to law collections deal directly with principles of government.

From the Sumerian period of the late fourth to the late third millenium, Mesopotamian civilization was based on city-states. Here people from different areas and ethnic groups intermingled. In contrast to Egypt, there were several important centres; different cities achieved hegemony at different times. The central region was periodically invaded by peoples from the periphery.

Cities first developed as focal points of trade and craft production, in which the great variety of goods produced in the river valleys and surrounding hill country were exchanged and distributed. Merchants and craftsmen managed their own affairs and played a significant role in jurisdiction and in civic life. Manufactured artefacts were exchanged for raw materials from further afield. Towards the end of the fourth millenium writing was used to record weights, measures, and receipts. Cities were where kings lived and justice was administered. These great cities were regarded as the height of both moral and economic achievement.

In the city of Nippur, it was said, the god Enlil would not tolerate 'the oppressor... the informer, the arrogant, the agreement-violator' (in Kramer 1963: 120). A late second-millenium text described Babylon as 'a place of abundance [and] wealth... the seat of kingship and power... the seat of justice... giving sanctuary and protection... the bond of heaven and under-world... the house of reason and counsel... perfect in all understanding' (in George 1997: 126–7).

What little is known of the life of the mind and heart has, as in Egypt, come down to us mostly in the form of religious beliefs and imagery. We may take it that this was the primary mode of experiencing and expressing human life and the world. And one important role of the city was as a cult centre. Temples were centres of administration, and for storing, distributing, and exchanging goods. Cities were identified with particular gods, the god being the true owner and king of the city (Garelli 1979: 323), watching over its fortunes. Enlil presided over Nippur, Marduk over Babylon, Ashur over Assyria.

These city-states were ruled by kings, sometimes alongside a civic assembly of elders, merchants, and others. The dominant, indeed the only, ideology was kingship. It was articulated in hymns, poems, and myths; monumental scupture, reliefs, and inscriptions emphasized a king's status, and recorded his achievements for all (especially the city's inhabitants) to see or read about (Mieroop 1997: 119). Royal inscriptions were also designed to gain the king favour with the gods, and fame among men (Paul 1970: 21). Under the Akkadian kings Sargon and Naram-Sin during the late third millenium, there was 'a new emphasis on the royal person in the public plastic arts and public display ceremonies' (Michalowski 1993: 87). Kings 'made art an instrument of their politics' and used it 'to express the imperial ideology'. The ruling circles of officials and scribes were imbued with 'technical, detailed, complex texts',[1] which 'provided an ideological continuity for a bureaucratic class' under succeeding rulers. Social hierarchy was also legitimized in this way.[2] What most people actually thought remains inaccessible; judging by analogous situations, one should not assume it was significantly different.

In the twenty-fourth century Semitic Akkadians took over and created the world's first empire under a 'Great King'. Two centuries later, this was dissolved and something like the previous pattern restored (the Ur III period). From the early second millenium, tribal confederacies of Amorites, a western Semitic people who had been immigrating into the cities, began to take over. Now Babylon rose to primacy (the Old Babylonian period), especially under Hammurabi (r. *c.* 1696–1654 BCE)—an Amorite sheikh.[3]

Further north, the city-state of Ashur saw off the Amorites. From around 2000 BCE it had established trading colonies in other cities; now, in the later part of the second millenium, it created its own empire, based on its military power, and extended its rule southwards into Babylonia and ancient Sumer. In 609 BCE the Assyrians were thrown out of Babylon, which was then ruled by a 'neo-Babylonian' dynasty. Finally, the Persians under Cyrus took over the whole region and conquered Babylon (539 BCE).

Thus there was less political stability, and also less ideological continuity, than in Egypt. Ruling groups came and went, sometimes without forging a socio-political identity within their empires. These different regimes represented different types of political culture. In the periods of Sumerian independence, autonomous cities formed leagues, the religious and cultural centre being Nippur, Enlil's city, 'the bond between heaven and earth' (in Westenholz 1979: 109). Sometimes there was a Great King holding undefined powers.

The Akkadians, and later the Amorites, on the other hand, were tribal and dynastic, focusing on the dynastic household and with a more top-down notion of authority (Postgate 1992). They emphasised the king as heroic warrior, leading his people in war and protecting them from enemies and rebels. King Sargon set a pattern for absolute monarchy. In the Old Babylonian period there was a development of individual self-consciousness; people became more involved with their own personal gods.

The Assyrian kings emphasized the role of the king as warrior and protector. They too practised royal absolutism, partly modelling themselves on Sargon, who had by now become a model monarch. 'With your just sceptre, extend the frontiers of the country', the Assyrian king was commanded at his coronation. But these kings 'were never deified either in the official cult or in popular devotion'.[4] New Babylonia returned to the more civic model.

There was thus a contrast between periods of civic political culture, and those in which tribal warrior aristocracies—the Amorites, Kassites, Elamites, and finally the Persians—predominated. One might apply here Ibn Khaldun's contrast between the civilization of the wilderness (*badawa*) and that of the city (*hadara*) (Black 2001: 173).

'Kingship' (*nam-lugal*: 'the Existence of the Great Man') referred to the office of the 'Great King'; that is, a large-scale ruler who 'exercised a nominal hegemony over most, if not all the city-states within the orbit of Sumerian culture'. He could arbitrate border disputes.[5] Such a Great King was at the same time the king of that city-state which had achieved hegemony in the region at any particular time. According to the Sumerian king-list (composed in the latter part of the third millenium), this office of overlordship went back to the beginning of history, when kingship 'was lowered from the heavens' (Reade 2001: 4). The minor rulers of the other states were 'small kings'; they stood in a reciprocal relationship to the Great King, owing him loyalty but also expecting protection from him (Liverani 1990: 68).

The Mesopotamians' view of kingship, like the Egyptians', was an integral part of their religious beliefs. Some hold that these very religious beliefs were a reflection of their theory and practice of kingship ('in almost every particular the world of the gods is a projection of terrestrial conditions', as Jacobsen put it (1943: 167)). Religion, heroism, and folklore could be metaphors for politics, all the more effective if unconsciously so. Royal language was used to portray the ideal life of the gods: 'Enlil who sits broadly on the white dais, the lofty dais; who perfects the decrees of power, lordship and pinceship; the earth-gods bow down in fear before him ... Only to his exalted vizier ... did he commission to execute his all-embracing orders' (in Kramer 1963: 120–1). It seems in fact impossible to say how far religious belief led to a strong theory of kingship, or kingship provided a model for the world of the gods.

The social order was also assumed to be continuous with, and part of, nature. The gods ordered and controlled both. Perhaps 'political and economic power and inequalities had to be portrayed as part of the "natural" order of things . . . rather than as stemming from human choice or innovation' (Pollock 1999: 189). But it seems also possible that people believed unquestioningly that the social order, with its elites, hierarchy, and kingship, *was* part of the natural order, just like the sun and the stars.

In the Mesopotamian cosmos there were many gods; and so they managed their affairs in a divine *assembly,* led by Anu (god of heaven). The gods discussed among themselves until all were in agreement, in the manner of tribal decision-making (above, p. 11). Then Enlil, Anu's son, carried out 'the verdict, the word of the assembly of the gods, the command of Anu and Enlil' (in Frankfort et al. 1946: 136–7). To what extent this corresponded to actual civic procedures on earth has been hotly debated. It is possible that it was, once again, an idealized picture in undefined relation to what actually went on (or indeed to what people thought ought to go on) in a human state. We hear no argument that the human polity *ought* to be modelled on this divine pattern.

What we can say is that kingship, as in Egypt, must have met socio-political needs which could not, perhaps, have been met by any other means: the need for stability and order in a society that had extended far beyond the ties of kinship. Kingship stood at a certain distance from the life of ordinary people, from civil society; the king stood outside society and delivered justice to it. And probably only someone who was believed thus to stand outside society could have had the authority necessary to enforce the requirements of justice, especially against rich and powerful people; so that without this phenomenon the life of the ordinary person might have been worse. Indeed, society might not have held together at all (we are all-too familiar with instances of this nowadays). The state had to be special—in some sense divine—in order to work in people's minds. It is clear enough in any case that the gods and power went together. When someone rose to be king, it was because he had the favour of the gods. When one city-state conquered others, it was because its god had been singled out by the assembly of gods.

Each city-state was regarded as the estate of a particular deity. If the gods were to get the sustenance and reverence they wanted from earth, there had to be order in society and the people must be governed. The human king was the god's estate manager (*ensi*), employed by the god to look after the land and its people, for the god's and the people's well-being.

An Assyrian proverb put a different argument for kingship. It presented kingship as a necessary part of the natural and social order, but *without* reference to gods: 'a people without a king is like a flock without a shepherd, a crowd without a supervisor, water without a pipe . . . a house without a master, a wife without a husband' (in Labat 1939: 373). This non-religious argument comes from an unofficial source. The same argument was later used in early medieval Europe.

In this Mesopotamian model, unlike the Egyptian, supreme authority *circulated* from one city to another. This was in accordance with the wish of the gods. The gods in their assembly had decided that a certain one of them—the god of the newly ascendent city-state—should have primacy. When, for example, Babylon conquered much of the region, this, according to the prologue to the laws of Hammurabi, was because Anum and Enlil had decided to transfer 'the Enlil functions over all mankind' to Marduk (god of Babylon); Enlil nominated 'me, Hammurabi, the devout, god-fearing prince' (*ANE* 164a). Thus the inscrutable fortunes of war were based on the gods' collective decision-making (Cooper 1993: 21), a divinely ordained revolution of power. The idea of a divinely ordained revolution of power recurred in Jewish thought. For similar reasons, the Assyrians held hostage the gods of conquered cities, in the form of their statues, until their rulers accepted defeat (Cogan 1974: 37).

The coexistence of many cities, each with its own god and king, did not mean that there was a plurality of *legitimately* independent power-centres, as there later was in Greece. By contrast, legitimate human authority was conceived as inherently *universal*—like that of the gods. In this, Mesopotamian and Assyrian ideology was the same as the Egyptian. This aspiration went back (according to later texts) to early Sumer: a Sumerian king was called 'king of the four quarters [that is, the universe]...who exercised kingship over the entire world'. 'Enlil...made all sovereign countries wait upon him, and made everybody from where the sun rises to where the sun sets submit to him...from the Persian Gulf along the Tigris and Euphrates to the Mediterranean.'[6] The Mesopotamian and Assyrian concept of the state was universalist: there could only be one state in the world.

This claim to universal empire took on a stronger meaning with the Akkadian dynasty; Sargon was 'king of the totality'.[7] This ideological claim was generated by the need to convince the core population of the greatness of their king, as well as by the religious logic of authority ('It is not so important truly to control the world as...to persuade the inner population that we control the world'—Liverani 1990: 47). It was partly for domestic consumption. Their own right to universal hegemony was a core belief in the Assyrians' monarchical state. They ruled some of the conquered provinces directly, others though native rulers as vassals (Cogan 1974: 37, 60). This added a practical nuance to the imperial project.

There was never any question of religious intolerance (in the later Judaeo-Christian sense). Acceptance of the gods of other peoples went with polytheism. Under Assyria, the annexed provinces simply had to include Ashur in their cult. Vassal states could worship as before; in fact, their cults were subsidized to win the hearts and minds of gods and men alike (Cogan 1974: 41, 60, 112).

Kings were said to have been personally selected by the god.[8] Enlil, the gods' 'executive', had to ensure that their wishes were carried out on earth, and so he sought out a suitable individual to be king. 'Thou didst single me out with the glance of thine eyes; thou didst desire to see me rule. Thou didst take me from among the mountains. Thou didst call me to be a shepherd of men. Thou didst grant me the sceptre of justice', said Ashurnasirpal II, king of Assyria 883–859 (in Frankfort 1948: 239) (compare Jahweh's choice of David). Some royal hymns tell of the god fathering the king (Kramer 1974: 165–6). This was close to the Egyptian view.

Sumerian kings were credited with ideal qualities: physical perfection, courage, profound wisdom, insight into people's hearts. Both god and king were 'sovereign', 'legitimate shepherd', 'lord of the lands', 'lord of the universe'. Once again, it was the Akkadian monarchs Sargon and Naram-Sin who took the final step towards divinizing the monarch; this was part of their policy of putting all other states and their gods in their subjection. Hammurabi called himself 'the sun-god of Babylon who causes light to rise over the land of the Sumerians and the Accadians'.[9]

From the language and concepts used, it seems clear that the gods had established not just individual rulers but an *institution*, with specific functions, which would outlast individual rulers—we can call this a state. It was symbolized by 'sceptre, tiara and [shepherd's] crook'; these 'lay deposited before Anu in heaven' before 'kingship descended from heaven'.[10] Among the fundamental cosmic and cultural essences were 'the exalted and enduring crown, the throne of kingship, the exalted scepter, the royal insignia, the exalted shrine, shepherdship, kingship'. Kingship was *bala*; that is, 'return or reversion to origin', or 'term of office'.[11] This sounds like the prototype of the Irano-Islamic notion of the state (*dawla*) (Black 2001: 50–1). Thus, it seems, theology led, or enabled, people to formulate the abstract concept of an authority that would transcend the vagaries and misfortunes of individual monarchs, and so provide a more effective political instrument for human survival and reproduction.

THE FUNCTIONS OF MONARCHY

What, then, did the gods expect of their estate manager? What *were* 'the Enlil functions'? What was the state for? On this subject we have the gods' point of view: the king is put there, first, to maintain the established order of the god's estate, including both the temple with its economic infrastructure, and justice among humans; secondly, to carry out specific divine commands, notably temple-building, war, and peace. He might receive special instructions in dreams. Certain decisions could only be made on the correct days. In other words, he is 'producer of wealth, pious supporter of the cult, war leader, circuit judge' (Jacobsen 1957: 115–16 n.).

First, then, it was the king's duty, as high-priest, to satisfy the gods by observing their cult: he was 'intermediary between the human community and its divine ruler'. 'This constituted the essential feature of kingship'. Thus, 'most Sumerian works of art show kings engaged in . . . ceremonial acts, such as carrying bricks to build temples . . . or standing piously before the god in perpetual prayer'.[12] A king was expected to undergo abstinence and observe complicated rituals on behalf of his people.

All this might have given power to the priests. They, however, were appointed by the king. From the mid-third millenium a kind of secularization seems to have taken place. In the early 2300s the king of Lagash 'proclaimed an edict ostensibly placing all lands in the hands of the city-gods, but in reality taking control of all temple domains himself'. Temples were 'incorporated into the palace hierarchy'.[13]

The king was also responsible for the prosperity of his subjects. This could include the practical tasks of building and maintaining irrigation canals.[14] 'All the most ancient inscriptions of Sumerian rulers are devoted to the construction or reconstruction of temples and canals'. A hymn to King Solgi of Ur III (r. c. 2000–1953 BCE) ran: 'In your shepherding in a tender mother's heart the land is at peace, the land grows; the peoples live in peace side by side; the prosperity of the people shines like the day.' There was a religious element in this, too: economic success depended upon the construction of appropriate temples. Moreover, 'the person of the king had a profound relationship with the life of animals and plants'. King Gudea (late twenty-first century) was promised by god that 'prosperity shall accompany the laying of the foundations of my house. All the great fields will bear for thee; dikes and canals will swell for thee . . . Oil will be poured abundantly in Sumer in thy time. Good weight of wool will be given in thy time'.[15]

In a more secular vein, Sargon II of Assyria (721–705 BCE) claimed he was able 'to provide the wide land of Assyria with food to repletion . . . as befitting a king, through the filling of their canals, to save the people from want and hunger . . . [and] to provide sumptuous offerings fit for the tables of god and king'. When the cities accepted Ashurbanipal (668–627 BCE) as king of Assyria, there occurred rainfall and wonderful crops. This 'economic' function extended to price control and social welfare. Sargon II acted so that 'no

interruption may occur in the offerings of the sick, so that the oil of abundance, which soothes men, does not become expensive...[and] the price of
every article had its limit fixed'.[16]

All these aspects were conveyed by the image, going back to we know not
when, of the king as shepherd. Lipit-Ishtar (r. *c.* 1838–1828 BCE) was 'the wise
shepherd' (*ANE* 159), Hammurabi 'the beneficent shepherd whose scepter is
righteous; my benign shadow is spread over my city. In my bosom I carried the
peoples of the land of Sumer and Akkad; they prospered under my protection;
I always governed them in peace; I sheltered them in my wisdom'.[17]

JUSTICE

Finally, the king existed to ensure justice. The Mesopotamians, unlike the
Egyptians, developed a theory of *law*. This was based on *kittum* ('truth and
right'), which (like *maat* in Egypt) 'belonged to a sphere of existence that
surpassed both the human and the divine'. This immutable justice was to be
spelled out and implemented by the 'just king (*sar mesarim*)'. He was its 'agent
rather than its source', and subordinate to it. 'What the god "gives" the king is
not "laws" but the gift of perception of kittum', so that the king, and he alone,
'becomes capable of promulgating laws that are in harmony with the cosmic
principle of kittum'. A king could then tell his subjects what the law was in all
the varieties of life's circumstances by means of royal *legislation*. The law in
this sense was 'an economic rather than a religious concern'.[18]

The just king, like god, should punish the unjust judge, and anyone 'who
handles the scales in falsehood', and reward those who refuse bribes (Sumero-
Akkadian hymn: *ANE* 388). As in Egypt, the king's role in protecting the poor,
weak, and oppressed from lawlessness or domination by the rich and powerful
was strongly emphasized in discourses about justice. In other words, the king
existed to *rectify the existing inequities* in society; getting rid, that is, of the
harmful effects of social hierarchy. This was modelled on the gods' activity:
Nanshe is one 'who knows the orphan, who knows the widow, knows the
oppression of man over man, is the orphan's mother, Nanshe, who cares for the
widow'. She will 'comfort the orphan...set up a place of destruction for the
mighty, turn over the mighty to the weak' (in Kramer 1963: 124–5). A late
third-millenium king was said to have 'left not the orphan at the rich man's
mercy, left not the widow at the mercy of the strong...On the neck of
lawlessness and of rebels he set his foot'. A nineteenth-century king promised
'the seized just man to deliver, the evil-doer to annihilate...that the weak
succumb not to the strong, but the powerless renew strength, that the mighty

may not act arbitrarily, nor do violence to the weak'. Hammurabi said he had been made king 'to cause justice to prevail in the land, to destroy the wicked and the evil, that the strong might not oppress the weak'; and he had his laws written down 'in order that the strong might not oppress the weak, that justice might be done the orphan and widow'.[19] The parallel with Egypt could hardly be closer.

Sometimes the intention was not only to redress a specific grievance, but to remove the weak from the power of the strong by putting them under the king's protection. Urukagina, a reforming monarch of the twenty-fourth or twenty-third century, was said to have 'joined the covenant with [the god] Ningirsu that he would not deliver up the weak and the widow to the powerful man'.[20] In eighteenth- to seventeenth-century Babylonia, 'the annulment of debts by the king became a common occurrence' (Mieroop 1997: 206). This suggests a desire to readjust the relationships of power, not simply to correct an injustice already done, but to create a situation in which it would not happen again.

One way of achieving this was to have the laws inscribed so that all could know their rights. This was one major difference between Mesopotamia and Egypt. Written laws were a feature of the Sumerian cities from early times. Urukagina claimed to have 'restored the ancient decrees'. Legislation was undertaken by several Mesopotamian kings prior to the famous collections of Lipit-Ishtar and Hammurabi. Such 'codes' were in fact reforms, 'modifications of an existing body of law', or 'executive orders' on matters needing further regulation. Hammurabi's code included regulation of wages.[21]

Such activities gave rise to sincere self-congratulation on the part of kings: 'When Marduk commissioned me to guide the people aright . . . I established law and justice in the language of the land, thereby promoting the welfare of the people', said Hammurabi. A later Babylonian king, it was said, 'did not rest night or day, but with counsel and deliberation he persisted in writing down judgments and decisions arranged to be pleasing to the great lord, Marduk, and for the betterment of all the peoples . . . He drew up improved regulations for the city, he built anew the law court'.[22]

Hammurabi himself spelled out the advantage to the ordinary person of having laws collected and written down: 'Let any man who has a cause come into the presence of the statue of me, the king of justice, and then read carefully my inscribed stela, and give heed to my precious words, and may my stela make the case clear to him; may he understand his cause' (Code of Hammurabi, in *ANE* 178). Publication of the laws was specifically designed to ensure justice *for the future*: 'let the king who appears in the land observe the words of justice which I wrote on my stela; let him not alter the law of the land which I enacted' (ibid.). In other words, such written codes were supposed to bind future kings.

Mesopotamians, like Egyptians, looked to their king as one who rights wrongs and restores order after chaos. Here too kings were acting on behalf of gods. Desolation and disorder were described in terms of 'a cultic experience', in which (in Engnell's words) 'the temples are profaned...the people are without protection...famine and diseases are rife' (1967: 49). The reforms of Urukagina, Lipit-Ishtar, and Hammurabi were written down as royal law-collections. Reform also meant restoration of liberty: Lipit-Ishtar had 'procured the freedom of the sons and daughters of Nippur...Ur...Sumer and Akkad upon whom slaveship had been imposed' (*ANE* 159).

CITY ASSEMBLIES

'The palace and the citizenry formed two separate political elements in the Mesopotamian city'. There were assemblies of citizens, but with the exception of Old Assyria not much is known about them, nor about their relationship to kings. There were 'guilds', based on common professions or crafts, in some cities, sometimes occupying separate localities.[23] It appears that, especially in Babylonia, civic assemblies had a good deal of autonomy in commercial and legal matters.[24] A document from early second-millenium Nippur speaks of various craftsmen and manual workers sitting in an assembly and taking part in a judgement of a case of homicide. Sometimes a kind of mayor was made responsible for law and order, and sometimes this person acted as intermediary between the citizenry and the palace (Mieroop 1997: 122–3, 130, 139). There are parallels here with medieval Europe (Black 2003: 47).

Jacobsen argued that city assemblies had been much more powerful in earlier times (Jacobsen 1943: 165). Stories about gods and heroes seemed to him to legitimate democracy. An incident in the Gilgamesh epic (late third millenium?) says that Gilgamesh, the hero of Uruk, when faced with the choice whether or not to resist an invasion, consulted first the 'elders' and then 'the men of the city'. (Within the citizenry, there was a distinction between 'elders' and 'men of the city'; sometimes there was a separate council of elders.) Another story tells of an 'assembly of all the gods', including goddesses: after they had had a good drink, the 'father of the gods' put forward subjects for discussion, and these were debated with 'intelligence, profundity and knowledge'. In the Flood story in the Gilgamesh epic, someone who has to explain why people are building a big ship asks: 'what shall I answer the town, the craftsmen and the elders?' (in Jacobsen 1943: 166 n., 168) (but this may just mean that craftsmen wanted reasons for the work they were going to do). It is possible that these were not portrayals of current practice, but what the author thought had happened in a remote past, or would happen in an ideal world.

Jacobsen found further support for his view in the twelfth-century Babylonian 'Epic of Creation'. Here the origin of kingship is traced to an occasion when Marduk offered to fight as champion of the gods against their common enemy, but only on condition that the *assembly* of gods transferred all authority to him: 'If I am to be your champion... then establish an assembly and proclaim my lot supreme... so that whatever I frame shall not be altered, and the command of my lips... shall not be changed'. Jacobsen interpreted this as indicating that power had originally been transferred *by the assembly of citizens* to a king. There was also an occasion when an individual was reported to have been made king by a city assembly after a popular revolt against his predecessor. Postgate thinks that, 'whether or not the event is historically accurate, it must reflect contemporary attitudes'.[25] This has led some to see parallels between the Mesopotamian city and the Greek polis (Springborg 1987).

But this view of 'primitive democracy' in ancient Mesopotamia has been disputed.[26] For in other passages, distinctly political language was used to describe the supreme god Anu as absolute sovereign: 'Wielder of the scepter, the ring... who callest to kingship, sovereign of the gods, *whose word prevails in the ordained assembly of the great gods*... What thou has ordered comes true!... O Anu! thy great command takes precedence, *who could say no to it?*' (in Frankfort et al. 1946: 140, my italics). It was widely accepted that royal commands could not be questioned: 'The command of the palace, like the command of Anu, cannot be altered. The king's word is right'. Assyrian kings assembled the whole population and made them swear by the gods to accept a particular son as sole legitimate heir.[27]

The quasi-democratic view receives support, however, from evidence unearthed in Old Assyria. Here, according to Larsen, the king had three roles: he was, as chief priest, the 'steward (or vicar) of Ashur', he was the head of the royal lineage, and he was leader of the city assembly, responsible for carrying out its decisions. Larsen thinks, nonetheless, that 'the terminology of the texts indicates that the fundamental powers were held by the assembly rather than the king. It was the assembly which passed verdicts'. The economic and administrative affairs of old Assur were controlled by a 'city hall', and this was run by an officer, selected annually by lot. The assembly, acting in the name of the city, supervised the city's colonies and their legal proceedings.[28]

In Old Assyria the word *karum* (lit. 'harbour') referred to the merchants of a city as a body; in the Assyrian trading colonies such a body could represent the city as a whole, and act independently.[29] Some Old Assyrian colonies appointed a group of individuals, designated by the collective abstract noun *limmum*, to act as their representatives and enter into contracts on their behalf. Was this an instance of corporate representation, some 2,000 years before the Roman jurists developed it? In the Assyrian colonies in Anatolia, especially Kanesh, there is evidence (between *c.* 1920 and *c.* 840 BCE) of an assembly. It was composed of 'small men' and 'big men'; government was formally in the hands of 'the colony, small and big'. The elders could represent the city, and the council of 'big men' decided when to summon the assembly, and what proposals should be put to it.[30]

Some scholars think that, rather than cities having originally been more democratic, they became more self-governing and obtained more privileges during the first millenium. Residents of certain cities, notably ancient cult centres such as Nippur, were given 'exemptions from taxation, corvée and military duties'; and, in the legal sphere, exemption from capital punishment and the right of appeal to the king. In the late second millenium, Babylon was called 'the privileged city, which liberates the captive'. Such privileges were sometimes inscribed on a stele.[31] In neo-Babylonia, ethnic minorities (such as Egyptians and Jews) acquired some judicial independence (Dandamaev 1982: 41). The citizens of Babylon requested that this same protection be extended to foreign residents; for Ashurbanipal had guaranteed them that 'whoever enters Babylon is assured permanent protection... Even a dog who enters will not be killed' (in Mieroop 1997: 136). This too had a parallel in medieval Europe.[32]

Similar views were expressed in a sixth-century account of the revolt of Babylon against Assyria. The revolt is explained by the usual model of a divine 'revolution' of power, but this time the crimes of the Assyrian king Sennacherib against Babylon were emphasized: he had destroyed the city's temples. The Babylonians said that this was caused by Marduk's anger against his own city (Babylon). When this anger abated, Sennacherib was overthrown for crimes against *both the gods and the people of Babylonia;* he had behaved 'without pity towards the inhabitants of the country'. Eventually, partly as a result of this, 'the days had rolled round, the fixed time came' (in Labat 1939: 117). This argument was based on divine protection; the divinely ordained circulation of power was being used to justify a popular revolt.

Another document from the first half of the first millenium stated that Marduk would cause a ruler who ignored Babylon's privileges to be defeated by his enemies (no right of popular resistance here). In Babylonia the citizenry came to identify themselves with the *temple* organization, they 'expressed their views in powerful temple assemblies'.[33] The Persian takeover was facilitated by clashes between the king and the priests (Labat 1939: 15). Dandamaev calls this 'self-rule by free and legally equal members of society united in a popular assembly' (in Mieroop 1997: 138). But juridical autonomy is not the same as self-government.

These different views may be partly reconciled by distinguishing between two levels of government: a larger unit (empire) ruled by a Great King whose power was, in theory, unlimited; and the subordinate cities, in which legal and commercial affairs—the domain of civil society—were managed by groups of citizens. This is reflected in the way in which imperial rulers—such as the Assyrians—negotiated agreements with cities under their rule. A similar two-tier system ('indirect rule') has functioned in several empires, both ancient and modern.

In ancient Mesopotamia and Assyria both the city as a whole and groups of citizens within it had at various times some degree of autonomy. Yet, in contrast with ancient Greece, this culture produced, so far as we know, no ideology, far less a philosophy, of civic self-government. There was no radical religious movement, as in India; no competing schools of thought, as in China; no sign of coherent opposition to the established order. But there was Israel.

What parallels and contrasts were there between Mesopotamia and Egypt? In both, the king was formally absolute, his powers unlimited. But never in Mesopotamia was his relationship with god so close as in Egypt; no Mesopotamian king was deified. In both cultures the image of the king as shepherd of the people was developed. The king's duty to implement justice, especially by fair adjudication between the powerful and the weak, was emphasized in both cultures, perhaps more insistently in Egypt. The most striking contrast was the judicial and, occasionally, political role of citizens in Mesopotamia, and the complete absence of such popular participation in Egypt.

NOTES

1. Liverani 1993*b*: 49 n.; and Liverani 1990: 28.
2. Michalowski, in Cooper 1993: 22; Pollock 1999: 169; Barrelet 1974: 39; Lamberg-Karlovsky 1986: 205.
3. I am deeply grateful to Dr Julian Reade (from whose conversation I borrowed this phrase) for clarifying a great deal about Mesopotamian and Assyrian history and thought for me.
4. Garelli 1979: 323; Labat 1939: 362, 368, 372.

5. Westenholz 1979: 109; Frankfort et al. 1946: 195.
6. Kramer 1963: 51; Jacobsen 1957: 135–6.
7. Michalowski 1993: 88; Liverani 1990: 44; Labat 1939: 20. 'Implicitly, the universal empire exists already from the beginning...It is the seat of the only king operating as a relay between gods and men' (Liverani 1990: 47).
8. Westenholz 1979: 109; Cooper 1993: 12.
9. Kramer 1974: 171–4; Engnell 1967: 23, 37–8.
10. In *CAH* i/2 102; Barrelet 1974: 38.
11. Kramer 1963: 116; Frankfort 1948: 218; Jacobsen 1943: 170.
12. Larsen 1976: 113–14, 149; Labat 1939: 361; Westenholz 1993: 165.
13. Mieroop 1997: 16, 33; Pollock 1999: 193; Labat 1939: 363–4; Frankfort 1948: 259–60.
14. Diakonov, in Larsen 1976: 112; Mieroop 1997: 119.
15. Engnell 1967: 39; Labat 1939: 278; in Frankfort 1948: 257–8.
16. Labat 1939: 295; in Mieroop 1997: 60.
17. Epilogue to his Code: *ANE* 178. See also Kraus 1974: 252.
18. *ANE* 159; Paul 1970: 5–8, 25.
19. Frankfort 1948: 274; in Engnell 1967: 40; *ANE* 164, 178, 440.
20. In *CAH* i/2 140, 142; Kramer 1963: 82.
21. Kramer 1963: 83, 289; in Labat 1939: 230; Postgate 1992: 289.
22. *ANE* 165; in Whitelam 1979: 21.
23. Mieroop 1997: 82, 128; Finer 1997: 217.
24. Jacobsen 1943: 165; Dandamaev 1988: 67.
25. Jacobsen 1943: 165, 169–70; Postgate 1992: 269–70.
26. Mieroop 1997: 119; Garelli 1979: 323; Labat 1939: 25.
27. Frankfort et al. 1946: 203; Labat 1939: 24.
28. Larsen 1974: 296–8, and 1976: 191, 369–70; Mieroop 1997: 39.
29. Jacobsen 1943: 161a, n.; Kraus 1982; Mieroop 1997: 204.
30. Larsen 1976: 162–3, 333–53, and 1974: 291.
31. Mieroop 1997: 118, 133–5; Brinkman 1974*b*: 415; George 1997: 126.
32. In the famous tag: 'City air makes you free after a year and a day'; Black 2003: 39.
33. Mieroop 1997: 136–8, Labat 1939: 21.

4

Iran

In the mid-sixth century BCE the entire Near East was taken over by Iran; Babylon was conquered in 539. Little is known about the early Iranian polity and religion. The sage-prophet Zoroaster may have lived between 1500 and 1300 BCE.[1] His teaching centred upon a 'fierce opposition between good and evil ... with man as an active and important factor in the outcome' (*CHI* iii/1. 353, 641). Early texts portray 'vertical social organization' of the family, clan or village, tribe, and country or province (ibid. 649). The first historically recorded dynasty were the Achaemenids (550–330 BCE); they have left no written texts. All that is known about their political beliefs is what can be gathered from inscriptions and policies. Yet that is not negligible.

Darius I (r. 521–486 BCE) claimed that the supreme deity, Ahura Mazda, had made him 'king over all the earth'. He owed his success to his special relationship with the god: 'whatever I did, by the will of Ahura Mazda did I do it ... to me Ahura Mazda was a friend ... Ahura Mazda is mine, I am Ahura Mazda's'.[2] *Farnah*, 'a kind of divine radiance or royal charisma' (Wiesehoefer 2001: 30; Ahn 1992: 305), was said to emanate from the king. The idea of the investiture of the king by the supreme god seems to mark 'the transition from a charismatic notion of power, bound up with tribal society and expressed in the Avesta', to a new view of monarchical sovereignty as 'in practice unlimited, extending to choice of a successor and substantially independent of the priesthood'.[3] Iran's adoption of sacred monarchy was thus part of its political development into a more unified and much larger state.

The king's favour with the deity was based on his 'righteousness'. As in Egypt and Mesopotamia (from which much of this could have been borrowed), this meant treating the poor and the honourable alike, favouring the weak against strong.[4] On his tomb Darius proclaimed how he rewarded 'the man who co-operates' and punished him 'who does harm' (in Wiesehoefer 2001: 33). From Zoroastrian religious ideas came the idea that the Persian[5] king is characterized by his 'love of truth'; his enemies and rebels belong to 'the Lie' (ibid. 21, 30).

In Iran, too, the king was perceived as having a dynamic relationship with the forces of nature; and he had a special role as protector and promoter of agriculture (Briant 1982: 447–8, 482–8). This was symbolized by the creation of magnificent gardens ('paradises'), constructed as havens of peace and models of productivity. The king sponsored irrigation-works; this 'politics of water' made the farming communities depend upon him (Briant 1982: 423, 429, 489).

The Achaemenids too claimed world sovereignty. Cyrus (d. 530) claimed to be 'king of the world . . . king of the four rims of the earth'.[6] And indeed the Achaemenid empire, extending from the Indus to the Aegean, from the Caucasus to the Nile, was the largest polity yet known, one of the largest in world history.

This achievement was facilitated by a new conception of sovereignty. The Iranian empire incorporated a multiplicity of tribes and nations by a policy of religious toleration. Their regime was more explicitly multicultural than any of its predecessors. They operated a policy of indirect rule, intervening as little as possible in the cultures of conquered peoples. The Iranian kings allowed conquered peoples to govern themselves to an unprecedented degree. They presented themselves as 'the legitimate heirs of the local monarchies'.[7] Darius reorganized imperial space into provinces, each governed by a satrap. This was the meaning of the title 'king of kings'.[8]

Achaemenid iconography showed the relationship between king and subject peoples as consensual. Tribute processions were portrayed 'as event[s] participated in voluntarily by dignified delegates of the subject nations' (Root 1979: 131, 282–3). The contrast with 'the brutal imagery of the Assyrian and Egyptian sculptural traditions' was surely deliberate.[9] There was a more generous attitude towards other people's cultures and religions. After he had conquered Babylon in 539, Cyrus claimed: 'I returned to these sacred cities . . . the sanctuaries which have been in ruins . . . the images which used to live therein . . . I gathered all their former inhabitants and returned them to their habitations' (in Wiesehoefer 2001: 45). This was the programme which allowed the Jews to return to their homeland and rebuild the Temple of Yahweh; Artaxerxes I (r. 465–24 BCE) gave the Jews legal autonomy, authorizing them to use the Mosaic law (Finer 1997: 245; Ezra 7: 11–26). The policy of 'world peace on the religious front' was applied throughout the whole empire.[10] Cyrus also claimed to have abolished forced labour. By officially tolerating other cults alongside their own, the Persian kings inaugurated a new phase in religious monarchy. It was by such means that the Persians linked together India, Mesopotamia, Greece, and countless tribes, with Aramaic as the common tongue.

The ancient Irananian views of sacred monarchy were revived and adapted by the Sasanian dynasty (*c.* 224–637 CE). The Sasanian king was said to rule by 'divine grace (*farr*)',[11] and to represent the supreme deity (Ahura Mazda) on earth (*CHI* iii(2). 864). There was a close relationship between the new regime and a revival of Zoroastrian religion[12] ('kingship and religion are brothers').[13] Iran also served as a connection between the Israelite and the Greek worlds. Cyrus freed the Jews; Darius and Xerxes failed to subjugate the Greeks. Both the Israelites and the Greeks put sacred monarchy behind them; but, while the Greeks were discovering science, the Jews were discovering Yahweh.

NOTES

1. Boyce 1984: 280; *CHI* ii. 684–5; Kellens 1991: 82–4.
2. In *CHI* ii. 684–5; Briant 1996: 195, 223.
3. Gnoli 1974: 163–4, 168; Dandamaev and Lukonin 1989: 117. This view is found in Achaemenid inscriptions but not in the ancient Iranian religious text, the *Avesta*. It probably owed much to the influence of neighbouring peoples, notably the Medes; Gnoli 1974: 118–22.
4. Wiesehoefer 2001: 33; Briant 1996: 224–5, 344.
5. As Iranians are sometimes called, following Greek precedent.
6. Darius styled himself 'king of the countries containing all races' (in Wiesehoefer 2001: 29, 45).
7. Dandamaev and Lukonin 1989: 97, 116; Koch 1984: 64; Gnoli 1974: 150.
8. Wiesehoefer 2001: 29; Högemann 1992: 357–8.
9. Root thinks this 'might reflect the persistence of an elusive Indo-Iranian vision of kingship' (1979: 226).
10. Gnoli 1974: 152–5; Högemann 1992: 334.
11. This was 'comparable with the Greek Tyche or Roman Fortuna' (Wiesehoefer 2001: 167).
12. Fowden suggests that they emulated the monotheistic faiths by formulating their own revealed scripture, the *Avesta* (1993: 81).
13. This was 'a late Zoroastrian design of an ideal state', though it may have 'emerged under Islamic influence' (Wiesehoefer 2001: 211). It became a popular saying; the Iranian Muslim sources ascribed it to the Sasanians (Black 2008: 23).

5

Israel

The ancient Israelites were not a major military or political power. But they produced an idea of what life is about, of god, humanity, and political society, which has for millenia dominated whole swathes of humanity. We encounter here the first phase of an ideology which has contributed to conflicts and constitutions almost everywhere, from India to America.

The political ideas of the Israelites are found in the various parts of the Hebrew Bible (the Old Testament). This consists of the Torah (or Law)—the first five books (Pentateuch)—the historical books (Joshua, Kings, and so on), the Prophets, and 'Wisdom' literature. Within the Torah and the histories, four layers of composition have been distinguished (Gottwald 1985). Two of these probably date from the tenth and ninth centuries BCE, subsequently edited between 722 and 609. A third was composed between 550 and 450 BCE, during and after the Exile in Babylonia (587–538). The fourth, the Deuteronomist History, emerged in 622 BCE (ibid. 137–9). The Prophetic writings range from the eighth to the second century. The Psalms and Wisdom literature were also written, or in some cases reworked, after the Exile.[1]

The history of the Israelites before the Exile is obscure. There was a pre-monarchical, or tribal, period. The Israelite monarchy appears to have been set up in the eleventh century. What happened before that is impossible to say. Norman Gottwald (1979; 2001) has suggested that the origins of Israel lay in the thirteenth and twelfth centuries; that then, during protracted wars between Egypt and Assyria, groups of Palestinian peasants and city-dwellers became disaffected with their overlords and with the class system of the cities. They established a new confederacy of tribes[2] with an informal military leadership (the 'judges'). It is possible that they organized themselves around a core of refugees from Egypt.

Such a process of 'retribalization' was highly unusual. And indeed Israel presents the only instance in the ancient world of an articulate, self-conscious tribalism. The melting-pot of Canaan–Palestine, intensely heated by the friction between Egypt and Assyria, had produced a new element.

This interpretation is compatible with, and may help to explain, some of the unusual features of Israelite thought. When they appeared in the light of history, the Israelites were a self-conscious group with their own ideology. As recorded in their own literature, when they entered the 'promised land' they were still organized along tribal lines.[3] Israel emerged from tribal society in its own unique way, not, as most societies did, by cohering around a king— that came later—but by cohering instead around the unifying authority of Yahweh and his Law. The Hebrew polity presents an utterly distinctive path from tribal to more heterogeneous association. As we shall see, the values of informal tribal society permeate, and often predominate in, the sacred texts. These values found unique expression in Israel.

Their greatest innovation was belief in one god (Yahweh), not only superior to all other gods, but eliminating them as either worthless or non-existent. 'Mono-Yahwism' focused 'on the deity as leader, ruler and defender of his people'.[4] The sharp delineation between insiders and outsiders, so character- istic of tribal societies, was also an integral part of mono-Yahwism.

Yahweh was so utterly above all else that no king could claim to represent him. In this sense, Yahweh was (as Gottwald puts it) 'politically unobtrusive'.[5] Since all humans are immeasurably below Yahweh, social distinctions are irrelevant and meaningless.

The other major innovation, according to the Hebrew scriptures, was that Yahweh had himself dictated a comprehensive legal and moral code to Moses after he had led the Israelites out of Egypt. Yahweh was the sole legislator; no king made laws, according to this view. As to the content of the Mosaic Law (or Torah), Gottwald argues that it was eminently suited to the kind of neo- tribal society which Israel aspired to be: in Finer's words, an 'egalitarian society of independent semi-literate small-holders—all warriors if need be' (Finer 1997: 244). For the Law stipulated that (in Gottwald's words) the 'means of production (land, herds and flocks)' should be owned inalienably by extended families. The Jewish laws 'inhibit[ed] social stratification', by, for example, prohibiting interest on loans and the sale of land outside the family. This mono-Yahwism, nowadays known as monotheism, was reproduced in Christianity and Islam.

Finally, Yahweh in his utter otherness did not need extravagant human gifts, which many of these hill people could ill afford anyway, so that no priestly class was necessary (Gottwald 1979: 646). This helped to ensure a relatively egalitarian society, based on 'the self-sustaining integrity of the household productive units'.[6] Social equality remained part of Jewish culture.[7]

An ideological innovation on this scale was perhaps necessary to ratify the social venture of the Israelites, and to validate their new political identity, which separated them so radically from all other peoples. It enabled them to survive as the type of economic entity which they aspired to be. Abraham's departure from the wealthy city of Ur, and his descendants' eventual escape from slavery in monarchical Egypt, may never have actually happened; they are certainly unverifiable.[8] But they were a potent myth for the Israelites' unique sense of their destiny as a people.[9] This may provide a better explanation for Yahwism than Assmann (1995), who argued that it was an adaptation of the radical monotheism of Egypt during the Amarna period (above, p. 25). For this there is no evidence.

The Israelites set up a monarchy (probably in the late eleventh century) as the most efficient means of organizing themselves to fight local rivals, such as the Philistines.[10] Yet throughout the monarchical period there remained tension between the central monarchy and the local structures of tribe and lineage (Halpern 1981: 247, 255). After a century-and-a-half the Israelite kingdom split in two, into a northern kingdom called 'Israel' and the southern kingdom of 'Judah', based on Jerusalem. Israel was destroyed by the Assyrians (722 BCE), and its ten tribes were absorbed into other peoples. In 587 BCE the Babylonians conquered Judah, destroyed the Temple at Jerusalem, and transported its leaders to Babylon.

When Cyrus of Persia (above, p. 47) conquered Babylon in 538, he allowed the exiled Jews to return to Judah, and to rebuild Jerusalem and its Temple. Judaea became a province, with religious and cultural autonomy, within the Persian, and later the Seleucid, empires. Then, from 167 to 63 BCE, 'Jewish nationalism flared into political independence' under the Maccabean monarchy (Gottwald 1985: 410). In 63 CE Judaea was conquered by Rome. The revolts of 66–73 CE and 132–5 CE led to the dispersal (diaspora) of the Jews. They maintained their cultural and ethnic identity. Alone among dispossessed peoples of the ancient world, the Jews regained their ancient territory in the twentieth century.

THE COVENANT

By the sixth and fifth centuries BCE, during and after the Exile, the Jews[11] had developed a distinctive view of what it meant to be a people and of the relationship between god, king, and people. The unique characteristics and cosmic status of the particular people of Israel were based on their unique relationship with Yahweh, the one and only true god. They, and they alone, had been chosen as god's beneficiaries. The fundamental relationship was not between god and the king of Israel, but between god and the people of Israel. This was expressed as the covenant.[12]

The relationship between god and the people was not exactly reciprocal. The covenant was not a contract in our sense. Yahweh would punish them for any fault, but he could never do wrong. When Yahweh made the covenant, he made a conditional promise of land and favour; Israel's promise to him was unconditional. The trade-off was that Israel was to recognize and worship Yahweh as the only existing god—this was said to be the essence of the Law— while Yahweh would recognize and treat them as his special people, his protectorate. Thus Yahweh denied entry into the promised land of Canaan to all those Israelites who had complained against him.[13]

The political fortunes of the Israelites were read entirely on the template of this relationship, and of the divinely ordained scheme, or theodicy,[14] resulting from it. If they failed to get into the promised land, or lost it, it was because they had failed to obey God and observe the Law. The disasters that befell Israel, on the other hand, were never Yahweh's fault. When it *appears* that Yahweh is not keeping his side of the bargain, for example when they can't get into the land, or are driven out of it, this is because *they* have done wrong. The purpose of the covenant was to instil into the people a dread of what will happen to them if they disobey 'the voice of Yahweh' and his law. Such a theodicy is terrifying.

According to the Hebrew scriptures, Yahweh promised the founding-father of the Israelites, Abraham, 'all the land that you can see', and made a pledge that Abraham would be 'the father of a host of nations'. Both pledges were made 'to you and to your descendants for ever... generation after generation, an everlasting covenant'. In return, Abraham was required to have himself and all his male descendants circumcised (Gen. 13: 15; 17: 4, 7, 9–14).

The terms of this covenant were expanded when Yahweh called Moses. Yahweh now promised the Israelites liberation from Egypt, by force if necessary ('I will rescue you from slavery there. I will redeem you with arm outstretched and with mighty acts of judgment'; Exod. 6: 6); and, secondly, a special relationship of patronage ('I will adopt you as my people, and I will become your God'; Exod. 6: 7): such patronage will be exclusive to Israel as 'a spiritual aristocracy' among nations (Paul 1970: 30). Thirdly, he promised them 'a land flowing with milk and honey'—the 'promised land' of Israel (formerly Canaan) (Exod. 3: 17; 6: 8; 23: 31). Finally, Yahweh promised military success against the inhabitants of this land: 'I will send my terror before you and throw into confusion all the peoples whom you find in your path. I will make all your enemies turn their backs' (Exod. 23: 27–8; 34: 11). Yahweh was, among other things, a warrior god, who revealed his power by destroying the pharaoh's armies and conquering the Canaanites. He smashes heads as well as Amun Re.[15] The Israelites in their turn undertook to recognize and worship Yahweh *alone*, observe the Law which he laid down for them (Exod. 19–30; Deut. 4–5), and obey his wishes in everything.

At certain critical moments in their history, the king or leader and the people of Israel renewed the covenant to obey Yahweh and his law. The terms of the covenant were expounded in greater detail by the Israelite commander Joshua, just before the Israelites entered the promised land. This time there was also a covenant between Joshua and the people, to the effect that they would 'banish the foreign gods' and worship Yahweh alone (Josh. 24: 25). Although this was clearly not a political contract between leader and people, it became the subject of political discourse in Europe and North America as just that.

There was a further agreement between Yahweh and the Israelite king, David. This time, Yahweh promised land, peace, a continuation of his dynasty for all time, and a father–son relationship between Yahweh and David's son, Solomon. (The term 'covenant' is not used.) Finally, King Josiah in 622 BCE supposedly 'rediscovered' a copy of the law, whereupon 'the king made a covenant before the Lord to obey him and keep his commandments . . . and so fulfil the terms of the covenant written in this book. And all the people pledged themselves to the covenant' (2 Kgs. 22: 8–23: 3).

The Israelite law was 'a code of moral behaviour coextensive with the everyday behaviour of everybody' (Finer 1997: 239). There was no distinction between crime and sin, since everything in the law was the command of Yahweh. What was unusual was that equal rights and responsibilities were ascribed to all.[16] King Zedekiah made 'a covenant with all the people in Jerusalem' that all 'Hebrew slaves, male or female' were to be set free (Jer. 34: 8–9). The dividing-line was drawn around, not within, the people.[17]

Who was involved in these covenants with Yahweh? The original covenant—between Yahweh and Abraham—was with a specific individual, and included a pledge to his many descendants. In other words, it involved a kinship group or race. In the first of the covenants with Moses, Moses was commanded to 'go and assemble the elders of Israel' (Exod. 3: 16); in the second, to 'say therefore to the Israelites . . .' (Exod. 6: 6); and on the third occasion, when Moses was about to receive the law (which included the 'Ten Commandments') on Mount Sinai, he 'came and summoned the elders of the people and set before them all these commands which the Lord had laid upon him'.[18] This was a uniquely awesome occasion: 'the people stood at a distance' (Exod. 20: 18, 21). Joshua, in turn, 'summoned all Israel, their elders and heads of families, their judges and officers' (Jos. 23: 2; 24: 1). In David's case the people were not involved.

One parallel with, and possible precedent for, these covenants was the 'ancient Near-Eastern international suzerain–vassal treat[ies] concluded between an imperial overlord and a subject ruler'. These are found in 'Aramean and neo-Assyrian texts of similar form [to the Israelite covenants] down to the seventh century'.[19] Some have also seen a parallel with the 'instructions' which Hittite kings gave to their subordinate officials; these were called 'bonds', the same as the Hebrew 'covenant/bond' (Weinfeld 1990: 182). These, however, were considerably earlier, in the fourteenth and thirteenth centuries BCE.

It was not unusual in the Near East, especially among the Hittites, to 'gather together all segments of the population to participate in the covenantal oath'. Even so, the Hittite 'bonds' included an obligation of unconditional loyalty to one's lord, whom one is bound to love 'with all the heart and soul' (Weinfeld 1990: 181, 184). The phrase 'for all the descendants in the future' was also used in Hittite covenants. One thirteenth-century Hittite king provides some parallel with Josiah's (much later) rediscovery of the law: Muwatallis made 'a prayer of confession for negligence in observing the laws of divinity as written in the law of covenant (*ishiul*) in ancient scripture and promised to do his utmost to rediscover the written covenant of the gods, and to fulfil it'.[20]

THE PEOPLE OF ISRAEL

It is important to see not just that there were precedents in the ancient Near East, but just where exactly Israelite political thought differed from that of other peoples, and by how much. And what leaps out is the absence of a king from the Hebrew covenants; that is, from the founding moments of society and state. The individual recipients of the divine covenant are Abraham and Moses: great leaders, but long dead. The agreement with David is not called a 'covenant'; it seems intended to add material about the state and royal dynasty, rather than as a recapitulation of what everyone knew to be the main body of the covenant, namely the Law. Rather, it was *the elders and the people* who were the politically active agents at the time.

The focal points of Israelite political thought, then, were Yahweh and the people or nation of Israel. Yahweh was the ultimate and ever-present authority, the sole legislator. The main organizing force in Hebrew, and later Jewish, society was the law (ascribed to Yahweh) and the religious worship and ritual it prescribed.

Divine legitimacy was bestowed not on the king but on 'the people', 'Israel', 'the Israelites', 'the men of Israel' (Gottwald 1979: 239). The Law had indeed been revealed to a historic leader, but he had transmitted it to the nation as a whole, not to a dynasty or institution. Through their role in the covenant, the people are positioned as the primary political actor.[21] The divine covenants were portrayed in the Hebrew scriptures as empowering not the monarch but the elders and the people.

This is what is most striking about Israelite political theory. Due to the absence of the king from the agreements, the people's role is much greater than it was among other peoples of the ancient Near East. The character of ancient Israelite political thought may be explained in terms of its neo-tribal origins. This was also how the texts saw it.

Yahweh's concern, then, was primarily with *the people of Israel.* All obligations to keep the covenant and obey its law are directed at them. The law is proclaimed to all the assembled people. This is to be repeated every seven years with *every individual present*—'the people, men, women, and dependants ... [and] aliens ... [and] children too' (Deut. 31: 11–13; Neh. 8: 2–3).

Yahweh insists time and again that the covenant be written down to preserve its exact words (Exod. 34: 27). Joshua 'wrote its terms in the book of the law of God'.[22] There was a requirement that every male be personally acquainted with the law (this was to be reproduced in Islam). Thus law, religious observance, and literacy all made the Jews in some ways more 'democratic', in some ways more conservative, than other peoples. We may say that from the Exile onwards they were the most articulate and politically aware people of the region.[23]

NATION

This view of the relationship between god and people gave rise to a unique form of nationalism. The nation of Israel was itself a confederacy of tribes, each tribe containing several clans, each clan several families. Gottwald notes 'the central importance of intertribal organization among the first Israelites'.[24] But it had the internal cohesion, the corporate identity of a super-tribe. The men of Judah saw themselves, at least in post-Exilic times, as a real collective body (in modern legal language, a 'corporation') with collective rights and obligations, which can act and be punished, or rewarded, as a unit.[25]

There was a strong sense of their own racial and cultural uniqueness, of 'tribalism' in the everyday modern sense. Cultural exclusiveness was asserted by insisting, unusually for this time and place, that all other gods were 'false'—impotent, irrelevant, or non-existent. Racial exclusiveness was asserted by the claim to common descent from the single male ancestor. Both the cultural and the racial elements were underscored by the first requirement of the covenant: male circumcision (also continued under Islam). 'This is how you shall keep my covenant between myself and you and your descendants . . . thus shall my covenant be marked in your flesh as an everlasting covenant'; the uncircumcised 'shall be cut off from the kin of his father. He has broken my covenant' (Gen. 17: 9–14).

This gave Israelites a strong sense of the 'other'. They viewed all other peoples as outsiders, aliens of inferior status and with fewer rights. They were told to drive out and kill, if necessary, the Canaanites (Josh. 23: 4–5).[26] Others may dwell in Canaan, but the people of Israel constitute an exclusive spiritual master-race. 'Out of all peoples you shall become my treasured possession; for the whole earth is mine. You shall be my kingdom of priests, my holy nation'.[27] Exclusive nationalism followed from exclusive monotheism: 'the Lord's name is the Jealous God' (Exod. 34: 14).

This had social and political repercussions. The Israelites were commanded to make no 'covenant with the natives' (Exod. 34: 14). They believed that they held their land from Yahweh on condition that they did not inter-marry or associate with 'the peoples that are left among you'.[28] They must 'demolish their altars, smash their sacred pillars' (Exod. 34: 13). This avoidance of other people is essential if they are to worship Yahweh and no other gods (Josh. 23: 7–8 and 24: 14, 22). The Hebrews were told that, if they associated with others, they would 'vanish from the good land which the Lord your God has given you' (Josh. 23: 7–16). One of the most important obligations of God's covenant, then, is national exclusiveness. For nation read '*umma*—a big leap, to be sure—and this too was to be replicated in Islam. Nationalism in all but name was born here, not in the French Revolution.

THE ELDERS AND THE PEOPLE

The transfer of divine authorization to the nation or people also took constitutional form. Both the elders and the popular assembly had important, if relatively informal, roles. 'The elders' referred to heads of lineages and households. They functioned as a collective body at local, tribal, and national levels (Halpern 1981: 198–205). In the cities, 'elders and notables' were said to sit in council alongside the ruler (1 Kgs. 21: 8). 'Elders' and 'people' sometimes play interchangeable roles, the elders being taken as 'reliable representatives of their constituents'.[29] They could negotiate agreements on their behalf.

'The people' (*'am*)—who were also called 'the men of Israel' or 'the people of the land'—referred to all able-bodied males—the tribal army, the nation in arms.[30] On any major decision, the people as a whole had to be consulted, negotiated with, won over. This did not necessarily imply (as in Greek and European democracy) that they had any right to get their way; it was more a fact of life. 'The body of free-and-equal males gathered for cultic celebrations, for periodic redistribution of land, and for exceptional deliberations on matters of war and of internal dispute'.[31] It was in the nature of Hebrew religion that the people bound themselves personally and individually to the covenant with Yahweh in an assembly of all.

For example, on receiving an unfavourable report about the promised land, the people 'one and all made a complaint against Moses and Aaron', and they would have stoned them had Yahweh not personally intervened (Num. 14: 1–10). The people persuaded Saul not to kill Jonathan (1 Sam. 14: 45–6). Serious policy issues were occasionally portrayed as being debated publicly in front of the people, on the divinely inspired initiative of a prophet. Thus Jeremiah is commanded to 'speak to the inhabitants of all the cities of Judah who come to worship' in Jerusalem—a kind of informal representation. On this occasion, 'priests, prophets and people' opposed Jeremiah; 'the people all gathered against Jeremiah'. But, on the arrival of 'the officers of Judah', both the priests and prophets and Jeremiah himself put their cases before 'the officers and the people'. These now, along with 'some of the elders of the land', supported Jeremiah and carried the day (Jer. 26: 1–17).

The elders and people together played a part in the establishment of the first king and in the subsequent choice of his successors. When Samuel presented Saul as 'the man whom the Lord has chosen', Saul was acclaimed by all (1 Sam. 10: 24), and he was also, at Samuel's suggestion, invested as king by 'all' (1 Sam. 11: 14–15). Acclamation followed the religious leader's declaration of the divine choice, but it was nevertheless part of the process.[32] Then there is the cryptic statement, 'Samuel then explained to the people the nature of a king, and made a written record of it on a scroll which he deposited before the Lord' (1 Sam. 10: 25). Was this a kind of 'written constitution'? It is the last we hear of it.

Besides this, becoming a king and remaining a king were subject to repeated negotiation. While this tends to occur in many cultures, no other tradition of the ancient Near East made it so explicit, if it was mentioned at all. Before Israel adopted monarchy, the problem was, rather, to persaude someone to take on the role of leader. Jephthah, the prospective war leader, has to be persuaded to take up the task, and (not unlike the god Marduk in Babylonian lore) he extracts a condition, namely, in this case, that, if he agrees to serve and the campaign is successful, the elders will recognize him as their lord (Judg. 11: 5–11). David's elevation as king is also preceded by negotiation with the elders and the people. After the Absalom disaster, David 'needs to campaign for re-election' (Halpern 1981). This involved regaining support by the kind of bandwagon effect one finds during succession disputes in many a pre-modern monarchy.

The people were portrayed as playing a decisive part in the break-up of the kingdom of Israel and in the appointment of a rival king. It was the *people* of the ten northern tribes of Israel who took the fateful decision to reject Solomon's designated heir, Rehoboam, secede from Judah, and appoint Solomon's younger son, Jeroboam (previously exiled by his father) as their king. 'All the assembly of Israel' made pointed requests to Rehoboam as a condition of accepting him as king (he should 'lighten the cruel slavery he imposed on us'). The elders who had attended Solomon recommended that Rehoboam should accept these conditions, but he refused. So 'when all Israel saw that the king would not listen to them', they 'went to their homes'—that is, refused him as king. 'The men of Israel' then 'called [Jeroboam] to the assembly and made him king over the whole of Israel'. This was how Israel seceded from Judah, and from 'the house of David'.[33]

In Judah itself, 'the assembly regained its strong position during the period after Solomon's death' (Mettinger 1976: 130). It sometimes played a critical role in deciding who was to be king. When Ahaziah (who had been made king by 'the inhabitants of Jerusalem') did what was 'wrong in the eyes of the Lord', he was assassinated. The priest Jehoiada then mustered support for one Joash. There was a bandwagon effect, and Jehoiada eventually 'gathered to Jerusalem the Levites from the cities of Judah and the heads of the clans in Israel'—that is, a wider constituency. There, 'all the assembly made a compact with the king', and accepted Jehoiada's choice of Joash as their king.

Thus the popular assembly could make and unmake kings; it played a much greater role than in Babylonia. But the assembly only functioned in a crisis. Israel and Judah were still quasi-tribal monarchies; the assembly had nothing like the regular and defined role it had in many Greek poleis. There is no sign of the kinds of clashes of interest between elders and people which occurred in the Greek poleis (but then the Hebrew scriptures were portraying an ideal situation). The assembly was usually called into play by others. But, once assembled, 'the people' seem to have played the role almost of de facto sovereign.

All of this may be compared with the well-known roles of elders and assemblies of male warriors among many tribal peoples. The prominence, unique among major ancient cultures, of elders and of the assembly of the male (warrior) population, is indeed the kind of thing one would expect if neo-tribalism played a significant role in the formation of Israel.

Thus, regarding the role of the people too, the Hebrew polity was unique in the ancient world; and indeed in the modern world until the French Revolution.

Neither Greek democracy nor European parliamentary institutions gave so much scope to an assembly of adult males. Here, too, Israel was a new *kind* of polity.

MONARCHY

The way in which monarchy is presented in the Hebrew scriptures almost certainly represents a later priestly and scribal view, not the actual situation under the pre-Exilic monarchy. This may have had considerable judicial and legislative powers.[34] In that case, the later theory adopted by the Hebrews was more 'original' than their pre-Exilic practice. The position of their king, as recorded in the surviving Hebrew histories and sacred texts, suggests a halfway house between informal tribal society and the fully fledged monarchy found in Egypt or Mesopotamia.

The outstanding difference between the Israelite or Jewish view of monarchy—as recorded in the scriptures—and the Egyptian or Mesopotamian views, was that for Israel the king in no way represented Yahweh. In the crucial matters of religious status and observance, he was on a level with the people. True, he sometimes acted as the agent of the people in a symbolic sense (not in the sense of representing their views). But he was subjected to criticism for religious irregularities, or for failing to live up to the increasingly high standard of justice expected by the legal and prophetic traditions. Such criticism came especially from 'prophets'. They were able to speak in this way because they were thought to have an independent line of communication from and to Yahweh. King and people were on a much more equal footing than in Mesopotamia or Egypt.

This low esteem for kingship is clear in the first version of the appointment of Saul as king of Israel. It was only because the people had rejected Yahweh that the elders asked Samuel to 'appoint us a king to govern us', so that they could be 'like other nations'—as indeed they would be: the trappings and ideology of monarchy appear to have been directly borrowed from Egypt. Samuel warned them that a king would take a tenth of all their goods, and that 'when that day comes, you will cry out against the king you have chosen; but it will be too late'. But the people persisted: 'we will have a king over us... to lead us out to war and fight our battles'. Yahweh reluctantly agreed.[35] The same peculiarly Hebrew theory of kingship appears in Deuteronomy, where the king is forbidden to have much in the way of horses, wives, or gold, in case he becomes too proud (Deut. 17: 16–20).

In the thought of ancient Israel as it has come down to us, the Law, not the king, was the primary agent of Yahweh, the foundation of the social and political order. The primacy of the Law was emphasized by the post-Exilic religious establishment. The (pre-Exilic) kings of Israel were portrayed as more limited by the law than kings in any other ancient monarchy. This is expressed in a 'constitutional' passage in Deuteronomy: 'When he has ascended the throne of the kingdom, [the king] shall make a copy of this law in a book at the dictation of the levitical priests. He shall keep it by him and read it all his life, so that he may...keep all the words of this law' (Deut. 17: 18–20). Difficult cases must be referred to the priests and judges, whose decisions have to be accepted.[36] There is, on the other hand, no evidence to show that, before the Exile, 'the king was in reality subject to the law of the kingdom' (Whitelam 1979: 220).

In the theory presented by the Jewish scriptures, royal authority is outweighed by the priests and judges as interpreters of the Law, and by prophets as voices of the ongoing will of Yahweh. Various individuals claimed divine inspiration as prophets, and denounced the king for deviating from the Law, or ignoring the current voice of Yahweh (Finer 1997: 239). On the other hand, there are signs that in practice a king could usually find priests and prophets to put his own view. Once again, there is a world of difference between the political ideology of Israel before and after the Exile.

Nor is there good evidence for the view that the relationship between king and people was contractual, with 'mutual obligations' on each side. According to the theory expressed in the various covenants, the relationship between Yahweh and the king was analogous to that between Yahweh and Israel, except that the king had the further reponsibility of ensuring that the nation as a whole kept the Law. This was indeed the condition on which Yahweh promised to secure the dynasty on the throne. When a king took part in the renewal of the covenant, he did so not on his own behalf but as the leading representative of the nation.[37] Thus when, under King Josiah, Deuteronomy was 'rediscovered', the king called together 'all the elders...the men of Judah and the inhabitants of Jerusalem, the priests and the prophets, the whole population, high and low', and 'read out to them all the book of the covenant discovered in the house of the Lord'. Then 'the king made a covenant before the Lord to obey him and keep his commandments...and so fulfil the terms of the covenant written in this book. And all the people pledged themselves to the covenant' (2 Kgs. 22: 8–23: 3). There was indeed no difference in status between king and people in relation to the covenant. This is principally because both stand immeasurably below Yahweh.

When the priest Jehoiada proclaimed Joash king, he 'made a covenant between the Lord and the king and people, that they should be the Lord's people, and also between the king and the people' (2 Kgs. 11: 17). But the point of this episode was to reaffirm Yahweh as sole god and to smash the temple of Baal (2 Kgs. 11: 18). A second decription of these events (2 Chron. 23: 16) made no mention of a covenant between king and people. If there was any 'covenant' between king and people, we have no idea what it was (a mutual pledge of loyalty, perhaps). There was anyway no suggestion on any of these occasions that there was a 'contract' between the king on one side and the people on the other, nor of limits on royal authority. (All this was read into these texts by Calvinist constitutionalists in the sixteenth and seventeenth centuries.) It is not, therefore, surprising that there was no procedure for dealing with either party's failure to keep a covenant between them.

The Psalms express a very different view of kingship; their language is often remarkably close to that of Egypt and Mesopotamia. This is of course poetry, not constitutional theory, and it is often not clear whether the author is speaking of an actual king of Israel, or what he would like the king of Israel to be, or whether he is giving an idealized picture of kingship in general. Sometimes the king is spoken of as a future prospect. The qualities ascribed to, prayed for, or hoped for in the king are similar to those found in Egyptian and Mesopotamian royal hymns: the king will bring peace, prosperity, and justice, especially for 'the poor and suffering' (Ps. 72: 2–3). This quickly turns to superhuman fantasy: he will live 'as long as the sun endures'; prosperity will last 'until the moon is no more' (Ps. 72: 5–7). At times the poet seems to be thinking of Yahweh coming to rule in person (Ps. 47 and 98).

Isaiah (Gottwald 1985: 417) replicates the Egyptian and Mesopotamian themes of physical and moral desolation ('The highways are deserted ... Covenants are broken'), followed by a restoration of order (see above, pp. 24, 40). But the Hebrew author(s) introduce two new themes: even in a time of desolation the upright man will have 'his bread secure and his water never failing' (Isa. 33: 15–16). And the rescuer is no human king, but Yahweh himself. There will follow, naturally, an ideal state of affairs, again characterized by Jewish themes: those who are at present disadvantaged will themselves 'take part in the pillage'; and 'the sins of the people ... shall be pardoned' (Isa. 33: 23–4). Such ideals may represent 'official national piety' (Keel 1978: 278–9, 355–6). Alongside this was an idealization of Jerusalem (Zion) and its Temple as the permanent earthly abode of Yahweh, sacred to his people. The Davidic king was thus seen as 'intermediar[y] between Yahweh and his people', as embodying piety, executing justice, and in 'a distinctive filial relation to Yahweh' (Gottwald 1985: 336).

There is, finally, talk not only of the land of Israel, but of conquering other nations, indeed *world domination* by Yahweh and the (ideal) king: 'I will give you nations as your inheritance ... you shall shatter them like a clay pot'.[38]

Here the relationship between god, king, and people comes into line with Egypt and Babylonia: 'tremble, and kiss the king, lest the Lord be angry'.[39] Such sentiments, together with coronation rituals and symbolism, especially the ascription of divine sonship to a king, may actually have come from Egypt.[40]

THE MESSIAH

The Israelite monarchy's greatest contribution to Jewish political thought was its failure. Military collapse demolished any strong theory of monarchy in Israel. The Jews tried a different strategy for survival, with, as it turned out, dramatic potential for cultural diffusion. The catalyst was the utter humiliation inflicted by the conquest of Judah and Jerusalem, the destruction of the Temple, the Exile. This experience of defeat and desolation, though far from unique among peoples of the region, seems to have transformed Jewish religious and political thought.

The experience of the Jewish community in exile in Babylon (587–38 BCE) reinforced and transformed the sense of their uniqueness as a nation. They became a highly self-conscious community with a new conception of government and politics. The basis of the community was its religion and law. Kingship was now seen as an optional extra, a temporary and accidental feature of public life.[41] In the sacred Jewish scriptures, kingship was presented as an alien graft, not part of the essential Israel, not an instrinsic part of its observance of the Law, nor of its worship of the one true god. They had learned to live, though not by choice—and, they hoped, not for long—as a stateless nation. To what extent they needed *any* form of governmental authority would be experienced and reflected upon over the ages, by Jews and then by others who associated themselves with this Jewish experience (notably, the early Christians and Shi'ite Muslims). Out of this came also anarchism and communism.

The conviction that they had been chosen by the only god that exists went through its most crucial test in the Exile. Conquest and exile interacted with the core Jewish tenet of the chosen people, destined by Yahweh for the lead role among all the peoples of the world. This gave rise to a new genre of prophecy, initiated by Jeremiah even while the monarchical state was in the process of collapsing.

What emerged was a consolidation and reinterpretation of what had gone before. The sacred texts were formalized and written down in a form that was to be authoritative from then on. There developed a new conception of the

Jewish deity, together with a new theodicy; both have influenced huge swathes of humanity. Defeat and suffering were interpreted as divine retribution for moral and legal transgressions, sin codified as central to the divine scheme. They were suffering the consequences of neglecting their side of the covenant with Yahweh. But—and here was the new emphasis—Yahweh was a merciful and wise god: he would use their sin and suffering to teach his people—*and through them all human beings*—a new way of thought and practice.

Out of this emerged an ideal which has embodied for many over millenia, and still today, central ideas about the divine nature and the human condition. These texts are known to millions; the monuments and godheads of those who conquered Israel had to be dug out of the sand. Defeat and disaster were explained in terms not, as in the Greek historians, of human expectations, interests, and conflicts, but in terms of a divine design for humanity. They created *the* counter-culture of the oppressed, making themselves superior in the divine scheme. It was an ideology which would empower marginalized people, notably the Arabs.

In the Jewish way of thinking, this new understanding involved a new interpretation of national history. The Jews had gained, then lost, their promised land. Any new hope would have to focus on the future, to add a codicil to god's promise. The Jews believed that, despite disasters, the covenant would be fulfilled. But this required, in the first place, moral and spiritual reform. Israel must—of course—turn away from its sins and return to its side of the covenant by observing the law. But there was more than this: Jeremiah prophesied a new covenant in which Yahweh would give the people 'law within them and write it on their hearts . . . No longer need they teach one another to know the Lord; all of them, high and low alike, shall know me' (Jer. 31: 31–4). This was a revolution within a revolution: it meant, obviously, that every individual Israelite would know Yahweh for himself/herself. The law was internalized. The implication of this for individualism and democracy are prodigious and clear.

The new prophetic writings proclaimed that 'a remnant', a small minority of the nation of Israel, would indeed 'turn again' (Isa. 10: 22), and for them the divine retribution would be lifted. They would be enabled to return to the homeland of Israel and rebuild the Temple. But, again, there was to be more. They would have a super-leader: someone would come from the old royal house, a 'Messiah',[42] who would possess in his own person all the qualities of the ideal just king that had been so lacking in their experience of actual kings (Isa. 11: 1–5). Isaiah envisaged him as a boy warrior who is 'prince of peace' (Isa. 9: 6–7).[43]

The themes of equal treatment under the law for rich and poor, redress of grievances for the weak against the strong, and prevention of their recurrence by some (unspecified) shift in power relationships, were particularly prominent in prophecies of the Messiah (Jer. 23: 5–6; see especially Isa. 11: 1–5). As we have seen, in Egypt and Mesopotamia these ideas had formed part of eulogies for kings and other powerful men, by themselves or by admirers. These same ideals are invoked in Hebrew literature, but relatively seldom, and in different contexts: first, as part of Yahweh's rebuke against people in power ('you ought to give judgement for the weak and the orphan') with the threat of divine retribution ('princes fall, every one of them, and so shall you'; Ps. 82: 2–8). Similarly, Jeremiah stated them to the last king of Judah as a divine command; here the threat was national devastation, for these values were part of the covenant (Jer. 22: 3–9). Secondly, they appeared in some of the royal Psalms and the Prophets, not in eulogies of an actual king, but in prayers that God would make the king just (Ps. 72: 1–2), and in hopes for a better future when a king will 'help those of the people that are needy' (Ps. 72: 4). The boasts of good deeds, which we met with in Egyptian and Mesopotamian literature ('I have fed the hungry', and so on), are absent. Such good deeds are only mentioned once as examples of what Yahweh requires (Isa. 58: 7; Job 22: 7). They reappear in the sayings of Jesus, as the criteria on which the Son of Man will judge every individual, in almost exactly the same words as those used in ancient Egypt (Matt. 25: 36; see above, p. 27). Christianity, Shi'ite Islam, and Marxism would each in its own way pick up on these themes.

The Jewish Messiah will bring righteousness and prosperity; he will 'defend the humble in the land with equity' (Isa. 11: 4; 42: 1–4). This future perfect ruler will be especially understanding towards the weak and helpless (Isa. 42: 3). He will not judge by external appearances (Isa. 11: 3); he will act quietly (Isa. 42: 2). Under this new ruler, there will be a utopia (Isa. 11: 6, 9).

So, in this version of their imaginary future, a highly idealized kingship did for the first time become central to Jewish thought. This king would have all the characteristics that contemporary political culture in the Middle East ascribed to the just king. Such messianic ideology can be seen as 'a continuation of existing royal ideology' (Whitelam 1979: 34–6), in response perhaps to the frustration of hopes placed in the actual kings of Judah. This, then, was one more mutation of sacred monarchy.

This was one part of the story of the future. The promised regime of the future would encompass not only the land of Canaan and not only the Jewish people. The Jewish Messiah would be a universal ruler ('all kings shall pay him homage, all nations shall serve him'; Ps. 72: 11). Yahwism mutated into messianic justice with a global reach. Part of the new moral understanding and internalization of spiritual values was a belief that what Yahweh had originally promised to the Jews was in some sense promised to all humanity. Thus the Jews' vocation was not just to secure for themselves a promised land, but rather to lead all peoples to Yahweh and justice. The Messiah would be a world ruler. Or, again, Yahweh himself will 'judge between nations' and bring universal peace ('nation shall not lift sword against nation'; Isa. 2: 4). The Jews were to be a revolutionary vanguard.

NOTES

1. Gottwald 1985: 334, 525. Regarding Proverbs, '[e]ven though many voices speak in Proverbs, the one that grew loudest over time was the dogmatic authoritarian voice that ripped wisdom out of its particular sociohistoric contexts and robbed it of its careful observational and inquiring mode of reasoning' (ibid. 575).
2. Is there a similarity with the story of the founding of Rome, and with the history of early New England?
3. Joshua was said to have 'allotted you your patrimony tribe by tribe, the land of all the people that I have wiped out'; Josh. 23: 4.
4. Gottwald 1979: 682, 685. The 'Yahwist' in the Pentateuch was 'the first Israelite writer to give extended graphic literary expression to a "personal" and "transcendent" mode of conceiving deity that has prevailed in popular Judaism and Christianity ever since' (and, one might add, in Islam) (Gottwald 1985: 328; 1979: 644).
5. When the Israelites asked Gideon to rule over them, he replied: 'I will not rule over you, nor shall my son; the Lord will rule over you'; Judg. 8: 22–3; Halpern 1981: 61–3.
6. Gottwald 1985: 285, 287. Mono-Yahwism may be seen as 'the function of sociopolitical egalitarianism'; it was capable of sustaining 'communal egalitarianism' (Gottwald 1979: 611, 616).
7. To give one example: even though mere craftsmen do not have time to 'become wise' and sit in 'the council of the people', nevertheless 'each becomes wise in his own work . . . they maintain the fabric of the world' (Ecclesiasticus 38: 24–39; 11, early 2nd century BCE).
8. None of this is mentioned in the Egyptian sources (Redford 1992). For the uncertainty of the Exodus story, see Gottwald 1985: 190–4, 201–2.
9. 'Whatever their actual numbers, the Exodus proto-Israelites, who had broken away from the grip of the Egyptian empire and survived a trek through the desert, became a powerful catalyst in energizing and guiding the broad coalition of underclass Canaanites'; Gottwald 1979: 496, see also 485, 489, 584–6; Gottwald 1985: 288. These sagas 'became exemplary for all Israel'.
10. Gottwald 1985: 319–23; Halpern 1981: 235; Redford 1992: 367.
11. As the people of Judah may be called after the Exile (Gottwald 1985: 410).
12. For the precise meaning of the Hebrew term *berith*, see Gottwald 1985: 202.

13. Num. 14: 26–35: 'your bones shall lie in this wilderness; your sons shall be wanderers in the wilderness forty years, paying the penalty of your wanton disloyalty till the last man of you dies there'.

14. Weber identified a 'consuming passion for theodicy, for justifying the ways of deity... as one of the primary characteristics of ancient Israelite thought'; Gottwald 1979: 687.

15. Halpern 1981: 72. See Exod. 15: 3–4; Josh. 23: 9–10; Ps. 47: 3–4 and 89: 10, 13.

16. This meant in practice 'men and especially those owning property—a small fraction of the population' (Nathan MacDonald, personal communication).

17. For the influence of other legal systems, see Paul 1970: 104–5.

18. Exod. 19: 7. Here the elders represented the people.

19. Gottwald 1985: 205; Assmann 1995: 100–1; Redford 1992: 276. But see Mettinger 1976: 229–30.

20. Weinfeld 1990: 184. Here the phrase 'young and old' was employed, as it was in Josiah's case (2 Kgs. 23: 1–3); and covenants were declared binding also on those who were absent, as in Deut. 29: 14 (Weinfeld 1990: 189).

21. Paul 1970: 36, 38; Weinfeld 1990: 218. 'The covenant mechanism associated the religious sovereignty of Yahweh with the historical sovereignty of the people' (Gottwald 1985: 204).

22. Josh. 23: 6, 8; and 24: 26. The 'Ten Words' (*sc.* Commandments) were inscribed by Yahweh himself 'on two tablets of stone' (Deut. 4: 13).

23. Israel may also have been more literate than other societies, but this is disputed.

24. Gottwald 1985: 284; Halpern 1981: 187–8, 194, 198.

25. 'The object of this legal corpus is to form a "holy nation"' (Paul 1970: 36). Within the nation, on the other hand, responsibility tended to be personal rather than collective: ibid. 39–40.

26. This may, however, have been directed against Israelites who followed other deities. At the time this text was probably written, there would have been no Canaanites in the land of Israel (Nathan MacDonald, personal communication).

27. Exod. 19: 5–6. See Gottwald 1979: 670 ff.

28. They could, however, marry captured women from other nations (Nathan MacDonald, personal communication).

29. Mettinger 1976: 109; Halpern 1981: 204–5.

30. Gottwald 1979: 241–2, 688–9; Halpern 1981: 190; Mettinger 1976: 109, 130.

31. Gottwald 1979: 243, stated as a strong impression, based on 'the total number of references to "the assembly" in demonstrably early sources'.

32. Mettinger goes further, claiming that the people or elders played a decisive role in choosing kings 'before and after Solomon'; and that 'the participation of the people or its representatives (the elders) at the royal investitures was a more or less constitutionally fixed feature of life in Israel and Judah' (1976: 108, 113, 118, 129).

33. 1 Kgs. 12: 3–20. See Halpern 1981: 252; Mettinger 1976: 118.

34. Whitelam 1979: 206, 209, 214, 217, 220. Evidence for a contradiction between the levitical theory and royal practice may be found in the rival versions of the

appointment of Saul as first king. In the more pro-monarchical version, Yahweh announces this as his intention in response to the people's pleas for help against the Philistines (1 Sam. 9: 16 and 10: 24–5).

35. 1 Sam. 8: 4–8, 18–22; Finer 1997: 253.
36. Deut. 17: 8–12. See McConville 1998: 277; Finer 1997: 268.
37. Mettinger 1976: 149, 229–30; Halpern 1981: 49. The anointing with oil may signify 'an exchange relation' (Mettinger 1976: 211, 295).
38. Ps. 2: 8–9; Ps. 47. See Keel 1978: 164.
39. Ps. 2: 11–12. See Keel 1978: 246.
40. Keel 1978: 244, 256–9; Mettinger 1976: 291; Voegelin 1957: 304–8; Weinfeld 1990: 30, 32. But see Redford 1992: 365, 369, 378, 381; Weinfeld 1990: 69.
41. Jeremiah 'drew the radical conclusion that his people's future was detachable from institutions of monarchy and cult'; Gottwald 1985: 397.
42. 'Messiah' means 'the anointed one', royal anointing being a peculiarly Israelite practice: see *Cruden's Concordance*, s.v. Messiah; Mettinger 1976: 211, 228–30.
43. On Isaiah, see Gottwald 1985: 379.
44. Psalm 72 then returns to the prayer mode: 'may he have pity on the needy...May he redeem them from...violence' (13–14).

6

India

Social and political thought developed in India somewhat later than in Mesopotamia or Egypt, during the late second and first millenia BCE, after the Indo-Europeans had invaded the subcontinent. But it went on developing over a much longer period. At first, it was embedded in ritual and philosophical texts: the *Rig Veda* (*c.*1300–*c.*1000 BCE), the *Mantric Vedas* (*c.*1200–*c.*1000 BCE), and the early Brahmanas (*c.*1000–*c.* 800 BCE)—explanations of ritual (Roy 1994: 13–14; KR 34). There was an outburst of creative thinking from *c.* 800 to *c.* 500, which produced the *Upanishads* (*c.* 800–*c.* 600 BCE) and Buddhism. The *dharmashastras* (writings on ethics) were composed from the third century onwards. These were commentaries on the sacred texts, 'a branch of Brahminical sacred literature dealing with civil and religious law' (Ghoshal 1959: 528). They expanded 'the ritualistic universe of the vedas into every corner of everyday life' (Smith 1994: 27). The duties of kingship (*rajadharma*) were expounded in the *dharmasutras*, following the sacred revealed texts (Ghoshal 1959: 189). The Laws of Manu were compiled from *c.* 200 BCE to *c.* 200 CE.

'Dharma' meant 'morality, piety, virtue, the social order'. Dharma did not, however, lay down general moral principles according to which one could judge a ruler's action.[1] In this it differed from natural law in Graeco-Roman and European thought.[2] Rather, it specified the duties of individuals and groups, and was thus integrally related to caste.[3] The distinctive feature of the Indian moral code was that dharma varied according to one's social position and stage of life (Derrett 1975: 127–8). In the *dharmasutras*, 'the authors conceive dharma... in the sense of the sum total of the distinctive duties of the constituent units of the social system comprising the four castes (varnas) and the four orders (asramas)' (on which see below), including the king (Ghoshal 1959: 43, 83).

These religious texts were written by brahmins (see below, p. 72), and were generally regarded as the basis of all valid knowledge. The characteristics of political thought in India were thus for the most part defined by its religio-philosophical culture. Like the Hebrew scriptures, these texts were thought to have been revealed by the godhead (Brahma) (though not through specified individuals). 'Absolute, transcendent authority... [was] vested in the Veda' (Heestermann 1998: 33); the truth so revealed was 'the law that governs the universe... that operates in ritual and sacrifice, and finally the moral law'.[4] These truths were handed down from teacher to pupil.

Such an attitude determined the form and content of mental life: 'what was best had been discovered by ancestors long ago... debate was confined to the question whether current versions correctly appraised what the past had achieved' (Derrett 1975: 135). The approach to moral questions was quite similar to that of the revealed monotheistic religions. This body of religious thought also dealt, implicitly or explicitly, with power relationships: power in the universe, power in the social order, power over people's hearts and minds. If anyone imagined political thought could not be more religiocentric than in Egypt and Mesopotamia, they were wrong.

But there was also a separate genre of writings on politics and economics: the *arthashastras*. These were 'the product of independent schools and independent teachers working more or less on lines distinct from the Brahmanical canon' (Ghoshal 1959: 80–2). Thus ancient Indian political thought developed in two directions, broadly expressed in the genres of *dharmashastra* and *arthashatra*. Kautilya, author of the sole surviving example of *arthashastra* (*KA*), writing in the second century BCE, defined *artha* as 'the subsistence of men' or 'the land supplied with men', *arthashastra* being the branch of knowledge which 'treats of the means of acquiring and guarding' these.[5] *Arthashastras* discussed how to achieve security and prosperity, the well-being and expansion of the state (meaning both the king and the people). In particular, they discussed the distinct skills needed for the use of coercive power (the Rod: *danda*) and for 'the maintenance of law and order by the use of punishment' (*KA* 1.4.3 and 1.2.1–9). They may have been composed for particular rulers or states, but they were summaries of knowledge rather than *pieces d'occasion*.

Arthashastras in general relied on observation, analysis, and deduction.[6] Their method of argument and subject-matter may be called 'secular'. Kautilya preferred experience and observation to earlier textual authority. Frequently, especially on foreign affairs, he rejected the views of earlier teachers. He said that 'philosophy is ever thought of as the lamp of all sciences, as the means of all actions (and) as the support of all laws (and duties)' (*KA* 1.2.12); this has been seen as a rare 'subordination of religion to critical reason'.[7] He was adamant that the king should be educated in philosophy and religion (which he should learn from brahmins) as well as in economics (which he learns from government ministers) and politics (which he learns from 'theoretical exponents of political science' and 'practising politicians') (*KA* 1.5.7–10).

'The Arthashastra's concern is with the terminology, arguments and method that should articulate debate and help in reaching appropriate decisions'.[8] It was appropriate, therefore, that Kautilya stressed the need for counsel (*mantra*) in taking political decisions. 'Rulership can only be carried out with the help of associates... therefore (the king) should appoint ministers and listen to their opinion' (*KA* 1.7.9; 1.15.41–4). One is more likely to take the right decision after a debate. But Kautilya disagreed with those who say that ministers are more important than the king; for it is the king who 'appoints the councillors' (*KA* 8.1.12).

Knowledge (or counsel) is preferable to might (the treasury and the army) and to valour or energy (moral and psychological influence) (*KA* 6.2.33). Discussing the relative weight that should be given to each of these in preparing for a military campaign, Kautilya noted that earlier teachers had said that energy is superior to might. '"No", says Kautilya'. And they said that might is superior to counsel. '"No", says Kautilya'. Rather, 'the power of counsel is superior. For the king with eyes of intelligence and science, is able to take counsel even with a small effort and to over-reach enemies possessed of energy and might, by conciliation and other means and by secret and occult practices' (*KA* 9.1.14–15).

In the *Dharmasutras*, too, reasoning was a recognized means of applying the sacred tradition to current situations. When there was no clear ruling in scripture, a council of ten qualified persons could decide. Public sentiment was also invoked.

The *Mahabharata*, a massive epic poem composed between the eighth century BCE and the third century CE (KR 45), contained a wider variety of ideas. It drew on both the religious canon and the *arthashastras*; and it contained a great deal of original thought by its own author(s). Political ideas expressed by the sage in the *Mahabharata* blend 'the old (brahmanical) tradition with the teaching of the technical arthashastras... Some duties are based on truth, others on reasoning and still others on good custom and expediency' (Ghoshal 1959: 46–8, 99, 189, 227). But the *Mahabharata* focused on kingship rather than the brahmins. The epic ends in triumph for the forces of good, when Yudhishthira, the king of righteousness (*dharma-raja*), becomes the actual king.[9] Here the conflicts of lineage are transcended by the monarchical state (Thapar 1984).

The Buddha also engaged in independent thought. In fact, he produced a radical alternative to the vedic, brahminical order. That there was no 'philosophy' or science in the Graeco-European, or again the Chinese, senses— open-ended argument from logical propositions and empirical observation without regard for current beliefs—did not mean there was no original thought.

CASTES

In India the transition from tribal to wider society was made through castes rather than through kingship. It was by means of castes and various occupational groups that tribes were assimilated.[10] The system of caste (*varna*: colour) was brought to India by the Indo-Europeans.[11] The theory of varna was coeval with Vedic religion. It was expounded in the *Rig Veda* and other sacred texts. Varna referred to an individual's occupation and also his intrinsic qualities. Indian religion further specified four 'stages of life (*asramas*)': child, student, married householder, ascetic recluse (Zaehner 1962: 111–14).

The four main social castes were brahmins, kshatriyas, vaishyas, and shudras. These were each given special innate functions: the brahmins' job was teaching and learning; the kshatriyas' was defence; to the vaishyas was assigned care of livestock, trading, and agriculture; the shudras—artisans, labourers, and indigenous slaves—were to 'serv[e] these other classes without resentment' (Smith 1994: 28; KR 39–40). Castes were distinguished by their graded roles in sacrificial ritual; the shudras were excluded altogether from these.

Thousands of local castes[12] were slotted into these four main categories. Caste differences were explained by an organic analogy similar to the one used in medieval Europe. According to a late passage (? *c.* 500 BCE) in the *Rig Veda*, the four varnas were made from the body of the creating deity: 'when they divided the cosmic Man...his mouth became the brahmin, his arms were made into the kshatriya, his thighs the vaishya, and from his feet the shudras were born' (Smith 1994: 27–8).

The top three 'twice-born' or 'initiated' castes were regarded as the full members of Aryan society (Smith 1994: 29). The brahmins and kshatriyas comprised the ruling class, and collaborated in social management (compare the philosophers and warriors in Plato's Republic, below, p. 151). They should be 'closely united' and 'speak with one voice' (cit. Smith 1994: 40). In theory, the brahmins held the monopoly of knowledge about cosmic truth, human fate, individual destinies, and moral duties. It was their function to transmit this knowledge to other members of society. Only brahmins could perform the all-important sacrificial ritual, with its 'message of dominance and subordination' (Roy 1994: 75). But they did not control politics or war.

This system was based on a combination of race, ritual, and socio-economic status. It was designed to maintain purity of the blood group, especially of the Aryans as a whole, who supposedly made up the top three castes; to prevent ritual contamination through contact with inferiors; and to reserve prestigious occupations for elite groups. It may be seen as a means of distributing and monopolizing status and power (Olson 1982: 152–79).

This was the basic scheme of social classification, shaping the way Indians saw themselves, other people, and social relationships. Enormous importance was attached to one's place in society, with its specific rights and duties. Varna was presented as the expression in human society of the nature of being, so that there was something inevitable about it.[13] It was the strongest manifestation in any recorded ideology of status and hierarchy. Social inequalities, though undoubtedly present in all early (and indeed later) human societies, were never taken so seriously as they were in India. The way this system worked constituted a unique strategy for organizing human relationships. It determined people's perceptions and their everyday lives.

To many, the caste system is a classic case of reification (compare Assmann's 'theologization', above, p. 32 n.): an existing pattern of social stratification provided the original mould for the world of thought. The strategy of the Vedic authors, from the later second millenium onwards, may be seen as an attempt to 'demonstrate'—or, more precisely, to have it be assumed—that this was just how things are in every department of existence. The special quality of religion was to reinforce authority by inverting what we see as the causal relationship: it presented the social structure as an inevitable *consequence* of cosmic reality. Thus, 'the Vedic varna system . . . is not represented as generated from the Vedic social structure . . . The social classes in these narratives find their source only in the divine . . . or the ritual'.[14] This went with a perception of the Vedic texts themselves as having no human authors.

Some see this process of religious legitimization as deliberate. 'The superiority of the Brahmin class was *ensured* by the Brahmin authors of the canonical veda . . . A classification system like that of varna is ultimately the *invention* of a specific group of people whose power and privilege were in part based on their very ability to "seize the enunciatory function" (as Michel Foucault might say) and expatiate on how the universe is organised'.[15] These people represented the social hierarchy as 'inherent in the original order of things' (Smith 1994: 60). It appears that in Sri Lanka, by way of contrast, 'the accoutrements of caste developed, but without sacred systematization as in India and hence with the retention of the essentially secular hierarchy of earlier times' (Chakravarti 1987: 115). The effectiveness of this 'hegemonic project' lay in the way it was inserted into the very roots and fibres of social awareness. This method of asserting collective self-interest as part of a sacred and natural order may have been masked even from its authors by their religious self-awareness, or their capacity for self-delusion.

This strategy had the advantage of apportioning privileges and so (on the whole) avoiding social conflict. It achieved this precisely by appealing to *all* participants in the system through the extraordinarily subtle doctrine of *karma*. According to this, one's status in one's present life is the result of one's actions in previous lives.[16] Those who found themselves further down the social scale could be consoled by their 'knowledge' that they were working out the bad effects of karma acquired in previous lives. By fulfilling the religious and social duties of their present life, they would be improving their own status in their next incarnation. 'Theodicies may serve as legitimations *both* for the powerful *and* the powerless, for the privileged *and* the deprived' (Berger, in Roy 1994: 17). As in Egypt and Mesopotamia, this Indian religious strategy was structurally dependent on belief in an afterlife; in this case, in numerous lives both before and after the present one.

One might compare this technique with the ideology dominant in Victorian Britain, and in the United States today, which combines laissez-faire economics with evangelical Christianity. In this case, even more than in ancient India, the better-off get mainly material benefits, the worse-off get spiritual ones (they 'know the Lord Jesus'). But their 'interests' coincide, nonetheless. And surely, in both cases, the amount of *deliberate* manipulation may be more or less minimal. No one may have sat down and said, 'now these are the views we should propagate to keep everyone happy'—or did they?

KINGSHIP

The process by which kingship developed out of tribal aristocracy and chieftainship, and the state developed out of lineage society, was uneven and long-drawn-out.[17] For a long time kings[18] were elected, and barely distinguishable from tribal chiefs. Their authority was limited by the tribal assemblies of the *sabha* (tribal elders) or *samiti* (general tribal assembly).[19]

Some have seen the more remote regions of India as having 'a republican or quasi-republican form of govenment'; but how far it actually differed from chiefdoms is disputed.[20] In the *Mahabharata*, bands (*ganas*) depend for their political survival on avoiding disunity and honouring 'wise and heroic' warriors (Ghoshal 1959: 238). Discussing how a king should deal with 'oligarchies', Kautilya recommended 'sowing dissension' (*KA*, book 11). In any event, such quasi-republics disappeared and left no trace in political thought, though they were a factor in the rise of Buddhism (below, p. 85).

A type of sacred kingship emerged between *c.* 900 and *c.* 500 BCE, under the influence of Vedic religion. Tribes (sing. *jana*) evolved into a people (*vish*) (KR 43). This was the political background to the *Mahabharata* and the *Ramayana* (third century BCE?) (Thapar 1984: 132–3, 141). The events of the *Mahabharata* are set against the backdrop of a dysfunctional royal family (compare the Greek story of the house of Atreus). The *Ramayana* dealt with the question of royal succession; its hero, Rama, was an ideal king, who would be 'the model for all future rulers'.[21]

The king was ritually legitimized by brahmin priests, and acquired something approaching the status of a Middle Eastern sacred monarch (KR 42). But the brahmins were always senior to a king in the religious sphere. The king had overriding influence over adjudication (Spellman 1964: 107). Judicial proceedings were supposed to be based upon dharma, the evidence of witnesses and custom, as well as royal edicts (*KA* 3.1.39). Kings could also legislate in order to re-establish right order (*KA* 3.1.38). Further, while *dharmashastras* override custom, royal edicts override *dharmashastras*.[22]

Members of the kshatriya caste acquired large estates; cities and a market economy developed. Villages continued as self-regulating communities with a headman, usually hereditary, and a village council (*panchayat*). According to Kautilya, the village headman is also 'responsible for preventing cruelty to animals'. In war, one should seek to win over the hearts and minds of 'chiefs in the country, towns, castes and corporations'.[23] According to one *dharmasutra*, groups such as 'castes, families, cultivators ... artisans, have the authority to formulate rules for themselves'.[24] Disputes within a caste or other group were generally settled within the group (Ingalls 1954: 35–6). India's uniquely resilient social order, based on local self-management and the thousands of caste groups, gave it a distinctive political culture down to modern times. Society was less dependent on sacred monarchy than in Egypt, Mesopotamia, or China. Dynasties came and went, but society remained relatively stable despite the frequent political upheavals.

During the sixth and fifth centuries BCE larger kingdoms (*mahajanapadas*) emerged in northern India. After the Greek invasion of 327–5 BCE this process culminated in the Mauryan dynasty which ruled from *c.* 320 to *c.* 185 and, under Ashoka (see below, p. 87), gave India the most extensive and unified state it has ever had. Even so, the Mauryan dynasty was—by comparison with other ancient empires—short-lived.

There developed an unusually clear notion of the state as a composite entity. Sacred tradition in India, as in Mesopotamia, expressed in abstract terms the office to which god (Varuna) appointed the king: as 'sovereignty', 'supreme authority', 'kingship' (Spellman 1964: 13). This was developed in the *arthashastra* tradition. According to Kautilya, the constituent elements of the state are: 'the king, the ministers, the country, the fortified city, the treasury, the army, and the ally'.[25] The 'ally' signifies that the state was supposed to expand. This definition also appears in the religious lawbook of Manu, where it was said that the components are of equal importance, like sticks tied together into a staff (Spellman 1964: 132). This idea of interdependence between the monarch and other parts of the state was unusual in ancient society.

According to the religious canon, kingship had been instituted by Brahma (the supreme godhead). In the *Rig Veda* the gods themselves arranged for Indra to be their king. In the *Brahmanas*, the gods, recognizing the evils of disunity, decided to come to an agreement and 'yield to the excellence of one of us' (in Spellman 1964: 2). In the *Rig Veda* coronation ceremony, the king is selected by Indra (ibid. 1, 13).

The *Mahabharata* gave three separate but related accounts of the *origin* of kingship. These suggest that it has a more fundamental and all-embracing role than was usually assigned to it in brahminical literature; more similar, that is, to what we find in Egypt, Mesopotamia, and China. These accounts also have parallels with modern Western political theory. The first is quasi-Hobbesian. People without a king devoured each other like fish. Indeed, it was widely held that, without kingship, society and cosmos would both descend into chaos. Collective agreements to outlaw such aggression failed; the people then pleaded with god for 'a lord...who would protect them' (Ghoshal 1959: 194). Brahma offered them the patriarch Manu. He agreed, in return for a stipulated revenue (compare Israel, above, p. 60).

A second version was quasi-Lockean: people at first protected themselves by means of ethics (*dharma*) alone without a king or coercion. But later they became deluded and lost their knowledge of morality; society became a mess, the Vedas were lost, the gods no longer got their sacrificial nourishment. So they begged the supreme god Brahma for help. Brahma responded by giving them 'his archetypal work' on the art of government (*dandaniti*) (Ghoshal 1959: 195). The gods then asked the god Vishnu to give human beings a king. Kings, however, turned out to be either too other-worldly or too self-indulgent. But eventually they got someone 'fully armed in the Vedas and their auxiliaries, the art of war and of government'. On him the gods and sages imposed obligations with a solemn oath.[26]

In a third version, Bhishma the sage made the same two points again but with a special reference to property:

If the king did not exercise the duty of protection, the strong would forcibly appropriate the possessions of the weak... [nobody] would be able to say 'this is mine'... the very idea of property would disappear...all restrictions about marriage and intercourse would cease...agriculture and trade would fall into confusion...the three Vedas would disappear. Sacrifices would no longer be performed...society itself would cease to exist.[27]

This 'state of nature' is hardly less dire than Hobbes's; in it, religion too is destroyed. The point of this explanation is that the king was entitled to raise taxes to enable him to fulfil his responsibility of protecting the people against violence, both from one another and from external attack.[28]

The king's office in the earliest Vedic sources was primarily military.[29] According to the Laws of Manu, his tasks were to protect the people, remove the enemies of society, and honour brahmins (Scharfe 1989: 14). The kshatriya caste as a whole had the task of defending the community, especially brahmins and the weak or helpless, against lawless individuals and external enemies.[30] One of the king's main functions was to maintain the caste system itself. He had a special duty to uphold the status of brahmins, and to ensure their exemption from punishment.[31] In the *Mahabharata* his duties were more ambitiously defined as 'casting away life in battle, compassion for all creatures, rescuing people from danger... relieving the distressed and the oppressed' (in Ghoshal 1959: 190–1). Indeed, according to a *Brahmana* commentary, he had a duty to provide for all vulnerable members of society: 'he shall support brahmins and people who are unable to work, even if they are not brahmins... no-one in the kingdom shall suffer hunger, sickness, cold...'. This especially emphasized the king's duties towards 'orphans, widows, diseased and distressed persons, and pregnant women in need of medical attention' (in Spellman 1964: 189). This paralleled the Egyptian and Mesopotamian views of a king's function.

Kautilya's *arthashastra* also spelled out the king's obligation to provide a wide range of social services. 'The king should maintain children, aged persons and persons in distress... as also the woman who has borne no child and the sons [of a destitute woman]'; again, 'brahmins, cattle... minors, the sick' are all his concern (*KA* 1.19.29; 2.1.26; see also 3.20.22). The king's responsiblity for social welfare was, in other words, at least as extensive (in theory) as that of a modern welfare-state.

Kingship and caste always interacted. The king was a kshatri (warrior: the second-highest caste). (According to some later dharma commentators, however, 'whoever holds *de facto* power is king, irrespective of his legitimacy, or, rather, lack of it'—he does not even have to be a kshatri).[32] The king had an essential and leading role in the ritual and moral universe. The king, as well as the brahmins, was charged with the supreme task of maintaining morality (*dharma*) itself, of upholding the four castes and the four life-stages, and keeping intact the boundaries between them: 'the king and the priest uphold the moral order of the world' (in Gonda 1956–7: i. 53). The moral authority of the brahmins and the coercive power of the king could thus be seen as interdependent. This view was also stated in the *Mahabharata*: 'Just as in the matter of holiness the [brahmins] are the source and stay of the other castes, so are the Kshatriyas in matters of good conduct' (in Ghoshal 1959: 190). Compare church–state relations in Europe (Black 2008: 18).

Castes were independent of king or dynasty. The king in India did not stand outside or above society. He was 'the nodal point where the relationships of cooperation and rivalry...are ritually expressed in communal festivals', but he was 'enclosed in the web of personal relationships that constitute the community' (Heestermann 1985: 131). Castes were conceived as more fundamental than a king to the structure of society and cosmos. In ancient Indian theory, caste came first, kingship second.

So this was sacred monarchy with a difference. Kingship, though sacred, was not the sole or supreme agency of the divine in society.[33] It is true that 'in the Vedic period the chief/king assumed identity with various gods during certain state rituals'; he could be regarded as a 'deva' with supernatural faculties. A good king could, as in Egypt, Mesopotamia, and China, have a beneficial effect on nature and the cosmos.[34] But he was not identified with the supreme god Brahma, nor was he Brahma's 'Son or representative'.[35] The fundamental role of sustaining the social order by ritual sacrifice and teaching the Vedas belonged to the brahmins. In the *Mahabharata* the relationship was expressed by saying that 'a brahmin is the root of the tree of Justice; the sovereign prince is its stem and branches; the ministers are its leaves and blossoms; just government is its fruit' (in Spellman 1964: 124). It is important to note, however, that in the *Mahabharata* the good king is generally portrayed as acting quite independently of brahmins.

A king depended upon brahmins for his knowledge of the Veda, without which he was unable to fulfil his task.[36] He was supposed to listen to the advice of brahmins.[37] The king was attended by a chief-priest (*purohita*, lit. 'one who is put ahead'). The *purohita* and the king were 'the divine representatives of the powers of brahman and kshatra, and also...two complementary principles': the brahmin-priest stood for intelligence, the kshatriya-king for action. Brahmins were credited with the ability to bring down an unrighteous king by cursing or magic.[38]

There was thus a considerable difference between sacred monarchy as understood in India, and as understood in Egypt and Mespotamia. The difference lay in the ideological and social context. In the Egyptian and Mesopotamian traditions, the king could intervene in all aspects of social life—he was theoretically omnipotent. In India, kingship functioned alongside, and within, the system of castes. Varna received 'most of the loyalty elsewhere felt towards king, nation and city' (Finer 1997: 1211).

MORALITY AND PRAGMATISM

The relationship between right (or duty: *dharma*) and interest (or necessity: *artha*), that is, between ethics and power politics, including war, was also conceived in an original way in India. A king was supposed to rule according to royal ethics (*rajadharma*)—'the means of controlling the world ... essential to the order of the world and to social order'.[39] Governing is a religious act: 'for the king, the (sacrificial) vow is activity, sacrifice the administration of affairs' (*KA* 1.19.35). 'A true king is dharmatman—an embodiment of dharma, of order, truth, norm and justice'.[40]

On the other hand, political pragmatism (*dandaniti*) had also been taught by Brahma (Ghoshal 1959: 195). It had 'almost canonical authority'; without *dandaniti*, 'the three Vedas would sink and all the dharmas be mixed up' (ibid. 188–92). According to the *Mahabharata*, *dandaniti* 'controls the four varnas so as to lead them on to the performance of their duties and, when it is employed by the ruler properly, it makes them desist from non-dharma' (in Spellman 1964: 11). The art of government seems to be identified with the divinely ordained ethic of kingship.

A king upholds the *varnas* and *asramas* by means of coercive power (the rod: *danda*). 'The advice of the spiritual preceptor and the punishment (*danda*) inflicted by the king ... protect the people' (Ghoshal 1959: 49). According to Kautilya, 'it is the power of punishment alone, when exercised impartially ... that protects this world and the next' (*KA* 3.1.42). As the Laws of Manu also stated: 'if the king does not sedulously employ coercive author-ity (*danda*) for punishing those that deserve it, the strong would torment the weak as ... fish devour each other' (in Spellman 1964: 5). The *Mahabharata* at one point identifies *dharma* with *danda*.[41]

Kings, in view of the unique predicament of their position, enjoyed im-munity from ritual pollution when carrying out their royal functions and maintaining public order (Ghoshal 1959: 45–9). In the *Mahabharata*, the hero Yudhishthira is only with difficulty persuaded to become king, 'for he has been told at very great length ... that the dharma of kingship involves not only wars of aggrandisement but also lying ... and it was Yudhishthira's proud boast that he had never told a lie' (Zaehner 1962: 116–17).

The relationship between the demands of dharma and the needs of the political community provoked soul-searching reflection in the *Mahabhar-ata*.[42] It offered a variety of solutions. In one dialogue, a brahmin 'pleads the individual's supreme right to self-preservation', while an outcaste expounds the authority of canonical rules. The wise Bhishma here drew the conclusion that self-preservation is the ultimate rule, since 'while a man lives, he can win religious merit' (in Ghoshal 1959: 231).

The practical and emotional conflicts arising out of the contrary demands of morality and political survival were explored in the section of the *Mahabharata* known as the *Bhagavad-Gita*.[43] Here there seems to be a tragic yet (within the terms of Vedic culture) triumphant working-out of the conflict between dharma and artha. On the eve of the final battle, the god Krishna gave Arjuna a transcendent justification of the doctrine of karma. Arjuna was in a quandary: 'facing us in the field of battle are teachers, fathers and sons... These I do not wish to slay, even if I myself am slain'. To this Krishna replies: 'if any man thinks he slays, and if another thinks he is slain, neither knows the ways of truth. The Eternal in man cannot kill: the Eternal in man cannot die... But to forgo this fight for righteousness is to forgo thy duty and honour: it is to fall into transgression' (1: 34–5; 2:19, 33). By doing one's caste duty here and now, therefore—in Arjuna's case, as a warrior—whatever the consequences, one will acquire benefits through karma in one's next life.

This was a unique resolution to the conflict between morality and practicality. It avoids the Machiavellian move of denying the validity of moral norms. It implies a statist sense of duty to the public order comparable to what we find in Roman tradition (where Brutus allows the execution of his own son) and in modern European practice (see below, p. 235).

KAUTILYA'S *ARTHASHASTRA*: APPROACH AND METHOD

The question of right and expediency is central to Kautilya. It is misleading to compare him to Machiavelli, as is so often done. The intellectual context was completely different; the term 'Machiavellian' is a category mistake. For all his focus on material welfare, the use of spies, and so on, Kautilya never ignores (far less contradicts) *dharma*. Both foreign policy and warfare are subject to moral norms—for example, 'to be in accordance with dharma, the place and time of battle must be specified beforehand' (*KA* 10.3.36). Non-combatants and those who surrender should not be harmed (*KA* 13.4.52).

Kautilya's work, the only surviving example of the *arthashastra* genre, was probably written *c.* 150 BCE, but was revised and added to up to the third century CE. It deals with the education and self-discipline of the king (Book 1). Books 2–6 deal with domestic policy, including agriculture, forestry, industry, trade, and transport; taxation and consumer protection; legal procedures, property, contract, labour law, prisons; and lastly the secret service. Book 2 is about the departments of goverment and the selection and regulation of civil servants; book 5 about secret activities. Books 7–14 (about one-third of the whole) deal with diplomacy and war, with a great deal on military tactics, ending (once again) with spies and covert operations. Most of the ideas and attitudes expressed in this work derived from the Maurya dynasty (*c.* 320– *c.* 185 BCE), but it drew extensively on earlier works. Kautilya set out to provide a model of the royal-imperial state in India, especially that of Ashoka (r. 268– 233: see below, p. 87).[44]

This is a work without parallel in the ancient world. It covered the whole range of practical politics, foreign as well as domestic, in great detail. Kautilya's approach to politics was pragmatic and down-to-earth. He considered a wide range of possible situations and alternative courses of action. How one should act—whether in treating seeds or negotiating with an ally—depends upon the specific situation. He is inventive in his search for practical solutions.[45] He explores the ramifications of alternative policies with the same thoroughness which Aristotle applied to constitutions (below, pp. 163–7). Precise punishments are spelled out for various misdemeanours: for example, 'failure to maintain an irrigation facility' incurs 'double the loss caused by the failure' (*KA* 3.9.37).

Kautilya asserted the primacy of the political over all the other modes of knowledge or approaches to life. Philosophy, religion, and economics are all rooted in political science (*arthashastra*) (*KA* 1.2.1; 1.5.1); for they all depend for their functioning on the use of coercive power. 'The means of ensuring the pursuit of philosophy, the three Vedas and economics is the Rod (wielded by the king)' (*KA* 1.4.3). It is coercive government which enables subjects to attain the three goals of life: spiritual good, material well-being, sensual pleasure (*KA* 1.4.11). The Rod underpins the social order, the caste system, and morality: 'the people of the four varnas and in the four stages of life, protected by the king with the Rod [and] deeply attached to occupations prescribed by their special duties, keep to their respective paths' (*KA* 1.4.16). Finally, 'it is punishment alone that guards this world and the other' (*KA* 3.1.42). So far, so Hobbesian.

Kautilya insisted that material well-being is more important than spiritual well-being or sensual pleasure, since both of these depend on material well-being (*KA* 1.7.6–7). His *arthashastra* is thus the polar opposite of the *Bhagavad Gita* in its estimation of spiritual values in action. This may have had something to do with why it was forgotten. His view of society is, one might say, materialist, but in an Aristotlian (or Marxist) sense: although the spiritual depends upon the material, it can also function independently.

And he is not as Hobbesian, nor as Machiavellian, as he at first appears. For he rejects the view of 'the ancient teachers' of *arthashatra*, that coercive power should be used severely or indiscriminately. Rather, 'the (king who is) severe with the Rod, becomes a source of terror to beings. The (king who is) mild with the Rod is despised. The (king who is) just with the Rod is honoured' (*KA* 1.4.5–10). It is 'administration (of the Rod), (when) rooted in self-discipline (that) brings security and well-being to living beings' (*KA* 1.5.1). He opts, in other words, for a middle way informed by justice. His *arthashastra* was written for a state functioning according to *dharma* (Derrett 1975: 130).

While there is much in Kautilya that sounds a bit Machiavellian, he envisaged no fundamental separation between power and morality or religion.[46] This was possible because the relationship between religious ethics (*dharma*) and political power (*artha*) was conceived differently in ancient India from the way it was conceived in modern Europe. The religious norms of Kautilya's society were of such a kind that one did not have to contravene them in order to deal effectively with ruthless opponents. Thus, a royal servant 'shall give his advice always in accordance with dharma and artha' (*KA* 5.4.11). Kautilya's advice on the treatment of newly conquered territories, for example, combined quasi-Machiavellian recommendations about winning hearts and minds with an underlying concern for reform in accordance with *dharma*. One might compare Kautilya's teaching with the almost exactly contemporary combination of Legalism and Confucianism in China (see below, p. 122), which was another attempt to combine ethics with political pragmatism.

KAUTILYA ON POLITICAL ECONOMY AND FOREIGN POLICY

The *arthashastras*, as represented by Kautilya, wanted royal government to be pre-emptive and interventionist.[47] Kautilya was especially concerned with management of the economy.[48] 'Being ever active, the king should carry out the management of material well-being' (*KA* 1.19.35). The purpose of the art of government is 'the acquisition of things not possessed, the preservation of things possessed, the augmentation of things preserved...' (*KA* 1.4.3).[49]

A king needs a sound economy for political stability and to achieve his political objectives. Economic and military power are interdependent.[50] 'Agriculture, cattle-rearing and trade—these constitute economics, (which are) beneficial, as they yield grains, cattle, money, forest produce and labour.

Through them the (king) brings under his sway his party as well as the party of his enemies, by the (use of the) treasury and the army' (*KA* 1.4.1–2). Foreign policy must be based on sound finances. Indeed, prosperity can only be maintained by expanding one's territory.

A flourishing economy depends upon a proactive royal policy. A government needs to manage the production and distribution of goods. The king should stimulate production 'in mines, factories and forests' (*KA* 1.2.19). The king is responsible for public goods and the economic infrastructure. He should establish trade routes, including 'water routes, land routes and ports' (*KA* 2.1.19); he should 'cause irrigation works to be built' (*KA* 1.2.20); he is responsible for 'the construction and maintenance of reservoirs, tanks, canals and wells... storage of grains for emergencies, construction and maintenance of trunk roads'.[51] The king should also manage supply and demand.[52] The aim of all this is to maximize the extraction of revenue for the state. Kautilya set no limit to the state's right to raise taxes, and to control the economy for that purpose.

At the same time, Kautilya envisaged an identity of interests between ruler and people: 'in the happiness of the subjects lies the happiness of the king and in what is beneficial to the subjects his own benefit' (*KA* 1.19.34). 'For a kingdom is that which has men. Without men, like a barren cow, what could it yield?' (*KA* 7.11.24–5). A king is acting in his own true interests when he benefits his subjects.[53] The well-being of the people will safeguard the tax base over the long term (Dumont 1970: 307). A king can 'attain popularity by association with what is of material advantage' (*KA* 1.7.1). Kautilya's *arthashastra* is a classic statement of the patrimonial economy, run by the king, but for the benefit of the whole community (Weber 1968: 1010–69).

Foreign policy is viewed in the same light. Unlike most political thinkers, modern as well as ancient, Kautilya (and, one may suppose, his predecessors in *arthashastra*) paid as much attention to foreign as to domestic policy. He saw a close connection between the two. The sole aim is to promote the interests of one's own king and country. One should 'trade with such foreign countries as will generate a profit', and 'avoid unprofitable areas', unless there are 'political or strategic advantages in exporting to or importing from a particular country' (*KA* 2.16.18–25). He subjects foreign policy to cost–benefit analysis: 'the king shall undertake a march when the expected gain outweighs the losses and expenses' (*KA* 9.4.3). The expense of war means that peace is usually preferable, other things being equal.[54]

Kautilya dealt in detail with the various methods of conducting peace, war, and neutrality (Ghoshal 1959: 93–4), and with different means of conducting war. These included covert operations (*KA* 13.1.3–6) and psychological warfare (*KA* 13.1.7–10).

Relations between states are compared to a wheel (*mandala*). The ultimate aim was a 'world ruler (chakravarti)', who would control the whole Indian subcontinent (*KA* 9.1.17–21)—as Ashoka did. Various states are 'bound by hostile, friendly or neutral relations with an ambitious potentate ... as [the] central figure' (in Ghoshal 1959: 93). A dominant ruler or 'conqueror' can 'control the members of his circle of kings' by conciliation, bribery, by sowing dissension, or by 'open, deceptive or secret war' (*KA* 7.16.3–8).

The conqueror who acquires new territory should act virtuously so as to win the hearts and minds of his new subjects. He should fulfil promises he has made to former supporters of his enemy. A new king should also adopt the 'way of life, dress, language and behaviour' of his subjects; he should promote their religious practices, and provide funds for their men of learning and piety (*KA* 13.5.3–11). He should, however, put a stop to customs which are 'unrighteous', 'harmful to the treasury and the army', or 'not in accordance with dharma'. He should replace them with 'customs which are in accordance with dharma' (*KA* 13.5.14 and 24). In all these respects, Ashoka was presumably his model.

Kautilya's *arthashastra* is unlike any other surviving document of the ancient world. There was nothing like it even in Greece or China, with all their philosophy, perhaps because of all their philosophy. It was written in full awareness of the practicalities of government; yet it drives no wedge between politics and ethics.

Kautilya's work was used by later Indian writers. Yet there was no further development of this genre.[55] The approach of the *arthashastras* found its way into Sasanid Iran, and from there into the Islamic Caliphate. Muslim writers, like the writers of *arthashastras*, were able to combine moral ideals with down-to-earth practical advice in a manner unknown to medieval and early modern Europe.

Kautilya's views on the social and economic responsibilities of royal government, especially regarding the economic infrastructure, also anticipated Muslim theorists of the Caliphate. He may well have influenced them. In Sasanid Iran, the interdependence between economic and military power was developed into the notion of a 'circle of power': justice, religion, the state, the army, prosperity are all linked in a causal circle (Black 2008: 104–5). Both the circle of power and the idea of four status groups were absorbed into Irano-Islamic political culture (ibid. 73).

BUDDHISM

The Buddha, the first individual in India for whom historical records exist (KR 49), lived in the sixth century BCE; the earliest Buddhist texts, the Pali canon, date from the fifth century. He was one of several religio-ethical reformers looking for a new way of seeing and acting in the world. He came from a remote region in northern India, on the fringes of Vedic culture, where there was as yet neither caste nor kings. The society of the Ganges plain, where he spent his life, was predominantly agricultural, with expanding trade and cities (Gombrich 1988: 49, 55–6).

Buddhism was the least political of the ancient world-views. Its focus was release from mental and physical suffering for oneself and other sentient beings (*nirvana*). This was to be achieved through recognizing that the source of suffering is desire or attachment, followed by a total renunciation of worldly desires, and the practice of compassion, a process which takes many lives. The Buddha retained belief in reincarnation. But no deity was involved.

The Buddha founded a new society for those who followed him (*bhikkus*): the Sangha, 'the world's oldest monastic order' (Gombrich 1988: 88).[56] This was a wholly new type of human group. Social and family background were no longer of any importance (Chakravarti 1987: 108–9). Any individual of any race, caste, gender, or age could, by dedicating themselves to the pursuit of enlightenment, enter the Sangha. Anyone could go right to the top of the moral-spiritual scale. Women had the same capacity for enlightenment as men. They could enter the Sangha, but their status in it was lower (ibid. 32–4). Seniority within the order was based on progress towards the spiritual goal. This was measured not by birth or caste but by the date when one entered the community. The teacher–pupil relationship was crucial to the development of the individual who had renounced the world. This made the Sangha formally a meritocracy, based on age and experience (Gombrich 1988: 113), a spiritual elite.

The Buddhist conception of the good life, and the Sangha itself, were at once highly individualistic and communal. Monks were 'islands to themselves, their own resorts', yet 'one in thought' (early Buddhist text).[57] The Buddha established certain rules for the Sangha (modelled on the clan-tribal 'oligarchies' among which he grew up—also known as *sanghas*) (Gombrich 1988: 49–50). According to an early Buddhist text, there were to be 'full and frequent assemblies' every two weeks, where all monks were to come together and confess their faults in public.[58] Disputes were to be settled by committees of senior monks in unanimity.[59] The Sangha as a whole was a confederation of local Sanghas (Chakravarti 1987: 56), with occasional general councils. The first of these was held (reportedly) following the Buddha's death in order to record his teaching (Gombrich 1988: 128). No one succeeded the Buddha as overall leader.

The Buddha was the first moral and philosophical teacher to establish a new social entity. This long outlasted him, and survives to this day. Plato's

Academy (closed down some 900 years after his death) required a different kind of commitment, to philosophical training and political reform. The monastic orders of Christianity, which also survive to this day, are a closer parallel.

It seems fairly clear that the Buddha did not intend his teachings 'to have political conseqences' (Gombrich 1988: 81). It is difficult to identify any political implications in Buddhism. The good life was separated from politics. The Sangha was separate from society at large.[60] Buddhism never underwent the kind of change that transformed Christianity when its adherents came to power (Black 2007: 16–17).

In fact, what Buddhism did was to reject the two distinguishing features of Indian political thought: caste and the moral acceptance of power politics. Whereas Vedic religion accepted the political and economic sphere of *artha* as a separate category, early Buddhist teaching regarded power politics as inherently selfish and not fit for discussion by bhikkus (Scharfe 1989: 218). There was some anticipation of the Christian view of the political, as represented by St Augustine: kingship requires punishment, the pursuit of enlightenment requires passivity, so the two cannot go together (Ghoshal 1959: 261). The family, property, and kingship were seen as consequences of the deterioration of human beings (Chakravarti 1987: 151). In this view, kings are predators, one of the disasters that befall men (Gombrich 1988: 81).

Buddhism removed the justification for caste. One overcomes the effects of actions in previous lives not by doing one's caste duties but by perceiving the truths, living virtuously, and joining the Sangha. Buddhism thus disconnected karma from the social structure. 'The caste system is nothing but a human convention... [the Buddha] saw men of all [castes] as essentially equal' (Gombrich 1988: 85, 105). Buddhists did not take caste with them when they converted non-Indian peoples. But, however critical Buddhists may have been of aspects of the caste system, they did not set out to change it where it already existed (Chakravarti 1987: 95–7, 114–18).

Buddhists conceived of 'a series of paternalistic relationships between parents and children, husband and wife, teacher and pupil, and master and worker' as 'the basis of an ordered society' (Chakravarti 1987: 180). Society is divided into warriors, religious teachers, and a new category of gentlemen-householders-farmers (*gahapatis*).[61] These categories had no religious status. One's duties towards others were determined not by one's caste but by one's ability to pay (Chakravarti 1987: 99, 107–9, 119). Householders played an important part in the Buddhists' view of social relationships. 'Within the Pali canon we can find a good deal of material which is primarily addressed to the householder and his family'. The householder was a landowning farmer, who might be engaged in trade, or else a craft-worker (ibid. 67, 81–4, 178).

Industry, self-control, and frugality were singled out for praise (Basham 1980: 17). 'The ideal layman [was] one who works hard, does not dissipate his wealth, but makes maximum use of it; preserves and expands his property, and saves a portion of his wealth for times of need' (Chakravarti 1987: 179).

Buddhism thus enhanced the social standing of agriculture, commerce, productive labour, and the wealth acquired through these.[62] Farmer-house-holders were the main taxpayers (Chakravarti 1987: 68–70). The duties of a king included support for agriculture:

the king should supply seed and fodder to those who are working at agriculture and animal husbandry; he should supply capital to those who are working at commerce; he should organise food and wages for those working in his own service. Then those people will...not harass the countryside...People will be happy, and, dancing their children in their laps, they will live, I think, with open doors. (reported saying of the Buddha, in Gombrich 1988: 82–3).

The payback was that people who practised these Buddhist economic virtues were more likely to be in a position to make donations to the Sangha.[63] One no longer needed to spend money on Vedic rituals (Chakravarti 1987: 69).

But Buddhists also envisaged a 'righteous king', under whom 'the wheel of power turns in dependence on the wheel of justice' and there is no need for coercion.[64] The duties of such a righteous king are to support the family and property—the two bases of the social order—and to eliminate poverty, identified as the source of violence.[65] The most suitable individual should be selected as king 'by the great multitude' (Ghoshal 1959: 258). A good king would consult assemblies of warriors, religious teachers, and farmers (Chakravarti 1987: 167). He should practise the royal virtues (*rajadharma*), such as impartiality (Ghoshal 1959: 69–70, 267). There were no gods and therefore no divine mandate, but such a person was compared to the Buddha (Scharfe 1989: 217–18).

The ideal Buddhist king would be a 'world ruler (*cakkavatti*)', one who conquered by moral principles (*dhamma*)[66] alone ('even his enemies would welcome him').[67] The emperor Ashoka (r. *c.* 268–39 BCE; the model for Kautilya's *arthashastra*) was the exemplary Buddhist righteous world-ruler, much as Marcus Aurelius was an examplary Stoic emperor (below, p. 191). After great conquests, Ashoka established hegemony over the whole of India. Then he became converted to Buddhism, and 'publicly declared remorse for the sufferings he had caused': from now on he would practise only 'conquest through righteousness'.[68]

Ashoka proceeded to promulgate Buddhist ethics and teaching by means of edicts inscribed on stone in prominent spots throughout his empire. He went on 'teaching tours', and appointed Buddhist teachers and welfare workers in various provinces.[69] *Dhamma*, he told his subjects, meant 'treating your slaves and servants properly, respecting your elders, acting with restraint towards all living beings'.[70] He also said, 'all men are my children ... I desire that they may be provided by me with complete welfare and happiness in this world and in the other world' (in KR 64). An important feature of his reign was that there was no persecution, no destruction of temples; he made provision for brahmins as well as bhikkus. It is wrong, he said in one of his edicts, 'to extol one's own sect or disparage that of another' (in Thapar 1966: 87).

Despite his distancing himself from politics, the Buddha was socially radical on caste, and socially creative in the Sangha. He was the first recorded founder of a new way of life, the first person to have established a new organization which has lasted.

NOTES

1. Basham 1975: 42 n., 128; Derrett 1975: 127.
2. See Thapar 1966: 46; Basham 1975: 127.
3. One might compare *dharma* in some respects with 'honour' in developing Europe, the obligations of which also varied according to one's status—knight, mason, and so on.
4. Zaehner 1962: 30; Heestermann 1985: 97; Smith 1994: 287–8.
5. 15.1.1–2, tr. Dumont 1970: 305; Derrett 1975: 139.
6. Ghoshal 1959: 80; Shah 2003.
7. Dumont 1970: 306; Heestermann 1985: 131.
8. Heestermann 1979: 130–1 f.; Spellman 1964: 43, 97.
9. Zaehner 1962: 64; Spellman 1964: 213.
10. Chakravarti 1987: 29; Thapar 1966: 51.
11. Dumezil suggested it was an example of the '*ideologie tripartite*' found among other Indo-European peoples, and therefore probably going back much further; Smith 1994: 5–6; Dumont 1970.
12. Called *jati*, meaning that into which one is born: KR 39; Smith 1994: 9.
13. 'Society becomes merely one expression of a universe created in the image of the Veda' (Smith 1994: 288).
14. Smith 1994: 81, 26. 'The social order in which Brahmins are placed at the top is simply part of creation, part of nature, part of the "way things are"' (ibid. 323).
15. Ibid. 288, 4 (my italics), 19, 81, 275. Roy is even more explicit: 'these texts were conceived of, to a great extent, as instruments with which to influence, control, direct and understand [certain processes], providing for the institutionalization of ideas relating to power' (1994: 16).
16. Zaehner 1962: 4; Thapar 1966: 46; Ghoshal 1959: 44.
17. Thapar 1984 and 2002: 18; KR 55.

18. Sing. *raj*, cognate to Latin *rex*; Scharfe 1989: 230.
19. Thapar 1966: 36; Sharma 1968: 18–19, 27.
20. Sharma 1968: 12, 15, 41–7, 109–11, 196–8, 237, 241; Thapar 1984: 78–9; Heestermann 1985: 13, 114.
21. Scharfe 1989: 41. I am indebted to Anthony Parel for these observations.
22. 'Where (a text of) the science may be in conflict with any edict, there the edict shall prevail': *KA* 3.1.43–5. See Spellman 1964: 105–7; Ghoshal 1959: 113.
23. *KA* 3.10.30–4; Finer 1997: 1225–6; Basham 1975: 5.
24. Thapar 1984: 127. On legal procedures see Ghoshal 1959: 114.
25. *KA* 6.1.1. See Spellman 1964: 9, 132–3.
26. According to another text, 'the creator created the king for the protection of the world when everything through fear ran hither and thither' (in Spellman 1964: 5). In the Laws of Manu, the divine origin of kingship is explained along similar lines.
27. In Spellman 1964: 5–6; Ghoshal 1959: 198.
28. Spellman 1964: 179; Ghoshal 1959: 194.
29. 'A leader in battle and protector of settlements' (Thapar 1984: 35 and 1966: 36; Roy 1994: 151–2, 185). He was also the supreme head of a household (Roy 1994: 281–2).
30. Laws of Manu, as summarized by Ghoshal 1959: 65. See ibid. 49–50; Scharfe 1989: 74.
31. Ghoshal 1959: 202; KR 43. Kautilya warned that a king should be particularly careful when dealing with 'the affairs of persons learned in the Vedas and of ascetics' (*KA* 1.19.31–2).
32. Heestermann 1985: lll; Scharfe 1989: 213 n.
33. There was no 'consistent overall scheme that would give substance to a consolidated theory of sacred kingship' (Heestermann 1985: 111).
34. Ibid. 131; Roy 1994: 114–15. The ideal king, such as Yudhisthira or Rama, was also a sage. See *KA*, book 1.
35. Gonda 1956–7: i. 59; Spellman 1964: 30; Scharfe 1989: 92.
36. Laws of Manu, in Derrett 1975: 131.
37. 'A Brahmin is to be approached by a Kshatriya who intends to take any action, for his success depends on the act having been impelled by a Brahmin' (*Brahmana*, in Smith 1994: 42). 'Rulers cannot adequately carry out their tasks without the aid of Brahmins' (ibid.). See also Spellman 1964: 74; Dumont 1970: 293.
38. Laws of Manu, in Scharfe 1989: 68; Smith 1994: 40. This may be compared to the relationship, as some saw it, between king and clergy in medieval Europe.
39. Gonda 1956–7: i. 53; Scharfe 1989: 214; Ghoshal 1959: 189.
40. Gonda 1956–7: i. 53; Scharfe 1989: 214.
41. Ghoshal 1959: 43, 48, 255; Spellman 1964: 98–9; Roy 1994: 152–3; *KA* 3.1.38.
42. One may see 'two separate and fundamentally incompatible worlds: on the one hand, the break-away transcendence of rationally systematised but meaningless ritualism; on the other hand, an unreformed social world of conflict and ambivalence' (Heestermann 1985: 103 and 1998: 33; Roy 1994: 14).

43. Written in the fourth or third century BCE (Basham 1975: 3). See Zaehner 1962: 116.

44. Ghoshal 1959: 80–1; Scharfe 1989: 103; Thapar 1984: 16.

45. Heestermann, however, criticizes him for being 'either too detailed or too vague to be of much practical use'; 1985: 129.

46. The work shows 'a strong reaction' against the 'immoral statecraft' of other *arthashastras* (Ghoshal 1959: 150).

47. 'The root of material well-being is activity, of material disaster its reverse'; *KA* 1.19.34.

48. This is emphasized in L. N. Rangarajan's edition and translation (New Delhi, Penguin Books India, 1992), which (regrettably in the view of some scholars) rearranges the text to address these specific concerns.

49. Compare Ps.-Aquinas' view that a king must first establish the good life, secondly preserve it, and thirdly improve it: Thomas Aquinas, *Selected Political Writings*, ed. A. P. D'Entreves (Oxford: Blackwell, 1954), pp. 78–80.

50. 'The treasury has its source in the mines; from the treasury, the army comes into being. With the treasury and the army, the earth is obtained' (*KA* 2.12.37).

51. Thapar 1966: 78 and Scharfe 1989: 213.

52. 'Both locally produced and imported goods shall be sold for the benefit of the public' (*KA* 2.16.2–3 and 6).

53. 'What is dear to himself is not beneficial to the king, but what is dear to the subjects is beneficial (to him)' (*KA* 1.19.34).

54. 'If there is equal advancement in peace or war, he should resort to peace. For in war there are losses, expenses' (*KA* 7.2.1–2).

55. Ingalls 1954: 40; Ghoshal 1959: 155.

56. *Sangha* was the term used for clan-tribal oligarchies in his homeland; Gombrich 1988: 49–50.

57. In ibid. 89, 114; Chakravarti 1987: 31.

58. Gombrich 1988: 109; Thapar 1984: 82.

59. Gombrich 1988: 113–14. There were also provisions for voting; Spellman 1964: 54–5.

60. See Chakravarti 1987: 170–2. In a fifth-century CE Sinhalese text, a king says to a council of bhikkhus, 'yours is the authority of the spirit as mine is of power' (in Chakravarti 1987: 174). This exactly parallels the view of many Christians on church and state.

61. Gombrich 1988: 56; Chakravarti 1987: 82, 98. They put warriors above religious teachers: Chakravarti 1987: 98–9. Some writings simply referred to 'high' and 'low' (ibid. 100–3, 112).

62. Thapar 1984: 82, 94; Chakravarti 1987: 112, 81; Gombrich 1988: 76, 80.

63. Thapar 1984: 109; Gombrich 1988: 78–9. 'In order to obtain the surplus to give to the sangha it was necessary to lead a relatively austere life and invest one's wealth with care and caution' (Thapar 1984: 110).

64. Ghoshal 1959: 262; Al-Azmeh 1997: 54–61.

65. Gombrich 1988: 84; Chakravarti 1987: 159, 165–6.

66. The Pali equivalent of *dharma*.
67. Chakravarti 1987: 164–5; S. Tambiah, *World Conqueror and World Renouncer* (Cambridge: Cambridge University Press, 1976).
68. Gombrich 1988: 129; Scharfe 1989: 220.
69. Lamotte 1988: 229; KR 67.
70. Gombrich 1988: 129–30; Basham 1980: 18.

7

China

Knowledge of ancient China has been revolutionized by archaeological discoveries which are still going on. These include discoveries of important philosophical texts. The Shang dynasty (c.1600–1046 BCE) was replaced in c.1046 by the Zhou dynasty. This lasted effectively till 771, and in attenuated form till 256. During the Spring and Autumn period (771–453 BCE),[1] there was still an overall cultural community, but the country was divided up into de facto independent states in competition with each other. The Zhou kings remained theoretical overlords, but actual power was divided among hegemons (ba), tied to the Zhou by lineage, but in fact independent. Confucius (c. 551–479 BCE) lived at the end of this period.

From 453 to 221 BCE (the 'Warring States' period), competition between states intensified. Smaller states were swallowed up by larger, more powerful states, which became increasingly centralized. During this period of political flux and frequent warfare, Chinese philosophy got started—much as it did during the age of independent poleis in Greece.

Reformers advocating different approaches to government competed for the ear of rulers. The followers of Confucius ('the gentle (ru)') (ST 41) specialized in advice on the traditional norms and ritual (li) enshrined in the Classics.[2] The followers of Mozi (c. 460–390 BCE) (Mohists) were specialists in defensive warfare.[3] Mengzi (c. 379–304 BCE) was the most famous and committed disciple of Confucius. Shang Yang (Lord Shang) (d. 338), chief minister of the state of Qin in western China, introduced a new realist way of thinking about public policy and the state. He and those who thought like him became known as Legalists, due to their emphasis on the written laws of the ruler. Xunzi (c. 310–218 BCE) was a Confucian, but also an original thinker who synthesized different approaches. We shall meet with others.

Between 231 and 221 the state of Qin conquered all the other states in a ruthless campaign, and unified the whole of China. Its king, Qin, proclaimed himself emperor (huangdi: lit. august thearch). In 209 a peasants' revolt resulted in the establishment of the more amenable Han dynasty, which lasted until 220 CE. By this time, the main contours of Chinese political thought and culture were well and truly established.

The Shang dynasty, like early states everywhere, was a sacred monarchy. The king was the lineage head ('I, the one man'); the state was 'inseparable from the king and the royal lineage' (Lewis 1999: 15). The royal ancestral line was 'the centre of the cosmos' (Aihe Wang 2000: 43). This view of the central role of the state in the scheme of things survived in China much longer than anywhere else, and is still in evidence today.

The Shang ruler had supreme authority. This was related to his religious functions: only he could perform divination rituals, interpret communications from ancestors, and offer the sacrifices which, it was thought, were needed for prosperity and victory. The well-being of society and the natural order were thought to depend upon due performance of rituals by the ruler. Already 'written documents played a major role in the organisation of the state';[4] bureaucracy had begun.

The revolution of *c.*1046 BCE was based on, or gave rise to, the belief that the 'Mandate (or Decree) of Heaven' (*tian ming*) had passed to the Zhou lineage, because of the Shang's misrule and the virtue (*de*)[5] of the Zhou. The Zhou took the title 'Son of Heaven'. This was the beginning of a distinctive theory of sacred monarchy in China. The Mandate played the same pivotal role in China as the Covenant played in Israel, except that the Zhou monarchy sought to monopolize access to Heaven. The Zhou succeeded in establishing 'an understanding . . . of the world that would undergird all subsequent Chinese intellectual discourse', and the 'canons of govermental propriety' (*CHAC* 351).

During the Spring and Autumn period government was still based upon kinship and hierarchy. But the rulers of the several states, while in theory representing the Zhou emperor as 'Son of Heaven', in fact relied on their own military force. Attempts to base inter-state relations on traditional norms failed. The power of these hegemons later devolved to warrior elites, based in cities though still organized in aristocratic lineages.

During the later Spring and Autumn period larger states emerged. These were still supposed to be part of the Zhou cultural community, and acknowledged, in theory at least, the same system of behaviour and ritual. But domestic and inter-state politics was now based on naked use of force and unrestrained warfare. The Zhou king, though still nominally 'Son of Heaven', was ignored. There was a legitimacy deficit.

Power was based 'on the unique person of the ruler'.[6] Hereditary office and obligation were steadily replaced by the direct control of all subjects by the ruler. Kings came to rely on a new stratum of government officials, the *shi*. These 'men of service' were chosen for their skill and mental agility, 'a class of men similar to the samurai of medieval Japan [and] originally serving as soldiers' (*CHAC* 566, 604). They were employed in civil and military roles, for purposes both technical and occult. Rulers relied on the *shi* as experts in politics, management, warfare, and cosmology. Such were the circumstances in which Confucius taught.

At the same time there appeared 'a new form of military commander, a specialist' who led 'through mastery of military techniques'. In place of aristocratic and lineage values, these leaders 'presented combat as an intellectual discipline', dependent upon 'the powers of mind and textual mastery', combined with 'the unthinking obedience and uniform actions of the troops'. The general was compared to a sage who discovered, or created, 'pattern in the chaos of battle' (Lewis 1990: 11, 97, 121, 230). This parallel chain of command during battle overrode that of the king.

The *shi*, if they were dissatisfied or could find a better post, would move from one state to another. This gave them a certain leverage, and contributed to their intellectual independence. It also reflected the cultural *oikoumenē*. The *shi* saw themselves as members of an intellectual community connecting them to their master regardless of time and place. For them, 'entering the service meant receiving a rank in the state hierarchy'; in this way a *shi* could become 'a legitimate member of the ruling elite'.[7]

This was of decisive importance for the development of Chinese political thought. It was one reason why the political order played such a dominant role in Chinese philosophy, in fact more dominant than anywhere else. In no other culture would the history of thought and the history of the state be so closely intertwined. Ethical and philosophical reflection developed in response to the increasingly problematic political situation. This was the period of 'a hundred schools'. China produced a greater variety of political ideas than any other monarchical agrarian civilization.

Traditional norms, though still respected by many, were widely disregarded in practice, and wielders of power resorted to unrestrained force. There emerged a variety of ideas about legitimate authority and public ethics. There was systematic debate of an intensity which we find nowhere else except in Greece. Knowledge entered the public arena; ethics and politics were opened up to discussion, argument, and proof.

But discussion was limited to monarchy and did not, as in Greece, consider other types of state.[8] Chinese and Greek philosophy and science may be fruitfully compared, as parallel and equally remarkable, although quite different, achievements (Lloyd 2002). But a similarly close comparison of Chinese and Greek political thought is less easy, because their accomplishments were quite different.

The role of the *shi* was one of the primary concerns of Confucius, Mozi, and Mengzi. The *shi* 'overwhelmingly opted for a political career as a main avenue of self-realization'. Confucius himself, who has been called 'the first intellectual leader of the shi', 'shaped decisively their approach to holding office', by upholding the moral commitment to serve the government, but only on their own terms (Pines 2009: 3, 145–6). For Confucius, the truly noble man (*junzi*)[9] was not necessarily an aristocrat, but someone who lived according to the code of behaviour known as 'the rites (*li*)' (below). The difference between the noble and the 'small' man was that the former 'concentrates on right', the latter on 'advantage', especially financial gain (*CA* 4.16).

Confucius' father, a warrior and administrator, died when Confucius was young. Confucius' *Sayings* (*Lunyu*: 'Analects') were probably compiled between *c.* 479 and *c.* 250 BCE by his followers.[10] They are 'the first text in which the term shi'—referring to 'people with aspirations'—'itself becomes an object of enquiry' (Pines 2009: 120). Confucius served as minister and counsellor in various states, often as an adviser on ritual. He repeatedly resigned from posts that proved unsatisfactory.

The *Sayings* take the form of miniature anecdotes, snatches of conversation, question-and-answer exchanges. They leave spaces to be filled in, questions in the mind. Confucius' unique teaching method was based on the understanding that people make mistakes; the important thing is to correct them (*CA* 15.30). Above all, his concern is with what *can* be done (*CA* 13.3). Indeed, the *Sayings* reveal a specific approach to the relationship between theory and practice. They communicate a method of moral judgment, an approach to life (B&B 197). The focus is on ethics and ritual conduct rather than on politics; this may have contributed to the work's lasting influence. The *Sayings* are comparable, in originality and profundity, with the founding texts of moral or religious development elsewhere.

THE MANDATE AND THE PEOPLE

During the Spring and Autumn period writings on political thought and culture began to appear: parts of the *Classic of Odes* (*Shi Jing*) and the *Classic of History* (or *Classic of Documents*: *Shu Jing*), though these were heavily re-edited and added to later.[11] These and other Classics[12] reached their final form under the early Han. Along with Confucius' *Sayings*, they became the textual basis of authority in China down to the nineteenth century (Lewis 1999: esp. 196, 217).

According to the tradition transmitted in these works, ancient sage kings, and especially the founders of the Zhou dynasty, received authority from heaven. Heaven was conceived as 'cosmic moral order';[13] the political order paralleled the order of the universe. According to the *Lüshi Chunqiu* (*Master Lu's Spring and Autumn Annals*), a compendium incorporating ideas from various schools of thought, completed at the court of Qin in 241 BCE, the ruler 'plays a crucial role in the cosmic order' as the Son of Heaven.[14] Human society, nature, and the world of spirits coexist in a continuum. This was later understood to mean that, for example, in a time of misrule there will be heavenly portents and natural disorders, as well as popular discontent.

The central tenet of the Zhou monarchy, and of political thinkers writing in the Zhou tradition (especially the followers of Confucius), was that the monarch ruled through the Mandate of Heaven. This Mandate was not unconditional: Heaven is impartial and decides 'the fate of people . . . according to a moral standard'.[15] The Mandate depended upon the ruler's possessing virtue (*de*).[16] This was used to explain the rise and fall of dynasties in the past (and, later on, throughout Chinese history). Heaven commands the removal of an unjust ruler, and it then transfers the Mandate to a new dynasty.[17] For earlier dynasties, which had once been 'cherished' by Heaven, 'have let the Mandate fall to the ground . . . because they did not care reverently for their virtue' (*Classic of Documents*: ST 36–7). Similarly, if rulers (during the Spring and Autumn period) 'deviate from the way of virtue and behave oppressively and licentiously, they will lose Heaven's Mandate', and it may turn out that they are overthrown (in Pines 2002: 58). According to Dong Zhongshu (fl. 152–119 BCE), 'unnatural portents [are] a warning to a badly-disposed monarch . . . and in the last resort [may be] a prediction of the end of a monarch's period of rule' (Loewe 1994: 95). Thus the Mandate had an ethical dimension.

The monarch alone represented Heaven, with which he was the supreme, indeed the only, mediator. In the *Classic of Documents*, the king's role is said to be to provide spiritual as well as material benefits: 'the sovereign . . . concentrates the five happinesses and then diffuses them so as to give them to his people' (*ST* 31). In contrast to Israel or India, there was no independent priesthood, no 'prophets' (Pines 2002: 61). In this respect there was no dividing-line between the sacred and the political. The drive towards administrative centralization and efficiency during the period 453–222 BCE 'did not eliminate the old model of the ruler as diviner' (Lewis 1999: 39). Similarly, in later times Daoist priests and Buddhist monks had nothing to do with the political order. All this helped to make non-monarchical forms of government inconceivable.

One key component of the ruler's virtue, and therefore of his claim to the Mandate, was that he should treat the people well. (The granting of the Mandate to the Zhou was sometimes taken to mean that it had been granted to the Zhou 'people', meaning the clan lineage as a whole: CHAC 315; Pines 2009: 190.) It was said that one reason why the Mandate had been transferred from the Shang dynasty to the Zhou was that 'our King of Zhou treated well the multitudes of the people'; he 'was richly capable of cultivating and harmonizing [the people]' (in Creel 1970: 84). A writer under the early Han repeated the view that Heaven favours a government that is good to the people; one that fails to provide for the people falls.[18]

Quite apart from the Mandate, the Way of the ruler was generally conceived as 'to benefit others' (*Lüshi Chunqiu*, in Pines 2009: 49); Heaven 'sets up the ruler to serve as [the people's] supervisor and pastor, not to make them lose their nature'; or, as a late fourth-century theorist put it, 'the Son of Heaven is established for the sake of All under Heaven', and the ruler 'for the sake of the state', not the other way round.[19]

The condition of the common people (*min*) was a major concern of Confucius and his followers.[20] The people, especially the poor and the disadvantaged or disabled, should be treated kindly by their social superiors ('lead them, work them … Do not weary them': *CA* 13.1).[21] This was in accordance with the view stated in the *Odes*: the people are 'indeed heavily burdened and it is time for them to rest a while'.[22]

The Classics sometimes said, or implied, that the existence of the Mandate—in other words, the ruler's legitimacy—could be discerned from the people's state of mind. For example, the *Classic of Documents* said that the king should behave virtuously 'in order that [he], through the little people, may receive Heaven's enduring Mandate' (*ST* 36–7). Another writer said that 'Heaven inevitably follows the people's desires' (in Pines 2009: 189). Mengzi cited a passage (now lost) from the *Classic of Documents* to the effect that 'Heaven looks through the eyes of our people, Heaven listens through the ears of our people' (Graham 1989: 116). Indeed, Lewis suggests that Confucians 'identified the people with, or substituted them for, Heaven', and that to Mengzi in particular 'the Mandate of Heaven was equivalent to the support of the people' (Lewis 1990: 236).

All this might be thought to imply that acceptance by the common people was necessary for holding the Mandate. An early Zhou document said that 'the awesomeness and intentions of Heaven are discernible from the people's feelings' (in Pines 2009: 189). Others said that those kings of Shang who were wise had 'feared the brightness of Heaven, and the little people'; a king should 'fear the danger of the people' (Creel 1970: 97–8). This view recurs in the Classics. A ruler should strive to be 'in harmony with the little people … [and] prudently apprehensive about what the people say' (*ST* 36). This suggests a fear of the unpredictable. A ruler would be well advised to listen to the people, by 'consulting the grass- and firewood-gatherers' (*Odes*, in *HCPT* 158).

With the decline of the Zhou monarchy, the concept of Heaven itself changed. 'There was an increasing tendency to identify Heaven as an impersonal, natural, and self-operating force', perhaps even unintelligible (Yang 1957: 273). During the period from 453 to 222 BCE, the transcendental basis of the state was also conceived as the Way (*dao*). This made political issues potentially more open to ethical and pragmatic criteria.

The dependence of the Mandate (in some sense) on the people may be related to the changing the concept of Heaven. For example, the ritual language affirming the quality of sacrificial offerings was interpreted as affirming the well-being of the state or the people (Pines 2002: 77). This may be seen as a kind of secularization of political thought. 'The Way of Heaven is distant, while the Way of man is near', it was said in 523 BCE (in ibid. 69). People began to think that 'the disasters of the people do not descend from Heaven but arise from men' (ibid. 59).

Quite apart from Heaven, gods in general were regarded with a certain scepticism. The people are more important. Confucius is famous for having dismissed ghosts and the spirits of the dead as irrelevant to the one important task, serving the people (*CA* 6.22; 7.21; 11.12). As early as 706 BCE, a political adviser is reported as saying: 'the people are the masters of the deities. Therefore sage kings carried out the people's affairs first, and then attended to the deities' (*Zuozhuan*, in Pines 2002: 76–7). But it was also sometimes said that the people express the gods' will, implying that if you please the people, you please the gods. 'When a state is to prosper, [rulers] listen to the people; when it is to perish they listen to the deities' (in ibid. 78). In other words, relying on the religious interpretation of phenomena is a last resort of a failing regime, and may be misleading. Or, as Pines puts it, 'it was the people, not the priests, to whom the deities were really attentive' (ibid. 71). Xunzi implied that prayers and divination are in reality a mere cultural ritual.[23]

Under the early Han there was a similar move to interpret omens in a more 'rationalistic' way, not as 'signs of natural order or destiny', but rather as 'indications of Heaven's intentions' (Aihe Wang 2000: 177). According to Lu Jia (fl. *c.* 206–180 BCE), 'Heaven communicates with human beings by rectifying them with catastrophes' (in ibid. 177). This too led (paradoxically, it may seem, but only superficially so) to a moralization and politicization of the interpretation of natural phenomena:

the decline of the world and the loss of [the Way] is not what Heaven makes happen, but rather what the ruler of the state causes to happen ... When the Dao of ruling is missing below, the pattern of Heaven will reflect it above. When evil government spreads through the people, insect plagues will be generated on earth.[24]

Social disintegration and natural disasters came to be seen by some as the result of bad government rather than of Heaven (Goldin 2007: 148–52). By these arguments, scholars could overturn the authority of shamans and religious specialists, and claim for themselves 'the highest authority in omen interpretation'.[25]

Confucians not only expressed compassion for the sufferings of the people, but were also concerned about how the people actually felt. Many *shi* were of humble origins. In the *Sayings,* humaneness (below, p. 104) is said to be closer to the people 'than water or fire' (*CA* 15.35). The man of simple means can act virtuously within his small domain. Confucius praised one who 'had a lowly hall and chamber, but put forth all his strength on ditching and draining' (*CA* 8.2).

It seems to us just one step from these sentiments to saying that the people determine who the ruler should be; or at least, who he should not be. The idea of Heaven revealing its will through events, among which manifestations of popular discontent may be one, could perhaps have given rise to an idea of the Mandate as bestowed directly by the people. It was from texts exactly like these that political theorists in Europe developed arguments justifying elections, representative parliaments, and the like.

Some Chinese writers seem to have come tantalizingly close to this. According to a sixth-century source, ministers who are members of the royal family could depose a ruler who persists in his mistakes; in doing so, they would be carrying out the will of Heaven and of the people. For Mozi, the ruler is appointed directly by Heaven, which could mean all kinds of things. For Mengzi, Heaven decides who should be Son of Heaven partly on the basis of public opinion. He was the thinker who came closest to what we call constitutionalism and democracy. He told a king on one occasion that, 'when the ruler makes a serious mistake', his ministers have a duty to admonish him; and if 'he still will not listen, they depose him'. But when the king appeared upset by this, Mengzi amended his statement to: 'they retire'. And he also said that 'nobody should claim he is a new recipient of Heaven's Decree' (for Heaven operates in mysterious ways).[26] The *Guanzi* recommended that a benevolent ruler should not 'keep the throne from generation to generation', but resign at the age of seventy.[27] In the later fourth century there was a groundswell of opinion in favour of abdication as 'the only means of ensuring orderly rule'.

Hereditary succession was modified as views of the Mandate of Heaven changed. Other methods of appointing the ruler were considered, and sometimes preferred. There was a tendency to apply the principle of appointment on merit to the ruler: a good ruler would give his throne, not necessarily to his sons, but to the worthiest of his ministers.[28]

But the idea of the people bestowing the Mandate was not developed in China. The connection between the Mandate and public opinion was never taken to imply a right to revolt. Rather, it meant that if, as a matter of fact, the people were alienated and disillusioned, this would signal that the Mandate had departed, and the government would in fact fall. The people express the will of Heaven tacitly and almost unconsciously; and to some extent after the event.

The Confucian view, similarly, was one of enlightened paternalism: it is the duty of government to look after the people, but there was no suggestion that the people were to be consulted about how this should be done. On the contrary, the people are, as a matter of observable fact, moulded by whoever is in power: 'if you desire the good, the people will be good. The virtue of the gentleman is the wind; the virtue of the people is the grass' (*CA* 12.17, 19). Similarly, 'if one day [the ruler] can overcome himself and turn to humaneness, the world will turn to humaneness along with him' (*CA* 12.1; 13.12). The Confucian ideal was a moral ruler and a moral ruling class who would give the people moral leadership. There was a tendency among Confucians to regard the people themselves as ignorant and small-minded. Confucians did not give 'the people' any authority to act on their own behalf; only the moral and intellectual elite were qualified to speak for them. But, when they did so, they had a kind of popular authority behind them (Pines 2009: 210).

There was thus no question of the people's active participation in the political process. Yet their opinions were not unimportant; and, if they were ignored, disaster could follow. One reason why thinkers did not develop the people's role further was perhaps the lack of any institutional means of expressing the will of the amorphous masses. But there seems to have been no inherent philosophical reason why a theory of popular sovereignty should not have developed (Chan 2007).

On the other hand, criticism of the government could be quite open, as when the *Classic of Odes* said: 'the people below are all exhausted. You utter talk that is not true' (in *CHAC* 335). Both the Mandate and the king's virtue were sometimes said to depend upon his consulting virtuous counsellors (*CHAC* 315). Confucius insisted that, if a ruler misbehaves, his minister has a duty to protest (*CA* 14.22).

STATUS AND MERITOCRACY: 'ADVANCE THE WORTHY'

Status and hierarchy were enshrined in the system of *li* ('rites': ethics and manners, ritual conduct). The obligations and privileges of hereditary status had been reinforced by ritual changes in the ninth century which reaffirmed differences in rank.

Alongside this, tradition assigned a distinctive role to ministers and advisers. In the period 771–453 BCE ministerial lineages acquired considerable power, and they dominated political thinking (Pines 2002: 90, 161–2). In the Warring States period, when the *shi* were replacing hereditary nobles as political advisers, there was renewed emphasis on the responsibilities and political standing of ministers, which was after all what the politically articulate *shi* aspired to be. The ideal type was the duke of Zhou, brother to the king who had founded the Zhou dynasty. He was portrayed as a model of the loyal and selfless adviser; as Confucius put it in his oblique way: 'How I have gone downhill! It has been such a long time since I dreamt of the Duke of Zhou' (*CA* 7.5).

Confucius' political priorities were in fact partially democratic and republican *in spirit.* He believed in equality of opportunity and an overriding duty to serve the state. The central plank in the reform programme of Confucius and his followers was 'advance worthy talents' (*CA* 13: 2): here Confucian values and the interests of the *shi* coincided. Confucians, nevertheless, balanced the claims of merit with those of noble birth.[29] The distinction between the 'noble person' and the 'little people' rationalized transference of power to newcomers without undermining the traditional social structure. Mengzi based status on the distinction between mental and manual labour: 'Those who labour with their minds govern others, while those who labour with their strength are governed by others' (*ST* 132). Xunzi was particularly insistent on the need for differences in rank if society were to be stable.[30]

The followers of Mozi (Mohists), on the other hand, went much further than the Confucians and rejected noble birth outright as a qualification for office: social distinctions should be based exclusively on merit. Both Mozi and Xunzi were less compromising here than Confucius. For Mozi, 'advancing the worthy' and 'employing the capable' should mean complete equality of opportunity.[31] One could perhaps say that Mozi pursued Confucius' thoughts more wholeheartedly than Confucius himself. He rejected the Confucian middle way between the claims of talent and noble birth; the sage-kings of the past had appointed peasants and craftsmen to high office (Graham 1989: 45). Pure meritocracy is essential if a ruler is to fulfil his function. Xunzi argued that descendants of kings and nobles who were unworthy should be reduced to the rank of commoners; descendants of commoners who 'have acquired culture and learning [and] are upright in their personal conduct' should be promoted to the highest rank (*ST* 167).

Legalist thinkers, said that office and status should be based solely on ability and achievement. But they rejected virtue as well as hereditary status as a qualification.[32] The best chief ministers and generals are those who had risen from the ranks (Han Feizi, *Basic Writings,* 124). Thus the slogan 'advance worthy talents' was proclaimed by Confucians, Mohists, and Legalists, but with different meanings.

PUBLIC SERVICE

Confucians hoped to implement their reforms through their influence as ministers with the right ideas and values. This emphasis on public service as the normal, the best, if not the only, way to exercise virtue, distinguished China from other civilizations. And serving the ruler was the best way of serving the people. 'Not to serve is to have no sense of duty' (*CA* 18.7). Government service 'was reinterpreted by mainstream thinkers' (especially Confucius and his followers) 'as the noblest way to self-realization' (Pines 2009: 220). Many passages in the *Sayings* are devoted to the ethics of public service; they emphasize hard work, selflessness, devotion to the interests of the people, and humaneness (e.g. *CA* 15.9, 15, 38). Mengzi records dialogues he had with various rulers.

One reason why public service played such an important part in Chinese political thought was that political ideas were written and promulgated by people who were *shi*. The development of ethics in China from the sixth to the third centuries BCE was more state-oriented than analogous developments elsewhere. There was no mention of rewards in an afterlife. The closest parallel is the Stoics (below, p. 196). Only the 'Daoist' Laozi and the *Zhuangzi* were opposed to political involvement in principle.[33]

This is not to say that Confucians in any way played down other activities and other aspects of life. Far from it. The family was the basis and focus of Confucius' moral teaching. And it is where the virtues of public life begin ('filiality and fraternity are the basis of humaneness, are they not?'; *CA* 1.2). The five most important human relationships are father–son, ruler–subject, husband–wife, elder brother–younger brother, and friend–friend. You can cultivate virtue among family and friends (*CA* 2.21). The concerns of a noble person, said Mengzi, should be his family, his reputation, and the education of talented youngsters. Thus Confucians saw improvement of morals and culture as an end in itself.[34]

Mengzi, like Confucius, was an itinerant teacher, trying to influence rulers through personal contact. But, living in more troubled times, he was particularly concerned about what to do when you cannot engage in public service without compromising your principles. A minister should resign rather than do that. You should only accept office if you can serve the people in a humane way; that is, by persuasion rather than coercion. Mengzi emphasized the possible alternatives to government service more than Confucius, although he personally engaged in public service most of his life. Partly due to the circumstances in which he lived, which meant that one had to look outside politics for fulfilment, Mengzi also emphasized the non-political aspects of *li* (see below), for example in personal relationships. Here one may see a parallel with the situation Plato found himself in. But government service was still seen by most as by far the noblest occupation.

CONFUCIUS ON *LI* (RITUAL CONDUCT) AND *REN* (HUMANENESS)

Li (lit. rites) referred to ritual, decorum, propriety, or ethics: 'the embodied expression of what is fitting'.[35] It included 'custom, manners, conventions, from the sacrifices to ancestors down to the details of social etiquette' (Graham 1989: 11): a code of conduct handed down from time immemorial. *Li* may be compared to Hegel's *Sittlichkeit* (communal ethics).[36] They were an important part of the traditional, and Confucian, view of how society is governed; as someone said in 516 BCE, *li* had been received by the ancient kings 'from Heaven and Earth to rule their people' (Pines 2000a: 16).

During the period from 771 to 453 BCE, the scope of *li* was extended from conventions of social intercourse to embrace 'a broad range of political activities, such as personnel policy, [and] proper handling of rewards and punishments', so that it came to comprise 'the entire way of governing' (ibid. 12, 14–15). Crucially, it included the correct relationship between both ruler and ruled, and a ruler and his ministers. *Li* were also supposed to regulate inter-state conduct within the proto-Chinese world.

Confucius saw his mission as, above all, to re-establish *li* as the norm of personal and public life. This he saw as the ultimate solution to all social and political problems. (This was presumably why the conservative thinker Michael Oakeshott admired Confucius, as someone who based politics on tradition, rejecting (so Oakeshott thought) 'rationalism in politics'.) But Confucius at the same time revolutionized the whole meaning and import of *li* by internalizing the notion, changing it from a formality into a moral ideal, 'a means of self-cultivation, self-restriction and proper conduct' (Pines 2000a: 18–19). Like the Hebrew prophets, he infused existing practices and social relationships with new moral meaning. Interpretation of the ethical and societal norms of *li* was the focus of Confucian thought. But the *Sayings* did not reference antiquity for its own sake. It would be misleading to see Confucius as a conservative thinker in a Western sense (see *CA* 9.23–4). *Li* involves asking questions (*CA* 3.15).

Confucius did not *identify li* with morality. There is, besides *li*, *yi*—justice. This too could mean, in the first instance, 'the conduct fitting to one's role or status, for example as father... or minister' (Graham 1989: 11). But *yi* could also refer to 'rightness' in a more general sense, the equivalent of justice in Greek and Western thought. And it included what we call procedural justice; for example, the *Classic of Documents* stated that 'rightness' involves governing 'without partiality... without onesidedness' (*ST* 32). Impartiality was a traditional ideal, also expanded by Mozi (below, p. 107). For Confucius, *yi* and *li* were two sides of the same coin, the inner and the outer aspects of human conduct: 'it is the right which the gentleman deems the substance, it is through [*li*] that he performs it'.[37]

The ethical principles of Confucius are as open to a 'democratic' interpretation as are those of Christianity, Islam, or Marxism, if not more so. They are certainly much more friendly to democracy than Plato's principles. This is even more true of Mengzi. Confucius identified the underlying principle which informed the whole system of *li* as *ren* (humaneness, benevolence).[38] This was a universal ethical principle; it also defined the noble person. *Ren* derives from empathy (mutuality: *shu*) (*CA* 4.15),[39] which may be seen as *the* fundamental Confucian value: 'if I do not wish others to do something to me, I wish not to do it to them'.[40] *Ren* meant being upright and generous; it is the basis of all human relationships, both in the family and in society at large. Confucius also said that *ren* requires one to question incisively and reflect on 'what is close at hand' (*CA* 19.6); this gives it an epistemological meaning. *Ren* also has a practical advantage: the government that treats its people humanely is most likely to prosper and to expand its territory, because it will attract officials, farmers, and travellers from all over the world.[41]

Confucius once defined *ren* as 'to overcome the self and turn to li' (*CA* 12.1). He saw *ren* and *li* as interdependent: to be put into practice, *ren* has to be made concrete in *li*.[42] But the *li* need *ren*: it is their inner rationale, it is what motivates people to observe them, without it they are just meaningless (*CA* 3.3).[43]

The Chinese in general looked down on non-Chinese people as savages, 'wild dogs and wolves' (*CHAC* 993). They thought they were different precisely because they adhered to *li*. Confucius and Mengzi were the only thinkers who had a notion of humanity at large. Confucius said that one should practise *ren* in dealings with foreigners as well as with fellow-countrymen (Roetz 1993: 126, 137).

Mengzi went much further. He took Confucius' thought in a particular direction, making it more consistently humanistic. He argued that humaneness, rightness (*yi*), and propriety (*li*) are rooted in the human mind. Knowledge of right and wrong and feelings of compassion and shame are 'possessed by all human beings'. The 'true nature [of the noble man]—humaneness, justice, propriety and knowledge—is rooted in his heart'.[44] This suggests fundamental features that are common to humanity. It is somewhat reminiscent of the Stoic view of reason and morality.[45]

But Mengzi also thought that humaneness and the people are the bases of political community. It is humaneness that legitimates the political order. Putting this slightly differently, one has to extend those sentiments that arise within the family, notably humaneness, to all other people, in order to establish a state based on morality. You have to treat members of other families in the same way as you treat your own family. He quoted the *Odes* on the person who 'set an example for his wife; it extended to his brothers, and from there to the family of the state' (*ST* 122). On this basis, Mengzi proposed a *federal* empire as the solution to the warring states: the empire is based on the province, the province on the family, the family on the self (*ST* 115).

Xunzi viewed *li* in a more schematic and metaphysical way. It was the guide in both public and private matters, 'the ridgepole of the human way'.[46] He gave *li* a cosmic dimension: 'the heaven and earth are harmonized by it' (Schwartz 1985: 301). Yet he insists that the ultimate foundation of *li* itself is nothing other than the noble person: 'rites and rightness are the beginning of order, and the noble person is the beginning of rites and rightness'. This passage contains a remarkable elevation of the noble person to a cosmic status, prior even to that of *li* itself. 'Heaven and Earth produce the noble person, and the noble person provides the patterns for Heaven and Earth . . . [he] forms a triad with Heaven and Earth . . . Without the noble person there would be no patterns in Heaven and Earth, no continuity in rites and rightness, no ruler or leader above, no father or son below' (*ST* 169). This is in a passage about 'the model of a king'. He seems to assign the noble person the kind of cosmic status others would assign to the emperor (below, p. 123). Perhaps it was his best last hope in a time of disasters. For, in general, he held the pessimistic view that 'human nature is evil'; men are born with 'a fondness for profit', and with 'feelings of envy and hate' (*ST* 180)—the very opposite of Mengzi.

PERSUASION, NOT COERCION

Confucius insisted that humaneness was the fundamental norm not only of human conduct, but of political conduct and civilized government. It laid down both the goal and the methods of politics; it stipulated a harmonious society in which the virtuous lead by example. Confucius believed passionately that people could become moral only through the *example* of the ruler and his officials.[47] Government works best when the ruler is humane. The Confucian praxis was government by consensus. This was to be achieved through education, and through justice on the part of the ruler and the upper classes. Xunzi too thought that people only become good through education (*ST* 179–80). So long as rulers and ministers devote themselves to *li*, justice and fidelity, the people will follow them—and the economy will flourish (*CA* 13.4).

Confucius was realist enough to believe that people should first be enriched, then taught (*CA* 13.9). Yet it is the ability to put up with poverty that distinguishes the noble from the small person.[48] Those in charge of a family or state 'should not worry that they have little, but worry that the little they have is unevenly distributed' (*CA* 16.1).[49] Confucius' approach to wealth may be compared to Solon's (below, p. 139). Mengzi, in the belief that poverty is the cause of immorality, proposed light taxes, minimal state control, and policies to attract commerce.[50] More idealistically, he wanted to see the traditional practices of communal farming restored.

Persuasion is better than coercion. Confucius saw violence as the breakdown of politics: a good example removes the need for coercion (*CA* 13.11; 12.13). Killing has nothing to do with governing; it is hardly sensible to 'kill those who have not the Way in order to uphold those who have the Way' (*CA* 12.19). This was the main point of contention between Confucians and their Legalist opponents (below, pp. 110–12). As the *Classic of Documents* put it, people should be governed with clemency and by example, rather than by 'harsh capital punishments' (*ST* 37). Confucius and his followers wanted first and foremost to change attitudes. They believed that good governance and social responsibility would spread by example. This was the Confucian model for education, leadership, and personnel management.

Mengzi, although (or perhaps because) he was writing at a time when rulers were resorting more and more to methods of coercion, went further. A government should educate its people, raise their moral standards, and by these means show them their innate goodness (*ST* 123). This can only be achieved by example and persuasion, not by force. 'If the ruler is humane, everyone will be humane. If the ruler keeps to rightness, everyone will keep to rightness' (*ST* 141). 'One who gains the allegiance of the peasants will become the Son of Heaven';[51] this was how Mengzi envisaged the pacification of China. He came close to advocating non-violence. Xunzi, too, though writing in harsher times than Mengzi, and despite his pessimistic view of human nature, still insisted that one cannot achieve one's goals by coercion alone: 'one who understands the way to use force does not rely upon force' (*ST* 168).

MOZI

Confucian moral teaching was challenged from one side by Mozi, from the other by Legalists. Like Confucius, Mozi saw the means to bring about reform as a right-minded ruler who would employ virtuous and intelligent ministers ('advancing the worthy', 'employing the capable') (*Basic Writings*, 48–9). Where Mozi differed from Confucius was in rejecting Confucius' presumption that *li*[52] were universal norms, and that the society they envisaged embodied justice. Instead, he proposed a radical extension of *ren* (humaneness) by proposing what he called 'impartial caring' ('universal love').[53] One should value *all* other persons, regardless of kinship or status, as one values oneself; all other families, as one values one's own family; all other cities, as one values one's own city; and all other states, as one values one's own state. Putting one's own family, clan, region, or class before others is 'partiality'. Mozi rejected offensive warfare on principle (*Basic Writings*, 50–62). His followers urged rulers to adopt a policy of non-aggression, and, on a practical level, to improve their defences.

In other words, everything should be subordinated to the general interests of society at large (compare Bentham's principle of utility). This was humaneness without social distinctions.

Mozi derived his principle of universal caring from Heaven, which he saw as an active supreme being with a will. Heaven is 'all-inclusive and impartial in its activities'.[54] Heaven 'desires' that powerful states, families, and individuals do not attack or oppress weak ones; that the strong help the weak; that 'those who understand the Way will teach others'; and that those with wealth share it. This was the closest any Chinese thinker seems to have come to the west-Eurasian view of god. Mozi's Heaven seems particularly similar to Zeus as perceived by his Greek contemporary Aeschylus, and subsequently by the Stoics.

Mozi claimed that one could deduce from observation that impartial caring is the best course of action, by comparing the consequences which different types of action incur. 'When there is rightdoing in the world, we live, without it we die; with it, we are rich, without it poor; with it, we are orderly, without it disorderly' (in Graham 1989: 48–9). He also used logic to defend impartial caring as a social strategy: if you want to benefit your parents, then you want other people not to injure them; but this you can only achieve by treating other people's parents in the same way as you treat your own. Experience shows that reciprocity is a general trait of human behaviour, and that 'one who loves will be loved by others, one who hates will be hated by others' (*Basic Writings*, 46–7).

Mozi insisted that impartial caring should override all special claims of family, rank, and the state, as taught by Zhou tradition and Confucius. In that view, these relationships impose special obligations which one does not owe to those outside one's own group. Mozi, on the other hand, applied impartial caring without reservations, without regard for sentiments of kinship, for traditional norms or expectations based on status. Conventional mourning ritual, for example, was simply a vast waste of resources (Graham 1989: 40). In other words, Mozi was appealing, not to what was considered reasonable in a particular society, but to what any human beings could expect in their dealings with other human beings on the basis of reciprocity (see above, pp. 8–9). Mozi used rational calculation rather than empathy as the tool of moral judgement. In this respect, and in his method of 'argu[ing] out alternatives'—'the beginning of systematic debate in China' (Graham 1989: 36)—he seems the most modern-Western of ancient Chinese thinkers.

THE ORIGINS OF THE STATE

Several Chinese thinkers put forward theories about the origins of the state. These formed an integral part of their political argument. Mozi was the first Chinese thinker, and perhaps the first thinker anywhere, to do this.[55] Originally, he thought, 'everyone in the world has a different morality', and everyone thinks that other people's moral opinions are wrong. Consequently, they think that all other people are immoral, and they attack each other, both within the family and throughout society, refusing to cooperate. The solution was a single ruler, the Son of Heaven. Here Mozi used an idealized past as the model for the future. In the original, ideal state, 'the most worthy and able man in the world' would have been 'selected' as the Son of Heaven: Mozi does not say who selected him, but perhaps he meant Heaven itself.[56] This Son of Heaven then 'selected the worthiest and most able men' to be his ministers. These would realize that the world was too large to be ruled by them alone; and so they 'divided it up into myriad states and established overlords and rulers of the states' (in Pines and Shelach 2004: 132). Mozi may have been referring to a hierarchy of village heads, heads of districts, and rulers of states, under the Son of Heaven.

The original problem of human discord, which arose from differing moral viewpoints, was to be overcome by everyone deferring decisions about what is right and what is wrong to the person above them in the hierarchy, all the way up from village head to the Son of Heaven. Everyone should conform with their superiors, and not with their inferiors ('conforming upwards').

If, on the other hand, 'the superior commits any fault, his subordinates shall remonstrate with him' (in Pines 2009: 50). This system would work, Mozi thought, because 'the Son of Heaven was able to unify the judgments throughout the world'. The Son of Heaven should 'conform upwards' with Heaven. Heaven can depose him in the last resort.[57]

Thus Mozi, not unlike Hobbes, saw the original problem as moral anarchy, and believed the solution to lie in a single ruler, who would have sole authority in deciding right and wrong. Pines see Mozi's most striking innovation as 'the concentration of power in the hands of the Son of Heaven' (2009: 33). Mozi believed, however, that this would only work if people identified themselves not only with the Son of Heaven but 'with Heaven itself'.[58] In other words, he thought a solution depended on the commitment of individuals to moral values (a touch of Augustine here). This differed from Hobbes, but was more humane and possibly more realistic.

Two things strike one about Mozi's theory of state development: his identification of *moral disagreement* as the source of social conflicts, and the solution of a single ruler with a quasi-federal hierarchy of authorities. Mozi's moral universalism produced another version of sacred monarchy. Hobbes and al-Jahiz[59] similarly thought that moral disagreements were a major cause of strife. Hobbes, like Mozi, advocated conformity of thought. All in all, Mozi was perhaps the most original political philosopher in ancient China.

Xunzi's theory of the origins of political society reflected to some extent the priorities of Confucius. He differed both from Mozi and from the *Book of Lord Shang* and Han Feizi (below) in his emphasis on ranks and ritual—Confucian values. Like Plato, Aristotle, and their followers in Islamdom and the West, Xunzi traced the very capability of human beings to outdo animals to their ability to 'form a social organization'. And this, he thought, was made possible by 'distinctions' (ranks). Without ranks, human society would be strictly impossible, because human beings are naturally competitive and therefore prone to conflict; our irrepressible desires would lead to strife.[60] Ranks in turn depend upon 'the sense of propriety'. This is why he argued—in the face of Legalist thinking—'it is impossible to abandon ritual and propriety'. The ruler exists to establish these 'norms of ritual and propriety'. The ancient kings established rites and morality because they 'abhorred chaos'.[61] Rulers and teachers are 'the roots of order'; along with Heaven-and-Earth and the ancestors, they comprise the 'three roots of rites' (*ST* 175). According to

Xunzi, then, human well-being depends upon ranks; these depend upon an agreed moral system; and this in turn has to be put in place by a ruler.[62]

These and other theories produced in China (below, p. 113) may be contrasted with the various ideas about the origin of states put forward by Greek thinkers at about the same time. These based the state (*polis*) on physical needs, language, and the need for justice; Plato emphasized the need for economic cooperation, and the division of labour (below, p. 150). The outcome of human development was, for them, a polis, not a monarchical state. All the Chinese theories, on the other hand, emphasized the need for a single locus of authority, a quasi-absolute monarch. Lewis thinks that Mozi's notion of 'conforming upward' actually makes 'the state the source of morality' (1999: 67).

SHANG YANG AND HAN FEIZI: COERCION AND *REALPOLITIK*

During the later fourth and the third centuries, a new, more realist approach to politics and war was articulated by Shang Yang (d. 338) and others. As prime minister of the state of Qin, Shang Yang undertook a radical reform of the government of Qin between 356 and 348. The text that developed his ideas, the *Book of Lord Shang* (*Shang jun shu*), was a programmatic explanation of the reasons behind his reforms. Shang Yang and those who adopted his approach became known as 'Legalists' because of the emphasis they placed on law (*fa*), and coercive law-enforcement, rather than on persuading people through teaching. They articulated a view of the state that was in many ways the complete opposite of the Confucians' view. They focused upon the methods necessary to maximize the military potential of a state, and so to achieve a pacification of China through *conquest*. One might call them 'authoritarians', even perhaps in some cases 'totalitarians'. These policies provided a model for the king of Qin, who unified China and became the First Emperor. Theirs too was an all-embracing political theory, which included psychology and military strategy.

Shang Yang's policies included universal military conscription, the compulsory registration of the whole population, and a tax on all households. He introduced 'a detailed legal code [for] the conduct of... government and the behavior of the peasantry' (*CHAC* 612). The economic and social order was reorganized in order to instil social discipline and maximize the military strength of the state. To increase productivity, the traditional system of land-ownership was changed to one of individual peasant holdings. Families were grouped into sets of five, with each group made jointly responsible for the actions of *all* its members; this meant 'joint liability for criminal actions and mutual responsibility to pass judgment upon one another'.[63]

The early and middle parts of the third century BCE saw the climax of inter-state conflict, with warfare and slaughter on an unprecedented scale. The state of Qin deposed the last titular Zhou king in 256 BCE. This period produced two of the most original writers on political theory: Xunzi (*c.* 312–219 BCE) and Han Feizi (280?–233 BCE). Han Feizi was Xunzi's pupil, but they were strikingly different. Xunzi developed Confucius' ideas, though he was more pessimistic than Confucius, and called urgently for a 'Son of Heaven' who would restore peace and unify China. Han Feizi combined the realism and statism of Shang Yang with mystical and philosophical ideas derived from the *Daodejing* (*Book of the Power of the Way*, written between 350 (?) and 250 BCE and also known as the *Laozi* after its supposed author). He produced a remarkable rationale for the aggressive policies of Qin. He is reported to have said, 'if only I could converse with [the king of Qin], I would die without regrets'. But, when he arrived at the Qin court, a rival had him imprisoned and killed. Nevertheless, Han Feizi's *The Way of the Ruler* impressed the ruler of Qin.

Success in this view depends upon prosperity and social discipline. As the *Guanzi* also stated, 'the means by which a country is made prosperous are agriculture and war'; 'an extensive territory, an affluent economy, a teeming population and a strong army' are the foundations of power.[64] Or again, 'food is the foundation of the people, the people are the foundation of the state and the state is the foundation of the ruler'.[65] This suggested the same view of the relationship between the state and the economy that we found in Kautilya (above, p. 83).

China's Legalists were unique in the lengths to which they were prepared to go in the use of social engineering in order to achieve agricultural prosperity. They recommended a combination of financial incentives and compulsion; this involved state planning, a population register, and government by decree (*fa*). In fact, they aimed to remould society as a whole in order to achieve the internal order necessary for expansion. Agriculture and military service must be made profitable. Shang Yang thought everyone should be either a farmer or a soldier (or both). Farming makes people hard-working, subservient, and dedicated to the ruler—indeed ready to die for him. Shang Yang's land reforms were also designed to establish a market economy in land, enabling individual farmers to buy and sell their land.[66]

He thought artisans and merchants were useless and overpaid. Most of all he detested the *shi*, 'itinerant scholars'. Public discussion he saw as enervating, indeed counter-productive, for it breeds laziness and dissent. Opinion must be controlled, intellectuals silenced. According to Han Feizi, even treacherous *thoughts* must be suppressed. State officials should take on the role of teachers, and the ruler's laws should be their only textbook.[67]

The Legalists made the written law (*fa*) of the ruler the primary instrument of government and the supreme textual authority. The traditional position was that kings should not resort to written law because it would make people 'lose their fear of authority' and become contentious (Bodde 1981: 177, 171–2). But Han Feizi declared law to be 'the great standard for the world . . . when all obey the law, this is called great good government' (in ibid. 182). Law, it was argued, had the advantages of universality and predictability; it was an objective measure which could be applied with minimum human intervention.

This was the very opposite of the Confucian approach of influencing people through teaching and example. Coercive law, as understood by Legalists, was a completely different method of controlling society from the method of *li*. Shang Yang and others thought that *li* had been tried for long enough as a basis of governance, and found wanting. Relying on good-will and persuasion has put us in the mess we see around us today. Confucian values are all very well for the few who are up to it, but the ruler has to concern himself with the *whole* population.[68]

These 'administrative realists' (as some call them) dismissed traditional values of family and social rank. Rather, the family was to be made the *instrument* of law-enforcement: family members were to denounce one another's crimes—a complete inversion of traditional priorities. And legal penalties must be applied irrespective of status. The morality of the ruler does not matter. The *Book of Lord Shang* put forward the somewhat 'Machiavellian' view that crimes are more likely to be punished if those in charge are wicked than if they are virtuous.[69]

This use of incentives and coercion was justified by a view of human nature propounded both in the *Book of Lord Shang* and in Han Feizi's writings. According to these, the springs of human action are not love but self-interest: human beings are rational maximizers. They viewed the relationship between ruler and subjects as 'an outcome of mutual calculation': 'their minds are attuned to utility since they both cherish self-seeking motives' (the same, Han Feizi observed, is true of master and workman) (Han Feizi, in Hsu 1965: 152–3). This obviously contrasted with the view of Confucius, Mozi, and Mengzi, that human behaviour can be improved by teaching and virtuous example. The Confucian policy of ruling people by humaneness, said Han Feizi, is based on a misunderstanding of human nature.[70] Political relationships within the state cannot be based on the same sentiments as relationships in the family. Rather, state policy and law-making should recognize that 'likes and dislikes are the basis of rewards and punishments' (*Book of Lord Shang*, 241).

The reason why we cannot nowadays take antiquity as a model, as Confucians do, they argued, is that the circumstances in which people live today have changed; 'as conditions in the world change, different principles are practised' (*Book of Lord Shang*, 227). To prove this point, they put forward a quite different view of social development from that of Mozi and Xunzi. According to Han Feizi, the reason why people in antiquity were more relaxed about material goods was not that they were more benevolent, but that goods were more plentiful. Coercion was, therefore, unnecessary. The reason why there is competition and conflict today is that too many people are chasing too few goods. The model kings of ancient times established rites and laws that were expedient and practical in *their* day, but these are of no use now.[71]

The *Book of Lord Shang* proposed a somewhat different theory of social and political development. At the start, it said, people acted on the principle of 'sticking to kin'; this meant they were 'selfish in their concerns'. But, as the population grew, so that people had to interact with non-kinsfolk, there was instability and disorder, because people had divergent aims, and they lacked a common standard of justice (Graham 1989: 271–2). To remedy this, 'the worthies established impartiality and propriety', and preached benevolence: this stage was based on the principle of 'elevation of the worthy' (Pines and Shelach 2004: 134), in other words, Confucian and Mohist ideas.

But then 'the worthy' vied with one other and disputes broke out among them. 'Therefore, the sages who came next'—by this the author of the *Book of Lord Shang* would appear to mean himself and those who thought like him—'originated divisions between lands, between properties and between man and woman'. These, however, were 'unenforceable without controls, so they established prohibitions'. These in turn required officials to enforce them. And these in turn needed a single ruler to unify them. Laws and ruler are therefore interdependent.[72] Therefore, 'elevating the worthy' was now replaced by 'honouring rank'. Thus the *Book of Lord Shang*, like Xunzi, saw *rank* as the most important factor. What is involved in this process of social and political development is neither progress nor decline, but adaptation to changing conditions (Graham 1989: 272).

One should not, therefore, according to the *Book of Lord Shang*, elevate the norms of either antiquity or modernity, but organize the state and law 'in accordance with the needs of the times': 'the enlightened ruler...makes law move with the times'.[73] This was the rationale behind the First Emperor's ban on private scholarship and thought: the past should not be used to criticize the present (*ST* 210).

Once a ruler grasps what people really want, he can manipulate and control them by decrees, punishments, and incentives. In doing so he may be ignoring their immediate desires, but he will be catering for their long-term needs. He undertakes policies which, even though 'people do not have the sense to rejoice in them', are for their long-term benefit (Han Feizi, *Basic Writings*, 128–9); he 'does not indulge the people's desires, he simply looks ahead for what will benefit them'.[74] Han Feizi insisted on putting 'the public' above the private or selfish (Moody 1997: 329). The ruler may have to enforce his measures 'against the will of the people' (Han Feizi, *Basic Writings*, 94). The goals of the state—prosperity, stability, and expansion—were the only ones which would make life tolerable for the majority of people, and they were ones which people would choose if they could see sufficiently far ahead. This was their justification for compulsory labour, taxation, military service, and severe punishments.

The aim, then, was still the welfare of the masses. The realist-legalists saw the two main obstacles to this as social disorder and oppression by the upper classes. Hence Han Feizi and others wanted 'to ensure that the strong do not override the weak' (in Bodde 1981: 182), for 'if penalties are heavy, men dare not use high position to abuse the humble' (Han Feizi, *Basic Writings*, 28).

This was the reasoning behind the policy, advocated by Shang Yang and others, and first implemented in the state of Qin, of making punishments exceptionally severe but predictable. With what would nowadays appear breathtaking honesty, they advocated rule by fear as the most efficient way of securing the greatest good of the greatest number (Han Feizi, *Basic Writings*, 104). Only when light offences are 'regarded as serious' do 'serious ones have no chance of coming'.[75] The psychological argument was that 'punishment produces force, force produces strength, strength produces awe, awe produces kindness. Kindness and virtue have their origin in force'.[76] 'Rely on punishments in order to abolish punishment'.[77]

War and killing are permissible so long as the aim is to abolish them. This means achieving what people want by means they do not want (*Book of Lord Shang*, 230, 285). It is only by going against the wishes of the people that you make them happy. 'What I call punishment is the basis of righteousness, but what the world calls righteousness is the way of violence' (Han Feizi, in Wang and Chang 1986: 46). In other words, they were implying that the outcome desired by Confucius could only be achieved by means he refused to contemplate. It simply could not be achieved by persuasion and example (*Book of Lord Shang*, 325). The true lesson of history was that a great king 'seized the world by force, but held it by righteousness'[78]—an almost prophetic statement when one looks at the first two dynasties of the Chinese empire.

The Legalists were speaking a language some of which has become familiar to us in totalitarian thought. The underlying psychology, nonetheless, was one which Adam Smith and Jeremy Bentham might recognize. There are some real parallels between this school of thought and Machiavelli. Machiavelli shared their view on the constancy of human nature over time, and the need to adapt one's behaviour and morality to changing historical circumstances. He shared their view—which in Europe appeared original—that physical coercion is the only effective method for governments to employ; traditional values and abstract moral principles are ineffective. He also shared their view of what a despotic ruler can achieve for a people: strong government and ruthless force can bring long-term benefits, and, by providing security, lay the basis for moral behaviour. Moral purity, on the other hand, can bring untold suffering to the people. But Machiavelli never advocated control of the family, nor of thought.

Striking similarities have been observed between some aspects of Legalism and the theory and practice of twentieth-century Chinese Communism. Indeed, Mao Zedong held that the People's Republic of China could trace its 'intellectual roots' to Legalism, and in 1973 he 'launched a nationwide campaign to popularize Legalist teachings' (Zhengyuan Fu 1996: 8, 123). The Chinese Communists shared the Legalist belief in the primacy of force in politics, in the centralization of power and the need to remould society from the top, and in historical relativity. Mao's assault on the professional classes had a precedent in the Legalists' condemnation of pursuits other than agriculture and military service. His destruction of books, and his attack on any independent thought, also had a precedent in policies advocated by the *Book of Lord Shang* and Han Feizi, and implemented by the First Emperor (below, p. 121). The Cultural Revolution was based on the same view of the past as that of the Legalists. Chinese Communism also advocated mutual denunciation within the family, and attempted to control what people thought.

Marxism was another text-based system for the authorization of power. Perhaps in China today we are seeing a division, not dissimilar from that envisaged by Confucians, between a 'Marxist' ruling group (no longer very text-based) and a populace bent on economic self-improvement. Once again, the elite do not have to be too concerned about what the people believe, provided they know their place.

A NEW KIND OF MONARCHY: THE *LAOZI* AND HAN FEIZI

A new concept of monarchy developed from the fourth to the second centuries BCE, before and after the unification of China. It was a combination of, on the one hand, traditional and Confucian ideas, especially as developed by Xunzi, and, on the other hand, a remarkable fusion of ideas from Legalist and proto-Daoist sources. This had been initiated by Shen Bu-Hai (Creel 1974), and was continued by Han Feizi, who wrote a commentary on the *Laozi* (Wang and Chang 1986: 13–33).

All thinkers, from the end of Zhou hegemony in 771 BCE until the unification of 221, regarded the fragmentation of the cultural unit bequeathed by the Zhou as a temporary and, as time went by, increasingly disastrous aberration. 'The Great Unity paradigm was not an outcome of, but rather a precondition' for, unification.[79] China was becoming more and more integrated economically. The development of military technology was making internal boundaries less sustainable. The upper classes had a shared cultural legacy in the Zhou Classics. Already by the late sixth century, statesmen were imbued 'with the feeling of belonging to a common economic, political and cultural realm', which they called 'All under Heaven (*tianxia*)' (Pines 2002: 134). This was reinforced by the migrations of advisers and intellectuals from state to state. Their primary loyalty was to All under Heaven and to the Zhou tradition, rather than to any particular state. Thus unification under a single ruler existed in theory long before it actually came about.

The view gained ground among all schools of thought that to the oneness of being must correspond a single political ruler. The Zhou Classics spoke exuberantly and longingly about the Son of Heaven, with never a hint that there could be more than one. Confucius may have been the first to suggest that the only way to end disorder and conflict was to concentrate political power once again in the hands of a Son of Heaven, whom he saw as 'the pinnacle of the ritual order'.[80] Mozi held that 'the disorder under Heaven derived from the absence of the ruler' (Pines 2000*b*: 303–4), and that strife could only be overcome by establishing a single Son of Heaven as the head of a uniform hierarchy, of whose morality he was to be the ultimate guardian. Mozi's principle of universal love was related to the cosmic unity of humanity. Mengzi looked forward to the day when a 'true king' would replace 'tyrannical government' and unify China.[81] For the *Laozi*, 'the unifying principle of Oneness on the cosmic level had to be matched by political unity below' (Pines 2000*b*: 305).

During the Warring States period, the Zhou guan gave 'a list of offices with descriptions of their tasks that offers a model of a world-state based on principles of cosmology' (Lewis 1999: 42). Encapsulating the general view on the eve of unification, the *Lüshi Chunqiu* synthesized the thought of the preceding centuries in such a way as to demonstrate the need for a new, unified monarchy (Sellmann 1999). 'There is no greater turmoil than the absence of the Son of Heaven; without the Son of Heaven, the strong overcome the weak, the many lord it over the few, they use arms to harm each other, having no rest' (in Pines 2009: 19). As Lewis says, 'the dream of writing the world in a single text prefigured...the enterprise of uniting the world in a single state'.[82]

Legalists advocated a single ruler on more practical grounds: 'authority should never reside in two places'.[83] Both the realist *Book of Lord Shang* and the Confucian Xunzi insisted that social and political order could only be achieved by the sovereignty of a single individual,[84] an argument also expressed in Europe during the rise of absolute monarchy (Black 1970). Furthermore, Legalists thought that this did *not* depend upon his moral qualities, though it did require an individual of exceptional capacities: 'he who can make decisions alone is able to become the sovereign of the world' (Han Feizi).[85] Xunzi also observed that laws cannot bind a ruler since he is the source of their coercive power. If the ruler violates the laws too much, however, the state will disintegrate. It is part of his moral perfection that he 'does not dare to violate [laws] nor to abrogate them once they have been established' (Huang-Lao text, in Peerenboom 1993: 78).

Meanwhile the *Laozi* and other proto-Daoist works proposed a return to primitive simplicity, withdrawal from the world, spontaneity (Robinet 1997: 27). They thought that society has become overdeveloped, overheated. 'The more prohibitions and rules, the poorer the people become...The more elaborate the laws, the more they commit crimes' (*Laozi*, ch. 57). What we need is 'small country, few people' (ibid., ch. 80). Graham suggests that such an approach may 'overlap Western ideas of liberty' (1989: 302). According to the work ascribed to Zhuangzi (d. *c.* 286 BCE), corruption and oppression were the inevitable results of civilization and were brought about precisely by those whom others idealized—rulers and sages (Pines and Shelach 2004: 140–2). In this view, the state is part of the problem, part of humanity's misguided attempt to control the world. Solutions to human problems are to be sought only in the individual mind.[86] This was the counter-culture.

Yet some 'Daoists' thought that the sage-ruler is himself 'the unmoving director of the world' (Robinet 1997: 28): his beneficence consists in going with the flow of events, like water flowing downhill. The *Laozi* spoke of a sage-ruler perfectly in tune with Heaven and Earth, and with 'the hearts and minds of the people' (*Laozi*, ch. 49; Ames 1983). 'When he acts, he takes no credit', for 'the people say "we did it ourselves"' (*Laozi*, chs. 2, 17).

The intentions of the author of the *Laozi* appear unfathomable. We can probably never be sure whether he was expressing mystical insights—it ranks alongside *The Cloud of Unknowing* as one of the most extraordinary products of the human spirit—and then applied this to rulership; or whether the mystical notions were all along intended—bizarrely and perhaps horrifyingly to a Western reader—to lead to a political conclusion.

The view that only a sage can be the 'true monarch' was in fact shared by thinkers of several persuasions,[87] though not, to begin with, by the Legalists. It was the genius of Han Feizi to pull the threads of realism and Daoism together, and so to create a new conception of monarchy and the state, out of the dialectic between Shang Yang's Legalism and the inaction (*wu-wei*) theory of the *Laozi*. The monarch is sole and absolute ruler, *but at the same time* a sage. As such, he is 'in a position of virtual equality with Dao, Heaven and Earth' (Pines 2000*b*: 306). This line of thought was developed by the Huang-Lao school in the third and second centuries BCE (Peerenboom 1993). It was already generally acknowledged that the true monarch was the counterpart in human society of Heaven and Earth. It is, therefore, Han Feizi emphasized, appropriate for him to live in a state of creative inaction. He does so by allowing *others*—his ministers—to rule on his behalf; and by leaving everthing to be regulated by *laws*. For the wise man (as the *Laozi* had taught) allows things to take their course, in human society as they do in nature; by not acting, he is in control. Such a person *has* to be the supreme ruler, because to be sage-like is the pinnacle of human achievement. Whatever the intentions of the *Laozi*, then, this idea of the sage was constructed in such a way that he and he alone could be the ruler of the world.

However one interprets the *Laozi*, this was the outcome. When we read Han Feizi, it is as if the inaction of the sage had been established as the summit of human excellence, and the obvious conclusion had then been drawn: this is how the true ruler must be. The *Laozi* contains a mixture of mystical and political thought found nowhere else in the world. And indeed, the ideal Han emperor was to be conceived as one who 'reigned with his arms folded, in a posture of ease, while his ministers and officials carried out the irksome tasks of administering the empire' (Loewe, in *CHC* 744–5, 694).

Xunzi put the same idea in Confucian language. Only 'the Heavenly Monarch' will be able to 'preserve the Way and virtue complete . . . to enhance the principles of refined culture, to unify All under Heaven' (in Pines 2009: 84). Only the 'True ("Heavenly" or "sage") Monarch' will be able to 'achieve the truly universal tranquillity' (Pines 2000*b*: 310).

Legalist writings, on the other hand, used the military idea of a 'power-base (*shih*)'[88] to mean something similar to the Daoist notion of force through inaction: 'the power that the ruler has by virtue of sitting on his throne'. *Shih* referred to the power inherent in the potentials of a strategic situation. This was conceived as 'something that one cultivates and then releases at the right moment'.[89]

The result, in any case, was a theory of government by non-intervention. And it was also, as Pines observes, the ultimate Chinese solution to the problem of the bad or inept ruler. The monarch 'reigns but does not rule'

(Pines 2009: ch. 4). 'The Son of Heaven's life appears as a purely ritual enterprise' (ibid. 96, on Xunzi). The Chinese had invented a special form of constitutional monarchy, one without a constitution. (In terms of its religious and ceremonial functions, one might compare the British monarchy.)

By being 'empty and still', the emperor is supposed to be able to identify the 'regulatory principles' of the Dao which operate in both the natural and the human worlds.[90] The *Guanzi* insisted that 'statutes, regulations and measures be modeled on the Tao [*Dao*]'.[91] These make up (in Pines's words) 'the perfect legal and administrative mechanisms'. Han Feizi actually referred to laws and administrative regulations as 'the Way' (Pines 2009: 101).

Once the right laws, in harmony with the cosmic principles, are in place, then the ruler just has to leave everyone to follow them. The actual business of government is in the hands of the chief minister and bureaucracy. This may be compared to Max Weber's notion of a rule-bound bureaucracy (which he saw as characteristic of a modern state) under a charismatic head.[92] It is bureaucrats who govern while the monarch maintains a 'mystical link to the cosmic flow': 'administration is not his business' (*Lüshi Chunqiu*, in *ST* 237). *The ruler does not need to make personal decisions as such.* As Shen Bu-Hai first put it, 'he does not act, yet as a result of his non-action the world brings itself to a state of complete order' (in Creel 1974: 64).

Han Feizi, however, sometimes speaks as if, in certain cases at least, the ruler's inactivity is only for show. He advises the ruler 'to take hold of the handles of government carefully and grip them tightly' (*Basic Writings*, 18), meaning that he should not let ministers and civil servants get a grip on them. The ruler, not his ministers, must control finance, appointments, and other important powers (Zhengyuan Fu 1996: 81).

On the appointment and conduct of ministers, the views of a Confucian such as Xunzi and of Han Feizi were totally opposed. According to Xunzi's Confucian philosophy, only morally upright individuals should be chosen. In Han Feizi's view, the law lays down clearly the criteria by which appointments are to be made, so that here too the principle of the ruler's 'inactivity' can and should be maintained. 'The enlightened ruler lets the Law choose men; he does not find them for himself. He lets the Law weigh achievement; he does not measure them himself'.[93] Both Shen Bu-Hai and Han Feizi wanted the whole relationship between ruler and ministers to be governed by managerial techniques of manipulation; once again, the ruler did not need to depend on 'his sagacity. He employs technique, not theory'.[94]

Han Feizi's view was partly Machiavellian. Ruler and minister have opposing interests; the ruler must trust no one close to him. He must check and double-check ministers' actions to ensure they are really doing their job. He should *feign* inactivity, not revealing his mind, but letting the minister speak, 'for if he reveals his desires, his ministers will put on the mask that pleases him' (*Basic Writings*, 16–18). He should take credit for his ministers' achievements but let them be reponsible for their failings. Here Han Feizi expressed the monarch's inactivity in an altogether ambiguous way, implying that the ruler still does something, albeit in the background: '[he] who knows how to govern the people thinks and worries in repose...After one becomes able to scheme well, one becomes able to control everything'.[95] Think of Stalin.

Shen Bu-Hai had said that the ruler is 'like a scale, which merely establishes equilibrium, itself doing nothing'. And in Han Feizi's view, the law is an objective standard for measuring human acts, like the 'inked string' or 'compasses' of the craftsman (Wang and Chang 1986: 50, 8). Han Feizi wanted to emphasize that human intervention is not required: one applies the measuring instrument, and the results automatically follow; they indicate what you should do. This may be seen as a development of the traditional principle of impartiality (Graham 1989: 274–5). It implies a kind of rule of law: the ruler simply allows the laws to take their course. But, just as the ruler needs the laws, so the law cannot function without the ruler (see Pines 2009: 46).

THE FIRST EMPEROR

In 221 BCE the king of Qin finally accomplished, in the words of the Han historian Sima Qian (whose *Records of the Grand Historian* were completed *c*.100 BCE), 'the unification of the world' (*ST* 208). This, as we have seen, had long been the goal of political thinkers. Belief in the necessity of a Son of Heaven with a Mandate to rule All under Heaven was a legacy of the Zhou, enshrined in the Classics, and advocated by political thinkers of all hues. Qin accomplished this thanks to his predecessors' centralization and militarization of Qin and his own ruthless warfare; in other words, by means approved only by the Legalist way of thinking.

It was unification in more than name. Under the First Emperor, government in China was centralized as never before. Feudal lords and vassal states were abolished, and the whole country was divided up into new administrative prefectures under central government (*CHC* i. 90). Qin 'deliberately broke the power of the indigenous aristocracies by removing the peasants from their communities and setting them up as individual farmers who owed taxes and military service to the state' (Elvin 1973: 24). This accorded with the Legalist agenda. In public inscriptions he boasted that he had—once again following Legalist principles—'elevated agriculture and proscribed what is secondary'. He justified his harsh policies by pointing out that they benefited the majority: 'the powerful and overbearing he boiled and exterminated; the ordinary folk he lifted and saved'.[96] His prime minister Li Si (280–208 BCE), an admirer of Shang Yang and also a pupil of the Confucian Xunzi, banned 'private learning' on the ground that it led to disorder. Independent scholars and teachers were persecuted and executed, their books burned. All this accorded with the *Book of Lord Shang*. Realists of the fourth and third centuries had provided the theoretical basis for a massive monopolization of the means of coercion.

Qin's supporters justified his policies by arguments drawn from cosmology and nature. According to a prevalent theory of 'correlative cosmology' (Aihe Wang 2000), phases in the heavens, nature, and human society correspond to one another. The *Lüshi Chunqiu* (perhaps 'prepared as a handbook for the young king': see above, p. 116) argued that a new 'phase' was imminent, and that it would be characterized by forceful action.[97] The emperor Qin himself 'advanced the theory of the cyclical revolution of the Five Powers': under the Zhou, fire had been dominant, but now it was the turn of the 'power of water', of the colour black, and of winter (Sima Qian, in *CHC* i. 77). The appropriate policy for this period (Qin declared) was 'harsh, firm, perverse and occult, with all affairs determined by law': 'be severe and strict rather than benevolent, kind, harmonic and righteous' (in Aihe Wang 2000: 141). But he also claimed to be 'humane and righteous', to embody the Way and its power; he proclaimed himself a sage and a god, the representative and enforcer of this new correlation of heavenly and earthly forces, due at this time.[98] He could boast that he had brought 'peace to All under Heaven', and stability to families and ranks (Pines 2009: 108).

For more than two millenia this imperial government seemed to have a staying-power and a power of self-renewal which one finds in religions— but less often in states—in other parts of the world. In ancient China, what I have been calling 'political thought' had a somewhat different function from the equivalent genre elsewhere. It brought together what we in the West divide into the sacred and the secular. Religions such as Hinduism, Judaism, Christianity, and Islam were similarly based on sacred texts. But these supported a system of belief and practice rather than a system of government. China was the only text-based *state*.

China's experience provides a striking contrast with what happened in Europe after the collapse of the Roman empire (Elvin 1973). Throughout the European Middle Ages and Renaissance, many longed, like the Chinese had done after the decline of the Zhou, for a 'revival' of universal empire. But it remained a dream.[99] It was overridden by nationalism, at least until the later twentieth century. Republicanism, democracy, and human rights were indeed advanced by theorists and only subsequently implemented. Ancient China was different in that political idealism was closely linked to a specific polity, namely a single empire for all China. This doubtless contributed to its longevity.

HAN CONFUCIANISM

After the emperor Qin's death, the first successful peasant rebellion in Chinese imperial history overturned the Qin dynasty, and set up the Han in its place. This dynasty lasted until 220 CE. The Han, while building on the unification and centralizion achieved by the Qin, adopted very different methods of government. Forced labour, taxation, and state controls were reduced. Free expression of opinions was once more permitted. The Han dynasty was the model for later imperial dynasties. 'The unity and order of the Han were remembered as a reality and the name of Han came to stand for a perfection that had been lost and a unity that was desired' (*CHC* i. 369).

This sequence of events approximated to the views of Han Feizi and others, that coercion could achieve the harmonious society which most people desired, but only by means they would never have chosen for themselves. The ruthless conquests, together with the reforms already imposed on the state of Qin and now, under the First Emperor, extended to the whole of China, had the effect of providing a milieu in which the gentlemanly culture of Confucianism could flourish.

There now took place a fusion of political ideas deriving from the Confucian tradition, correlative cosmology, Daoism, and some (unacknowledged) Legalist sources. 'Han Confucianism' (as it has been called) was thus a conflation of earlier Confucianism, mystical cosmology, and authoritarian statism (*CHC* i. 107, 652). The Zhou notion of monarchy had been transformed, but the nature and extent of the change was not apparent in the language used. The 'institutional framework' was and remained a 'legalist autocracy' (Wang and Chang 1986: 12). But the state could now afford to be benevolent. Chinese historians have called it 'outside Confucian, inside legalist' (Zhengyuan Fu 1996: 8). As Bodde put it, 'it is the Legalist/Confucian symbiosis evolved during the Han, with administrative controls at the top merging into self-administered behavioural standards below, that gave to the

Chinese state the necessary combination of firmness and flexibility that enabled it to survive' (*CHC* i. 90).

The *Lüshi Chunqiu*, summarizing previous thinkers, had portrayed the state as an organic development of the natural world, and at the same time as created by men in order to achieve order and stability. Under the Han, the emperor's sacrifices to Heaven were expanded 'to demonstrate the transcendant bases of the emperor's might' (Lewis 1990: 162). The theory of the Mandate of Heaven was fully stated in a work of the early first century CE, *On the Mandate [Destiny] of Kings*, by Ban Biao (Loewe 1994: 109). It was becoming the norm that actual government should be done by professional civil servants, a significant proportion of whom came from humble backgrounds.[100] This was in accordance with Confucian and Mohist thought. This rule-following bureaucracy contributed to the relative stability of sacred monarchy in China.

During the first century of this unified empire, Confucian teachings were combined with correlative cosmology to become the dominant political ideology of the state, the bureaucracy, and the landed classes. Confucian thinkers adopted metaphysical notions which rooted polity and power in the very structure of the universe and nature. Thus the Confucian Dong Zhongshu (fl. 152–119 BCE) reflected on how 'Heaven, Earth and humankind are the foundation of all living things: Heaven engenders them, Earth nourishes them, humanity completes them with music and the Rites'. They interact like the parts of the body (*ST* 299). Class distinctions and family structures were believed to reflect the order of nature and Heaven. In fact, 'everything, from the grand movements of history to the minute workings of the human body, was the outward expression of one of five metaphysical powers: earth, water, fire, wood or metal' (*CHC* i. 360). The heavenly, natural, and human worlds were thought to go through interrelated cycles of creation, decay, and rebirth (*CHC* i. 107). Each cycle was identified by specific phenomena in Heaven, Earth, and the state. And each phase has its own abuses: in the phase of fire, these would be 'disregarding the laws, expelling meritorious ministers'; in the phase of metal, 'ignoring the well-being of the people'.[101]

Under the emperor Wu-di (r. 141–87 BCE), Confucianism gained the upper hand among the various 'schools' of earlier political thought. Within the Confucian school, the star of Mengzi, with his greater optimism about human nature, rose, while that of the more pessimistic Xunzi declined (Goldin 2007). An imperial academy was established for the education of officials; the examination system was based on the Confucian Classics, subject now to official interpretation. The political culture of Confucianism steadily gained ground among the elite; the emperor Wang Mang (r. 9–23 CE) tried to present himself as a Confucian sage.[102]

The Confucian Classics were transmitted by an elite of landowners who had a vested interest in ensuring the perpetuity of this text-based state, because they alone, in virtue of their literary learning, were authorized to run it (Lewis 1999: 10, 361). These men and their families in turn depended on state service to maintain their status and wealth. Local elites adopted the Confucian ideal of the cultured gentleman who fulfils his aspirations by leading an exemplary life in his family and local community, while still 'participating, even if very indirectly, in national...political affairs' (Patricia Ebry, in *CHC* 643). The Chinese empire enjoyed much greater cultural unity than the Roman (see below, p. 198). There was a genuine cultural *oikoumenē* among the educated elite, who went to school together, were posted to every corner of the empire, but kept in touch with each other. The country was intersected by recognized landmarks of past exploits. The landscape was viewed through the eyes of those who had gone before, and had celebrated it in poetry.[103]

Among the masses there was greater diversity. They looked to shamanism, Daoism—'the indigenous religion of China'[104]—and Buddhism. One should not assume that China would have remained unified, and so relatively peaceful, if it had not been for the gentle way of Confucianism and the predominantly non-violent orientation of Daoism and Buddhism. One key to explaining the stability of the Chinese state may be the kind of accommodation arrived at between refined culture and popular thought.

The Confucian idea of leading by example and teaching meant that government had philosophical reasons for leaving well alone. Similarly, Daoist inaction theory suggested that 'the court should refrain from excessive interference in the operation of government at lower levels and in the life of local communities' (*CHC* 767). These ideas favoured the clan and the small community, together with a tradition of government through 'kinship organisations, village communities or trade corporations well adapted, not to replace but to evade...power at the centre' (Graham 1989: 300).

Nevertheless, both the Mandate and the notion of successive and contrasting phases in human and natural affairs could justify occasional changes of dynasty. Pines argues that the significant, albeit passive, role assigned to *the people* in classical Chinese political thought was partly responsible for the fact that, throughout imperial times, 'the most massive and steady collective actions by commoners in human history' recurred. Members of the elite might see rebellion as 'ipso facto proof of the dynasty's failure' (Pines 2009: 217), legitimizing a change of dynasty that had already happened, though not actually bringing one about. Indeed, no human action was thought necessary to effect a change, since moral failure would *automatically* entail loss of cosmic status. 'When the ruler fails in all the Five Duties...he loses his presidency over the Center'.[105]

CONCLUSION

In ancient China one encounters ways of thinking which one finds nowhere else. In other cultures the state was often held in high regard as an institution with a cosmic function. In China, however, unlike everywhere else, reforming thinkers, rather than questioning this state tradition, reaffirmed it. They made the Son of Heaven a focus of their ethical and mystical aspirations. Confucius, even more than Plato, saw a particular kind of polity as essential to the solution of human problems.

The peculiarly Chinese solution to the problems of socio-political organization would never have happened without the Legalists. In several parts of the world today, a dose of Legalism would probably reduce the sum of human suffering, by achieving what people want by means they would never choose. But this would require the cultural back-up of something equivalent to Confucianism. This combination was surely the most successful of ancient political outcomes in matching results to aspirations.

Confucianism and Legalism offer two alternative approaches to the organization of large communities: the affective and the calculating. Confucians based their idea of the state on the family. This gains strength from the evolutionary origins of human societies (see above, p. 8). The Legalists saw the state as clockwork. In both ancient and modern times, an attempt has to be made to combine these two approaches.

NOTES

1. Named after the annals describing it.
2. Confucian*ism* is a Western construct.
3. Mo Tzu, *Basic Writings*, 2; Graham 1989: 44.
4. Keightley 1983; and 2000: 98–9, 557; *CHAC* 289–90.
5. Referring to 'political, symbolic and moral potency' (Aihe Wang 2000: 60).
6. *CHAC* 566, 597; Lewis 1990: 243.
7. Pines 2000a: 19; 2009: 86, 119, 126, 140.
8. 'Not a single known text challenges the concept of the ruler's monopolization of the ultimate administrative authority'; Pines 2009: 16, 52–3.
9. Sometimes translated 'gentleman'.
10. B&B 201–56. The *Sayings*, and also the texts ascribed to Mozi, Mengzi, Xunzi, and others, were compilations based on the teaching of the master, but considerably edited and added to after his death.

11. The *Zuozhuan* also contains records of political ideas expressed in speeches of this period (Pines 2002: 7).

12. The *Classic of Changes, Record of Rites,* and *Classic of Music.*

13. *ST* 27, 170; Aihe Wang 2000: 101.

14. Pines 2009: 43. The *Lüshi Chunqiu* was ostensibly a history of the period from 771 to 453 BCE.

15. Pines 2002: 58; *CHAC* 314, 332–4.

16. 'If it is virtue that the king uses, he may pray Heaven for an enduring Mandate' (*Classic of Documents*, in *ST* 37).

17. *ST* 27, 35; Loewe 1994: 88–9; Shahar and Weller 1996: 39.

18. Jia Yi, writing in the early second century BCE (*ST* 291–2).

19. In Pines 2002: 71–2; 2009: 22.

20. 'The people (*min*)' are mentioned fifty-two times in the *Sayings*: de Bary 1991: 19; Roetz 1993: 124–5.

21. There is praise for someone who 'relieves the needy, but does not enrich the wealthy' (6.4, according to B&B written *c.* 460); 'the gentleman esteems the good but pities the incapable' (19.3; de Bary 1991: 19–21). When someone declined a gift of grain, Confucius replied: 'was there no way you could give it to the neighbouring households or the county associations?' (6.5, written perhaps *c.* 460).

22. In Paul Wheatley, *The Pivot of the Four Quarters* (Chicago: Aldine, 1971), 446; Creel 1970: 99.

23. The people look upon them as 'dealing with deities', whereas '[noble] persons regard these as refined culture' (in Pines 2002: 55).

24. In Aihe Wang 2000: 178–9. 'Success or failure are determined not by the natural order of the universe but by the moral conduct of the ruler' (ibid. 178).

25. They 'turned omens from a mantic practice into a symbolic system used in constructing emperorship and a discourse for political persuasion' (Aihe Wang 2000: 177).

26. In Graham 1989: 117; Pines 2002: 212; and 2009: 22, 75–6. The *Zuozhuan* said one could 'expel' a really bad ruler (*ST* 185).

27. In Graham 1989: 294–5. On this work, see Lewis 1999: 27.

28. Yuri Pines, 'Subversion Unearthed: Criticism of Hereditary Succession in the Newly Discovered Manuscripts', *Oriens Extremus*, 24 (2005), 159–78; Pines 2009: 57–8, 63–7.

29. The *Classic of Documents* said that the emperor should appoint as minister 'someone who is already illustrious, or raise up someone who is humble and of low status' (*ST* 30). Patronage and what the Romans called 'friendship'—acquaintance and contacts—do not seem to have featured in these discussions.

30. *ST* 168; Roetz 1993: 72.

31. *Basic Writings*, 48–9; *ST* 67; Schwartz 1985: 157.

32. *Book of Shang Yang*, 235, 239–41, 315; Han Feizi, *Basic Writings*, 20. According to Shen Bu-Hai (d. 337), prime minister in the state of Han, one should appoint only for ability and reward only for achievement (Creel 1974: 33).

33. Pines 2009: 155–61. On the *Zhuangzi*, see Lewis 1999: 60.
34. Bodde 1981: 180; Roetz 1993: 86; Waley n.d.: 115, 64.
35. Herrlee G. Creel, *Confucius and the Chinese Way* (New York: Harper and Row, 1949), 84; Roetz 1993: 46–7.
36. This is satisfactorily explained only by Charles Taylor, *Hegel* (Cambridge: Cambridge University Press, 1975), 376.
37. *CA* 15.18, trans. Graham 1989: 11.
38. Pines 2002: 184–7. It is the concept most often mentioned in the *Sayings* 'by a large margin' (de Bary 1991: 30). Moreover, 'by the time of Confucius *ren* was widening to the ordinary word for human being' (Graham 1989: 19).
39. See also 1.16; 15.24; 6.30; de Bary 1991: 32; B&B 159; Graham 1989: 20–1.
40. *CA* 5.12; 12.2; Roetz 1993: 138, 145.
41. *ST* 119, 123, 151; Graham 1989: 115.
42. B&B 89; Bodde 1981: 179. This is again reminiscent of Hegel.
43. 'Emotion underlies ceremony', as B&B say (p. 81); see also de Bary 1991: 34.
44. *ST* 147, 149, 154. Pines translates this passage thus: 'every man possesses the mind of pity... [and] shame... every man possesses the mind that distinguishes right from wrong... Benevolence, propriety, ritual and wisdom are not infused in us from outside; we definitely possess them [within ourselves]' (2000*a*: 28). This 'view of human nature would ultimately become dominant, not only in China but also in the rest of Confucianized East Asia', both among intellectuals and 'in the value system of an entire culture'; *ST* 116.
45. Below, p. 210. See Lloyd 2004: 159–60.
46. In Pines 2000*a*: 39. See ibid. 27–8; Sato 2003: 425.
47. 'If one day [the ruler] can overcome himself and turn to *ren*, the world will turn to *ren* along with him' (*CA* 12.1; 13.12).
48. *CA* 6.11; 15.2; 4.9; 7.16.
49. Under a humane ruler, even if he receives 'the revenues of the whole empire', the lowliest in society 'will not feel themselves to be deprived' (Xunzi, in *HCPT* 186).
50. *ST* 127–8. Xunzi similarly argued for the unimpeded circulation of goods, no customs barriers, and no taxes on forests, marshes, or weirs (*ST* 169; *HCPT* 187).
51. *ST* 157; Graham 1989: 115.
52. He consciously avoided the term (Pines 2000*a*: 22).
53. *ST* 70; Graham 1989: 41, 49; Schwartz 1985: 146, 149.
54. In *HCPT* 243. And it is 'the ultimate source of morality and the politically active deity in charge of maintaining the sociopolitical order' (Pines 2009: 33).
55. *ST* 68; Graham 1989: 46. Democritus and Protagoras would have run him close: see below, p. 146.
56. Or possibly the people (Pines and Shelach 2004: 133).
57. I am grateful to Yuri Pines for guidance on this point.
58. *ST* 68–9; Graham 1989: 46–7.
59. A ninth-century Muslim thinker; Black 2001: 27–9.
60. For comparable statements in Muslim philosophers and Marsilius of Padua (early fourteenth century CE), see Black 2008: 44–53.

61. *ST* 168, 175; in Pines and Shelach 2004: 143; Pines 2000*a*: 35; Roetz 1993: 112.
62. 'The law cannot stand alone ... Without the right man, they are lost ... The noble man is the source of the law', as Xunzi put it (in Schwartz 1985: 296).
63. Lewis 1990: 96; *CHAC* 605, 611–15; Yates 2001: 363.
64. *ST* 194; Zhengyuan Fu 1996: 39.
65. The *Huainanzi* (*c.* 139 BCE), in Ames 1994: 163.
66. *Book of Lord Shang*, 41, 45, 203, 219, 237, 282; *ST* 195; Han Feizi, *Basic Writings*, 110; *CHC* i. 38.
67. *Book of Lord Shang*, 49, 177, 220, 282; Han Feizi, *Basic Writings*, 116; Zhengyuan Fu 1996: 90; Pines 2009: 176. Xunzi thought likewise (Pines 2009: 177).
68. Bodde 1991: 181–2; *Book of Lord Shang*, 243.
69. *Book of Lord Shang*, 212–13; *ST* 196; repeated by Han Feizi: *HCPT* 405.
70. Most rulers cannot 'rise to the level of Confucius', nor can 'ordinary people be like Confucius' disciples' (Han Feizi, *Basic Writings*, 102–3).
71. Pines 2000*b*: 138; Graham 1989: 273; Hsu 1965: 155.
72. Compare classical Islamic thought, especially al-Jahiz (Black 2008: 44–51).
73. *Book of Lord Shang*, 228; Bodde 1981: 181; HPT 408; Han Feizi, in Wang and Chang 1986: 51. Compare Li Ssu (above, p. 121), in *CHC* i. 69.
74. In Graham 1989: 291, Han Feizi also said that 'you cannot rely on the wisdom of the people (because) they have the minds of little children' (*Basic Writings*, 128).
75. *Book of Lord Shang*, 231, 239; *ST* 196. Punishment of guilty officials 'should be extended to their family for three generations' (*ST* 197).
76. *Book of Lord Shang*, 204, 120; 'impose rule upon them and they will become upright; when they have gained a sense of security, they will become upright': the *Guanzi*, in *HCPT* 330.
77. Sunzi, in Zhengyuan Fu 1996: 66; *Book of Lord Shang*, 233, 285.
78. *Book of Lord Shang*, in Pines 2000*b*: 313.
79. Pines 2000*b*: 282. See also Yuri Pines, 'Serving All-Under-Heaven: Cosmopolitan Intellectuals of the Warring States as Creators of the Chinese Empire (fifth–third centuries BCE)' (2009).
80. Pines 2000*b*: 301–2; and 2009: 27.
81. Schwartz 1985: 285; *HCPT* 167.
82. 1999: 287; Graham 1989: 5.
83. Han Feizi, *Basic Writings*, 27; the *Guanzi*, in Zhengyuan Fu 1996: 81; *HCPT* 333.
84. Pines 2009: 44–6, 50–1, 83–5.
85. In Zhengyuan Fu 1996: 85.
86. The *Guanzi*, in Graham 1989: 172; Schwartz 1985: 231–3.
87. Lewis 1999: 39; Pines 2009: 42–3.
88. 'Position of strength'; *shih* was a military term for 'the power inherent in a particular arrangement of elements and its developmental tendency' (Kidder-Smith, in *ST* 215, on Sunzi); see also Graham 1989: 268, 278; Zhengyuan Fu 1996: 36.
89. Kidder Smith, in *ST* 219; Graham 1989: 280. Some see this as implying a theory of sovereignty; Moody 1997: 318–20.

90. Wang and Chang 1986: 9. This, they add, 'has become a characteristically Chinese philosphical outlook'. Xunzi speaks of 'guiding principles'.
91. Karen Turner, 'The Theory of Law in the Ching-Fa', *Early China*, 14 (1989), 55–76, at 68, 60; Peerenboom 1993: 80.
92. Schwartz 1985: 336; Creel 1974: 100–1, 293.
93. Han Feizi, in Waley n.d.: 178; the *Guanzi*, in *HCPT* 363; Pines 2009: 139.
94. Shen Bu-Hai, in Creel 1974: 65; Graham 1989: 268; *CHC* i. 74.
95. In Wang and Chang 1986: 33; Pines 2009: 100–1.
96. In *CHC* i. 38; see ibid. 76, 104–6, 187–9, 198–9.
97. Sellmann 1999: 195; Yates 2001.
98. Pines 2009: 109; *CHC* i. 78.
99. For a comparison between the Warring States period and early modern Europe, see Victoria Tin-bor Hui, *War and State Formation in Ancient China and Early Modern Europe* (Cambridge: Cambridge University Press, 2005).
100. *CHC* i. 753. 'Of the men who held the highest office … during the second and first centuries BC, at least 22% came from poor or humble families' (Creel 1970: 7).
101. Fu Sheng (early second century BCE), in Aihe Wang 2000: 158.
102. *CHC* i. 464–5, 753, 756, 768–9, 773. But see Michael Nylan, 'A Problematic Model: The "Han Orthodox Synthesis", Then and Now', in Kai-wing Chow et al. (eds.), *Imagining Boundaries: Changing Confucian Doctrines, Texts and Hermeneutics* (Albany, NY: SUNY Press, 1999), 17–56.
103. *Grand Canal, Great River: The Travel Diary of a Twelfth-century Chinese Poet*, trans. Philip Watson (London: Frances Lincoln, 2007).
104. Its continuous organization dates from the second century CE (Graham 1989: 171).
105. Fu Sheng (fl. *c.* 221–170 BCE), in Aihe Wang 2000: 166.

8

The Greeks

THE POLIS

In contrast to China, the Greeks were seafarers, split up into tiny communities; and, while sacred monarchy existed, it was the weakest form in any literate civilization. When the Greeks emerged from nomadic tribalism, they settled in territorial groups called *poleis* (sing. *polis*: citizen-state).[1] Ancient Greece consisted of 'more than a thousand separate political communities stretching from Spain to Georgia' (Cartledge 1997: 4), especially on the sea coasts. The many small islands and the mountainous terrain, dotted with inlets and coves, enabled relatively small communities to remain independent, and to communicate with one other through trade and a common language and culture. In contrast to Mesopotamia, sovereignty remained with the separate poleis. The classical Greek world, from at least Homer onwards, was geographically dispersed yet culturally close-knit.

The first Greek poleis were warrior and pirate bands which had found a permanent territorial base. The polis was based on a band of warriors, an all-male fraternity on which everyone's survival and freedom depended.[2] In Homer's epics (probably composed 750–700 BCE, but depicting a much earlier society), we find people already organized in territorial units called polis or *dēmos* (lit. a 'people'), consisting of (generally speaking) a warlord, his family and followers, and others. In contrast to nearly every other ancient developing society, these were face-to-face communities, small enough for all citizens to meet together in one place, the agora, both market-place and assembly.[3]

Most striking when we compare the poleis with other early states was the absence of sacred monarchy (see below). The polis itself, with its temples and walls, was the sacred political object (Scully 1990). Within it there was no specific agent of religious authority. The state was conceived as an abstract, impersonal entity, separate from any individual or dynasty, a forum rather than an authority.

Poleis were less hierarchical than other ancient societies. The Greeks travelled widely, with a relatively high proportion engaged in trade and craft manufacture. Hesiod (a seventh-century poet) portrays the outlook of the hard-working farmers who formed the backbone of the polis. It was an ethic of work and trade. Hard work brings virtue, a good name, and wealth (*Works and Days* 288–312). Peaceful competition is a 'good' kind of 'strife', because it stimulates the lazy to work: 'a neighbour competes with his neighbour who is hurrying to get rich... potter with potter, craftsman with craftsman'.[4]

Independence and self-government were made possible because it was the mass of citizens who comprised the predominant military force, the hoplites (heavy infantry), 'a block of identically equipped troops', comprising a large, and increasing, part of the citizenry.[5] The Greek poleis defied, for a while, anything a sacred monarchy could hurl at them. There was thus a connection between military and political participation (as Machiavelli later noted in Renaissance Italy). In fifth-century Athens, *dēmokratia* was justified on the ground that the state's power rested on a navy manned by the common people (*CGR* 100).

The polis was evolutionarily successful because members were on the whole willing to die for it (despite a slender belief in life after death). Greek political culture was based on public shame (*aidōs*) and glory for one's descendants. Virtue (*aretē*: excellence, greatness)[6] was said to consist in standing firm in close combat: 'this is a common good for the polis and all her people'. Citizens look out for one another (Scully 1990: 111). If someone dies fighting, 'his grave and his children are conspicuous among men, and his children's children and his line after them'.[7] Just as sacred monarchy was based on the instinct of extended kinship, so too the polis made genetic sense as a way to ensure survival of one's kin, and gave reproductive advantage to descendants of the glorious dead.

The polis retained certain features of 'primitive' society that other early civilizations lost partly because of its size. One's whole life depended upon this tight-knit community; the individual without a polis is a nobody.[8] One's own survival and that of one's family depended on people with whom one had face-to-face contact. This was the only time that such relatively intimate communities flourished as independent and self-managing states. 'Everyone acquired a certain stature in relation to whatever happened in the world, an ability to influence the course of events that is scarcely conceivable today' (Meier 1990: 23). This produced a unique kind of patriotism towards a 'fatherland' which (in Aeschylus' words) embraces 'children, wives, the seats of the ancestral gods, the tombs of our forbears' (*Persians* 403–5). And eventually the polis 'became the focus of a man's moral, intellectual, aesthetic [as well as] social and practical life' (Kitto 1951: 11). And yet, far from discouraging individual self-awareness and independence of thought, the community of the polis could, in some instances, foster these (Meier 1990:

138). It may have helped that sexual and romantic love (*erōs*) stood at the centre of religion, aesthetics, and thought, especially at Athens where social ties were multiple and people generally tolerant.

And yet actual kinship could be less important in the polis than in some other early types of state (*CGR* 54–7). The significant family unit was nuclear rather than extended. The polis itself controlled the family, lineages, 'rituals of death, military organisation, rites of commensality', and religion.[9] Poleis tended to be subdivided into artificial 'brotherhoods', subordinate to the polis as a whole, but not based on actual kinship.

Considerable variations developed between the constitutions and political cultures of different poleis. Sparta became a rigidly hierarchical oligarchy based on social conformity and strict military discipline. Athens became a *demokratia* with an astounding freedom of self-expression; social ties were multiple and people tolerant.

The Greeks recognized the special character of their political institutions, and the role these played in their whole way of life. For them, 'the good life was possible only in a polis... the good man was more or less synonymous with the good citizen' (Finley 1983: 125). Only in the polis does one develop the *aretē*, which includes competence in public affairs (*Gorgias*, in *EG* 205), proper to a human being. Greeks believed that the polis gave them an advantage over other peoples, because being the citizen of a polis develops people's courage and understanding (Hippocratic corpus, in *EG* 165). In stark contrast to China and India, in the classical period no school of thought—indeed hardly a single individual—seriously considered opting out of the polis. The state and its politics were probably more central to the way people lived and thought than they were in any other ancient culture.

The polis and knowledge

Language and the human brain first evolved in the context of competitive social interaction (above, p. 7). Scientific and philosophical enquiry (natural philosophy) started among the poleis of Ionia (the eastern Aegean) during the sixth century BCE. The Greeks emphasized the importance of checking things out and weighing alternatives even before science began. Craftiness was the characteristic of Odysseus, a type-case of Greek heroism. And 'by far the best man is he who checks everything out for himself, looking round to see what will be better in the long term' (Hesiod, *Works and Days* 293).

The development of natural philosophy, based on logic and observation, was probably made possible by the kind of society and self-government that existed in the polis.[10] Citizens would spend hours in 'talk in market-place, colonnade, gymnasium, in the political assembly, in the theatre and at religious celebrations' (Kitto 1951: 37). Dialogue was a feature of public life and of politics.[11] *Logos*, which meant word, speech, argument, reasoning, disourse,[12] was conceived to underlie both the human mind with its decision-making, and the physical world (*kosmos*). The social dynamics of early human society was replicated and intensified by interaction between large numbers of individuals, with decision-making still in the hands of social equals. (Indeed, Aristotle thought that the development of the intellect was the purpose of the polis.) One must remember, however, that science and philosophy also arose in China without any polis.

In *dēmokratiai* especially, and at Athens most of all, political and judicial decision-making took place in a context of argument and counter-argument: 'the Assembly expected . . . to choose between alternative proposals or policies on the basis of the facts and the arguments they had heard' (Finley 1983: 79). Athenian drama enshrined dialogue in religious ritual (compare Confucius in the *Sayings* 3.5, above, p. 104). Aeschylus (525–456 BCE), Sophocles (496–406 BCE), and Euripides (c.480–406 BCE) portrayed the agonies of human uncertainty, and struggled to understand the things that happens to human beings.

Sophocles and Euripides displayed confrontation between fundamentally opposed viewpoints, neither of which necessarily gained the upper hand. In plays such as *Philoctetes* and *Electra*, Sophocles does not seem to know which side is right; he certainly does not do the deciding for us (perhaps he thinks the case equally balanced). Both he and Euripides test out what each side can say. In Euripides' *Trojan Women* this becomes a sympathetic dialogue with the (Trojan) other.[13] It would be surprising if the stimulation of such interactions between different people's opinions, of having to look at questions from several different angles, did not do something to stimulate the latent functions of the human brain. Heraclitus (c. 500) insisted on the public nature of mental processes—'reason is common to all but most people live as if thinking were their own affair'—and saw reason as the inner principle of the cosmos itself.[14] In other words, understanding nature, like politics, involves public discourse; evidence has to be considered and certain procedures followed. With increasing reliance on evidence and testimony, 'legal proceedings brought into operation a whole technique of proof, of reconstruction of the plausible and the probable, of deduction from clues'; judicial activity 'contributed to the development of the notion of objective truth'.[15]

What the Greeks called philosophy (love of wisdom) was not the kind of academic pursuit it has become (even though Plato founded the Academy, and with it the academic way of life and the university tradition). It meant pursuit of knowledge of all kinds, including (and for Socrates and Plato pre-eminently) knowledge about how to conduct our lives, both as individuals and as members of a polis. It referred both to practical knowledge, and to the understanding of ourselves and our lives—all that we do—in connection with the world around and beyond us; both to knowledge (as, for example, taught and pursued in universities today) and to 'wisdom' in the modern sense (which is definitely not).

Natural science used the language and concepts of politics.[16] 'Cosmos' (world) meant 'order' but it could also mean government.[17] 'The notion that natural phenomena are regular and subject to orderly and determinate sequences of causes and effects is expressed partly by means of images and analogies from the legal and political domain' (Lloyd 1979: 247). Heraclitos found 'the same materials and the same laws' in both the natural and human worlds (KRS 203). Indeed, the very idea that 'the events in the world are all governed by law' may be related to the role of law in the polis ('the people should fight for their law as for their city-wall', as Heraclitus himself said) (Barnes 1982: 128).

There seems to have been a further connection between science and the 'democratic' notion of political equality. According to Empedocles (c. 495–435 BCE), the four elements (or 'roots') of the cosmos are 'equal in power', and they rule in turn; he saw the cosmic forces as holding one another in check, so that none can gain 'violent supremacy' or 'monarchy' over the others.[18] Health was conceived as equality or balance (*isonomia*: the very term used for equality before the law) between the 'powers' of the body.[19] Heraclitos, on the other hand, said that, just as among humans war is 'the father and king of all', so too in nature 'war is common [to all] and right is strife' (KRS 193–4).

Political wisdom (*sophia*) was itself much in demand. There were numerous proverbs about how to behave in public: 'do not speak ill of neighbours', 'obey the laws', 'forgiveness is better than vengeance', 'win bloodless victories', 'moderation is best', 'counsel the polis for the best' (Bryant 1996: 96–7). The sixth-century philosopher-poet Xenophanes claimed that his *sophia* was better than gymnastics because it alone could give a polis good governance (*EG* 38). According to Aristotle, what the first humans meant by wisdom was the ability to organize a polis and make laws; this, in his view, preceded both science and theology (Vernant 1982: 69). Solon applied causal and empirical reasoning to the political problems of Athens just at the time when Thales was initiating natural philosophy (*CGR* 40–1; below, p. 139).

Religion, ethics, skill (*technē*)

The non-monarchical and non-authoritarian nature of the polis was to some extent reflected in the Greek view of the supernatural world. The gods were not as exalted as they were in Persia, Egypt, or India; Zeus was supreme, but he was neither the creator nor the master of the universe.[20] Human destinies were, rather, controlled by impersonal 'fate'. Punishment and reward in an afterlife were less important than those meted out in one's own life and on one's descendants (*OHG* 321). The tragedians analysed the effects of wrong-doing and the causes of human catastrophes; they tended to point to inscrutable supernatural action, but this was not taken for granted.

It was thought that Zeus had rebelled against his father, Kronos, and replaced him as chief god. Following this successful revolution, Zeus exercised paternal power, which could be tyrannical. Homer wrote about gods in a relaxed, self-consciously artistic, sometimes deliberately fanciful way. They are not particularly benevolent (as they became under sacred monarchies); Zeus is hardly loving;[21] nor are they, for the most part, personally interested in the fate of humans. They are, however, bound by their promises.

There was no divine revelation or divinely authorized code of law, no 'divine warrant for any specific magisterial or legislative decision'. Virtues were more important than rules. Priests were lay state officials without political power. It was the polis which 'had the right to punish offences against the gods, to censor or ban religious practices'.[22] This probably made it easier to apply to the natural world the kind of reflection and enquiry that all cultures applied to social relationships. It probably also made it easier to apply these to theology.[23] This was a relatively relaxed ideological environment.

But Homer and Hesiod emphasized that the moral code was protected by the gods, and that offenders, whether kings or commoners, would be punished.[24] Hesiod contrasted justice (*dikē*) with common practice (*nomos*); he portrayed Zeus as, above all, 'avenger of the poor and oppressed' (Dodds 1951: 32). It was only to humans that Zeus gave justice, which means giving 'straight judgements' to strangers and citizens alike (Hesiod, *Works and Days* 225–6, 274–85). Hesiod was particularly concerned with telling the truth in court (ibid. 284–5). One finds parallels in Mesopotamia, Egypt, and Israel (*CGR* 54). The corresponding quality of a person or group was *dikaiosunē* (uprightness, integrity).

Greek craftsmanship and art,[25] like their science and philosophy, were part of a more confident relationship with the cosmos. Greeks did not, on the whole, look down on manual crafts (Kitto 1951: 239). The gods Hephaistos and Athene 'taught glorious crafts to mortals on earth'. Early literature dwelt on the wonders of craftsmanship and art. Homer is always interested in what domestic objects—seats, doors, cups, jugs—are made of. Odysseus prides himself on his DIY ability: it was when he explained the construction of their marriage-bed out of a living olive tree—'and I made it straight (*ithuna*) on the line'—that Penelope finally recognized him (*Od.* 23.197). It was technology that enabled humans to make the transition from cave-dwelling to civilization.[26] Theories of social evolution emphasized the role of manual crafts (below, p. 145). Plato was particularly fond of analogies from craftsmanship (*Rep.* 341c, 353d).

Artists portrayed the human figure as accurately as possible. Experts used technical skills and town-planning to redesign nature. The founding of a new polis involved detailed consideration of how best to plan both public space and the distribution of power.[27] Aristotle defended the study of animals and their organs on the ground that, if art is beautiful, nature is more so (Lloyd 1968: 69–70).

Greece was the only ancient society in which a new relationship with the world was sealed by the canonization of the beauty of the human body. More than in any other ancient culture, art portrayed *human* scenes. No sculptures, male or female, in any other ancient culture are nearly so sexually attractive. Judging from poetry and sculpture, people saw and experienced themselves as human beings more sharply than in any other culture—without a veil.

Natural philosophy in turn fed back into moral and political thought. Politics is a craft (*politikē technē*) (Democritus, in *EG* 158). The notion of a moral law ingrained in the cosmos appears in Heraclitos; in him, 'ethics is for the first time formally interwoven with physics' (KRS 211). He saw nature as 'self-regulating' (*autonomos*: 'a law to itself'; in Vlastos 1947: 168 n., 175 n.). There is 'one divine law' which nourishes 'all the laws of humans'.[28] Here we have the origin of one of the most important ideas in Western political thought: natural law. According to Empedokles, 'that which is lawful for all' extends throughout the cosmos (KRS 319–20). In other words, moral principles are embedded in the scheme of things. Sophocles' Antigone appealed against the ruler's mere 'proclamation' (*kerugma*) to 'the unwritten and eternal ordinances of the gods: and no-one knows where they have come from' (*Antigone* 450–7).[29] Aristotle went on to distinguish between those laws which are common to all peoples because they are 'in accordance with nature', and those laws which are 'determined by each people for themselves' (*Rhetoric* 137b4–6).[30]

Athens and the other Greek citizen-states were conquered by King Philip of Macedon in the 330s. At this point, Athenian *demokratia* was unable to offer effective resistance to a large-scale monarchy. They never regained their independence.

Constitutions

Greeks kings (sing. *basileus*) did not have such a high status as sacred monarchs elsewhere. Homer's Agamemnon, who leads a coalition of forces from all over mainland Greece, gets his way, but with difficulty and much argument. Early poleis were dominated by the chief of the leading clan, but his position was not as stable or dominant as that of chieftains and monarchs in most cultures (Roussel 1976). Great families had to earn their status in each generation. Leadership had to be earned by ability and consensus. The prestige and authority of the chief 'depended on networks of carefully nurtured personal relationships with peers, subordinates and inferiors' (Donlan 1998: 55; *Iliad* 9. 37–9).

Indeed, Homer's Agamemnon is no hero, and not an attractive character (*Iliad* 19.80; *Odyssey* 2.170 ff.). Other kings are even less favourably portrayed: Priam vacillates, Menelaus is 'good at shouting'. Homer's real heroes are warrior-lords: Achilles, Hector, Odysseus. They are leaders of war-bands; they have the respect of their men on account of their ancestry and leadership qualities.[31] The relationship between Odysseus and his men on the voyage home is one of comradeship and reciprocity; their status is 'uncertainty of the leader's control over the group' (Donlan 1998: 58–62). Plunder is distributed equally, or by lot; although an act of prowess can earn Odysseus a lion's share. Something else, however, seems to be suggested when, after his homecoming, Zeus imposes on Odysseus and his opponents 'a faithful oath that he should be king for always' (*Odyssey*. 24.483, 546). This suggests a more stable monarchy, and seems rather out of character with the rest of the poem.

Hesiod, like the Hebrew prophets, threatened divine sanctions against those kings who give 'crooked judgments…not paying attention to the wrath of the gods' (*Works and Days* 250–63). There was a sceptical attitude towards rulers in general. The fifth-century Athenian dramatists portray kings as only slightly apart from those they rule; people know who has been sleeping with whom in the royal household. Each king was familiar to his people. They are fallible. The authors emphasize kings' subjection to fate and divine censure; great dynasties are liable to have tragic and ludicrous outcomes. Several Greek tragedies are about disasters that attend those in power. The cause of these is the *hubris* (being too pleased with oneself) that usually comes with wealth and power. The comic dramatist Aristophanes (*c.* 448–380 BCE) made fun of leaders in Athens' 'democratic' polis; the Old Comedy playwrights were the only people in the ancient world who regularly and publicly criticized active politicians without fear of reprisal.

Important decisions were taken in the assembly of citizens (*agora, ekklēsia, boulē*) (Vernant 1982: 33). Parallels might be found in Israel under the Judges, or the forest-republics which nurtured Buddhism. 'The evidence of Homer is overwhelming that in the long run the *demos* has the final say' (Donlan 1998: 69). From the seventh century BCE poleis tended to be ruled by a council of the better-off citizens, with varying degrees of input from an intermittent assembly of small farmers, craftsmen, and traders. High office was the preserve of the wealthy upper class (Finley 1983: 45). A gulf arose between the poor ('the many' or 'the people'), often described in current parlance as 'mean, knaves, the mob', and the rich ('the few'), generally described as 'the worthy, best, well-born' (Finley 1968: 51; 1983: 2). From the early sixth century BCE the ideologies of rich and poor began to be conceptualized as *eunomia* (good order) versus *isonomia* (equality of rights). Slaves, who might number up to a quarter of the population, had no rights.[32]

Conflict between rich and poor became endemic. Should 'the few' or 'the many' have power? In some poleis, a strong ruler (*tyrannos*) emerged, often a noble who had sided with the populace. Thus a variety of constitutions appeared, and also of political cultures. From now on, forms of government within the polis would vary considerably. Poleis tended to have a history of 'revolutions' (constitutional changes). Athens and Sparta in particular developed opposing ideologies, representing demokratia[33] and freedom, on the one hand, and aristocracy and social discipline on the other.[34]

ATHENS AND DĒMOKRATIA

Solon

The Greeks were unusual in trying, at least some of the time, to resolve their social problems by negotiating over the political constitution. At Sparta, power remained with two hereditary kings and the aristocratic Council of Elders; all citizens ('the equal ones') met in an assembly. At Athens, which with its silver mines was fast becoming a focal point for commerce and craftsmanship, reconciliation between the elite and the masses was undertaken by political means. The citizens elected (594 BCE) Solon ('the wise'), an itinerant Athenian merchant, as a special chief officer with full powers to sort out the class war between rich and poor. This tactic of calling in a 'wise lawgiver with unlimited power' (*CGR* 42–3) was a major innovation.

Solon was both a philosopher-poet and a master of the art of politics. He sought a moral conversion as well as political reform. He 'preached to his fellow citizens a new moral programme' (Bryant 1996: 94). What he tried to instil was *sōphrosunē* (self-control, discretion, moderation); this became a fundamental value, moral and political (Greenhalgh 1972: 195–6). He spared no pains in pointing out to the Athenians that their polis was in danger of being destroyed by its rich citizens, who, 'lured by wealth... know not how to restrain their excess'. Their injustices are reducing the polis to slavery. This is a public evil, affecting everbody 'even [in] the innermost recesses of his bed-chamber' (in Bryant 1996: 94).

He repaired the political structure by carefully thought-out innovations, based on factual analysis of the existing situation. He more than anyone enabled Athens to develop the rule of law and, eventually, *dēmokratia*. His solution was to establish a *balance of power* between the wealthy and and the populace: 'I set up a strong shield around both parties by not allowing either to overcome the other unjustly'.[35] He highlighted *eunomia* (good order), which, 'often put[ting] the unjust in fetters...makes rough things smooth, stops excess, weakens hubris...straightens crooked judgments...puts a stop to divisive factions' (*EG* 26). He saw the problems as both economic and political, and sought to address both spheres. His methods were compromise and consensus; he refused 'to do anything by force of tyranny' (in Greenhalgh 1972: 193). He freed debt-slaves and secured the writing-off of debts accumulated by poorer farmers, who could from then on reclaim free ownership of their land. He then drafted a new law code, the aim of which was to establish equality before the law: 'I wrote laws equally for poor and rich' (*EG* 27). He appears to have given greater powers to the assembly, partly by providing it with a new deliberative organ, the Council, to prepare its business (*CGR* 40–2). He extended political participation to less wealthy property-owners. He did something for everyone.

The poems in which Solon explained and justified his actions expressed a distinctive ideology. He had set 'black Earth' *free*. The central idea was eunomia (good order) and a sound legal system.[36] Eunomia meant generosity (*euergesia*: doing good works) as opposed to *pleonexia* (being grasping). He claimed to have done something for everyone: the people should realize that 'what they have now they would never have seen, even in their dreams'; the powerful should thank him for preventing the populace from destroying their wealth. 'I took my stand like a boundary stone...between them' (*EG* 28). Solon was both a moral thinker and a politician: he put his solutions into practice by combining might and right (*EG* 27), and by piecemeal political engineering.

This established security of tenure for poorer peasants and an opening-up of the political system to all citizens (Finley 1963: 33–4). Other poleis followed Athens's example; they too resolved the class-conflict between rich and poor by calling in an esteemed outsider to mediate. In a somewhat similar way, the city-states of medieval Europe attempted to balance political power between well-off and less-well-off citizens; they too appointed outside arbitrators to mediate disputes. But there is no evidence that they borrowed these practices from ancient Greece.

What differentiated the poleis and their constitutions from other types of state and regime was now said to be 'rule by laws, not by men'; that is, equality before the law (isonomia), which gave all citizens the right to defend themselves and their property rights in a fair trial. This ideal was espoused by oligarchs and democrats alike.[37] 'Equality permits business to be carried on in contractual exchange'.[38] The prevailing ideology of many poleis was that political power should reside 'in the middle', meaning both in the public arena and with those of middling wealth. 'Many things are best in the middle; I wish to be middling (*mesos*) in the polis', said the poet Phokylides (fl. 544 BCE, in Bryant 1996: 97). The key virtue was moderation. The polis was 'a political identity unique in world history, weighted towards the middle and lower ranks of society' (Meier 1990: 21).

In other cultures 'wise men' conveyed ideas as messages from the gods. Isaiah projected some of what Solon set out to achieve by legislation onto a future messianic utopia (above, p. 65). Again, Solon and Confucius had similar views on the merits of poverty and how the rich should treat the poor, but Confucius sought to achieve his goal through a reformed sacred monarchy.

Dēmokratia

During the fifth century Athens became the most 'democratic' state in the Greek world. Under Cleisthenes (in 508/7 BCE) the citizen body was reconstituted so as to embody 'a new, positive conception of active, democratic citizenship' (Cartledge 1997: 23). In 462/1 BCE, after the defeat of the Persians (480), when Athens had become the head of a naval confederacy (in effect her empire), the aristocratic Council of the Areopagus was abolished and the power of the assembly further increased. Members of the Council of 500 which acted as steering committee for the Assembly were chosen by lot and in rotation. At the same time, both the hearing of lawsuits and the calling to account of officials were transferred to people's courts with very large juries (up to 6,000); these were also chosen by lot. But every juror had to swear never to allow cancellation of debts or redistribution of property (Finley 1983: 109). Wealthy individuals were expected to contribute large sums to public causes, and many did so.

The assembly had sole legislative power, and it made policy. Some officials were elected by the assembly, some chosen by lot, all with limited tenure. In the assembly all citizens had the right to speak and make proposals.[39] 'A man was a leader so long, and only so long, as the Assembly accepted his programme in preference to those of his opponents'. For Athenians, demokratia meant not only the opportunity but the obligation to serve on the Council of

500, the juries, and the administrative offices at some point in their lives. Pericles noted that it was only at Athens that those who don't take part in public affairs (*ta politika*) were looked down upon (Thucydides 2.40.2). By these means the citizens 'gained control over the constitution as a whole'.[40] After Athens' defeat by Sparta (404 BCE), constitutional checks on the power of the assembly were introduced, but there was no fundamental change.

Benjamin Constant suggested that the main difference between ancient and modern democracy was that ancient democracy meant personal participation in government, while modern democracy means government by elected representatives. This was partly because in classical times political units remained small. Representation was attempted when poleis formed confederations against a common enemy. Thales of Miletus (seventh-sixth centuries), the first natural scientist and philosopher, suggested that the poleis set up a common 'bouleuterion (parliament)' to deal with the Persian threat (Herodotos 1. 170). Faced with Philip of Macedon in the fourth century, poleis sent representatives to interstate conferences. The Achaean League of the third century (Tarn and Griffith 1930: 68–77) was, according to Polybius, 'favourable to freedom of speech and true demokratia'.[41]

The main restriction on Athenian *demokratia* was the limited membership of the citizen body, and the difficulty of attending regularly. It excluded women and slaves. The ideology of freedom coexisted with a massive proportion of slaves in the population, possibly greater than in China, Israel, or other ancient societies (just as it did in the old American South). There were up to 40,000 citizens out of a total population of around 250,000. Actual attendance was at most about 6,000 (Finley 1983: 73). Payment for attendance in the assembly and the courts made participation possible, in theory, even for the poorest citizen. But obviously those living outside the city, notably farmers, and anyone with pressing business could only attend very rarely. Nevertheless, there was far more popular control over domestic and foreign policy, far more political participation, than anywhere else in the ancient world, or in the vast majority of modern states.

Law and liberty

The political ideals of fifth- and fourth-century Athens were freedom, equality before the law, and government by the people (demokratia). All of these were interconnected. Freedom and equality could not, it was thought, be achieved under one-man rule, whether this came about by family succession (called

'despotism') or by force and manipulation ('tyranny'). One meaning of freedom was government by the people. Participation in debates and decision-
making obviously entailed freedom of speech. Freedom also referred to the
independence of the polis from foreign rule, above all by a monarchy. This
was what had been contested in the Persian wars. The Athenian ideology was
put into the mouth of Theseus (Athens' legendary king-hero) in a play
presented by Euripides during the war with oligarchic Sparta: Athens 'is not
ruled by one man but is free. The people governs, taking turns each year'
(Suppliant Maidens 404–7). To be free means to have an equal right to take
part in deliberations about public policy.

Euripides' Theseus recalled the Solonic basis of Athenian political culture:
in the free polis of Athens the people 'do not give too much [political power]
to the wealthy; even the poor have an equal share ... With written laws, the
weak and the strong have equal rights; the lesser man with justice on his side
can overcome the great man'.[42] Here constitutional dēmokratia is seen as a
means not of representing civil society but of counteracting its inequities.

The Greeks thought that what differentiated the polis and its political order
from other types of state and other regimes was 'rule by laws, not by men'.
Eunomia (good law) meant isonomia (equal law): secure property rights for *all*
citizens, guaranteed by the right to a fair trial. And they further identified
isonomia with dēmokratia because, first, equality under the law protected all
citizens alike, and second, it was the laws which prescribed who held office and
on what terms (Finley 1963: 33, 50). The polis 'requires its citizens to rule and be
ruled' according to law.[43] Dēmokratia meant constitutional government, in the
sense that powers, offices, and functions were distributed by law. Freedom and
equality also depended upon each other. Freedom and demokratia meant
equality of political power among citizens.

But dēmokratia was not justified (as it is today) by the Athenians or other
Greeks on the ground that it enables each individual to promote their own
self-interests in public decision-making. In that respect, Athenian dēmokratia
was more 'corporate' than modern democracy; an identity of interests between the individual citizen and the polis community was generally assumed
(Thucydides 2.60.2).

Herodotus put forward another argument for freedom: that it stimulates
people to work for themselves (5.78, in Sinclair 1988: 13), a point taken up in
the European Renaissance and by Adam Smith and political economists since.
Democritus balanced this by saying that 'poverty under dēmokratia is preferable to so-called prosperity under a dictator to the same extent as freedom is
preferable to slavery' (Democritus, in *EG* 158).

In his praise of the dead at the end of the first year of the war with
Sparta, Pericles (as reported by Thucydides) singled out the fact that Athens

was a liberal, tolerant society. He emphasized freedom in private life: people could do what they wanted without incurring resentment or sour looks (Thucydides 2.37.2–3). It was a genuinely pluralist society with numerous opportunities for informal encounters, including philosophical symposia.[44] Economic and intellectual incentives attracted leading thinkers, including the so-called sophists,[45] to Athens, where they could find wealthy patrons, such as Pericles himself (Kerferd 1981: 18). Athens became the intellectual and artistic centre of the Greek world. It produced masterpieces of architecture and sculpture for all to see; the greatest works of literary art were performed in public.

Such was the background to the 'continuous, intense and *public*' political discussion at Athens (Finley 1983: 123), and the first rational and empirical analysis of society and the state (outside China). Without Athenian demokratia, there would have been no Western political philosophy.

Aeschylus

Playwrights, in front of mass audiences, explored the implications of moral and social norms.[46] The growth of the dramatic genre more or less coincided with the rise of dēmokratia.[47] In their search for meaning, they were concerned with justice both in the cosmos and in human relationships. For them, the problems of the family and the state overlap; personal tragedies have a political dimension.

Aeschylus reinterpreted the juridical structures of the polis in *The Eumenides* (*Furies*), the final play in his *Oresteia* trilogy, performed three years after the constitutional revolution of 462–461 BCE. (Some see it as a defence of the ancient Council of the Areopagus, whose powers had been greatly reduced.)[48] In the story, set out in the first two plays of the trilogy, the *Agamemnon* and *Libation-Bearers*, Agamemnon had consented to sacrifice his own daughter in order to get to Troy. On his victorious return ten years later he was murdered by his wife. Their son, Orestes, was told by the god Apollo to avenge the murder of his father by murdering his mother. At the start of the final play the Furies (or Eumenides, spirits of retribution) are driving Orestes mad; they demand his life in retaliation for the murder of his mother. Apollo begs that Orestes be allowed to expiate his offence by other means, but the Furies insist on 'an eye for an eye'. The goddess Athene resolves the problem by setting up the Council of the Areopagus to be 'judges of homicide'; from now on this is to be the forum for the punishment of crime—'an ordinance for all time' (*Eumenides* 484).

But first she has to convince the Furies. This she does by enshrining them within the polis as guarantors of law. By this means, respect for justice, for parents, and for strangers is established (*Eumenides* 540–55). The Furies are won over. From now on, conflicts are to be resolved by argument and Persuasion (personified as a sacred being: l. 885). Power goes 'to all things in the middle' (ll. 526–9, 696)—a triumph, declares Athene, for Zeus 'of the public space (*agoraios*)' (l. 973). The Furies then denounce faction and civil war; citizens must be of one mind, loving one another and hating their enemies (ll. 976–87).[49] The effect of this was to sanction the law of the citizen-state. Anarchy and tyranny are outlawed. It is also (in modern language) a triumph of reason over superstition.

Aeschylus seems to be showing his audience where and how the polis fits into the scheme of things. This was for Athens—or any polis—an equivalent of the social contract in modern political thought. Aeschylus' solution to the religious, moral, and psychological problem was to authorize an *institution*— the supreme law-court of the polis—as the forum for the settling of disputes. The judicial function passes from religion to the state; but the state has religious authority built into it (Meier 1990: 106).

All this is related to a new conception of justice. The automatic vengeance exacted by numinous forces is replaced by a trial based on witnesses and evidence: in other words, a *public dialogue*. As Meier puts it, 'self-perpetuating revenge yields to the law of the polis, self-help to citizenship, and the high-handed power of the house or the individual to the sovereignty of the [polis]' (ibid. 91). This is how dilemmas of conscience are to be resolved from now on. (One could call it the invention of legal rationality.)

The *Oresteia*, unlike a Shakespearian tragedy, has a 'happy' ending. Athene and Zeus come down on the side of human concord (as they also did at the close of the *Odyssey*). Aeschylus' work has both religious and political significance; sinister, numinous powers are appeased by incorporation into civic institutions and the civic code of morality. There is something of St Paul here, as well as of John Locke.

Socrates, Plato, and Aristotle probably watched the *Oresteia*; it was widely known throughout the Greek and Graeco-Roman world (and in Europe from the fifteenth century). Yet it was not mentioned in discussions of political or moral theory.

Education

It was obvious to everyone that the corollary of the way power was allocated in 'democratic' Athens was that political influence and status depended to a considerable degree upon oratory. Performance, ability, and reputation also counted for a great deal. Finley thinks that 'the Athenian demos displayed [great] discrimination in their selection of leaders' (1983: 140). Throughout the golden age of Athenian dēmokratia, Pericles, a wealthy aristocrat, was re-elected to the highest political office year after year: he was 'sober, incorruptible and reserved' (*OCCL* 313a). Thereafter the quality of leadership declined markedly.

Decrees, treaties, accounts, public notices, and archives were diplayed in public places.[50] A high rate of literacy may have been connected with dēmokratia (Goody and Watt 1968: 40–2, 55). Solon had (probably) introduced compulsory education in reading and writing; there was 'a well-established system of primary schools'. Books circulated widely.

Those who wanted to succeed needed to excel in public oratory and argument. A group of professionals emerged who taught aspiring citizens how to express themselves effectively, how to make out a convincing case in assembly or law-court. These 'sophists' got an extremely, and probably unfairly, bad press from the aristocratic Plato and the comic dramatist Aristophanes. We know little about them at first hand.

Reflection and debate about morals, politics, and religion intensified under dēmokratia, as people began for the first time to think systematically about these things, just as they were doing simultaneously in China. It was a wide-ranging debate and involved a significant number of people.

Protagoras

Protagoras—not himself an Athenian—was the first philosopher known to have discussed the polis systematically (he was also the first teacher to charge fees: *CGR* 92). Unfortunately, we know his views only through his opponent, Plato. Apparently, he argued that democratic citizenship required the political virtues of respect (*aidōs*: sense of shame) and justice, and also certain skills; that these are not innate but have to be *taught* (by people like Protagoras); but that *anyone* can acquire them (Plato, *Protagoras* 322d). This would maximize his class size, but it was also a truly democratic hit.

To prove his point, Protagoras made the first attempt (outside China) to explain the origin of states. Humans differ from all other animals in being 'naked, unshod, coatless and unarmed' at birth.[51] They therefore have to have certain skills to make what they need (they also developed religion and language); this was how humans acquired houses and clothing. But they still lacked *political* skill (*politikē technē*: how to live in a polis community); they lived separated from each other and so were unable to defend themselves. They *wanted* to unite and make poleis; but to do this they needed the qualities of respect and justice. But these are different from all other 'skills' in that, while a single doctor can meet the needs of many people, for there to be a polis *everyone* has to have the sense of shame and justice. (Indeed, those who don't have them should be killed: Plato, *Protagoras* 321c–322d.) This was, if you like, a technological theory of social development, and also of the political process.

Protagoras' was only one of several explanations suggested at this time for the origins of society, religion, and the state. Euripides suggested (*c.* 420 BCE) that some god gave us intelligence, language, agriculture, the ability to exchange goods by trade, and, for what we could not otherwise know, auguries (*Suppliant Maideus* 200–20). Democritus (*c.* 460–380 BCE) said that humans initially had an 'unruly and bestial life', but that then they began to help one another and 'learned each other's ways'; they developed language (in fact several languages) and crafts (*EG* 156–7). Someone else argued that, when faced with disorder and violence, 'men enacted laws for punishment, so that justice would be ruler'. But secret violence continued; therefore, clever people 'invented fear of the gods for mortals' (in *CHG* 89). These explanations of why humans live in society and the state may be compared with the roughly contemporary views of Mozi and others in China (above, pp. 108–10).

Protagoras proceeded now to what, according to Plato, was his main point (a self-interested one). To judge from the way people usually talk and behave, they *assume* that these civic virtues *can* be taught. Citizens are taught virtue first of all by their parents; then by their teachers at school; and finally by the polis itself (*Protagoras* 325–6; *EG* 181–3). Protagoras thus made a necessary connection between demokratia, civic virtue, and education: the polis depends on everyone having the political skills of civic virtue.

This was indeed a democratic point of view. The poet Pindar (518–*c.* 440) had argued (rather like Michael Oakeshott in his attack on 'rationalism in politics') that the best things come from nature and cannot be taught (Bryant 1996: 106). This would clearly give aristocrats a head start, because they were more likely to have acquired political skills from their upbringing and (private) education. Protagoras' was the only argument that was truly democratic (in either the ancient or the modern sense). He is also famous for having said (according to Plato), 'man is the measure of all things, of that which is, that it is, and of that which is not, that it is not'. This, if I understand it right (and it can be interpreted in several different ways), is one of the first statements of an anthropocentric view of the universe. It is no coincidence that it came out of the first democracy. There is surely a connection between running one's own affairs and believing oneself to be (or to be capable of being) in charge of nature as a whole (compare Marx); just as there is a connection between sacred monarchy and a theocentric view of the universe.

Plato was also to argue that citizenship depends upon certain virtues and skills, and that these have to be taught. But he insisted that only a few outstandingly gifted individuals would be able to learn these, and only very highly qualified specialists were capable of teaching them. In other words, Plato argued that politics *is* like the other crafts, in that here too we have to depend on specialized experts. He thus detached the argument for education from dēmokratia.

What survives in the philosophical record from 'democratic' Athens is only the counterblast (antithesis if you like; only there was no synthesis) which reinstated an elitist view of government. In subverting Protagoras, Plato was taking leave of the political culture of Athens, and perhaps of the polis generally.

Socrates

Socrates (469–399 BCE) was first and foremost a moral rather than a political thinker. His question was 'how one should live so as to make living most worthwhile' (*Republic* 344e, 352d). Above all, he was a remarkable personality. Nor did he charge for teaching; he said that his exclusive commitment to moral enquiry had landed him in 'boundless poverty' (Plato, *Apology* 23c). He wrote nothing (in this, he resembled the Buddha, Confucius, and Jesus). We know about him from his friends and admirers, Xenophon (*c.* 428–*c.* 354) and Plato (*c.* 429–347). Particularly remarkable seems to have been his method of enquiry, to tease out the truth by question and answer (dialectic). By this means, he led people to see that they did not really know what they thought they knew. Building on the way others in the Greek world were already framing questions, Socrates and Plato saw philosophy as a universal enquiry into how human beings should conduct themselves at any time and in any place. Socrates was executed on charges of introducing new deities and corrupting the young, both of which were manifestly false. He embodied in his way of life and in the way he died the method and qualities he had sought out in his discussions.

In the *Apology*, Plato's account of Socrates' speech in his own defence at his trial, he said that he had undertaken philosophy in response to a voice within him: 'something divine and spiritual (*daimonion*) comes to me' (*Apology* 31d); ever since childhood, 'a certain kind of voice comes upon me'. This god commanded him 'to spend my life searching for wisdom' (Plato, *Apology* 28e),[52] constantly enquiring of others what it is to be good; and, if they didn't know, at least making them acknowledge their ignorance as he did. This, Socrates argued, was the greatest service he could give to others and to the polis (*Apology* 30a). This was not secularization but internalization. (To an Israelite, it might have seemed the language of prophecy.)

While in most of Plato's dialogues—intellectual dramas—much of what is ascribed to 'Socrates' is Plato's construction (see Hare 1982: 14–15), the *Apology* and the *Crito* probably indicate Socrates' own attitude towards politics and the state. The *Crito* is set after Socrates has been condemned to death; his friends have an escape plan, but it means disobeying the law: should he go along with them? Socrates, as always, applies reason to ethics unreservedly: 'for I am not only now but always was someone who follows nothing else within me other than reason (*logos*), whichever logos seems after consideration the best' (*Crito* 46b). Socrates proceeds to argue that he would be being inconsistent if he disobeyed the laws of Athens at this moment, because, as an Athenian citizen, he had always lived by them. Besides, he would be undermining the authority of those very laws which had protected him all his life. He could at any time have gone to live somewhere else; and, by not doing so, Socrates argues, he has entered into a tacit agreement with 'the laws and the community of the polis' (*Crito* 51e–3a).[53] This was the first expression of a social contract between citizen and state.

Socrates also invoked patriotism: 'do you not see that your country (*patris*: fatherland) is more reverent and holy than your mother, father, and all your ancestors, and that you should respect, obey, and humble yourself before her... and either persuade her, or do whatever she commands? In war, law-court, everywhere, you must do what *polis* and *patris* command' (*Crito* 51b–c). He had done his utmost to persuade his fellow-countrymen to acquit him, and he must accept their verdict, as he had on other occasions.

Besides, if he did escape to some nice haven, what would he do there? What could he talk about? He would be alive, but could he go on saying that virtue, justice, law, and morality are the most important things for human beings (*Crito* 53c)? He would never again be happy. In other words, Socrates, faced with death, applied to himself the same principles which he had taught throughout his career (a perfect example of Kant's categorical imperative). But, unlike Kant, he was also convinced that only virtue brings happiness.

Thus Socrates referred to the rule of law but not to demokratia.

PLATO

Plato had become disillusioned with Athenian politics:[54] the 'democratic' polis had executed his mentor. In the *Republic* and the *Laws*, Plato directed

Socratic enquiry onto the state. In him, philosophy and the polis, thought and society, entered into a new relationship, one which, for some, they have had ever since: that is to say, philosophy takes priority over any particular social order, and the polis is to bend to its demands.

The *Republic*

The *Republic*[55] is an enquiry into the nature of *justice*.[56] This required redesigning the polis from first principles. Much of the dialogue is about how we know the true nature of things (epistemology). 'Socrates' leads Glaucon, his discussant, to the conclusion that things as we see them are mere appearances (or instances) of underlying realities (essences): of horse, dog, human, for example. These 'forms' or 'essences' (*ideai*) have their existence in an intangible world. It is only by knowing the forms that we can have true knowledge of things in the world of the senses. In the *Republic* Plato argued that truly good conduct and the truly good state have to be based on true knowledge of things in themselves; that is, of the forms or ideas that underlie the world of appearances. Plato seems to have had an unlimited (and untested) faith in the power of the mind.

Plato starts by looking at justice in the individual and then, to make things clearer, in the state. He seems to invert the usual relationship: rather than seeing our ideas as arising out of social discourse, he treats the state as an *illustration* of the mind.

The *Republic* begins with the conventional definition of justice: 'to pay everyone what is owed to him' (*Republic* 331e). This is promptly deconstructed by 'Socrates', who points out that, according to this, one should harm one's enemies and help one's friends, but 'it can never be just to harm anyone' (335e).[57] As we shall see, the whole debate hinges on what it is that is 'owed' to people.

'Socrates' insists that one cannot base justice on self-interest or convention. Glaucon feels instinctively that justice must be one of those qualities (such as sight, intelligence, and health) which are loved *both* for their beneficial consequences *and* 'for their own sake' (*Republic* 357c). Justice, he feels, is not merely a matter of convenience but something deeply embedded in human nature, an 'outstanding quality of personality' (*aretē psychēs*), without which we cannot 'live a blessed and happy life'. 'Socrates' undertakes to demonstrate that justice is indeed one of the 'greatest goods', valued both for its consequences and for itself; that it is (as we would say) intrinsic to human nature; that without it we would not be truly human. The argument that immediately follows is primarily about human nature (353e–4a, 357b–8a, 367c).

Now justice may belong either to an individual or to a state (polis). (This assumption that justice is fundamentally the same in individual and state is not scrutinized.) Since the polis is larger, one will get a clearer picture by identifying justice there first (*Republic* 368e).[58]

The division of functions; classes

Plato began by examining the origins of the polis. His analysis follows a slightly different tack from that of Protagoras. Plato observes that no one is self-sufficient (*autarkēs*): people need things from each other, so they gather in one place to help one another; this is called a polis. 'Socrates' describes mutual aid and the division of labour with considerable insight and a degree of light-heartedness. He introduces in turn the handicrafts, commerce (noting that there is a division of labour between states); then entertainers, artists, doctors, warriors (*Republic* 369c–376e).[59] Protagoras' and Plato's explanations of the origin of society and the state depend upon the need for collaboration rather than, like similar explanations in other milieux, the need to contain conflict.

Plato asserts a fundamental distinction between those who engage in trade and industry—the 'economic' pursuits we need in order to live—and the 'guardians' who watch over, defend, and regulate society. The warrior or guardian is a particular type of person. He is both high-spirited and, because he constantly has to distinguish between friend and foe, a lover of wisdom (*philosophos*) (*Republic* 376b). Plato goes into great detail about the guardians' education, which he considers crucial. Among the guardians, only some are capable of attaining the higher grades of enlightenment, and these will be the philosophers, those who deliberate and legislate.

Plato regarded it as fundamental to understanding human life and society that we recognize that people have to specialize in a particular profession—shoemaking, fighting, or whatever. Here sociology interacts with psychology: there are different *kinds* of people who have natural aptitudes for different tasks in the community. Both Plato's sociology and his psychology were rooted in this notion of craft-specialization. It was also intrinsic to Plato's argument that he was analysing the condition of humans (sing. *anthrōpos*: *Republic* 376b) as such, not of a particular race (see below, p. 204). His whole argument was based on a conception of human nature, with momentous consequences for the future development of political theory.

Plato thought he had now established the basic layout of human society and the state. In the polis 'based on nature (*physis*)' (*Republic* 428e), there will be three groups or classes: (1) philosophers; (2) warriors; (3) those pursuing gain through production and trade. To these correspond three parts of the soul or person (*psychē*) in every individual: (1) the rational, or wisdom-loving; (2) the ambitious and courageous; (3) the appetitive and pleasure-loving. Which part of society you belong to depends upon which part of your personality is most developed, or most capable of development. The crucial point, then, is the division of labour, based on differences in innate physical and mental abilities. Plato implants individual vocational aptitude at the heart of both personality and society.

This was an almost brahminical conception of fundamental differences between human beings (see above, pp. 72–3); indeed (as if to make this very point) Plato used a mythical tale to argue that people occupy their positions in society because of their behaviour in previous lives.

Of the four conventional virtues—wisdom (or knowledge), courage, self-control, justice—wisdom is concentrated in the philosophers, courage in the warriors. But self-control is 'a kind of harmony' suffused throughout the whole of society.[60] It is through this that 'the desires of the inferior mob will be controlled by the desires and wisdom of the elite few'. This is, crucially, because 'rulers and ruled will share the same conviction about who should rule' (trans. Cornford 122, adapted). Finally, justice is defined as every individual and group doing their own job, the one for which they are best fitted, minding their own business, not trying to do other people's jobs ('the possession and performance (*praxis*) of one's own affairs'; *Republic* 433a–434a). Justice, in other words, means respecting the contours of human nature; Plato's is the paradigm of a naturalistic theory.

But justice is not just one of several virtues; it is the master virtue, enabling all the others to exist, by ensuring the correct distribution of functions (Annas 1981: 118–25). Returning to the original definition of justice as paying everyone what is owed them, Plato concludes that justice in adjudication does indeed consist in each person being assigned what belongs to them and not what belongs to others (*Republic* 433e). It is the conception of what people are entitled to which has been quite radically altered here. This was a new notion, both of social justice and of what it means to be human.

What is peculiar to Plato is that he sees this distribution of roles and status as the necessary characteristic, indeed the very essence, of a just society. This view of justice was new; and no other thinker has adopted it since. Others, including later many Christian and Islamic thinkers, would follow Plato in proposing fundamental class-distinctions; but justice they would define as what humans may or may not do to one another, regardless of their socio-economic status.

Rule by philosophers

For political society thus constituted to function well, it is crucial that each 'part' fulfil its appropriate function, like the organs of a body, and that the three parts be properly related to one another. And this, Plato thinks, means that a few, properly qualified persons must rule. Here, he said, comes our 'biggest wave' that is likely 'to wash us away in laughter and contempt'. It is this: 'unless either the lovers of wisdom [philosophers] become the kings in the poleis, or those now called kings and rulers undertake to become truly wise, so that political power and love of wisdom are combined, there will be no end to our troubles in the cities, nor (I think) among the human race' (*Republic* 473d). What Plato was advocating was a complete inversion of existing power relationships.

Whereas Protagoras was happy to speak of the pursuit of politics as 'the political craft', Plato insisted that true politics consisted in a highly specialized form of knowledge (*epistēmē*), one which would combine outstanding moral virtue with (for example) mathematical skill. Government is a specialized form of knowledge requiring extensive education. He compares it to the skills of the doctor or navigator: you do not trust any old person to cure you or steer a ship, and 'in moral conduct too there is a measure which is absolutely right' (*Republic* 342c–e). He is not, of course, referring to how to acquire and retain power; for the 'art' of politics in this sense he had complete contempt. Rather, government requires a knowledge of basic philosophical truths and of the nature of the good life for humans.

Wisdom-lovers are fitted to rule because they have been trained to know the full truth; they are at home in the higher world of pure knowledge. Indeed, now that they have struggled painfully from dark, obscure images up to the sunlight of the forms and the good, they actually have to be persuaded and compelled to return to this dark world and give guidance to others (compare the Buddha: above, p. 85). Plato presents the ideal of a ruling class utterly dedicated to the welfare of the state.[61] The first criterion for the selection of such guardians is that they recognize the identity of interests between the polis and its members, and act accordingly (*Republic* 412d–e). The best rulers are those who would rather be doing something else (520d, 347c–d).

Plato modified this view in the *Statesman* (*Politicus*), to suggest that, since the requisite knowledge is so rare and so hard to come by, it will usually only be found in one individual. The best form of government, therefore, is monarchy.

In the *Republic* Plato gave no further attention to the form of the constitution; this was to be the subject of the *Laws*. Rather, the emphasis is on the character of the rulers. Among the guardians, there are to be no family units nor private possessions; women, children, possessions will be held in common. Marriage and the birth of children will be regulated. Female guardians are equal to male ones and may graduate to become philosopher-rulers. Whereas in other cultures these ideals led to the formation of separate monastic communities, here the moral-intellectual elite are not only in the polis, they rule it.

This was a counterblast not just to dēmokratia but to plutocracy. Whatever sympathies Plato may have once had with the attempt in 404–403 BCE, following defeat by Sparta, to turn Athens into an oligarchy, the programme of both the *Republic* and the *Laws* is something quite different. It was slightly closer to the Spartan model of military oligarchy, but, considering the central role of philosophy and philosophers, only slightly.

Here, then, we see an early endorsement of communism; in the *Laws* a rough economic equality is proposed (see below). Mengzi was thinking along similar lines in China at almost exactly the same time (see p. 106). Plato—like Confucius as well—regarded the pursuit of wealth with contempt ('all wars', he noted, 'arise from the acquisition of money'; *Phaedo* 66c). In all of this, Plato's modern descendants have been people like Marx and Ruskin. In the capitalist world today, economic science has persuaded almost all policy-makers and many political philosophers that communism is unworkable; and that equality is dysfunctional, and, since it fails to reward effort and ability, immoral.

If all this makes Plato appear unrealistic, he was well aware of the problem of reconciling his theory with reality (Annas 1981: 187). He knew that he could probably not bring about the ideal state in practice ('do not force me to demonstrate that what we have gone through in theory (*logos*) must be brought about in practice in every respect'). Philosophy (he says) may have taken control of a state 'in the infinity of past time, or now in some foreign region far beyond our knowledge, or it may do so in the future' (*Republic* 499c–d). What he has been doing is to paint a picture, provide a pattern (*paradeigma*), so as to show what the ideal state would look like. Here we meet Plato the artist: nature (he says) never conforms to the artist's ideal. Just as an artist paints a picture of 'the ideally beautiful man' without being able to prove that such a person exists, it does not matter if you cannot achieve a complete likeness of the model state in practice (472c–3a, 500c–1c).

Plato faced up to the prospect that his kind of state would never exist. In that case, what he has said will (he says) enable individuals to develop justice in their private lives. Similarly, in corrupt poleis such as 'democratic' Athens, philosophers 'must stand aside, powerless to help society, and can only save their own souls' (trans. Cornford 189). This exactly paralleled Confucius' advice (and later that of al-Farabi). This ideal of solitary virtue, and of the predicament of the philosopher in a corrupt state, would indeed appeal strongly to Muslim Platonists (Black 2001: 71–2).

But 'Socrates' has promised to demonstrate that justice is desirable not only in itself, but also for its consequences; that is, that it makes the individual and society happy. He proceeds to do this by means of ideal-typical descriptions of psychological types and political constitutions. These are: timocracy and the rule of honour; oligarchy and the desire for possessions; dēmokratia and the person who constantly changes their mind in pursuit of shallow, transitory pleasures of the moment. The way people live will depend on the kind of polis they live in. The trouble with dēmokratia is that 'the polis is filled with liberty and free-spokenness... the constitution distributes a kind of equality to the equal and unequal alike' (*Republic* 557b–558c). Here we can see how Plato set out to discredit the 'democratic' element in Greek thought and culture, which had developed furthest at Athens.

Book VIII of the *Republic* (543–76) was the first psychological and sociological analysis of how different types of individuals and regimes function and mutate. Plato analysed the degeneration of the ideal state into timocracy (rule by men who seek honour); this in turn declines into oligarchy (rule by the wealthy); and this into demokratia (rule by the fickle, pleasure-seeking masses whose ideal is liberty); and finally into tyranny (rule by a single, self-seeking individual). This whole passage pioneered the ideal-typical approach later used by Max Weber: behaviour and institutions are explained by laying bare the inner rationale of the way people think.

The *Laws*

In the *Laws*, probably his last work, Plato undertook a fundamental revision of his political ideas.[62] Here this incredibly fertile thinker approached the state and its constitution a second time. His purpose this time was to enquire what was the best *possible* constitution. Here he carried his investigation into every detail of political life. He concerned himself now not with the absolutely ideal constitution of state and society—the three psycho-social classes and the philosopher-rulers are absent—but with the 'second-best'. This is, to put it mildly, John Rawls and Walter Bagehot rolled into one.

There are two massive changes in Plato's new conception of the good state. The laws, which are to be laid down by 'a true legislator', are now said to be the essence of the state, its 'golden string', flexible yet consistent. He now classified the different possible constitutions according to whether power was in the hands of one, few, or many, and—Plato's own innovation—whether or not the rulers govern in accordance with the laws. He defines the good regimes as monarchy, aristocracy, and moderate dēmokratia; the bad ones as tyranny, oligarchy, and extreme dēmokratia. This straight away brought Plato's ideal constitution into the orbit of normal Greek political life, and quite close to the Athenian model. It is the laws, not philosophers, which set up the various public bodies and magistracies.

The purpose of laws is not to punish but to guide;[63] this overlaps, at least in part, with the function of law in some religious systems. Laws are to complement a system of universal education,[64] moral and physical, under professional teachers, paid for by the state. The minister of education is 'the most important magistracy in the city' (Laks, in *CGR* 282). Moral conduct is further to be encouraged by a state-sponsored religion. Monogamy is to be enforced, atheism and homosexuality banned.

In complete contrast to the *Republic*, the good constitution is a mixture of monarchy with dēmokratia. This, Plato thinks, will combine wisdom with liberty (*Laws* 693), balancing the representation of citizens' views with competent government. Plato thus took on board elements of the 'democratic' polis.[65] There is to be an assembly of all adult male citizens, but this assembly is severely restricted in what it may do. The 'guardians of the laws' (consisting of thirty-seven citizens aged over fifty) comprise 'the most influential organ of the state' (Stalley 1983: 188). Moral and social order are ensured by a special council of 'experts' chosen for their moral excellence: the 'Nocturnal Council'. The one area where Plato still thought equality desirable was material possessions: each citizen is to have at least one unit of land, none more than four (ibid. 102). Solon had not quite been forgotten.

Plato has been accused of being an enemy of liberty and of democracy, authoritarian, and even totalitarian. All of these charges are strictly true if we look at the *Republic*. But this is hardly fair to Plato, and hardly conducive to constructive debate, since Plato himself revised his views so extensively in the *Laws*. (To see him as the founding father of totalitarianism in the twentieth century, as Karl Popper did, is a textbook example of how to read a work out of context.)

In attempting to bring about something of what he has prescribed, Plato relied on education and persuasion. Those who are wise in Plato's sense could not rule by the methods associated with modern totalitarianism. His dialogues themselves were a new kind of writing, aimed to reach as wide an audience as possible. He founded the Academy in 385 BCE to train promising young men to become rulers, or advisers of rulers. He tried to persuade the dictator ('tyrant') Dionysius of Syracuse to take his advice.

Yet there is indeed an extraordinary contrast between Plato's whole approach in the dialogues and his conclusions in the *Republic*. The method

of Socrates and Plato was open-ended enquiry; no assumption goes unques-
tioned. Yet in the *Republic* Plato recommended indoctrination and censorship:
the truth is to be taught, but without the option of questioning it; the young
must first have the right opinions instilled into them, and only later is it to be
explained to them why what they believe is right.[66] So the culmination of
Plato's unrestricted pursuit of truth for its own sake was to be a new set of
dogmas about the way things are and how people should behave. In this respect,
Plato does not qualify as the starting-point of Western political thought.

Parallels and influences

Plato based his theory of justice and the state on his observation of human
nature and his theory of knowledge. He deduced from human nature what
form a state should take; there were parallels to this in China—in Mozi, the
Legalists, and Xunzi. But patterning the state on a theory of knowledge was
unique in the ancient world, and at any time. Plato's correlation between
knowledge and power is precise and uncompromising (in the *Republic*). Plato
was the first person outside China to attempt to analyse so systematically why
states exist, and how they should be organized.

In book VIII of the *Republic* Plato became the founder of political science.
The *Republic,* and still more the *Laws,* were the first detailed treatises on
constitutional theory anywhere in the world. The mixed constitution of the
Laws was taken up by Aristotle, Polybius, and Cicero (Laks, in *CGR* 259), and
then by medieval and early modern Europeans. The *Laws* was also the first
work of jurisprudence, establishing the distinction between public and private
law (trans. Taylor, p. xiv).

But I would argue that Plato was not, as is so often said, the *founder* of
political *philosophy, tout court.* Socrates and Plato may have been the founders of
moral philosophy, of epistemology, and of metaphysics (though this does scant
justice to the pre-Socratics); and Plato exerted a massive influence on Christian,
Muslim, and Jewish theology. And he may justly be called the found of *ancient*
political philosophy. Cicero's *Republic* and *Laws* (below, p. 186) were inspired by
Plato. The thought of al-Farabi (*c.* 870–950 CE), the first major Muslim political
philosopher, was an application of Plato's ideas to Muslim teaching. As their
titles indicate, al-Farabi's *Virtuous City, Aphorisms of the Statesman,* and *Sum-
mary of Plato's 'Laws'* followed on from Plato's three political dialogues. This
established Plato's influence among Muslim philosophers.

But when it comes to Europe and modern political philosophy, it is a
different matter. Plato's influence on European and Western political thought
was, I would contend, marginal. The first work of modern European political

philosophy was Marsilius of Padua's *Defender of the Peace*. And this effectively restarted political philosophy. Insofar as he was influenced by other thinkers, Marsilius drew on Aristotle and Ibn Rushd (Averroes), but not on Plato (Black 2008: 51–6). Hobbes marked yet another new start.

Plato's preference for monarchy in the *Statesman* contributed to the development of monarchical thought in the Graeco-Roman world (below, p. 164). And the standard definition of justice in Roman and European law became precisely the one which 'Socrates' had dismissed as too indeterminate: 'giving to each his due' (or 'right': *ius suum cuique reddere*, as Roman law had it; below, pp. 192–3). This definition was not, of course, what Plato ended up with.

Plato's idea of social stratification circulated widely in the Muslim world, with the sole difference that vocational groups were, in theory at least, given parity of esteem, as religion required. It was less influential in Europe, though the analogy between the division of labour and the organs of the human body was taken much more seriously. In both the Muslim world and Europe the main inference was that one should stick to one's own job and to one's own position in society (which often didn't happen, especially in parts of Europe). Hegel gave new expression to the ideal of a stratified yet harmonious society, also based on a division of functions according to people's different and unequal capacities.

The idea of philosopher-rulers appealed to many Christians, Muslims, and Marxists. Of course, by 'wisdom' or 'knowledge' these schools of thought each meant something radically different both from Plato and from each other. Following the lead of al-Farabi, Muslim philosophers used Plato's notion of a legislator to explain the function of prophecy.[67] They also promoted the primacy of virtue, education, and spiritual enlightenment in any rightly ordered political system. Royal wisdom became part of the Christian and European ideology of political authority from the fourth to the eighteenth centuries. Future kings should be educated by churchmen. Ever since Plato, the education of rulers was a major preoccupation of political savants and reformers. The Christian fathers also took to the notion that moral purity plus spiritual enlightenment are qualifiers for true authority, and used it to justify the subordination of secular to religious authorities.

Churchmen and mullahs could find support in Plato for the suppression of 'false' opinions; for the ideal of mystical enlightenment on the one hand, and a closed authoritarian system on the other; and for the entrenchment of a sharp divide between the enlightened few who teach, and the unenlightened masses who learn and obey. Al-Farabi and other Muslim philosophers fully endorsed Plato's view that the promotion of virtue and right belief are the main aim of government (Black 2001: 66–7). Plato's *Laws* was used to justify the essential role of law in any society, and of the Shari'a in a Muslim one.

At times it seemed as if Muslims and Europeans were reading different Platos. The Muslim version was closer to the original.

No sooner did political Platonism disappear as a Christian strategy in the early modern period than Platonic idealism took new shapes in Rousseau, Hegel, and utopian theory. J. S. Mill believed that the more morally and intellectually advanced should have a greater say in government. Today, the Islamic Republic of Iran attempts to reconcile rule by an orthodox moral elite with elections and legislation by representatives of the people: legislation by the elected Assembly is scrutinized by a 'Guardian Council' of twelve jurists. Plato's *Laws* lives on.[68]

Plato inspired his pupil Aristotle to think systematically about the polis, both as an ideal and as a reality. Plato's discussion of the imperfect regimes of oligarchy, dēmokratia, and despotism was used extensively by Muslim thinkers. In Europe it was superseded by the Aristotelian categories (below, p. 162). Benjamin Franklin's contention that the US Constitution 'is likely to be well admired for a course of years, and can only end in despotism... when the people shall become so corrupted as to need despotic government, being incapable of any other' could have come straight from the *Republic* (562–4).

ARISTOTLE

Aristotle (384–322 BCE) did more than anyone to integrate political philosophy with science. He came from the northern Greek kingdom of Macedon, where his father was court physician to King Philip. Philip conquered the poleis of mainland Greece in 338. In mid-career Aristotle spent two years (342–340) tutoring Philip's son, Alexander, who went on to conquer the East as far as India (334–324). These two monarchs terminated the independence of poleis in the eastern Mediterranean.

Aristotle thus moved between the worlds of kingdom and polis; he also influenced one of the greatest minds in political history. He was at pains to distinguish the household and kingdom from the polis (*Politics* 1251a–3b). He argued that the relationship between rulers and ruled in a polis differs categorically from the relationship between lord and subject. This is because the polis, as 'a community of free persons', aims at its members' well-being, whereas the lord aims at his own (*Politics* 1279a17–22). The philosopher had been close to power.

Aristotle studied at Plato's Academy. He started by revising Plato's theory of knowledge, playing down the role of pure thought, and emphasizing the role of sense-perception. He proceeded to work on logic, the natural sciences, cosmology, moral philosophy, and metaphysics. For study of the physical world, empirical research was required, and Aristotle left the Academy and travelled all over the Aegean Sea and western Asia Minor, identifying and classifying as many animal and plant species as he could find. He returned to Athens in 325 BCE, and established the Lyceum as a research institute.

In the *Nicomachaean Ethics* (hereafter *Ethics*) and the *Politics* (Aristotle's last work, composed at the time of Alexander's conquests), he applied the methods of analysis and observation, which he had developed for the natural sciences, to the study of human behaviour and the polis. He combined systematic reasoning with factual investigation. He regarded politics, meaning study of the polis in all its forms, as the master-science. He did not study kingdoms or inter-state relations.

Aristotle saw the study of the state and the study of nature as related. Both human beings and states are part of nature; but, while other animals live 'mostly by nature', humans live by 'nature, custom (*ethos*) and reason (*logos*)' (*Politics* 1332a40–1332b70). This is still a timely reminder that, in studying ourselves, we need to combine natural science, social science, and philosophy.

In all species of being, Aristotle drew a distinction between, first, matter (what things are made out of), and second, form (*eidos*: shape, or essence; genome, almost), for example oak or gorilla. This is only fully apparent in the developed specimen. Third, 'efficient' causes bring entities into existence and make them grow. Fourth, all things have an inbuilt purpose (*telos*) towards which their energy drives them.

At the same time, Aristotle linked politics closely to ethics. The *Politics* is a continuation of the *Ethics*. In the *Ethics* he had argued that there must be something which we do for its own sake, rather than for an ulterior motive (otherwise 'our desire would be empty and vain'; *Ethics* 1094a22). He calls this 'the good and the best', 'the human good' (*to anthrōpinon agathon*; *Ethics* 1094b7). Knowledge of this good will be of critical importance for everything we do in life, not least politics.

The polis

The polis, like all natural species, has a 'form'. This is defined, as for all entities, by its purpose. As in other species, you cannot grasp the essence of the state by reasoning alone, as Plato had once tried to do. Rather, Aristotle applied the methodology he himself had developed for biology and botany (he calls this 'the normal method'; *Politics* 1252a18). That is, he combined empirical investigation with analysis, drawing up models (of *demokratia* and so on), and refining these in the light of further evidence.[69] One examines as many examples of a species as possible in order to determine the form of the species. You need a thorough knowledge of what is already there (as in medicine); that is, of the various legal and political systems (constitutions) which exist or have existed. These have not previously been studied (*Ethics* 1180b28–1181b24). As in his researches on plant and animal species, Aristotle sought to understand the polis by collecting all available data and comparing the results; he organized a research team which sifted the constitutions of 158 poleis.[70]

Aristotle never doubted that every species has a form and purpose; the developed specimen shows us what the species is. The main aim of political study, therefore, is to determine the overall form and purpose of the polis, by examining as many case-studies as possible.[71] Aristotle provides the clearest example of the influence of natural science on social science in Greek, and perhaps any, culture.

But there are differences between ethics with politics, on the one hand, and other disciplines. For one cannot expect the same precision in morals, politics, and law as one can in mathematics, because in the former there is 'much difference of opinion and uncertainty' (*Ethics* 1094b12–27). Further, politics is a matter of action (*praxis*), not of pure knowledge (*gnosis*): to understand it, therefore, one needs practical experience; and so it is not for the young (*Ethics* 1095a1–6). Aristotle's views on methodology in the social sciences have some resonance today, even though the theory of knowledge on which they are based is no longer accepted. Thus, the dour northerner scrutinized Plato in the light of factual evidence. He observed human attitudes with the detachment of a scientist. He observed the polis as an outsider.

The purpose of the polis is to enable humans to fulfil themselves: that is, to perform noble acts of courage and justice for the common good, and to engage in the contemplation and understanding of being (*theōria*). Intellectual understanding is an end in itself; it is the ultimate purpose of human life.[72] The polis is what makes it possible for humans to be virtuous, by engaging in war and justice, and by 'legislating on what people should do and should not do'. Development of virtue requires good laws and, for some, coercion (*Ethics* 1179b7–1180a22). The state is, therefore, concerned with people's character, with making citizens good. This is what Aristotle meant when he said that the purpose of the polis is that people should 'live well' (*Politics* 1252b30). Above all, the state enables people to develop their minds, by providing them with material goods and a suitable environment (*Ethics* 1094b1–7, 1099b29–32). Legislation must ensure that there is an educational system to achieve these goals (*Politics*, book VIII). But Aristotle did not mean that the state should control knowledge.

The polis or state, then, is what makes possible the life of thought and science. Philosophy and polis are integrally related, but not quite in the way Plato had envisaged. This was a completely new way of looking at politics; Aristotle had a different view of the state from anyone else.

Aristotle, as we have seen, identified the essence or purpose of the species 'polis' as 'to live well'. The polis is 'the most supreme (or sovereign) community' because it aims at the highest human good (*Politics* 1252a4–7). It is *the* social environment for humans because in it, and in it alone, do we have sufficient material goods (*autarkeia*) to develop the potentialities of human nature to their fullest: the ability to perform noble actions and to seek for and understand the nature of things. Economic and military self-sufficiency are necessary, but not sufficient, conditions for a polis to exist. This is what Aristotle meant by saying that 'the human (*anthrōpos*) is by nature an animal in a polis (*politikon*)'.[73] (This expression does not mean what we mean today when we say 'man is a political animal'. It does not mean that we are by nature prone to getting what we want by manipulation—'politicking'.)

The polis provides the environment in which human beings are most likely to achieve their potential: opportunities to exercise courage in the army, justice in the law-courts, good sense in the assembly; and, thanks to the division of labour, it provides leisure for the intellectually gifted to pursue science and philosophy. For virtue has to be realized in action,[74] although activity may be purely intellectual (*Politics* 1325b17–22). It follows that the main purpose of the polis is the pursuit of the good life and of virtue, not military or economic goals (*Politics* 1280a–1281a). Aristotle stressed more than thinkers in other cultures, and more than many Greeks, the dependence of human development on a very specific institutional environment.

The polis is peculiar to humans because they alone have *logos* (speech and rationality) which makes clear to them their common interests and, consequently, justice ('it is peculiar to humans that they alone have perception of good and bad, just and unjust'; *Politics* 1253a14–18). Aristotle equates justice with the common good (as people tended to) (*Ethics* 1160a14).[75]

What is good—virtue—is the same for individuals as it is for the polis (as Plato had also assumed). The good of the polis, however, is 'greater and closer to the purpose', and to attain it is 'nobler and more divine' than the good of a single individual.[76] This was already a new perspective: the common good is more important than the good of one individual, because (by definition) it includes a great number of individual goods. Aristotle put the collective above the individual good in the same way as Jeremy Bentham in his 'utility principle': the yardstick for legislation is 'the greatest happiness of the greatest number'.

Human beings come together not only because of physical needs but also because they cannot be happy without each others' company. They are 'designed by nature to live together'. Indeed, they form all kinds of groups apart from the polis, both for specific needs and for comradeship (*sunousia*: being together). These communities (*koinōniai*) are 'like parts of the political community'; and they are subordinate to the polis.[77] Thus Aristotle was the first to recognize the role of lesser associations, and to assign them a place in the political order.

For the citizen to develop his virtue, he has to be an active participant in the army, the law-court, and the assembly. Again, in both adjudication and election one has to know the character of those one is dealing with. All this imposes an upper limit on the size of an effective polis (*Politics* 1326b15–20). Aristotle here provided reasons for some of the unique features of the Greek state. European civic humanists followed this line of thought, though without always being fully aware of its philosophical basis (Black 2003: 102–9).

The polis, then, has to be examined both as a phenomenon of nature and as the vehicle for virtue. In the former respect, one has, as with all natural objects, to break it down into its constituent parts, to see how it is made up and how the parts fit together; just as with animals and their organs. This involves examining the development of the polis out of its constituent parts. Aristotle classified these, first as families and villages (*Politics*, book I); then as the citizens (book III); and then again as occupational (i.e. functional) groups: farmers, craftsmen, merchants, labourers, soldiers, judges, land-owners, public officials.[78]

All along, Aristotle is searching for the generic essence of the polis: what it is that is common to them all. This is what drove him to examine all the existing poleis. It was here above all that Aristotle's philosophy of science led him, more than anyone else in the ancient world, and indeed for some two millenia after him, to develop political science. The amount of data he and his colleagues collected and sifted through would be impressive even by today's standards. But no less—perhaps more—remarkable were the methods he used to analyse this data.

Aristotle identified the core of any polis as its constitution (*politeia*).[79] First, he attempted to classify constitutions on the basis of whether, on the one hand, the sovereign is one, few, or many, and on the other, whether these aim at the common good (in which case they are upright and just) or at the good of the ruling body (in which case they are faulty and deviant). The good constitutions are kingship (*basileia*), aristocracy (rule by the best people), *politeia* (constitutional government).[80] The deviant ones are tyranny, oli-garchy, and dēmokratia (*Politics*, book III, ch. 7: 1279a–b). Here Aristotle was following Plato's *Laws*, but with the important difference that he made pursuit of the common good, rather than observance of the laws, the criterion for differentiating good from bad constitutions. He did, nonetheless, consider observance of the laws essential for a regime to qualify as good.

Political science

At this point (perhaps on the basis of data that were coming in), Aristotle refined his definition of the aims of political science. He listed four separate but overlapping approaches. First, one should work out the best constitution ('what one would most like it to be without any external impediment'); second, one should consider 'what constitution is suited to which people'; that is, what is best under existing conditions. Third, one should explore how various types of states develop and how to maintain them as long as possible; this should include those which do not have the right conditions, and ones which are not even the best in their circumstances; this, as we shall see, includes all existing states. Fourth, one must ask which constitution is most suited to *all* existing states, taking into account their real needs, something which (he says) most writers on politics (Plato, no doubt, included) ignore. For 'we must examine not only the best but the possible, including what is more attainable and common among all states'.

For the statesman (*politikos*) must be able to offer assistance to *any* state (*Politics* 1288b). Hence, like a doctor, he has to know how states in general function, but he also needs the skill to apply this general knowledge to specific cases. Methodology has to be adapted to subject-matter; the *politikos* should not seek the certainty of the mathematician.[81]

This led Aristotle to enquire 'what constitution and what way of life is best for most poleis and most human beings', assuming a level of virtue within the reach of ordinary people, and 'a life which most people can take part in, and a constitution which most poleis are able to attain'.[82] The qualities looked for must include both justice and stability. Here Aristotle was putting forward a new *kind* of political ideal, something which would be a 'common denominator' of existing arrangements. Practicality was an essential component of any ideal.

Aristotle here set an agenda for the empirical and systematic study of politics. At the same time, he insisted that the collection and analysis of data must be combined with the search for what is best, or for the best possible. (To use modern jargon, he insists on correlating fact with value.)[83] He was looking for features that were widespread, but also ones that were morally desirable in the light of the polis's purpose. Books IV, V, and VI of the *Politics* are a comparative analysis of existing states, with a view to determining which, of various alternatives in various branches of the constitution, is preferable from the viewpoint of both justice and stability. If some of these passages are not wholly clear, this is because of the complexity and novelty of the task he set himself. From his biological studies Aristotle had learned how to look for structure and variety in the same set of organisms. It was because he saw the polis as part of nature that he took the trouble to look at how people actually think—and he discovered tremendous variety.

In this part of the *Politics* moral principles and empirical data were inextricably interwoven. Yet Aristotle does not seem to have allowed his own moral preferences to bias his presentation and analysis of data. There is, especially for a modern reader, an extraordinary open-mindedness in his discussion of what is best in a particular kind of state, or in a particular situation. Throughout Books IV–VI the discussion swerves in different directions, depending on a multiplicity of relevant factors. His discussion of the advantages and disadvantages of oligarchy and dēmokratia are on the whole sensitive and undogmatic, ever watchful for exceptions to any generalization he is about to make. He inserts many reservations, and sometimes reaches no firm conclusion. One can sense him changing his mind in response to data. The style is maddening, the results fascinating. He was the political theorist who best appreciated how difficult it is to be certain in social science.

When he looked at the way most poleis actually function, Aristotle found that most of their constitutions were either some form of oligarchy (rule by the rich few) or some form of dēmokratia (rule by the many poor).[84]

On the whole, Aristotle thought that it was people's different views about justice and the good life (their 'ideologies', as we would say) which have led to different constitutions.[85] Every constitution is based on certain values. This fitted in with his general view of the polis; it is also the view of a moral philosopher.

Monarchy

Aristotle devoted a section of the *Politics* to kingship (book III, chs. 9–end). He had a relatively favourable view of monarchy: 'when a whole family, or one individual among the rest, happen to be so outstanding in virtue that they exceed all the others, then it is just that this family be royal and sovereign over all, and that this individual be king' (*Politics* 1288a15–35). This, no doubt, came naturally from a familiar of the Macedonian court, a former teacher of Alexander.[86]

Aristotle was not the only fourth-century Athenian intellectual to take the monarchical alternative seriously.[87] Xenophon, a close friend of Socrates, admired the Persian monarchy (see his *Cyropaedia*, written between 397 and 354 BCE). Isocrates (436–338 BCE), in a treatise written (*c.* 368) for the king of Cyprus, argued that monarchy was the best system of government, on the grounds that it recognizes people's different abilities, and awards offices to the best people. A lifelong ruler gains the benefit of experience. A king is motivated to take the interests of the polis more seriously, because these are his own personal interests. Whereas Aristotle distinguished sharply between state and household, Isocrates urged the king to 'manage (*oikei*) the polis as if it were your own ancestral estate (*oikos*)'.[88]

These were the first examples of the 'advice-to-kings' genre, which became one of the dominant modes of political discourse in the Islamic world. Indeed, Isocrates anticipated some of the leading themes of Islamic advice literature: for example, that the most important thing is the moral quality of the ruler; that virtue pays; that a king must be very careful to administer justice impartially; and that he must combine sternness with kindness (*To Nicocles* 51–9). Monarchy was not here treated as in any way sacred, simply as the most rational form of government—a significant contrast with other cultures.

Oligarchy and demokratia

Data coming in from his research team revealed to Aristotle the enormous variety of oligarchies and dēmokratiai, ranging from pure extremes to more moderate forms. Within each of the three branches of government—the deliberative, executive, and judicial—oligarchy and dēmokratia may be implemented to different degrees.[89] This depends partly on how thoroughly they each implement their particular notions of justice. These are based on inequality and equality, respectively (*Politics* 1289b13 ff.).

Now, the more moderate versions of each form approximate more and more to one another, until they actually merge in *politeia* (constitutional government); this, 'to put it simply is a mixture of oligarchy and dēmokratia' (*Politics* 1293b). This provides the answer to his fourth question in political science: what constitution is best for most actual states?

Aristotle feels his way to it by several routes. First, what characteristics enable people to contribute to the polis's goal of the good life? To what extent do wealth, noble birth, political ability, virtue and justice, or numbers make a contribution? He concludes that each factor has something to contribute, but virtue most of all. Nevertheless, no single factor has an exclusive claim, because to give all power to any one group would lead to dissatisfaction, and hence instability. Moreover, the many *collectively* have more wealth, ability, judgement, and virtue than even the most outstanding individual.[90] It is right, therefore, that in public bodies, such as jury-court, council, or assembly, authority should lie with the whole rather than with individuals (*Politics* 1281b, 1283b33–5).

Aristotle looks next at the claims currently made on behalf of oligarchy and dēmokratia. This involves an examination of the political language of Greek civic culture. He finds that there is something to be said for both schools of thought: for citizens *are* unequal in some things, such as property and ability; but they are equal in others, such as free birth. He observed the connection customarily made between dēmokratia and freedom (which can mean either 'governing and being governed in turn' or 'living as you wish'; *Politics* 1317b). Both justice and stability, therefore, require that one combine these two principles (or ideologies). One may combine them by allowing only those with high qualifications to hold office, while empowering everyone to elect and audit them (*Politics* 1318b28–19a6). This, says Aristotle, is *politeia* (the constitutional constitution, as it were): dēmokratia with checks and balances. For here constitutional law determines the way offices are distributed, and everyone takes a share in ruling and being ruled (*Politics* 1287a16–20). Finally, this realizes the principle (which Aristotle took over from Plato) that sovereignty should reside in the laws (*Politics* 1282b2–6). The very term 'politeia' seems to suggest that this type of state best represents the essence of—is most typical of—the species polis.

Aristotle's final argument was based on sociology and economics. In every polis there are three 'parts' or classes: the rich, the poor, and those in the middle.[91] Aristotle here appealed to the traditional view, that 'moderate and middle is best' (*Politics* 1295b4, 1287b4–5; see above, p. 140). He was also applying his own notion of the good (worked out in the *Nicomachean Ethics*) as the mean between two extremes. Justice and the law are also a kind of mean (*to meson*) (*Politics* 1287b3–4). Thus the middling people come closest to realizing the inherent nature (*physis*) of the polis, as a community of people who are similar and equal. The best polis, therefore, is one in which middling people are numerous and dominant.[92] The constitution based on the middling people is both just and stable, being 'closer to the people' (*Politics* 1296a8–10, 1302a13–6). It spreads political and legal participation widely, and thus maximizes the opportunity for as many as possible to develop the virtues of justice and good sense. Therefore, moderate democracy is the best constitution available to most states. Isocrates expressed the same view.[93]

This was an implicit criticism of the Athenian form of dēmokratia, which Aristotle regarded as too extreme. He was also somewhat less liberal than Athenian practice.[94] On the other hand, in criticizing Plato's communism, he insisted that the polis consists of persons 'differing[95] in kind' (*Politics* 1261a25).

Aristotle was as aware as any modern scholar of the variety of factors that influence, and may severely distort, formal political institutions. For example, a constitution may look like a dēmokratia, yet the distribution of wealth may make it function as an oligarchy; and vice versa. This mismatch between the formal actual distribution of power is a common cause of constitutional change (revolution, diagnosed in *Politics*, book V). He paid a great deal of attention to class.[96]

Conclusion

In his analysis of the various permutations of dēmokratia and oligarchy, Aristotle was using what Weber called 'ideal types' (for example, *Politics* 1317a–b). He used these to see just how far actual states correspond to particular patterns; he would then modify his 'models' accordingly. The purpose was to formulate an accurate language in which to describe what was going on, and to identify what constituted the essential core features of dēmokratia and oligarchy, and of the polis itself. He was at the same time trying to identify the *best*, in the sense of the most just and stable, constitution for the average state.

Aristotle's *Politics* virtually disappeared. No other ancient author adopted the same (in my opinion) very promising approach. This may have been because poleis ceased to be significant powers. The world Aristotle described was disappearing as he was describing it, partly due to the activities of his own pupil. And some of what he identified as the core characteristics of the polis could not exist in any other type of state.

Aristotle's method of investigation, combining conceptual analysis, empirical research, and moral assessment—and this across a whole class of political entities—has never been attempted again. After it was 'rediscovered' in thirteenth-century Latin Christendom, the *Politics* provided a mine of arguments for different types of regime in Europe. But in the scholastic syllabus it was treated as an encapsulation of ancient facts rather than a live research tool. Ibn Khaldun (d. 1400 CE) perhaps came closest to reviving Aristotle's method. But his work likewise promptly disappeared from sight. Max Weber combined conceptual analysis with empirical research across an even greater range of political phenomena, taking all the world and its histories as his province. He, like Aristotle, used models in the process of accumulating and interpreting data, in order to highlight what might be causally significant, and to generate useful hypotheses. But Weber explicitly rejected moral assessment as part of the social scientist's task. No modern political scientist has combined such a range of political, philosophical, and sociological discourses as

Aristotle did. Political philosophers are less well-informed about the world than Aristotle was, and the political scientist of today is faced with an inordinately greater volume of data.

CONCLUSIONS

In the West we have always thought that the culture of classical Greece was utterly different from anything else in the ancient world, or since. Its achievements (to speak most crudely) in art, philosophy, and self-government seem unique. I believe they were. However trite this view may seem, when one studies other ancient cultures and then turns to the Greeks, one is reminded that the trite is sometimes true. The more angles you look from, the more amazing Greek achievements are. They were 'a people who had a totally new conception of what human life was for' (Kitto 1951: 7). They teach us in a special way what it is to be human.

The Greeks were the only ancient people who discovered a viable alternative to monarchy. There was a degree of political equality and participation that is unimaginable to us in the age of (say) Vladimir Putin and Rupert Murdoch. Political equality in the modern West is confined to occasional acts of voting. On the other hand, it *is* supposed to include everybody.

Some Greeks, notably Athenians—but not Plato, nor Aristotle—insisted that freedom is an essential ingredient of the good life. In this too they differed from every other ancient culture. At Athens there was an exceptional degree of intellectual freedom, though this contrasted starkly with the practice of slavery. Equality before the law was, for many, an even more fundamental value than dēmokratia.

To the Athenians, freedom meant the ability to express one's opinions and live as one wished, plus independence of one's polis from foreign powers. On the other hand, it was widely accepted—contrary to modern liberal views— that the public organs of the polis intervened in economic and religious affairs. Aristotle defined the role of the state as religion, war, public finances; the upkeep and good order of the market-place, city, harbour, and country-side; law-courts, fines, and prisoners (*Politics* 1322b30–7). But every Athenian juror had to swear never to allow a cancellation of debts or redistribution of property (Finley 1983: 109). Aristotle seems to have expressed the general view, when he said that property should be privately owned, but used for the common good (*Politics* 1263a–b, 1320b10–12). This is somewhat different from liberal democracy, which sees 'the economy' as in principle separate from the state. Democritus said that 'poverty under dēmokratia is preferable to so-called prosperity under a dictator to the same extent as freedom is preferable to slavery' (*EG* 158). Most political thinkers today regard economic inequality as a price worth paying for prosperity.

Did the Greeks, as Meier suggests, 'invent politics'?[97] If this refers to strategies for achieving consensus in a large society, thereby making it possible to pursue collective goals, several others had got there before them. What they did invent was a way of conducting public affairs by debate and voting. When Solon was asked to resolve the social crisis of Athens, he did so by constitutional innovation (though Delphi was still consulted; Dodds 1951). While Solon and Confucius may have had similar views about wealth and poverty, Solon used piecemeal political engineering to achieve social justice, while Confucius looked to traditional values and sacred monarchy. Much of this specifically Greek 'invention' has been irretrievably lost. The political processes of the polis were attenuated under the Hellenistic and Roman empires, and had vanished by the time of the emperor Justinian.[98] They have been revived only patchily since. 'Politics' meant more to the Greeks than it does to us.

Did 'Western political thought' begin with the Greeks?[99] There were radical breaks between the Greeks of the poleis and the Greeks under the Hellenistic kingdoms and the Roman empire; an utter gulf between the classical Greeks and the Byzantines. Knowledge of Greek (as opposed to Roman) political ideas did not reach Europe until relatively late. European political thought had by that time already been moulded by the church and its relationship to the state. The institutions and political culture of medieval and Renaissance city-states were indeed similar to those of the Greek polis; but this may well have been convergence rather than influence (Black 2003: 53–65). The Europeans had to start all over again (Black 2008: 17, 152–3).

In the long European revival of Greek culture after the twelfth century, we need to distinguish, first, between Plato and the rest. People too often speak as if Plato in some way summed up Greek thought, or was typical of it. As we have seen, this was far from the case. Plato's ideas were, in fact, commandeered, not unreasonably, to underwrite the authority of clergy.

We must further distinguish between the influence of Greek political thought in general,[100] and of Greek ideas about freedom and dēmokratia in particular. While the influence of the Greeks on philosophy, science, and literature was everywhere, dēmokratia was regarded with suspicion. Rousseau and the French revolutionaries—not to mention the Americans—looked to 'republican' Rome, not 'democratic' Athens. Only in the nineteenth century did thinkers as diverse as Marx and Mill look to the Greek polis, and specifically Athenian dēmokratia, for a model of what a political community could and should be like.

Political philosophy began in China and in Greece at almost the same time. But only the Greeks went in for systematic analysis of political institutions and behaviour. This was without parallel elsewhere. The aims and methodology of Plato and Aristotle have been those of political philosophy and political science ever since. On the other hand, they did not look at international relations.

If it was in Africa, and only in Africa, that humans evolved, it was above all in Greece that these decisive cultural developments took place. There may, after all, be something in what Aristotle said: to develop their full potential, humans needed to live in a polis. In both cases, once the initial developments were there, they could and did spread elsewhere, although with considerable difficulty, bottlenecks, and setbacks. The diffusion of humans was more predictable and continuous than the subsequent diffusion of what had begun in Greece.

NOTES

1. Donlan 1998: 57; Finley 1963: 23; Raaflaub, in *CGR* 24; Scully 1990. *Polis* should be translated 'citizen state' rather than 'city-state' since country-dwellers were equal partners with those in the fortified market town, and 'were conceived as a single unit'. This differentiates them from medieval and Renaissance 'city-states' in Europe, and from those of Mesopotamia, which were ruled by kings and temple aristocracies (above, p. 34).
2. The connection between seamanship and citizenship was marked in classical Athens; both involved sitting side by side on benches. Weber's term 'warrior-guild' (*Kriegerzunft*; Weber 1986: 809) is not appropriate.
3. *Agora* also referred to the assembled citizens; Scully 1990: 101–2.
4. *Iliad* 18–26; Bryant 1996: 117.
5. Humphreys 1978: 164; *EG* 165; Meier 1990: 37.
6. Connoting especially 'manly' military qualities (cf. Latin *virtus*); derived from Ares (god of war); often translated 'excellence'.
7. Tyrtaeus, a warrior-poet of seventh-century Sparta; in Bryant 1996: 92–3.
8. *Odyssey*. 9.115. As Democritus (*c*. 460–380 BCE) put it, 'a well-managed city is the greatest support, in this is everything, if this is kept safe everything is safe, if this is destroyed everything is destroyed' (Diels and Kranz 1956: 195–6; *EG* 157).
9. Murray 1990: 19, 12–15; Bryant 1996: 25; Schmitt-Pantel 1990: 206.
10. 'The origin of rational thought must be seen as bound up with the social and mental structures peculiar to the Greek city' (Vernant 1982: 130); 'the *degree* of political involvement had important and widespread repercussions on intellectual life as a whole' (Lloyd 1979: 250—my italics). On the spread of literacy, Goody and Watt 1968: 43.

11. Debating contests were held in Athens (*EG* 166).
12. Lloyd 1979: 83 n; Vlastos 1947: 164 n.
13. Dialogue was introduced into drama at Athens about the time when dēmokratia developed; Cartledge 1997: 22–3. As dialogues, Plato's works seldom reach this pitch; Socrates always wins.
14. 'The formula or element of arrangement common to all things...Logos was probably conceived by Herakleitos at times as an actual component of things, and in many respects it is co-extensive with the primary cosmic constituent, fire' (KRS 186–8).
15. Vernant 1982: 81; Lloyd 1979: 247, 252–3, 258.
16. Vlastos 1947; Vernant 1982; Lloyd 1979.
17. Meier 1990: 128; *CGR* 50 n.
18. Vlastos 1947: 157–60; Vernant 1982: 121–3.
19. Vlastos 1947: 156–7. 'There was a profound structural analogy between the institutional space in which the human cosmos was expressed and the physical space in which [the first natural philosophers] projected the natural cosmos'; Vernant 1982: 126.
20. See Dodds 1951; Lloyd-Jones 1971.
21. 'It would be eccentric for anyone to claim he loved Zeus': *Magna Moralia*, in Dodds 1951: 35.
22. Finley 1963: 38 and 1983: 94–5; Ostwald 1986: 93.
23. 'Concerning the gods, I am not in a position to know either that they exist or that they do not...the subject is obscure and human life short' (Protagoras, in *EG* 186–7).
24. Zeus punishes those who resort to force rather than justice by destroying their crops (*Iliad* 16.386–92). See also *Odyssey* 19.109–14; Hesiod, *Works and Days* 5–10, 227–37, 256; Lloyd-Jones 1971.
25. Greek technology was at the same stage of development as that of the Near East; Lloyd 1979: 235–6. The Greeks made no clear distinction between craft and art.
26. Archaic hymn: *EG* 35. See Bryant 1996: 114; Plato, *Protagoras* 322b. Compare Aeschylus, *Prometheus* 450–70: Prometheus has been punished by the upstart tyrant Zeus for enabling humans to progress from caves to culture by teaching them about fire, astronomy, medicine, metals, and auguries.
27. Meier 1990: 40; Vernant 1982: 125.
28. KRS 210–11; Barnes 1982: 128–9, 132.
29. The ruler had forbidden the prescribed burial of a corpse: a 'ritual' act but with the gravest consequences. Tony Burns argues that this is a contrast between customary and statute law rather than (as most have thought) between natural and positive law: 'Sophocles' *Antigone* and the History of the Concept of Natural Law', *Political Studies*, 50 (2002), 552.
30. Tony Burns, 'The Tragedy of Slavery: Aristotle's *Rhetoric* and the History of the Concept of Natural Law', *HPT* 24 (2003), 16–36. See also *Ethics* 1134b18–1135a5, and Tony Burns, 'Aristotle and Natural Law', *HPT* 19 (1998), 142–66.

31. On other hand, Alcinous in *Odyssey* 7 is a model king: a beneficent ruler, people do jobs for him, he gives banquets, and honours gods by hospitality (see also *Odyssey* 19.114).
32. At Athens, with its silver-mines, they are estimated at 60,000–80,000 out of a total population of *c.* 250,000 (Finley 1983: 45, 63; Humphreys 1978: 148).
33. I use 'dēmokratia' throughout to avoid confusion with modern democracy.
34. Finley 1963: 77–80; *OHG* 22–3.
35. *EG* 26.
36. Solon, in *EG* 25–6; Vernant 1982: 97; Greenhalgh 1972: 195.
37. It was also retrospectively ascribed to monarchies of the archaic period (Finley 1983: 135–6).
38. An early fourth-century writer (Vernant 1982: 96).
39. *Isēgoria*, the equal right of public speaking; Sinclair 1988: 13; Ober 1989: 296.
40. Meier 1990: 10–11, 87; Ostwald 1986: 66–7, 77–8, 516–17.
41. Polybius 2.38 (Loeb edn. i. 336).
42. *Suppliant Maidens* 405–8, 433–7; *EG* 64–5.
43. Protagoras, in Plato, *Protagoras* 325–6; Meier 1990: 168–70.
44. Humphreys 1978: 250; *OHG* 245–7.
45. A misnomer, given the current meaning of 'clever-clever'. See Kerferd 1981; *EG*, pp. xxii–xxiv.
46. See Cartledge 1997: 15, 17, 21. Modern equivalents might be the novels of Tolstoy and Dostoevsky.
47. Dionysus, in whose honour the plays were performed, was sometimes known as 'the liberator'; Cartledge 1997: 23.
48. Ephialtes, the proponent of the reforms, had recently been assassinated (see Cartledge 1997: 22).
49. Athene calls the citizens of Athens 'my townsmen', 'my citizens'.
50. Kerferd 1981: 37; Humphreys 1978: 228.
51. Compare Marsilius of Padua, writing at Paris in 1324 CE, *Defender of the Peace* I.4 (Black 1992: 63).
52. Lit. 'philosophizing', 'loving wisdom'; *sophia* encompasses what we mean by knowledge as well.
53. John Locke put forward an identical argument in his theory of the social contract.
54. He may have been very briefly involved in the uprising of the oligarchic 'thirty tyrants' in Athens (404–3 BCE), which had been led by a relative of Plato (*EG*, pp. xi–xiii).
55. Greek *Politeia*, meaning citizenship or 'the condition of being a citizen' (Schofield 2006: 33). (I regret that this study came out too recently for me to take full account of it.) The *Republic* was probably written in the early–mid 380s; Hare 1982: 21–2.
56. *Dikaiosunē*: righteousness (Annas 1981: 11).
57. 'One should not repay wrong with wrong (as most say) nor treat any human being badly, whatever one has suffered from them' (*Crito* 49c–d).
58. See Annas 1981: 320.

59. See also Aristotle, *Politics* 1291a12–30.
60. One might have expected self-control to be the virtue peculiar to the third group (Cornford, note to his translation, p. 117), but this would not have suited Plato's argument.
61. For the aim is not the pleasure of any one class but the welfare of the city as a whole (*Republic* 412d–e, 519e–20a).
62. For the relationship between the *Republic* and the *Laws*, see Sabine and Thorsen 1973: 85–6; Laks, in *CGR* 268–9. That neither McClelland nor Coleman consider either the *Statesman* or the *Laws* leaves their accounts of Plato's political thought incomplete.
63. Introduction to Taylor's translation, p. xv.
64. 'The unfortunately better-known treatment of *Republic* III is a mere sketch in comparison with this more mature discussion' (introduction to Taylor's translation, p. xl).
65. Laks, in *CGR* 279–80; Taylor translation, p. xxvii.
66. 'Plato doesn't attach importance to educating people to be autonomous, to be critical of their beliefs rather than relying on authority' (Annas 1981: 91). See Hare 1982: 50.
67. To Moses, Jesus, Muhammad, some added Socrates, meaning Plato's *Republic* and *Laws* (Black 2001: 68; Kraemer 1992, appendix: 158–60).
68. Sabine perceptively noted 'a disagreeable flavour of clericalism about the Nocturnal Council' (Sabine and Thorsen 1973: 91).
69. 'In medicine one must pay attention . . . to experience and reason (*logos*) together' (the Hippocratic corpus, in Kitto 1951: 189).
70. Aristotle himself analysed the constitution of Athens to provide a model of how this should be done.
71. *Politics* 1290b24–38. See Lloyd 1968: 68–70, 88, 92, 248, 255.
72. *Ethics* 1179a27–31; *Politics* 1334b15; Lloyd 1968: 238.
73. *Politics* 1252b27–1253a9; alternatively, 'the human being is a living thing designed by nature to live in a polis'.
74. 'Happiness is activity, and the actions of just, sensible persons attain fulfilment of much that is noble' (*Politics* 1325a). Aristotle, like Milton, could not 'praise a cloistered virtue'.
75. 'Righteousness (*dikaiosunē*: being just) is a political quality, for justice (*dikē*) is the ordering of the political community, and justice is deciding what is right (*dikaion*)' (*Politics* 1235a38–9).
76. *Ethics* 1094a27–11; restated in *Politics* 1252a5–7, 1323b40–1324a2, 1333a12–13; Lloyd 1968: 214.
77. *Ethics* 1159b20, 1160a9–22, 29; *Politics* 1278b20–3. See Schmitt-Pantel 1990: 205–6.
78. *Politics* 1290b25–1291a11; or, alternatively, food, handicrafts, arms, money, priesthood, decision-makers-cum-adjudicators (*Politics* 1328b4–24).
79. 'The constitution lays out the organisation of positions of authority and their distribution, the sovereign within the constitution, and the purpose of each part

of the community; the laws are separate . . . [stipulating] how those in authority should govern and guarding against transgressors' (*Politics* 1289a).

80. In *Ethics* 1160a31–1160b2, he called this a constitution based on a property qualification (*timokratia*). In both cases, but especially in *Ethics*, he has in mind a limited or moderate form of dēmokratia.

81. See also *Ethics* 1180b15–1181a15; Mulgan 1977: 9.

82. *Politics* 1295a25–30, adapted from Everson.

83. 'It is by no means certain that, in political science, one can separate normative propositions from descriptive propositions without misunderstanding what is going on': J. W. M. Mackenzie, *Politics and Social Science* (Harmondsworth: Penguin, 1967), 41.

84. *Politics* 1280a; books IV–VI *passim*. In the ensuing discussion he used these terms in their current sense, rather than as signifying 'defective' constitutions as defined in book III, ch. 7.

85. *Politics* 1328a–b, 1301a. On the other hand, he also remarked that 'among most peoples, most customs are established more or less at random'; and again that, 'when laws do have one focus, they all aim at power' (*Politics* 1324b7–8).

86. See Lloyd 1968: 266; *CHG* 316–17.

87. In fact 'discussion on monarchy and the qualities that make a king occur in many fourth-century writings' (*CAH* vii/1. 75–6).

88. *Nicocles*, in Loeb, vol. i. 85–9; *To Nicocles* (written *c.* 372) in Loeb, vol. i. 51.

89. *Politics* 1297b–8a; Mulgan 1977: 57–8.

90. See James Surowiecki, *The Wisdom of Crowds: Why the Many Are Smarter than the Few* (New York: Little, Brown, 2004).

91. The term 'middle class(es)' has so many other meanings today that it is best avoided here.

92. *Politics* 1295b25–40. Elsewhere he argued that farmers are the best material for democracy (*Politics* 1318b10).

93. *Areopagiticus* (*c.* 354), Loeb edn. iii. 113–23; see *CGR* 143.

94. Mulgan 1977: 26, 32–4, 78–9.

95. Or 'unlike' (*Politics* 1276b29 and 1277a6). They are alike in all being free citizens (*Politics* 1277b8, 1328a36).

96. This inspired the one passage in the *Politics* which looked for comparisons beyond the Greek world of the polis (*Politics* 1329b).

97. 'The political arose only among the Greeks' (Meier 1990: 3); Finley 1983: 53.

98. A. H. M. Jones, *The Greek City from Alexander to Justinian* (Oxford: Clarendon Press, 2000).

99. See the sage remarks of Coleman 2000: 3, 277.

100. This came to Renaissance Europe primarily via Aristotle, who put his own spin on things.

9

Rome

CICERO AND THE ROMAN REPUBLIC

Rome, founded as a city-state in *c.* 753 BCE, expelled its kings in 509, and was governed, broadly speaking, by 'the senate and the people of Rome' until 48 BCE. From 31 BCE onwards it was governed by a single ruler. The political thought of Rome falls into two distinct parts, with many links between them.

In its method of government, the early republic was not unlike a Greek polis. It may have been influenced by the Greek poleis which dotted southern Italy. There was certainly Greek influence on the one major political philosopher of Rome: Marcus Tullius Cicero (106–43 BCE), born in the township of Arpinum,[1] the son of a Roman citizen and knight. There had been a cultural invasion of Rome by Greece in the second century. As the Augustan poet Horace put it, 'captured Greece led her savage conqueror captive, introducing culture into backwoods Italy'. Cicero studied in Greece under the Stoic philosopher Poseidonius (79–76), became a successful lawyer, and embarked on a political career. He became consul in 63 and was subsequently caught up in struggles between rival generals (below, pp. 184–5). He died trying to save the republic. Cicero's letters reveal intimate thoughts about himself, his friends, and family, as well as his hectic public life and anxiety about the state of Rome. They express concern for individuals, including household slaves. In 46 he divorced his wife and married his ward. Next year his daughter died; Cicero, deeply upset, was offended by the apparent indifference of his new wife, and divorced her.

The constitution

The Roman term for state was *res publica*: 'public affairs', 'the public sphere', 'public space', 'the political community'. It is, said Cicero, *res populi*, 'the people's affair',[2] everyone's concern—a more extensive concept than 'the state' nowadays. *Res publica* implied shared and constitutional government; absolute monarchy (*regnum*) was incompatible with it. But it did not always mean 'republic' in the modern sense; under the principate there was still a *res publica.* The Romans regarded their state as the *res publica* par excellence, 'the common fatherland (*patria communis*)', which was to provide public space for all humanity (below, pp. 205–6). The Romans developed the idea of the state more than any other ancient people; it was principally from them that it came to Europe and the West.

Res publica referred to both institutions and values.[3] For Cicero, it included 'religious observances, auspices, the powers of magistrates, the Senate's authority, the customs of our ancestors, the legal sphere and law courts, probity (*fides*), our provinces and allies, the reputation of our empire, the military sphere, the treasury'.[4] It attracted strong emotions: 'the whole community of our countrymen, even the poorest [hold dear] these temples, the panorama of the city, the possession of freedom, this very light and the shared soil of our fatherland (*patria*)'.[5] The Romans reckoned time 'from the founding of the city'. Roman epics focussed on the history of the state.

Cicero was extremely sensitive to the whole range of human social instincts, and the types of group to which these give rise. But he concluded that 'when you have gone over everything in your mind and heart, no social relationship is more serious or dear than that which binds each of us to the *res publica.* Parents, children, friends are dear, but all affections for everyone are summed up in our country' (*De Officiis* I.55–8).

The ethic of the political class put the political community above the individual. One should be prepared to sacrifice oneself and one's relatives for the public good.[6] For Cicero, taking part in the government of one's country was an essential part of life. Public enterprises bring greater renown and are more beneficial to humanity than philosophical contemplation.[7] We are born to serve others; our country that reared us expects us to devote our energies and skills to her service (*De Republica.* I.8). Cicero could have led a quiet and scholarly life—the kind of life the poet-philosopher Lucretius liked—but preferred to expose himself to the dangers of politics for the sake of public peace. Cicero inspired the Western ideals of public service and political participation.

Glory, so much more valuable than wealth, is acquired by service to one's country in war or in politics: 'arms, not furniture, confer grace', said the popular general Marius (Sallust, *Jugurthine War* 85.40). What you do for your country, according to Cicero, affects your status among future generations and in the afterlife: all who have contibuted to their country have an assured place in heaven.[8] In his last speech, Cicero called soldiers killed in battle 'most holy (*sanctissimi*)' (*Philippics* XIV.33). He numbered among the immortal gods 'the Brutuses, Camilluses, Scipios...and countless others who have made this state secure'.[9] Such sentiments, repeated throughout the European Middle Ages and Renaissance, were the archetype of patriotism, not nationalism.

The Roman constitution,[10] like the British, was unwritten, based on convention and not formally defined. Under the republic, the Roman state consisted of 'the senate and people of Rome' (*Senatus Populusque Romanus: SPQR*). The senate was composed of former executive and judicial officials (*magistratus*) and their descendants (the 'patriciate'). The senate had moral prestige (*auctoritas*) and the power of initiative. By convention, magistrates acted only on the senate's advice.

The assemblies[11] had powers of legislating, electing magistrates, and making war or peace. By long-standing convention, proposed laws were first discussed and agreed upon in the senate; the assembly usually endorsed decisions taken in the senate. At an election, candidates (who would be men of rank and wealth) canvassed for popular support, thus creating a 'nexus of reciprocal obligation between elite individual[s] and the People' (Morstein-Marx 2004: 260). Deference was important; Polybius (*c.* 202–120 BCE), a Greek statesman who lived in Rome from 168 to *c.* 150, believed that a true democracy is a society 'in which ancestral ethics prescribe reverence for the gods, service to parents, respect for elders (*seniores*) and obedience to laws' (Polybius VI.4. 4–5). Only a magistrate could convoke an assembly, and bring forward proposals to be voted on. The assembly also elected tribunes (a post peculiar to Rome), who came from the upper classes but whose job was to represent the interests of ordinary citizens. Any citizen convicted of a crime could appeal to the assembly.

The principal magistrates were the quaestors (financial administrators), the aediles (municipal administrators), the praetors (judges, provincial governors), and the two consuls. The consuls exercised supreme executive power (*imperium*) and supreme civil and criminal *jurisdictio.*

There were consistent attempts to prevent too much power falling into the hands of any one individual. All offices were for one year only. Either of the two consuls could veto the action of the other; tribunes could veto anyone's proposals. There was, on the other hand, provision for a *dictator* in a national emergency; he had authority over all other magistrates, but only for six months. Thus, Rome's constitution was one of checks and balances.

Magistrates usually came from the old-established landowning families who had held high office for generations. Some, however, came from wealthy non-senatorial families ('knights'), some from landowning families outside Rome.[12] Hence some 'new men' were able to hold office, enter the senate, and join the political elite. Cicero was proud of being just such a 'new man'.

Historians used to regard the Roman republic as essentially an oligarchy, with senators using their social and economic leverage to manipulate the popular assemblies: the upper classes thus effectively ran the state. It is now thought by many that the assemblies were more independent than this view suggests, especially during the last hundred or so years of the republic, the period about which most is known.[13] One should not forget 'the sheer range of issues over which a popular vote...was indispensable' (Millar 1984: 18). The public meeting (*contio*) which preceded the official assembly became 'the main locus of legislative decision' (Morstein-Marx 2004: 126, 124; Jolowicz and Nicholas 1972: 34). Opponents as well as supporters of a bill could speak, provided they were senators. The audience, though often merely an ad hoc crowd, was deemed to stand in the place of the Roman people. They had to be assiduously courted, and they made their views felt (Morstein-Marx 2004: 165–90). This was where debate and oratory became crucial. Here leading politicians 'typically addressed whatever crowd stood in front of them'—whoever turned up—'as the actual embodiment of the [Roman people]'.[14] According to Polybius, 'one might reasonably say that the People have the greatest role, and that the constitution is democratic' (VI.14.12). Despite all this, one could hardly call Rome 'a "direct democracy"' (Morstein-Marx 2004: 8)—a myth propagated by Rousseau.

Polybius attempted to explain 'how and by what kind of constitution almost the whole world' had fallen under Rome's sway during his lifetime, 'in less than fifty-three years' (VI.2.3). He singled out the combination of elements of each of the three 'good' constitutions: monarchy, aristocracy (rule by the best), and democracy (rule by the people, usually meaning the less-well-off). He thought that at Rome 'each of the parts can, if it wants, *counteract or cooperate* with the others'.[15] Hence there was an element of checks and balances. By tradition, and until the late republic in practice, the senate held preponderant power, so that checks tended to be stressed by supporters of the people. On the other hand, Cicero reported the opinion that 'without dissensions among the nobles, the kings [of Rome] could not have been driven out', nor the guarantees of personal liberty for the people introduced (*De Oratore* 2.198–9). This was later seized upon by Machiavelli, and widely used in support of constitutional government with checks and balances, and of political parties, in modern Europe.[16]

Neither Polybius nor Cicero, however, enlarged on the merits of checks and balances as such, as do modern European constitutionalists. They preferred to stress the *cooperation* of the three components. Polybius thought that Rome derived her strength from the way in which, in an emergency, the three parts were able to 'think and act together'; they could even compete to come up with the best strategy. This ability of the different parts to act in harmony was, Polybius thought, what made Rome's constitution superior to others (VI.18.1–4). Cicero concurred.[17]

The traditional view was that government should be conducted by consensus between senate and assembly (patriciate and plebs)—in Cicero's words, 'the collaboration of all good men (*conspiratio omnium bonorum*)' (*In Catilinam* IV.22). This was supposedly based on a settlement concluded after the major conflict between patriciate and plebs in 494. *Concordia* was the ideal; it even had its own temple (Morstein-Marx 2004: 55, 101). As different voices sing in harmony, Cicero said, 'even so a state sings together (*concinit*), combining the highest, lowest and intermediate orders, with agreement among dissimilars (*consensu dissimillarum*)'. But this can only be achieved if there is justice.[18]

According to Polybius, these three types of 'good' constitution and their degenerate opposites (tyranny, oligarchy, mob rule) follow one another in a natural cycle; but he thought that Sparta, and still more Rome, thanks to their *mixed* constitutions, managed to escape this cycle. Even they will eventually decline; in Rome's case this will be due to natural causes rather than external intervention.[19] Polybius' view that a mixed constitution, composed of monarchy, aristocracy, and democracy, was the best, was endorsed by most political theorists in medieval and early modern Europe. The notion of a natural cycle of constitutions was adopted by Machiavelli.

Political culture

Rome's elite had a strong sense of corporate solidarity. They regarded the state as their collective patrimony, inherited from glorious ancestors, to be passed on undiminished, or rather increased, to their progeny. Yet they were relatively open; one could go up or down. They combined traditionalism with flexibility; they were willing to adapt and compromise in both foreign and domestic policy.

They were men of practice, less inclined to theorize than the Athenians. Even Cicero, by far the most original Roman thinker, preferred the 'ancestors' custom (*mos maiorum*)' to philosophy. Lofty ideas, he said, achieve less than 'a state well grounded in public law and morals (*publico iure et moribus*)'; norms of justice and decency come from lawmakers and statesmen, not from philosophers.[20] Romans valued the Aristotelian virtue of practical reason (*prudentia*), and came closer than the Greeks to Aristotle's ideal of a stable mixture of oligarchy and democracy (above, pp. 165–7). In all of this Burke and Oakeshott were Rome's disciples.

And indeed, Rome produced no work of political theory until the onset of Greek culture and ideas during the mid- to late second century BCE. This Roman 'enlightenment'—the first of several 'renaissances' of Greek thought—

produced the first political theory based on the Roman experience, when Polybius undertook his historical analysis of Rome and her achievements, making a special study of her constitution.

Polybius thought Rome unique because her constitution had developed naturally without external interventions (VI.9.10–14). And her unwritten constitution did indeed develop in stages over long periods. Whereas Lycurgus had planned Sparta's mixed constitution, the Romans arrived at theirs 'not through reasoning but through many conflicts and difficulties. Through the experience of reversals, they always chose the best'.[21] Cicero too said that the Roman state was the work not of a single genius or of one generation, but of many men over many centuries (*De Republica* II.2).

During the later second century, Greek thought began to provide 'the moral vocabulary for weighing alternatives and justifying decisions' (Griffin 1989: 36) among the educated classes. It influenced the way that people expressed themselves in political debate in senate, law-courts, and public meetings. To what extent Greek ideas affected the *substance* of political attitudes is a different question. Cicero was an avid learner from several strands of Greek philosophy, an apostle (one might say) for Greek rationality; but at the same time he remained close to the central values of Roman tradition.

Roman political discourse emphasized the *moral* qualities required of citizens and politicians as much as constitutional norms. The citizen body was defined not by race, class, or creed but by one's ability to contribute to the state (*CCRR* 6). It was character and 'virtue', as much as lineage, which qualified people to hold office. Character was an issue at elections (and in law-suits against former officials). The moral qualities required of magistrates, senators, and people generally was Cicero's most persistent theme. He himself was a 'new man', 'known for myself, not born of any illustrious ancestors'. He was as passionate as Confucius in advocating the *carrière ouverte aux talents*. This, he thought, had been crucial in the development of the republic, and was essential now for its salvation. 'I will urge on you of noble birth to imitate your forebears, and I will encourage you who are capable of acquiring nobility through ability and virtue, to that course in which many new men have distinguished themselves with honour and glory'.[22] Cicero refused to accept that the problems of the mid-first century might lie with the system rather than with individuals.

This emphasis on character (*virtus*) in public life derived partly from the military nature of the Roman state. From *c.* 350 to *c.* 50 BCE 'there was probably not 12 years when a Roman army was not engaged abroad' (Finley 1983: 17). And it was the Roman people who made up the army, the senate their generals. Rome's political culture was permeated by the moral and psychological demands of war.

Some advocates of greater powers for the assemblies went even further than Cicero. Marius, one of Rome's most brilliant generals who had risen from the ranks, emphasized the sheer hard work, as well as the dangers, faced by both generals and ordinary soldiers. Thus, he said, 'authority with a purpose... (such as is exercised) over citizens (*utile... civile imperium*)' comes from sharing the labours of your men; and 'I will not earn *my* glory out of *their* labours... I have learned that the best way to contribute to the state is to strike our enemies... fear nothing but dishonour... and be prepared to work on short rations'.[23] This was the labour theory of authority. The ancestors of the Roman aristocracy, said Marius, had earned their nobility by their virtue.

Religion was interwoven with political life. State and religion were inseparable. There was something sacred about the state itself;[24] 'human virtue comes closest to the divine mystery (*numen*) when one is founding new states or preserving existing ones' (Cicero, *De Republica* I.12). The priesthoods were part of the state. Before an important action was undertaken, religious specialists had to examine the behaviour of birds or the entrails of animals, to see whether these were auspicious.[25] Cicero frequently appealed to the gods to save Rome. Polybius was impressed with the religiosity of the Romans, in both public and private life, which he contrasted favourably with the attitudes of the Greeks (VI.56.7). Temples were dedicated to Concord, Faith, Liberty (Brunt 1989: 177) (we might call these personified political values), as well as to *Roma* herself. Cicero in particular emphasized the religious dimension of the fatherland: 'the life of all citizens, arch and Capitol, the altars of our homes, the everlasting fire of Vesta, the temples and statues of all the gods, the walls and houses of the city' (*In Catilinam* IV.18).

Both Polybius and Cicero thought that religious observance brought tangible social and political benefits. 'Every mass of people needs to be restrained by invisible terrors'; that was why the ancients introduced the idea of gods and hell (Polybius VI.56.6–15). Cicero thought fear of divine punishment helped to maintain moral standards.[26] The same view was later adopted by some Muslim and Jewish thinkers (Black 2001: 74), and more recently by Leo Strauss and his followers in the United States. The Epicurean Lucretius thought otherwise.

The crucial difference between Rome and other ancient cultures was that divine authority was not ascribed to specific persons, or even specific institutions. Rome provides the clearest possible evidence that in the ancient world it was perfectly possible to separate religion from sacred monarchy. Her constitution offered scope for political decision-making and participation by both commoners and elite, yet this did not dim their concern for religious rectitude nor their fear of the gods.

Mutual trust (*fides*: loyalty) played an important part in Roman politics. Polybius noticed that Roman officials entrusted with large sums of money 'behave correctly because they have pledged their faith on oath' (VI.56.14–15). Military discipline was based on the solemn oath (*sacramentum*) which the soldier swore to his commander.

Fides was just as, if not more, important in foreign affairs. The Romans relied on alliance (*foedus*) sealed by solemn oath as a means of stabilizing relations with former enemies. Cicero thought that religious sanctions were especially important in the case of oaths and treaties (*Laws* II.16). The role-model was Regulus, a one-time consul captured by the Carthaginians in 255 BCE. The Carthaginians sent him to Rome to negotiate an exchange of prisoners; the condition was that, if this failed to materialize, he would return to Carthage, where he would face death by torture. In the senate Regulus opposed such an exchange, arguing that this refusal would demonstrate that Rome would not flinch from heavy losses. Despite the pleas of colleagues, 'he preferred to go back to be tortured rather than betray faith given to an enemy'.[27] *Fides* too had its own temple.

Conquest and empire

Rome engaged in competitive struggle as a land power, first for survival, then for control, first of Italy, then of the western Mediterranean, and finally of the entire Mediterranean world and the former Hellenistic kingdoms of the Near East. For Rome, the modern term 'empire'[28] is confusing because it fails to distinguish the constitutional transition from republic to principate from the territorial expansion of Roman power. Absolute rule and territorial empire are distinct as concepts, and in fact. Several non-monarchical states have run empires: Athens, Venice, the Dutch Republic, Britain. In Rome's case, the territorial empire was mostly acquired under the republic.

By the early third century BCE, the Romans controlled most of Italy, and entered into alliance with the Greek city-states of southern Italy. They fought two protracted wars against Carthage, a Phoenician city-state, the great sea power of the western Mediterranean. They finally defeated it in 202 BCE. This gave them control of Spain and the seaboard of north-west Africa. They defeated the Greek king of Macedon (196 BCE), and established hegemony over the mainland Greek city-states. They acquired western Asia Minor in the first century BCE; Egypt too came under Roman control.

Rome was driven to expand by both economic and political factors. The economic logic was land hunger and the opportunity for exploitation of men and materials. 'For centuries the Roman state [was] an exploitative instrument unique in antiquity in strength, brutality and the scale and reach of exploitation' (Finley 1983: 120). To their victims the Romans were 'the world's great robbers. When there is no more land left to devastate, they search the seas... Plunder, slaughter, theft they falsely call authority (*imperium*); they create desolation and call it peace'.[29] For ordinary citizens, satisfactory military service, especially a campaign leading to conquest, held out the prospect of land-ownership. ' "Public land" [was] never far beneath the surface of consciousness among the citizenry when some question involving conquest or empire was being discussed' (Finley 1983: 114). For members of the elite, military success became a route to political power; for emperors, it was a means of enhancing their reputation.

Romans were sometimes reluctant to start wars, partly because, under the republic, those who took the final decision to go to war were those who would have to do the fighting. One guiding principle of Roman foreign policy and conquest throughout her history was the perception that, in order to remain secure, you had to demonstrate that it did not pay anyone to attack you. They had to maintain a reputation for ruthless retaliation (Mattern 1999). They were very aware of the psychological component of relations between peoples: a mere insult had to be punished. In order to secure peace, it was essential that the honour and *dignitas* of the Roman state be upheld.[30] The ideology of *gloria* was thus replicated in the international arena.

This was the rationale behind the acts of brutality for which Rome became notorious, both under the republic and under the principate. 'Any military defeat, breach of treaty or revolt... should be repaid... with invasion, conquest, and the humiliation or even attempted annihilation of the enemy' (Mattern 1999: 183–4). Carthage was razed to the ground, the men killed, the women and children sold into slavery.[31] Caesar, whose invasion of Gaul was motivated partly by domestic ambitions, sold an entire tribe into slavery. But Rome also liked to show that those who submitted would be rewarded. Once she had conquered, she could afford to be benevolent.

The just war

You would not deduce much of this from reading Cicero on the 'just war (*bellum iustum*)'. Cicero outlined 'rules of war (*iura belli*)' which all should observe. A just war was one undertaken, in accordance with Rome's traditional priestly code, to right a specific wrong; certain rituals had to be followed, culminating in an official declaration of war.[32] Rome frequently justified wars by saying it was acting in defence of its allies. Augustus claimed that he had never made war merely for land or prestige, but only for just and necessary causes (Mattern 1999: 184). Cicero viewed war as a last resort: one should try to resolve disputes by negotiation before resorting to the 'bestial' method of warfare. In victory one should punish only the guilty, sparing the masses unless they have acted barbarously (*De Officiis* I.34–5, 82). (This was not always reflected in Roman policy.) Cicero looked back wistfully to the times when 'the height of glory for our magistrates and generals was to defend our provinces and allies with justice and honour... War was waged either for our allies or [to uphold] our authority (*imperium*)'. Rome's relationship to the rest of the world should, he said, be like that of patron to client: a world protectorate (*patrocinium orbis terrae*).

Cicero's was the first statement of the theory of the just war. This was to be further developed by Christian thinkers. The idea of war being part of a legal process was profoundly original, as commentators on Grotius point out.

The late republic

During the last century of the republic, ordinary Roman citizens claimed a larger share in Rome's increasing wealth and the spoils of her rapidly expanding empire. This led to a breakdown in the traditional consensual polity; differences between the interests of ordinary citizens and the landed aristocracy came into the open. Roman politics entered a new phase when Tiberius Gracchus, a tribune, proposed (in 133 BCE) that the size of holdings in public land should be limited, and the surplus redistributed among ordinary Roman citizens. This was an attempt to transfer 'a larger share in the rewards of the Empire which as soldiers they had helped to win' from the wealthy few to the Roman poor.[33] The assemblies of the people asserted their independence.

The military reforms of Marius—a popular general who won the consulate six times despite his plebeian origin, and saved Rome from a German invasion (102–101 BCE)—increased the dependence of soldiers on their generals for land and booty. This gave a successful general the chance to seek political power. It was disastrous for the authority of 'the senate and people of Rome'.

The political ambitions of rival generals began to undermine the authority of both the senate and the assemblies of the people. First, Marius engaged in a savage and bloody power-struggle (83–82 BCE) with the champion of the wealthy aristocrats, Sulla. Sulla won, and attempted a solution to the constitutional impasse by concentrating power in the senate, at the same time making it more widely representative. But this did not last.

In 66–63 BCE Pompey, a former supporter of Sulla, brought Asia Minor and Syria-Palestine under Roman rule. Following an attempt to carve up power between Pompey, the more populist Julius Caesar, and the fabulously wealthy Crassus (the 'first triumvirate', 60 BCE), Caesar set out on his conquest of Gaul[34] (58–49 BCE). On his return he seized power by entering Rome at the head of his army—he 'crossed the Rubicon' (the river at which generals returning to Rome were supposed to lay down their command)—thus making himself effectively a military dictator (as well as *dictator* in terms of the Roman constitution).[35] He was assassinated (15 March 44 BCE) by a group of senators in an attempt to restore the power of the senate and assemblies. Further civil wars continued until the victory of Octavian, Caesar's adopted son and heir. He became the first 'emperor' (*princeps*), with the title Augustus (below). The growth of the empire and the pressures of war had helped to destabilize the republic. It was impossible, as many contemporary observers and later historians have said, to rule so large a state without a fundamental change in the organization of power at home. Absolute monarchy was by far the easiest solution.

'Democracy' versus 'aristocracy'

The last century of the republic was an era of intense political and constitutional debate, which has influenced the Western world ever since. The issues raised by Tiberius Gracchus opened up divisions within the political class. Broadly speaking, those called *optimates* wanted to maintain the senate as the overriding authority, and to retain the existing landholdings of the wealthy. Those who became known as *populares* wanted to expand the powers of the tribunes and assemblies, and to equalize distribution of the spoils of empire.[36] The conventional constitution began to fracture.

From now on there were conflicting views about the proper distribution of political power. Both sides claimed to represent ancestral tradition. Despite the increasingly independent political clout of generals and their armies, both of these groups tried to impose their view of the existing constitution.

The ideology of the *optimates* was aristocratic in the sense that they argued that authority should reside with 'the best' (themselves). Virtuous men in the senate were fully capable of protecting and promoting the interests of the Roman people by guiding them with wise advice (*consilium*).[37] This was 'an elitist and paternalist ideal [which] set great store by the superior capacity of certain men of recognised excellence to discern the genuine interest of all (as ordinary men could not) and to pursue it honorably' (Morstein-Marx 2004: 276).

Cicero on the whole favoured the optimate view of giving the senate and its leading families a predominant role, but, as we shall see, he sought to synthesize this with what he saw as good points in the democratic outlook. To begin with, he proposed alliance between the political (senatorial) and commercial ('knightly') upper classes (and when necessary others too) (*In Catilinam* IV.14.19). He called this *concordia ordinum* (harmony between the estates). Beyond that, his solution to the recurrent crises of his time was a moral one: the senate and magistrates should lead selflessly; they must *earn* the consensus of the people. Only if they did so could the senate and people of Rome continue to function in the traditional manner. On the whole he supported Sulla's programme but not his methods. He sympathized with lower-class aspirations for liberty and equality under the law, but not with their demands for land reform.

Cicero did not pay much heed to the independent power of the Roman armies, though he realistically allied himself with one general, Pompey (a supporter of Sulla), because, Cicero thought, he had greater respect than others for the constitution. His opposition to the first triumvirate was 'perhaps the most principled stance of his political life' (Ungern-Sternberg 2004: 102). On his return from exile in 58 BCE, he was acclaimed as the spokesman of the senatorial traditionalists (*optimates*).

His theoretical works on government, the mainly Platonic *Republic* (much of which is lost) and the *Laws* were composed soon after (55–54 BCE). Cicero was firmly opposed to Caesar's coup d'état in 48; he later denounced 'the temerity of Caius Caesar, who overturned all laws human and divine to gain the supreme power on which he had basely set his mind' (*De Officiis* I.26). But he was not included in the conspiracy to assassinate Caesar, though he endorsed it strongly after the event: 'what more glorious deed, or one more to be commended to the everlasting memory of men, was ever in all the world accomplished?' (*Philippics* II.32).

Cicero's final campaign was a series of speeches (the *Philippics*: September 44 to April 43 BCE), urging senate and people to resist Mark Antony's attempt to take over Caesar's dictatorial role. His invective was both principled and personal. Cicero saw this as a last chance for senate and people to reclaim their authority. He knew that he endangered his own life by attacking Antony. When the second triumvirate (Octavian, Antony, Lepidus) was formed in May 43, Antony had Cicero put on the death-list. He was killed on 7 December 43. He was perhaps the only major political theorist who died for his political convictions.

In his legal and political speeches Cicero articulated and developed several traditional Roman ideas. His philosophical writings brought Platonic idealism and Stoic moral thought into line with the value-system of Rome. And it was through Cicero that medieval Europe picked up on these.

The democratic view of the *populares* was expressed in speeches by Marius and others, which were reported in the *Histories* of Sallust (86–35 BCE) (Morstein-Marx 2004: 31). Marius urged the people to stand up for their rights: *maiestas* (sovereignty) belongs to the people; 'all power is in you, citizens'.[38]

One crucial issue was the independence of the assemblies from control or interference by the senate. Way back in 148 BCE, 'the people shouted that, by the "laws of Tullius and Romulus", the people was sovereign in the elections and could validate or invalidate laws' (Millar 1986: 9). This, to the *populares*, was the meaning of liberty: the right to a free vote in the assemblies (a secret ballot had recently been introduced), representation by tribunes independent of the senate, trial by jury, and no executions without popular consent.[39] According to Sallust, the tribunate was 'a weapon designed by our ancestors for liberty' (*Hist.* 3.48.12); 'won't you do all in your power for the liberty they bequeathed to you?' (1.155.3–4).

Cicero articulated a position intermediate between this democratic view and the view of the *optimates*. Public office (he said) is a trusteeship, and therefore it is to be exercised in the interests of those entrusted to the magistrate. He must 'understand that he represents the state (*se gerere personam civitatis*), and he must, therefore, uphold its dignity and honour, maintain its laws, dispense its rights' (*De Officiis* I.124; *De Republica* I.51). Those who serve one section, whether *populares* or *optimates*, ought to recognize that they are there to serve the interests of all.[40]

Public offices in republican Rome were, of course, elective: the Roman people had a final say over to whom their interests should be entrusted. Cicero duly referred, in various contexts, to 'the voice and will of the whole state', the 'mind, will and voice' of all ranks of society acting in agreement (*In Catilinam* IV.18). In pleading a case before the judicial assembly, he told them that 'all the power of the immortal gods has either been transferred or at least shared' with them (*Pro Murena* 2); indeed, the people have the same 'power and awe' as the gods (in Morstein-Marx 2004: 224 n.). His combination of popular sovereignty with the idea of representation was crucial: Cicero's was one of the languages that was adopted when representative government began to develop in Europe.

What the people's party were also defending, according to Sallust, was 'liberty, our own homes and not to obey anyone except the laws' (*Hist.* 1.55.1–5). Equality under the law was central to their view of their rights. Cicero too saw the logic in saying that you could not have true liberty 'if it is not the same for all (*si aequa non ese*)' (*De Republica* I.49). The historian Livy put this in words that would one day ring through Europe: 'the authority of laws is greater than that of men (*imperia legum potentiora quam hominum*)' (II.1.1).[41]

Cicero, especially in the final speeches of his life when he was defending the republic against the autocrat Antony, agreed with the *populares* that liberty is the supreme political value. It is, he said, the greatest gift of the gods and 'nothing could be sweeter'.[42] Indeed, he pointed out that one *could* argue that the people can only secure their liberty in 'a state in which supreme power belongs to the people' (*De Republica* I.47). But, while for the *populares* the goal of politics was 'peace with freedom (*otium cum libertate*'; Sallust, *Hist.* 1.55.9), for Cicero it was 'peace with status (*cum dignitate otium*)'.[43] Even so, of all the political theorists in the ancient world, Cicero was the one who set most store by liberty.

But, whereas Cicero and the *optimates* would insist that equality before the law was quite separate from, and in no way implied, equality of property, advocates of popular liberty were indignant at the gross inequalities in wealth that had accumulated with the growth of empire. They saw politics as a conflict between a rich and powerful few and the Roman people as a whole (Wirszubski 1950: 45–6). On the distribution of property, Cicero supported the elite view. The idea of equalizing property was abhorrent to him. The redistribution of property and the cancellation of debts are beyond the legitimate powers of the state. States were founded to preserve property, and the first duty of government must be 'that everyone should keep what belongs to him, and that the goods of private individuals should not be diminished by state action'.[44] This later dovetailed with the bourgeois-capitalist view of the state in John Locke.

The Roman-republican view of liberty was transmitted to Europe through Cicero's writings. Whereas the *populares* saw liberty and economic equality going together, Cicero aligned it with freedom from economic intervention by the state, and so produced something very like a prototype for John Locke and, indeed, the 'Glorious Revolution' of 1689.

In addressing the assembly, the *populares* appealed to the pride and self-interest of the Roman commoners by contrasting their servile status at home with their glorious conquests abroad. The Roman people, as they put it, 'born free and for sovereignty (*in imperium*)...unconquered by their enemies [and] rulers (*imperatores*) of all nations...are being brought into slavery (*servitudo*) under the *dominatio* of others...the few want to dominate, you want to be free'; but are now being 'stripped of *imperium*, glory, rights'. They 'do not even have a slave's rations'.[45] Cicero too took this up: 'It is immoral that the Roman people, whom the gods chose to rule all nations, should become slaves ... Other peoples can endure slavery, but to the Roman people belongs liberty (*populi Romani est propria libertas*)' (*Philippics* VI.19).

What we hear from ancient Rome is, therefore, hardly the voice of Rousseau; it is imperialist democracy. Similarly, nineteenth-century Europe and the twenty-first-century United States have boasted of liberty and democracy at home, while practising imperialism abroad—only without saying so.

Cicero's political theory

Because he so often articulated conventional norms and ideals, it is easy to overlook—and most people have—the ways in which Cicero was an original political thinker. His theory of cosmopolitanism (to be examined below) was part of a new perception of social life, which he saw as developing at many different levels and as giving rise to a multiplicity of morally grounded associations. Bonds of affection begin, he said, with the family and friendship, but they extend to many other associations, including the state (*res publica, patria*), and eventually the whole human species (*De Officiis* I.13–14). Among these various types of society, the *res publica* held a special place for Cicero.

Alone among ancient thinkers in all cultures, Cicero held that people associate primarily because they want to, because they have a liking for each other's company, not because this is the only way they can meet their material needs or prevent conflict. Nor is it because they are coerced. His was thus the only *voluntarist* theory of the state. European and Western ideas of society and state, especially theories of social contract, derived from this.

Cicero grounded his view of the state on a Stoic theory of nature. Morality and society are expressions of the intrinsic way human beings are. It is *ratio* (reason) and *oratio* (speech, eloquence) which bring humans together, transforming savages into gentlemen. These are the basis for the (Roman) ideal of a free and peaceful political society, a consensual polity, in which leadership is established by good men using the skills of oratory and persuasion, and government is by law rather than by force.[46] So too the Stoic Epictetus (below) would later insist that you can only lead *men* (as opposed to animals) by teaching and persuasion. The first aim of law is not to resolve conflicts but to induce moral sentiments. Oratory turns out to be as central to Cicero's political thought as it was to the Roman republic in practice (Morstein-Marx 2004).

Humans form these different kinds of association not only for instrumental reasons but also for personal fulfilment and satisfaction. Cicero argued that, just as Plato had said that one must seek justice both for its own sake and for its results, so too should humans recognize that they seek a common life (*communis vita*) for its own sake, as well as for its evident advantages. Of the latter he stressed technological feats (aqueducts, roads, harbours, irrigation, and so on).[47]

In his last work, *De Officiis* (*On Duties*), Cicero discussed the conflict between morality (*honestum*: the honourable) and expediency (*utile*: what is useful).[48] His Stoic predecessors, he said, had not discussed this problem (*De Officiis* III.7). *On Duties* was written in extraordinary haste, at the very time when he was risking his life to save the republic, the first two books being completed in nine days (Long 1995: 221); the third book does not read like a work composed at leisure. It was finished in December 44, and dedicated to his son.

On Duties consisted of a sustained attack, with numerous examples from Roman history, on the subordination of morality to expediency. It is as much rhetoric as philosophy; the other side is not really heard. Only honourable or honest moral actions, Cicero urged, can be truly useful; that is, useful in the long term. Cicero 'detach[ed] "the honourable" from the traditional (Roman) honour code' and redefined it 'in terms of what is intrinsically or naturally good' (Long 1995: 218). One should do what is right whatever the cost—and not just for interests of state—because it is inscribed in our nature as humans. This theme, and the passion with which it is put, must be seen in the context of the stand Cicero was taking against Antony.

Cicero was killed while setting out for Athens, where he had hoped to join his son. 'I defended the state in my youth, I will not desert her in my old age; I cared nothing for Catiline's swordsmen, I will not be afraid of [Antony's]. I would gladly offer my body if the liberty of the state could be achieved by my death . . . I ask only that by dying . . . I leave the Roman people free' (*Philippics* II.118–19).

Cicero was the model of Latin prose for generations of Europeans, but he has been underestimated as a political theorist. Like Solon, he combined political activity with original thought. It is hard to grasp him, to believe in him as he appears to us both from his writings and from what we know about him, so different was he from us in his priorities, his apparently unending self-belief, and his self-giving. The fullness of his public commitment coloured his whole personality. His most interesting ideas—the primacy of social life and the universality of human values (below)—remain on the threshold of our accomplishments.

On Duties was, it turned out, Cicero's chief legacy to posterity. Book III was a perfect companion to Christian teaching. It was also a target for Machiavelli, and a precursor of Kant's 'categorical imperative'. It was partly thanks to Cicero that the fall of the Roman republic was not the last chapter in the history of constitutional government. Cicero's ideals of republican government may have been unrealistic in his own day, but they became more realistic in times Cicero did not know about. He did not save the Roman republic, but he perpetuated many of its political ideals.

STOICISM AND THE PRINCIPATE

When Octavian (Augustus) defeated his last rival at the sea battle off Actium (north-west Greece) in 31 BCE, this adopted son of Caesar was in unchallenged control of the Roman state and its dominions. He arranged that 'power was restored to the laws, authority to the courts, supreme dignity (*maiestas*) to the senate. The venerable and ancient constitution of the public order was restored'.[49] This was a masterstroke of inclusive statesmanship, almost entirely fictitious. He kept tight personal control over the entire civil and military apparatus, including the Roman armies, and appointed carefully selected subordinates to the main offices of state.

But a myth of popular sovereignty remained. Had not the Roman people 'transferred' their powers to the ruler voluntarily?[50] The senate was indeed still consulted, but only about minor matters. This remained the constitutional position. Augustus called himself neither king nor monarch but first citizen (*princeps*) and *imperator* (commander of the armies). The actual empire continued to be ruled in the name of the Roman people, and often to their material benefit. The idea of *res publica*, the public domain, 'the common affairs of the people', survived. When a triumphal arch was erected in the Roman forum in honour of the emperor Septimius Severus (r. 193–211 CE), it said (as one can see to this day) that he had 'restored the *res publica*, and extended the *imperium* of the Roman people'. By achieving stability, Augustus gained the support of Rome's governing and landed elite. It was a masterly way of masking new practice behind an old theory. And in some ways it worked. Neither allegiance to Rome, the 'common fatherland', nor Italian patriotism changed.[51]

This was a new kind of monarchy. What differentiated the Roman principate from the other ancient monarchies was, however, not the extent of the ruler's powers, but the way these powers were conceived, the language in which they were expressed (and perhaps occasionally the manner in which they were exercised). The emperor Marcus Aurelius (r. 161–80 CE) told himself always to be willing to change his mind on better advice. Although the Roman senate and people had lost the power to make political decisions, the liberties of Roman citizens were, nonetheless, unchanged in law (Wirszubski 1950: 158–9). Marcus Aurelius believed in a monarchy which respected above all else the liberty of its subjects (*Meditations* 1.14). In practice, however, such liberties depended on how the emperor decided to exercise his power. Some said that the regime was a mixed form of government, and therefore sound.[52]

When one compares the Roman empire of this period with what came after, one is struck by the freedom of thought and expression. The great historian Tacitus (*c.* 65–*c.*117 CE) thought he was living in one of those rare periods 'when you can think what you want and say what you think' (*Histories* 1.1). Since Hellenistic times, Jewish communities had, in some places, been self-governing associations (*politeumata*), which 'managed their own internal and religious affairs' (Tarn and Griffith 1930: 220, 226), and became a model for other ethnic groups—a form of local self-government which continued under Islam. 'Each nationality observes the ritual of its own family and worships its local divinities', wrote Celsus (? *c.*180 CE) in defence of non-Christian religion, noting (in anticipation of J. S. Mill) that this accords with the very uncertainty of our knowledge about 'the universe and [god]'.[53] It was now that the Jewish communities, following two failed revolts, traded their messianic expectations for the tightly ordered communal world of the Talmud, and political quietism (Baron, S. 1952).

The freedom of individuals, especially their ability to think for themselves and adopt what stance they chose about the great issues of life, was considerable. Early Christianity was part of this. To someone like the poor and disabled ex-slave Epictetus—and no doubt to many early Christians—the glory of this freedom was that it did not depend on one's political or even personal circumstances. It is easy for a modern author to despise such an attitude (Wirszubski 1950: 167). One may ask how many people living even in 'free' countries today are as free as many Romans of this period were.

The Roman empire embodied what we nowadays call 'civil society'.[54] Free men could engage in trade. Certain state activities, such as tax-collection, and construction of roads and aqueducts, were let out by contract either to private individuals or to 'semi-public corporate organisations, *collegia* and *societates*'.[55] There was considerable freedom of association, social, economic, and religious. Towns (*municipia*) enjoyed municipal autonomy. Corporations (*universitates*) were defined in law as 'capable of enjoying and exercising legal rights'.[56] They could be independent of kinship. Roman society had a diversity of affiliations that was probably unique in the pre-modern world.

Stoic doctrine bore fruit in the code of Roman law compiled and published under the emperor Justinian, known as *The Digest*. The Roman-law jurists of the second and third centuries CE combined the Roman and Stoic approaches to law,[57] and in so doing articulated legal principles which became the basis of Western law. Justice was defined as 'to give each his due (*ius suum cuique tribuere)*' (*Digest* 1.1.10).[58] (This followed the preliminary definition of justice in Plato's *Republic* (331e; see above, p. 149).) Was this definition deliberately open-ended? It was to be used in support of many different agendas in European history. It could be applied to justify whatever social order existed, or, if one believed that 'each' is 'due' certain things, it could be a slogan of change.

Roman jurists tended to interpret existing Roman law in the light of Stoic principles. They said that by the law of nature all men were 'born free' and equal: slavery was only introduced by the laws of all nations.[59] Stoics recommended that one should go beyond legal requirements in the treatment of slaves.[60] The jurists' greatest contribution was to try, so far as was possible under monarchy, to impose the rule of law. The poet Virgil implied that Rome spread the rule of law over the whole world.[61] Of particular importance was their notion of a 'constitutional office exercisable only within legal limits' (*CGR* 618); in other words, the application of constitutional limits to the exercise of power.

The problem was, of course, the *princeps* himself, who, as 'the living law', was not bound by the law. But he should, it was stressed, act as if he were, and be restrained by 'reason in himself'.[62] Tacitus recorded, with studied indignation, many outrageous cases of imperial abuse; but during the second century this seemed to him a thing of the past. The Younger Pliny (*c.* 61–*c.* 113 CE) also expressed his happiness that nowadays 'the prince is not above the laws but the laws above the prince . . . we are subject to you but in such a way as [to be subject] to the laws' (in Wirszubski 1950: 130). The emperor Trajan himself dismissed anonymous accusations as 'a very bad example that does not belong to our time'.[63] This suggests increasing concern for due process on the part of an emperor himself.

Many people in the provinces saw the right of appeal to the emperor as a precious privilege (we do not know how effective such appeals were). There was a general 'feeling that Caesar was there to protect the rights of the underprivileged against injustice' (Hopkins 1979: 222). One of the 'virtues' looked for now in an emperor was *clementia*, the exercise of mercy (Seneca, in *CGR* 540).

Christians were persecuted—intermittently—not for what they believed, but for refusing to show even 'the outward marks of respect' to the emperor (Veyne 1990: 317). Strictly speaking, it was political rather than religious persecution. People were perhaps right to fear Christianity, for it turned out to pose a threat to civil society. When Christians came to power, they did all they could (and more than Islam did later) to suppress religious and intellectual freedom.

A theory of monarchy

This was the least ideological monarchy of the ancient world, a reluctant monarchy, a kingship that hardly dared speak its name. There was no theory of monarchy, apart from what had been written centuries ago in 'democratic' Athens, by Plato, Xenophon, Isocrates, and Aristotle (above, pp. 164–5). In fact, more monarchical theory was produced in fourth-century Athens than in the three centuries of the Roman principate. The general view was that this concentration of powers in a single individual was simply the least bad option. Pliny said that people could now see how much better universal monarchy is than 'a divided and distracted liberty' (*EB* 253). After Nero's terrible reign, the new emperor Galba (according to Tacitus) introduced his chosen successor with the words: 'if the immense body of the empire could keep its balance without a ruler, I would be the one to start a republic. But...' (*Hist.* 1.16). It was generally agreed that the greatest benefit of monarchy, and of the Roman empire as a whole, was peace. If this was your goal in life, then the monarchical empire was your answer. Most Christians would also come to see things this way.

Arguments for monarchy were ad hoc rather than systematic or deeply philosophical. They were based on simple observations of nature or of human experience. Herds and swarms have one leader (Dio of Prusa, in *EB* 307). 'There had been no other remedy for our discordant country than that it should be ruled by one man' (Tacitus, *Annals*, 1.9.5). Seneca, the most prominent philosopher of Roman Stoicism, used an organic analogy: 'the immense number of people, encircling one soul, is ruled by [the monarch's] spirit, guided by his reason...He is the bond through which the public domain (*res publica*) sticks together'; he is 'the soul of the state (*animus rei publicae*)', the state his 'body'.[64]

The prevailing view now was that the best way to serve the *res publica* was by being loyal to the *princeps*. Awareness of the 'other' at the borders allowed no let-up in military preparedness (Mattern 1999). Emperors might be despised or loathed, but opposition was to the person rather than the system. It usually took the form of principled, occasionally quite blatant, disengagement from politics altogether (Wirszubski 1950: 138 ff.). There was no serious movement, even within the senate, to restore the republic. Stoic teaching reinforced the Roman tradition that what matters most is the moral fibre of ruler and ruled.

One strength of the principate was that it could appear to be, and in many ways was, less class-based and less Rome-centred than the republic had been. It offered protection by law to a significant proportion of its subjects, and made more and more peoples of the empire feel part of 'the system of man and god' (Epictetus, *Discourses* 1.9.4). In appointments, there was less emphasis on glorious ancestors, more on merit (Mattern 1999: 19–20). The emerging political value was *universalism* (see below, Ch. 10): whatever their background, all men had the potential for excellence, and therefore for the highest office.

Outside Rome, on the other hand, things were different. Julius Caesar was 'the first living Roman noble to claim descent from a god . . . the first Roman to be recognised as a god in a public state cult' (Hopkins 1979: 202). This had not gone down well in Rome itself, and Augustus learnt the lesson: he was not officially deified till after his death. Westerners took a more modest view of the prince's status (Sherwin-White 1973: 402–6). He was *augustus* (worshipful), *imperator* (victorious general), *pater patriae* (father of the fatherland), and Augustus became chief priest (*pontifex maximus*). The Younger Pliny said that an emperor 'functions in [god's] role (as world parent) towards the whole human race' (*Panegyric* 4.4 and 80.3), a reference to the prince's duty as well as his prestige.

In the Eastern provinces, however, people could hardly wait to include living emperors alongside 'goddess Rome' in the pantheon, and to build them temples. The conventional ideas of sacred monarchy were applied to the new rulers.[65] The deified figure of the emperor himself provided an overarching symbol of unity in a heterogeneous and relatively fluid society (Hopkins 1979), providing social glue for the 'multiculturalism'—the racial, linguistic, and cultural diversity—of the areas covered by the *res publica romana*. The Roman emperor, like the Hellenistic king, was hailed as 'doer of good (*euergetēs*)', 'lover of men (*philanthrōpos*)', 'saviour (*sōter*)', and of course shepherd.[66] In the third century, emperors were compared to 'the unconquered sun', Apollo, and the Persian Mithras (*EB* 352).

There was thus already a difference in political outlook between the western and eastern halves of the Mediterranean world. In the East, there was a well-established tradition of sacred monarchy. In Italy, the memory of republican Rome was strong, and the peoples of Spain, Gaul, and Germania had not developed sacred monarchy to anything like the same degree as in the East.

Fourth-century Christianity completed the process of sacralizing the Roman emperor. An emperor could not now *be* god, but he could be the next-best thing, god's representative on earth. And that is what all Christian emperors claimed to be. Christianity provided a metaphysically overwhelming case for monarchy by analogy with the universe. It is interesting that the emperor Julian (r. 361–3 CE), who opposed the Christianization of the empire, also wanted to return to the more modest aspirations and participatory practices of the early principate (Dvornik 1966: ii. 664–5).

Political philosophy

'Politics ceased to be a centre of live interest in its own right' (Trapp 2007: 232). People wrote ethical treatises, histories, panegyrics, satire, but not works of political theory. There was no public debate about constitutions or policy, no 'politics' as known in the Greek poleis or republican Rome. Nor did rulers aspire to be philosophers, at least in public. Marcus Aurelius (possibly the closest there had ever been to a philosopher-king) advised himself not to 'hope for Plato's constitution' (*Meditations* 9.29).

The most prominent philosophy among the elite was Stoicism.[67] This became grafted onto *Romanitas*. Augustus himself was taught by a Stoic. In the view of Roman Stoicism, the function of the ruler was to promote the well-being of his subjects. Everyone was agreed that the whole purpose of the unlimited power allowed to the *princeps* was to maintain peace and prosperity and enforce justice. 'Beneficence', defined as 'to be able to do the greatest good for the greatest number' (EB 304), was the clearest sign that the ruler represented god. It could include some social welfare. Under princely rule, the rhetorician Aelius Aristides (*c.*120–89 CE) said, people get what they want just as much as they do in a democracy (EB 326). The Stoic view of a ruler's duties was frequently alluded to in Marcus Aurelius' personal 'meditations'. He gives us a quite extraordinary insight into the mind of one absolute ruler; he urges himself to be gentle, concerned, infinitely patient, attentive to the smallest detail (*Meditations* 2.5 and 4.12), always prepared to do what 'reason, which inheres in the royal and law-making power, prescribes for the welfare of mankind'.[68]

Stoicism reinforced the Roman respect for tradition, implying that 'the moral law required performance of traditionally accepted duties and respect for conventions' (Brunt 1975: 16). It offered 'a framework [in which] the Romans can have their empire, but . . . in which they can have it well' (Shaw 1985: 29–30, 36, 39). It accepted the existence of social classes, and urged people to perform the duties of their status. Stoics also saw a connection between virtue, beneficence, the performance of public duties, and the nature of the cosmos. They were in the business of showing how life could be made more tolerable at the edges. Virgil applied the Roman-Stoic virtues of hard work and patience to agriculture: the simple rural life, the way of the common man, the ancestral way, is better than luxury or fame.[69] To fulfil the duties of one's allotted role in civil society and the state—that was their religion.

In the Stoic view, moreover, the duties and rights inherent in beneficence and public service, potentially at least, apply to everyone. For all humans possess reason (*logos*), and should perform their own duties to the best of their ability, and be treated with respect; humane treatment of subordinates, including slaves, helps preserve public order (Shaw 1985: 38–40). Epictetus' reply to the official who said 'I can have anyone I want beaten to death', was: 'so you can a donkey. This is not the government of men; men, as rational beings, should be governed by being shown what is desirable and what is not desirable' (*Discourses* 3.7.32–6). Both the similarities and the dissimilarities between Stoicism and Christianity deserve more attention.

Stoics also 'urge[d] active participation as the norm' (Trapp 2007: 221). They recognized, like Confucians, that circumstances could make it impossible to participate in public life and practise virtue at the same time. In that case, withdraw, pursue virtue and knowledge in private.[70] Epictetus taught that everyone has a duty to promote the public good by carrying out whatever their specific duties are, whether as father, son, worker, or manager. He told a visiting official who (being an Epicurean) thought there were better ways to spend one's time than public service: 'drop those doctrines, man'; they are 'subversive of the state, destructive to the family'. Rather, 'you live in the ruling city [Rome]: you should hold office, make just decisions' (*Discourses* 3.7.19–21).

POWER AND PHILOSOPHY IN ROME AND CHINA

The Roman empire stepped into the shoes of the Hellenistic monarchies, in which 'what was missing was true belief' (Ehrenberg 1969: 206); there was no common ideology to bind people together. A few classical Greek thinkers did put the case for monarchy (above, p. 165). But, remarkably, their ideas were not developed during the monarchical period of Greek or Roman rule. We have seen that, under Rome, what political thought there was had little basis in philosophy. There was, furthermore, a 'poverty of religious thought about the Empire'; there was 'no attempt to relate the structure of the Empire to the structure of the divine world' (Momigliano 1987: 316, 318).

The monarchical state with which Rome was most comparable in terms of political outlook was China. From about 200 BCE until the third century CE, the Roman and Chinese imperial monarchies were predominant in their regions (Elvin 1973: 18–20). In each of them, the breakthroughs in philosophical thinking, going back to the sixth century BCE, had reached a certain maturity. In both, a powerful state professed alliance with ethical idealism: Stoicism, and later Christianity, in the Mediterranean; Confucianism in China. Why did the Chinese synthesis of power and philosophy last so much longer?

In the second century CE the Roman imperium looked stable enough. But within a short time it was shaken by military disasters and succession conflicts. These also occurred in Chinese history. But, whereas the Chinese imperial project was re-established time and again, when the Roman empire collapsed in the West it was never revived. I suggest that what the Roman empire lacked was a public ethic, or an ideology of empire, something which could serve as a model for the ruling and wealthy classes, and be acceptable to others. Han Confucianism was a theology of power and authority: the empire and the emperor's right to rule derive from the Mandate of Heaven. Imperial power was believed in as an essential part of the cosmic and natural forces. Dynasties came and went, but each new dynasty could rely on this philosophy of power.

The Roman empire, unlike the Chinese, had been unplanned. The fusion between power and philosophy was more casual than it was in China. Too much was left to brute force. In China, by contrast, unification was indeed achieved by brute force, but it had long been the ideal of philosophers. People saw it as the only polity harmonious with the general scheme of things. Under Rome, there was no sense of the meaning the empire might have in the scheme of things. (Even in India, the Laws of Manu had divine sanction, and philosophical reflection was anchored in traditional religion.)

During the second century CE Stoicism might have filled the gap. But it had only a marginal connection with religion, and it lacked widespread popular support. It demanded much but offered little, and was therefore unattractive to the masses. Christianity demanded much, but it also offered a great deal. In any case, both Stoicism and Christianity were less politically focused than were either Confucianism or Legalism. Stoicism was to a large extent apolitical. It did not have the advantage of a religion which could engage the public's imagination. Instead, people resorted to the spectacle of the public 'games'. Indeed Marcus Aurelius referred to the Christians as too 'melodramatic' in their martyrdoms (*Meditations* 11.3).

In the end, the Roman empire did look for support to Christianity (the offshoot of a quite different culture). The adoption of Christianity as the official, and soon the exclusive, religion of the empire may have given Rome something of the ideological cement which China had. Latin and Byzantine Christianity in a sense reunited religion with philosophy. The emperor was henceforth the representative of god on earth. Christian monotheism offered a justification of absolute bureaucratic rule. Or, as Theodor Mommsen put it,

Christianity 'merely expressed in the religious field what had already been accomplished in the political' (in Baron 1952: 151). In other words, the Roman empire lacked a viable ideology *until* it adopted a (doctored) version of Christianity. In this respect, Gibbon's argument that Christianity undermined the Roman empire may be missing the point.

But Christianity may have been less amenable to political use than Confucianism. As the western and eastern halves of the Roman empire drifted apart, the East suffered from a new source of instability in the doctrinal disagreements between Christians. Enforced religious conformity, combined with admininstrative centralization, made the late Roman empire the most authoritarian pre-modern state. It was the 'pagan' emperor Julian who, in his attempt to restore polytheism, wanted universal toleration;[71] the Christian bishops made sure this did not last (Jones 1966: 69). In China, by contrast, Confucianism, like Stoicism, coexisted quite happily with folk beliefs.

It is possible that the East Roman empire might have fared better had not Islam produced its own quite different, and more militarily successful, combination of cosmology, law, and power. Islam's rise was facilitated by disenchantment with the religious conformity imposed from above. And in the West the Christian church soon showed itself unwilling to act as the servant of empire.

NOTES

1. About 60 miles south-east of Rome.
2. 'Res publica, id est res populi' ('the affairs and interests of the populus', in Schofield 1995: 77).
3. 'A form of government and a way of life'; Wirszubski 1950: 88.
4. *Pro Sestio* 46, 98. Sallust defined it as 'laws, law courts, the treasury, the provinces and (allied) kings' (speech of Lepidus: *Hist.* 1.55.13). Cf. Kautilya, above p. 75.
5. Cicero, *In Catilinam* IV.16. What was at stake was '[the Senate's] and the Roman people's ultimate security: so think of your wives and children, altars and hearths, sanctuaries and temples, the homes and dwelling-places of the entire city, power and freedom' (*In Catilinam* IV.23; *Philippics* XIV.37–8).
6. The elder Brutus, who led the expulsion of the kings and later allowed his own brother to be put to death, showed that 'when it comes to preserving freedom, no-one is a private citizen' (Cicero, *De Republica* II.46).
7. Cicero, *De Officiis* I.69–73; Greece's seven wise men 'nearly all involved themselves in affairs of state' (*De Republica* I.12). Such passages contributed to the debate in

Renaissance Europe about the rival merits of the 'active' and 'contemplative' life; Baron 1966: 106–13.

8. 'Where the blessed ones enjoy everlasting life' (Cicero, *De Republica* VI.13), from the 'Dream of Scipio', which attained classic status in medieval and Renaissance Europe. See also Virgil, *Aeneid* VI.

9. 'Those who have expanded, defended or served this great state by their counsels and labours' have surely obtained immortality in glory just like Hercules (*Pro Sestio* 68.143); though life is short, 'the memory of a life well given up is everlasting' (*Philippics* XIV.32–3).

10. See Lintott 1999; Jolowicz and Nicholas 1972: 33–4; Millar 1984: 18; Wirszubski 1950: 23–33.

11. The Roman people were organized in different ways for different occasions.

12. Senators were barred from government contracts, tax-farming, and commerce; these were the domain of knights. Tradesmen were ineligible for office.

13. Millar 1984, 1986; Lintott 1987; North 1990.

14. The *contio* was '*the* authorised locus of face-to-face communication between the Senate and the populace' (Morstein-Marx 2004: 15, 70; Jolowicz and Nicholas 1972: 84).

15. *Hist.* VI.15.1 (my italics).

16. Machiavelli, *Discourses* I.4; Pocock 1975: 194.

17. *De Republica* I.69. 'With us are all men of all ranks, every stock, and every age' (*In Catilinam* IV.14, 19).

18. *De Republica* II.69. Cf. Plato, *Republic* 443.

19. *Hist.* VI.9.10–15; based on Plato, *Republic,* books VIII–IX.

20. *De Republica* I.2–3 and 34, and II.57, I.34; Morstein-Marx 2004: 78–9.

21. *Hist.* VI.10.12–14, based on Loeb translation.

22. *Pro Sestio* 136; *In Verrem* II.180–3; *Philippics* II.119. See Wirszubski 1950: 36–8, 53.

23. Sallust, *Jug.* 85.17–37, my italics.

24. Ando 2003; Cicero, *Pro Sestio* 147.

25. 'Divine consent for the leading figures of the community... was no less important than majorities of human votes' (Ruepke 2004: 182; Finley 1983: 26).

26. Cicero, *Laws* II.15; see Diodorus Siculus (active 60–30 BCE), in Griffin and Barnes, 1989: 179. Cicero admired the way religious rites at Rome had been made complex but inexpensive (*De Republica* II.27).

27. Cicero, *De Officiis* I.39 (my italics) and III. 114; Horace, *Odes* III.5. 49–55.

28. '*Imperium*' meant the 'power to command' bestowed by the people on a magistrate in charge of an army.

29. Tacitus, *Agricola* 220 (after EB 241), ascribed to a Caledonian chieftain.

30. Mattern 1999: 216–18. 'They seem to have perceived foreign relations as a competition for honor and status between Rome and barbarian peoples' (ibid. 171, 181).

31. After the war of 148 BCE 'whole districts [of Greece] were half depopulated' (Tarn and Griffiths 1930: 43).

32. *De Officiis* I.34–6; Mattern 1999: 217; Harris 1979: ch. 5.
33. *OHR* 41–3; Millar 1986: 9.
34. This included the Low Countries as well as France. A temporary office with powers over other magistrates.
35. Appointed for six months with supreme military and judicial authority.
36. These were not 'parties' in the modern sense: Millar 1984; Morstein-Marx 2004: 279.
37. Morstein-Marx 2004: 223; Schofield 1995: 78. Cicero believed that the decline of Athens resulted from the abolition of its aristocratic council of the Areopagus (*De Republica* I.43): see above, p. 143.
38. Sallust, *Jug.* 31.9; *Hist.* 3.48.15.
39. Sallust, *Jug.* 31.5–25; Wirszubski 1950: 3, 24–6. 'Nothing in the state should be as incorruptible as the vote' (Cicero, *De Republica* V.11).
40. *De Officiis* I.85; Schofield 1995: 78–81.
41. Wirszubski 1950: 11–12. For Cicero on rights; Schofield 1995: 76–7.
42. *Philippics* II.119; *In Catilinam* IV.16. See *Philippics* IV and VI *passim*.
43. See R. Gardner in Cicero, *Pro Sestio* (Loeb, 1958), 302–4; Wirszubski 1950: 93–4.
44. *De Officiis* II.73; Schofield 1995: 77–81.
45. Sallust, *Jug.* 31.18–20, and *Hist.* 1.55.11 and 3.48.27.
46. *De Officiis* I.13, 22, 50–1, 153, and II.13–14; *Laws* I.49; *De Inventione* I.2; *De Oratore* I.30–1; *Pro Sestio* 90–2.
47. *De Officiis* II.13–14; *Laws* I.49, 352.
48. Unlike its Greek equivalent (*to kathekon*), *officium* here refers not only to appropriate actions but also to roles (e.g. consul) and relationships (e.g. friendship) (*CGR* 505–6; Brunt 1975: 15).
49. EB 230; Wirszubski 1950: 107.
50. Ulpian, in *Digest* 1.4.1. This passage, known as *lex regia*, was hotly debated in the European Middle Ages: could the people reclaim their powers?
51. Horace, *Odes* III.3; Virgil, *Aeneid* I.1–7 and IV.345–7.
52. Dio Cassius (*c*.150–235 CE; EB 232); Aelius Aristides (*c*.120–89 CE; EB 326).
53. *NE* 190; EB 431–3.
54. Ironically, this term derived, via Hegel, from Cicero's generic term for the state.
55. *OHR* 190; Polybius, *Hist.* VI.17.2–3.
56. *CGR* 618, 629–31. See P. W. Duff, *Personality in Roman Private Law* (Cambridge: Cambridge University Press, 1938).
57. 'True philosophy' is invoked in *Digest* 1.1.1.
58. Or 'to attribute to everyone his own right'; *CGR* 622.
59. *Digest* 1.1.4 and 1.17.32. See below, p. 211.
60. See also the laws of Antoninus Pius: *Digest* 1.6.2, *Institutes* 1.53.
61. *Georgics* VI.562; *Aeneid* IV.230; *OHR* 204.
62. Trapp 2007: 173; Wirszubski 1950: 133.
63. 'Pessimi exempli nec nostri seculi est': EB 252. The case in question was against Christians. During his trial in 257 Cyprian, a Christian bishop, remarked that 'by

an excellent and beneficial provision of your laws you have forbidden any to be informers': *NE* 260. See also *CAH* xi.217, and the emperor Hadrian, in *NE* 17.

64. Seneca to Nero: *On Mercy* 1.3.5–4.1 and 1.5.1.

65. 'It was considered all right publicly to entitle Caesar "God", provided it happened in the provinces' (Hopkins 1979: 204).

66. Veyne 1990; *CAH* xi. 210–11. For Hellenistic examples, see Ehrenberg 1969: 160, 162, 175, 178; *CAH* vii/1(2). 63, 66, 71, 74, 82–3; G. J. D. Aalders, *Political Thought in Hellenistic Times* (Amsterdam: Hakkert, 1975), 22–4.

67. See Trapp 2007: 215–57; Wirszubski 1950: 144–7. Stoicism offered 'a common ideological field, a common language of political thought and behaviour' (Shaw 1985: 49).

68. *Meditations* 4.12, trans. Hammond (adapted).

69. *Georgics* I.506–7, II.458–514, 532–4, IV.130–4. On the virtues of farming, see the Stoics Musonius Rufus and Dio of Prusa: *CGR* 602, 606.

70. Brunt 1975: 9; Trapp 2007: 221, 256.

71. Men should be won over by reason, not blows (toleration decree of 362; Dvornik 1966: ii. 20). The non-Christian Themistius (*c.* 317–88) told the emperor Jovian (r. 363–4) that to make one form of worship compulsory is 'to deprive man of a power which has been granted to him by god' (EB 379).

10

Graeco-Roman Humanism

The idea of the 'unity of mankind' was developed under the Roman empire, in both its republican and monarchical modes. This was originally a Greek idea. It arose out of the way Greeks thought, and the way they saw their own culture in relation to other people (Baldry 1965). In most cultures, people assigned to their own ethnic and cultural group characteristics which set them apart from other peoples. Many (perhaps most) Greeks also thought they were special. Herodotus said that Greekness rested upon 'shared blood, shared language, shared religion and shared customs'.[1]

The Hippocratic writings, on the other hand, ascribed differences in temperament to climate and political institutions, regardless of whether one is Greek or foreign (*EG* 164–5). There was, therefore, no inherent reason why other peoples should not acquire the virtues possessed by the Greeks. Some went further: 'by nature we are all at birth in all respects equally capable of being both barbarians and Greeks' (Antiphon, in *EG* 244; Kerford 1981: 114). According to Aristotle, however, 'the Greek race' alone combines energy with intelligence; 'it remains free, the best organised politically, and capable of ruling everyone else if it were one state' (*Politics* 1327b22–34). Non-Greeks are like slaves, fit to be ruled by Greeks (*Politics* 1252b5–10). He too ascribed such differences to climate, but he made no mention of a capacity of non-Greeks to develop out of their inferior status.

Greeks in general seem to have assumed that the generically human was in some ways the prior category. For Greek poets and thinkers, from Homer to Euripides, from Heraclitus to Plato, the group under discussion was as a rule just 'mortals'. Their moral and philosophical reflections were based upon what it means to be 'human (*to anthrōpinon*)'. Society and the state were conceptualized and discussed as *human* phenomena; discussion of the unique merits of the polis was based upon analysis of human conditions, not as something that was peculiar to the Greeks. The focus was on what *humans* can or should expect of one another; on why *humans* form poleis. As Protagoras put it, 'the human being (*anthrōpos*) is the measure of all things, of things that are, that they are, of things that are not, that they are not'.[2]

This humanist universalism underlay the arguments of Socrates and Plato. Socrates argued at his trial that what he had been teaching was 'human wisdom' (*anthrōpinē sophia; Apology* 20d). Plato's argument in the *Republic* was about the human species; he argued from the human condition; what he said was meant to be relevant not just for Greeks but for the whole human race (*Republic* 473d). 'Is not justice a human virtue (*anthrōpeia aretē*)?' (335c). (It is difficult to see how one *could* have a *philosophical* discussion about the characteristics of a race. This may be why there is hardly a trace of nationalism in early modern European political philosophy.)

Humanist universalism was implicit in Greek science: there are moral principles inherent in the cosmos, which are therefore common to all humans (see above, p. 136). As Aristotle put it: 'there is, as everyone senses, by nature a common standard of justice and injustice, even if men have made no society and no contract with one another'.[3]

But did this 'human' include females? In Homer and the fifth-century tragic plays, females played a prominent part.[4] Plato envisaged them as philosopher-rulers. Slaves, on the other hand, were tacitly ignored in discussions of 'the human'.[5] (Perhaps this was why classical Greek culture was so nearly swept away by Christianity.)

Humanist universalism was expressed in a deliberately provocative way by Diogenes the Cynic (*c.* 400–323 BCE).[6] He it was who introduced cosmopolis, the city of the universe: 'asked where he was from, he said: "[I am] a citizen of the universe" '.[7] His pupil Crates said he was 'a citizen of Diogenes': 'I don't have one country as my refuge, nor a single roof, but every land has a city and a house ready to entertain me'.[8] This sidelined family, nation, and polis.

Zeno (*c.* 333–262 BCE), the founder of Stoicism (he had been taught by Crates), developed this into a more general and explicit principle: 'we should not live in *poleis* (states) and *dēmoi* (localities), each separated by its peculiar system of justice, but should regard all men as fellow-inhabitants and fellow-citizens; and there should be one way of life and one cosmos' (Plutarch, in EB 7, adapted). This (according to Plutarch) was Zeno's 'one main point'. Chrysippus, the leading Stoic of the late third century BCE, saw cosmopolis as the only true community; in his view, it consists not of all men, but of 'gods and sages wherever they may be' (in *CHP* 768).

This must be seen against the background of the Macedonian conquest of mainland Greece, which brought the independence of most poleis to an end, and Alexander's conquests. These brought people from the Adriatic to the Aral Sea into a single Greek-speaking cultural unit (*oikoumenē*: the inhabited world). Alexander himself (a pupil of Aristotle) is said to have argued for 'oneness of mind (*homonoia*)' between peoples.[9] It is said that he deplored those (such as Aristotle, indeed) 'who advised him to treat the Greeks as friends and the barbarians as enemies'.[10] Plutarch (46–120 CE) portrayed Alexander as someone who 'believed he had a mission from god to harmonize men generally...He drew men together by appeal to principle (*logos*), not force of arms'. He wanted everyone to share each others' customs, and to 'consider the whole inhabited world their country'.[11]

GLOBALIZATION

The Roman empire, which on a good day extended from the Irish Sea to the Euphrates, once again created conditions in which such ideas could have political meaning.[12] Diodorus Siculus (active *c.* 60–30 BCE) praised the Romans for attempting 'to bring the whole of mankind, which is one in mutual affinity though divided in space and time, into a single system and under one comprehensive view' (EB 287–8).

The most original contribution of Stoicism to Roman political thought was this idea that human beings comprise a single worldwide society: cosmopolis. This way of thinking became widespread under the principate. The world came to be seen as a unity with Rome as its centre.[13] The globe itself became a popular symbol.[14] Virgil hailed Rome as an empire 'without limits in space or time' (*Aeneid* I.279). He celebrated the economic advantages of globalization, put agriculture and the exchange of commodities into a global context, and recounted with particular delight the various species of plants and trees grown all over the world. The empire parallels the natural diversity of fruits and animals (*Georgics* II.83–135). Pliny the Younger (d. *c.*113 CE) referred again to the comparative advantage of global commerce and a division of labour between regions. He praised the emperor Trajan for connecting 'East and West so closely by mutual commerce that all nations can learn from each other what exports each can offer and what imports each of them needs'.[15]

PAX ROMANA

But it was above all the *political* advantages of Roman rule that were uppermost in people's minds. As the usually rather cynical Epictetus put it, 'Caesar seems to secure us a world of deep peace' (EB 315).

The political culture of the Romans was unusually inclusive: they were willing to extend citizenship—and membership of the senate—to people from different parts of the empire. As their historian Livy (59 BCE–17 CE) put it, the Romans were 'a diverse people made up from earliest times of many immigrants from different backgrounds'.[16] A freed slave could become a Roman citizen; a freedman's son could become a magistrate. 'Neither the sea nor the wide space of intervening land prevents any man from becoming a citizen; with [Rome], there is no division between Asia and Europe, but everything is set out in the open for everyone to enjoy' (Aelius Aristides, in EB 324).

Rome had a unique capacity for absorbing not only foreign individuals but whole foreign communities into her political system. 'The two guiding principles of Roman policy were incorporation and alliance' (Scullard 1980: 146). Citizenship was first extended to neighbouring towns. Latins who migrated to Rome could become full citizens. But 'far more important as a means of creating new Roman citizens was the incorporation of entire Italian communities as citizens' with private civil rights, though without the vote (*OHR* 28). Some were bound by treaty as 'federated cities', others left formally independent as 'free cities'. These were allowed 'full independence in civil and ordinary internal affairs', with their own magistrates, councils, and assemblies. They were formally subject to Rome only in foreign affairs.[17] The Roman empire made a point of demanding of its allies troops, rather than money, thus making them party to Rome's conquests. As Aelius Aristides said, referring to the empire as a whole, cities are kept loyal 'from within themselves... the great and influential in each city garrison it for [Rome] themselves' (EB 325).

After the 'social war' with the Italian cities (98–91 BCE), Roman citizenship was extended to the whole of Italy. Out of this came 'a unified Italy that soon became Romanised' (*CCRR* 97). This vastly increased the constituency of 'the Roman people', not so much politically (since most non-Romans could never make it to the vote) as culturally: it brought the families which gave us Lucretius, Cicero, and Virgil into the orbit of Roman allegiance and into membership of the Roman state. The Italians, said Tacitus, 'yield nothing to us in their love for this fatherland' (*Annals* 11.24).

Rome attempted to pursue the same policy in Greece. In 196 BCE she proclaimed herself protector of the liberty of the Greek poleis: their historic right of self-government was guaranteed 'under the protection (*tutela*) of the Roman People' (in Sherwin-White 1973: 187–8). Right up until the third century CE, the empire was a confederation made up of many different 'peoples'.[18] In 212 CE all free inhabitants of the empire were given citizenship. A non-Christian philosopher could defend polytheism on the ground that it corresponded to the diversity between nations. The Roman empire allows each nation and each city to worship its own gods and observe its own laws.[19]

Such a non-nationalist approach to inter-state affairs had been endorsed by the poet Ennius (239–169 BCE) as early as the first half of the second century.

Quoting Hannibal,[20] he said: 'any man who smites our enemy shall be, so far as I am concerned, a Carthaginian, whoever he is, and whatever his country'.[21] Tacitus contrasted the successful Roman policy of incorporation with the failed imperial projects of Sparta and Athens, who treated those they conquered as aliens: 'but our founder Romulus was wise enough to treat many peoples as enemies one moment, citizens the next'.[22]

COSMOPOLIS

The Roman Stoics developed further the idea that there are two types of human community: the polis or state of one's birth, and cosmopolis, the community of all rational beings in the universe—humans and gods (or god). Roman Stoics thought that the things most fundamental to human beings are reason (*logos*) and moral choice (*prohaeresis*), and that these are things which all humans share. There exists a universal society, not defined by race or location, place of birth, or citizenship. What really matters is one's membership of this world community. This is more important than the city you live in or the state you belong to.

This idea was only found in Graeco-Roman culture. The subsequent Christian and Muslim ideas of a universal community of true believers similarly transcended race and statehood, but demanded more in the way of specific beliefs and practices as a condition of membership, and so became, from a cosmopolitan point of view, less than universal societies.

Seneca (*c.* 4 BCE–65 CE), the most influential Roman Stoic, said that we belong at one and the same time to two communities: first, the 'truly common society, which contains both gods and men', and secondly the society we are born into, for example Athens or Carthage (EB 234). He called these two *res publicae*, implying that cosmopolis too was in some sense a political society.[23]

This idea of cosmopolis was formulated in an especially original way by Cicero, writing during the late republic (above, pp. 189–90). Though not himself a Stoic, he drew widely on Stoic ideas. Cicero explored these issues more systematically and more deeply than any other thinker. In him, for the first and only time, cosmopolis became an integral part of a fully worked-out political philosophy.

The gods have given us the whole world as 'a common home and fatherland'; one can recognize oneself as 'a citizen of the whole world as of a single city'.[24] This arose, he argued, out of the very nature of human society and moral obligation. Cicero, like the Greeks before him (above, p. 136), deduced social and political norms from the nature of human beings (*Laws* I.27–31), but with new consequences. For justice and morality, which, as Plato taught, are to be pursued for their own sake and not for any advantages they bring (above, p. 154), are based upon 'men's solidarity with one another...and affection for the human race (*coniunctio inter homines hominum...ipsa caritas generis humani*)'. Friends, family, citizens, 'and finally everyone (since we want to be one human community) is to be considered for their own sake (*propter se expetendi*)'. Such affection arises, from 'the moment we are conceived', in parents' love for their children, and all the ties of family. Yet love (*caritas*) 'gradually seeps outwards, first to blood-relations and in-laws, then to friends, neighbours, then to fellow-citizens...and finally it embraces the whole human race'. One may say, therefore, that human nature has an inborn 'civil and democratic quality, which the Greeks call "politikon"'. This human 'affection and association' is what provides the emotional incentive for moral action. Cicero, then, believed in the fundamental unity of the human race: all humans share reason and the capacity for language; they resemble one another as much as do members of any other class of things. Similarly, the Roman general Marius (above, p. 184) had said 'I believe in one common nature of all men' (Sallust, *Jugurthine War* 85.15). In other words, the universal society is based on human nature, just as Aristotle had said of the polis.[25]

This argument was based on the Stoic doctrine of *oikeiosis* (affiliation, or familiarization), according to which our natural affections can be extended to ever-wider groups.[26] We can extend the natural affection and closeness, which we feel for family and friends, to others, both to fellow-citizens and, ultimately, to all human persons. This is because we do have real connections with these wider categories, sharing with them what is most constitutive of our own personality—*logos* (reason) and the capacity for virtue. This was a markedly similar idea to Confucius' notion of humaneness and Mozi's idea of universal caring (above, pp. 104, 107).

In *On Duties*, his final statement on political thought, Cicero drew out the practical impplications of this. The first principle (*principium*) of human society is 'what is found in the association of the whole human species (*in universi generis humanae societate*)': that is to say, 'reason and speech'. These are what distinguish us most from other animals and 'join men together in a kind of natural community'. Within this 'widest society of men as such, all with all', we should preserve common ownership of those things 'which nature has produced for the common use of men' (such as water and the coastline: *Digest* 1.1). Other things are differently assigned by the laws of states. Next come associations of race, tribe, and language. Then there is the (city-)state (*civitas*); here 'forum, sanctuaries, walkways, roads, laws, rights, judges, voting' are held in common. There is, finally, a still closer bond within family and household; here everything is held in common.

Cicero made two new points in *On Duties*. He inserted a further category of association, namely friendship based on shared moral values. This, he says, is the 'firmest and most outstanding' human group. Secondly, he insisted—no doubt because of the political crisis he was living through (above, pp. 184–5)—that the society which we hold dearest of all is the state (*res publica*): 'parents, children, friends are dear, but our native country (*patria*) includes all forms of affection for everybody (*omnes omnium caritates*).' A good man is prepared to die for his country (*De Officiis* I.50–8; III.69).

Epictetus (*c.* 60–*c.* 140 CE), a committed Stoic less affected by Roman tradition than Cicero, said that you are 'first a human being' and 'in addition, a citizen of the cosmos'. You do also have domestic and civic roles; these carry specific duties (2.10.1–10). But the most important system (*sustema*) is the one which consists of men and gods (1.9.4). This means, he explained, that you only choose what is good for the whole (the cosmos).

For Epictetus, membership of the cosmos had a more personal meaning: one's own sufferings—and he had plenty—are made comprehensible, even meaningful, when one can see that they are necessary for the well-being of the whole. The drive of Epictetus' thought is not so much that all humans belong to a single community and therefore potentially to a single state, but rather that our membership of the cosmos, though it goes far beyond politics, should be regarded as no less significant than membership of a polis. You should look on the cosmos as you would on your own city-state. Cosmic 'political' values are in fact what we call moral values: 'political' obligation here became moral obligation.

'What is a human being? Part of a city (*polis*); first the one that consists of gods and humans, and after this the one that is called closest to (the first), which is a small copy of the universal one' (*Disc.* 2.5.27). Here the contrast is between cosmopolis, on the one hand, and the *Roman empire* (not any old polis), on the other. The empire is 'closest to', 'a small copy of', cosmopolis; yet there is no question of the empire being some kind of realization of cosmopolis in the actual world we live in. Plutarch thought that Alexander the Great had actually *implemented* Zeno's idea of a single cosmos under a common law, in which people of all nationalities would be treated equally.[27] But Roman Stoics did not equate cosmopolis with the Roman empire; they did not see the latter as an expression of the former.

This reflects the detachment of philosophers from the Roman state (Trapp 2007: 256; above, pp. 197–8). They were perhaps all too aware of the Roman state's dependence on brute force, which comes out time and again in Epictetus. Here too, then, the empire seems to have been viewed, even by its most loyal subjects, not as an ideal but as the least bad deal going. Marcus Aurelius, who, despite his office, was more Stoic than Roman, was deeply influenced by Epictetus. He deduced from the rational and political nature of humans that we are citizens of the *cosmos*. This is, therefore, 'as it were a polis' (*Meditations* 4.2, 4). On one occasion Marcus did refer to *Rome*, but not necessarily the Roman empire, as his polis: 'my nature is rational and political; my polis and fatherland as [Marcus Aurelius] is Rome, as a human being it is the cosmos'. Only what is advantageous to these communities (*poleis*) is advantageous to me (*Meditations* 6.44). It is possible that here Marcus did not differentiate between Rome as city and Rome as empire. Even so, no other Roman thinker of this period spoke of the Roman empire in this way, as a polis.

The empire thus lacked philosophical status and moral meaning. The community with which philosophers identified themselves was cosmopolis, not the empire (Trapp 2007: 232–3). Seneca, when outlining the two cities, made no mention of Rome or the Roman empire. Both Seneca and Epictetus saw their own work as philosophers as a kind of public service, but on behalf of the *cosmic* polity.[28] In this respect, Christians were at an advantage. By seeing the tangible organization of the church as *the* earthly manifestation of the city of god, they could offer a closer relationship between aspiration and reality.

NATURAL LAW

One important consequence of Cicero's thinking was the cosmopolitan nature of morality: right and wrong are laid down, not by local custom, national ethos, or state authority, but by nature itself and our one common master, god, ruler of all.[29] Cleanthes (*c.* 330–231 BCE), head of the Stoic school after Zeno, had spoken of Zeus guiding everything through a 'common reason (*koinos logos*)'; morality is based on 'the common law (*koinon nomon*) of god'.[30] For Cicero, the basis of justice is our natural disposition to love human beings (*Laws* I.43, II.8). This ultimate 'law' follows nature, is common to all human beings, and is immutable. It would be impious to change or diminish it; it cannot be overridden by senate or people; it is the same at Athens as at Rome; it is for all peoples and all times.[31] To disobey it is to depart from human nature.[32] Thus all humans share the same fundamental moral sense, and recognize the same virtues of justice and benevolence. This became almost part of Roman political thought; Tacitus speaks quite casually of a 'human sense of justice (*ius hominum*)'.[33] St Paul observed that non-Jews observe the (moral) law 'by the light of nature', because it is 'inscribed on their hearts' (Rom. 2: 14).

Morality is, according to Cicero, cosmopolitan in the further sense that our obligations extend not only to kinsmen and fellow-citizens but to all human beings. Here we have a classic statement of universalist ethics:

> nature prescribes that a man should consider the interests of another man, whoever he is, for the very reason that he is human ... We are all bound together (*continemur*) by one and the same law of nature ... It is absurd to say, as some do, that one should not deprive a parent or brother for one's own sake, but it is different when it comes to other citizens. (*De Officiis* I.99)[34]

The practical consequences would seem to be no different from those which follow from Kant's categorical imperative.

Cicero drew out the implications of this, in the first place, for the state: to deny legal and social obligations towards one's fellow-citizens would undermine society and the state. But he made it clear that this also imposes moral obligations towards those outside one's own society and state: 'those who say one should take account of fellow-citizens but not of foreigners destroy the common partnership of the human race (*communem humani generis societatem*)'. This would be an act of impiety towards the gods who constituted *societas* among all humans, and also prescribed care for all people, including 'Europe, Asia, Africa'.[35] To confine moral obligation to fellow-citizens is contrary to nature. Seneca similarly said that every human being, simply because he is human, must be treated well (*On Mercy* I.1.3–4 and 18.2).

Cicero's argument, then, is that if one bases morality on human nature, it is logically impossible to stop short of universalism. It amounted to the strongest statement yet—and for a long time to come—of the universalist version of natural law.

Jurists of the second and third centuries CE identified a category of laws which are more specific than natural law, but which nonetheless all peoples have in common: for example, laws about war, boundaries, government ('kingdoms'), private property, commerce, and contracts (*Digest* 1.1.5; *Institutes* 1.2.2). They called this 'the law of [all] peoples' (*ius gentium*)—now known as the law of nations or international law. Their point was that the principles upon which these rules operate are not peculiar to any one race or legal system, but common to every human society.

This Romano-Stoic notion of natural law, and the cognate notion of a law of nations, were to have a profound influence upon Western jurisprudence. Yet the Stoic and Ciceronian notion of a world society was sidestepped by the vast majority of later European political thinkers and statesmen, in the early modern, modern, and above all the post-modern world. It was explicitly rejected by Hobbes; neither Locke nor Rousseau made anything of it. Muslims traditionally draw a fundamental distinction between moral obligations towards believers and unbelievers; Marxists, between what is due to members of one's own class and others; nationalists, between members of one's own nation and others. In the post-Roman world, moral status became contingent on one's faith, class, nationality.

Cicero appears to have believed in the *human species* as a social reality more strongly than anyone before him or, perhaps, after him. But did he see this as, potentially at least, a political unit? He used political language when speaking of it, but only, it seems, metaphorically (like many before and after him). When speaking of obligations towards the whole human race, Cicero used language which could imply political activity: for example, we should 'respect, guard, maintain the common union and fellowship (*conciliationem et consociationem*) of the whole human race' (*De Officiis* I.149). On one occasion he implied that commitment to the universal fatherland must come before everything else: 'in our affections that fatherland must come first in which the phrase "common interest" signifies the universal state (*qua rei publicae nomen universae civitatis est*). We must be prepared to die for it, give ourselves wholly to it, consecrate our all to it' (*Laws* II.5).

Cicero clearly thought that there are moral demands and social loyalties that transcend one's own state. It was, of course, to the *res publica Romana* that he devoted, and eventually sacrificed, his life. But this model patriot of the ancient world was also a cosmopolitan.

NOTES

1. In *OHG* 144. He was the father of social anthropology and comparative politics, and one of the chief sources on the ancient Iranian peoples and their history.
2. Or, 'of things that are as to how they are, and of things that are not as to how they are not': Protagoras, quoted by Plato (*Theaetetus* 152a), trans. *EG* 186 and Kerferd 1981: 85.
3. *Rhetoric* 137b4–6, in Kerford 1981: 113.
4. For the role of women in public life, see Cartledge 1997: 26–31.
5. See Stalley 1983: 107 for Plato on slaves.
6. A pupil of one of Socrates' pupils, he was the originator of the Cynic school, which 'preached the "natural" life and rejected with contempt the customs and conventions of society, thinking nothing of wealth, position, or reputation' (*OHG* 424).
7. Diogenes Laertius, in *CGR* 423.
8. In *CHP* 631, 423: cf. Matt. 8: 20.

9. He was thinking in particular of Greeks and Persians.

10. According to Eratosthenes (a geographer, 275–200 BCE), as reported by Strabo (*c.* 64 BCE–18 CE); Baldry 1965: 169; EB 6.

11. EB 6–8; Baldry 1965: 114; Schofield 1991: 104. Plutarch, perhaps influenced by Stoicism here, went on: 'Alexander added act and deed to the principle (*logos*) of Zeno' (EB 8): in fact, it was Zeno who was influenced by Alexander; Baldry 1965: 126–7.

12. Polybius (*c.* 202–120 BCE), for example, said that, in order to explain how Rome had conquered 'almost everything in the inhabited world', he was writing the first world history (Loeb edn., vol. i. 332, 268; Baldry 1965: 174–5).

13. Augustus entitled his record of his achievements (which was inscribed in Rome and provincial cities for all to read): 'Accomplishments of the divine Augustus, by which he subjected the world to the rule of the Roman people'. Aelius Aristides compared Rome to 'the surface of the globe, which is all men's abode'; she 'receives men from all the earth just as the sea receives the rivers' (EB 324–5).

14. Mattern 1999: 164, 169, 196. The globe featured on coins of the first century BCE. Marcus Aurelius was said to rule 'for the good of the human race' (inscription, in Hopkins 1979: 224).

15. EB 253. Caracalla (r. 212–17 CE) argued the advantage of exchanging Persia's spices and textiles for Rome's metals and manufactures (Fowden 1993: 25).

16. Livy, the main source for early Roman history, in *CCRR* 6. See *OHR* 189.

17. Scullard 1980: 148–9; *OHR* 39; Sherwin-White 1973: 174–5, 187.

18. *OHR* 396; Sherwin-White 1973: 263, 438–9; Celsus, in EB 431–3; Mattern 1999: 5.

19. Celsus, writing *c.*180, in Momigliano 1987: 319. On the same ground, the emperor Julian supported the rights of Jews and wanted to give Jerusalem back to them: ibid. 324–7.

20. Leader of Carthage in the Second Punic War.

21. Quoted by Cicero, *Pro Balbo* 51.

22. *Annals* 11.24; see Cicero, *Pro Balbo* 31 and also 22–7, 30.

23. Such dualism came readily to a culture long familiar with the Platonic contrast between 'the divine realm of immutable Forms' and 'the world of becoming' (*CGR* 560).

24. *De Republica* I.19; *De Natura Deorum* II.154; *Laws* I.61.

25. *De Finibus* V.65–8; *De Officiis* I.107; *Laws* I.29–30; Schofield 1995: 81–2.

26. *CHP* 677–8, 761. There is 'progression from instinctively rooted concern to impartial concern for any human just as such' (Schofield 1995: 82).

27. EB 7–8; Aelius Aristides, in EB 324.

28. Schofield 1991: 93; EB 234, 301, 305, 316; *CGR* 607. See also Epictetus, in EB 313–14; Marcus Aurelius, in EB 320.

29. 'What is right (*ius*) is based not on opinion but on nature': *Laws* I.43.

30. In Aalders 1975: 87; EB 37–8; Phillip Mitsis, 'The Stoic Origin of Natural Rights', in K. Ierodiakonou (ed.), *Topics in Stoic Philosophy* (Oxford: Oxford University Press, 1999), 120–40.

31. This followed 'the Stoic idea that there is a natural law which provides an absolute standard by which to correct human laws' (Griffin 1989: 19).
32. *De Republica* III.33. This passage survives only in the Christian philosopher Lactantius.
33. *Histories* 3.51. See also Seneca, *On Mercy* 1.18.2.
34. Cicero used *humanitas* to refer both to the condition of being human and to humane conduct. Lactantius (*c.* 250–317) equated humanitas with Christian love (*agapē*) (EB 463–4).
35. E.g. *De Republica* I.19; *Laws* I.61; *De Natura Deorum* II.154, 165; *De Officiis* III.27–8, I.22.

11

The Kingdom of Heaven
and the Church of Christ

The early Christians had few overtly political ideas.[1] But their teachings were brimming with suggestions for society and the state. Interpretations of the Christian message came to vary wildly, from political quietism to revolution, from sacred monarchy to democracy, and from liberalism to socialism.

Jesus of Nazareth was born and conducted his campaign in Galilee, an area of Palestine populated by Jews but different in ethos from Judaea and Jerusalem. Judaea had been brought under Roman rule from 6 CE; Galilee remained under indirect Roman rule until the Jewish revolt of 66 CE. It produced several rebel movements during and after Jesus' lifetime; in 6 CE Judas the Galilean led the Jewish 'zealots' in a bid for political independence (Vermes 1973: 42–8). Expectations of divine intervention on behalf of the Jewish 'remnant' (above, p. 64) circulated in mystical movements, such as the Essenes.

The synoptic gospels of Matthew, Mark, and Luke portray Jesus as a charismatic healer, teacher, and leader.[2] He was typical of charismatic Judaism, though perhaps better at it than others (Vermes 1973: 58–82). His originality lay in his idea of the 'Kingdom of Heaven' (*basileia tōn ouranōn*: lit. of the heavens) (Meier 1994: 237 ff.). This was the focus of his teaching and activity. These mutually reinforced each other (as they did in Confucius' case). This Kingdom was supposed to end oppression and reward the virtuous, and it was to be expected within the lifetime of his audience. Those who 'believed' and 'followed' him would be members of it, those who did not would be excluded. In this Kingdom, god the father will reign unopposed, the devil, and with him all suffering and evil, having been finally vanquished.

This idea was original in several ways. 'The Kingdom of Heaven' (or 'of god') was not a term 'widely used in previous Jewish writings or traditions' (Meier 1994: 452; Baron 1952: 68–73). Jesus' idea of it combined future and present in a new way; it was coming but it was also here. God himself was supposed to initiate it, and there were clear signs that this would happen soon. It was being brought into existence here and now, especially through the actions of Jesus himself, such as healing, exorcism, and the banquet of believers enacted at the Last Supper (Meier 1994: 349–50, 450–4).

The most original part of Jesus' teaching was about what the Kingdom of Heaven meant in terms of personal and social orientation and action. This is what has given his message lasting appeal, despite frustrated hopes for the looked-for metamorphosis. He presented his ideas through stories, similes, his own actions, and countless innuendos. His method of teaching was (like Confucius again) part of the message, and part of his originality.

Nothing approaching Jesus' notion of this Kingdom of Heaven is found in the other cultures which we have examined. It was new even within Judaism. This was, in part, precisely because it excluded all familiar political aspirations, such as the restoration of the Jewish kingdom in all its glory. Spiritual transcendence was seen to be achievable for all in the immediate future; it was signified, and could be hastened, by the simplest of actions. In a peculiarly direct way, divine otherness was brought into the here-and-now.

Jesus had a programme for transforming people's lives in both their moral and their material aspects. How he thought the world should, and could, be changed was different from what we find in other ancient political programmes. Of all the thinkers of antiquity, Jesus merits the name 'revolutionary' as much as any.

This idea of 'the Kingdom of Heaven' may, indeed, be seen as Jesus of Nazareth's original contribution to political thought. Its role in the New Testament has long been understood by biblical scholars and theologians. But it has not been appreciated as a political idea. One only has to read—but who nowadays does?—the gospels to be struck by something unique in ancient political thought, expressed partly in words, partly in actions and atmosphere. But we have been blinded to this, partly by gospel-fatigue and partly by the abuse of Jesus' ideas in much later so-called Christian thought.

Putting it bluntly, Jesus was saying that the perfect society is both in the process of being brought about, and will be with us very soon. For evidence, he said, look around you: at the healing and exorcizing of the sick, the communion and poverty of his followers, and various signs in nature. Of course, it all depends on the unknowable disposition of god (Yahweh).

The synoptic gospels are full of the countryside, lakes, hills, fishing, and harvesting (Vermes 1973: 48–9). Much of Jesus' teaching is about social behaviour. His target audience were the sick and the poor and those despised in Jewish society. He is often among crowds and is 'moved to pity' by 'the sight of the people' (Matt. 9: 36). Wealth is incompatible with membership of the Kingdom; if a rich man wants to follow Jesus, he must give away his possessions.[3] In general, whether or not you help those in need will determine whether or not you get into the Kingdom.[4]

The ideas of Jesus were certainly revolutionary in the Graeco-Roman world. What set Christianity apart from other ethical systems, such as Stoicism, was that it swept its hearers into an unfolding story.[5] To its severe moral demands, it added psychological excitement. It combined a radical ethic with the immediacy of Yawhism: act now, final judgement may come any time (Rom. 13: 11–13; Rev. 22: 20). Indeed, the extreme ethical demands only made sense (and, I suppose, only can make sense) in this extreme eschatological context.

Christianity, especially as it evolved under the influence of St Paul, was no less revolutionary in a Jewish context. Judaism had long been attractive to non-Jews disillusioned with Greek religion. Christianity broke the link between Yahwism and Jewish nationality. The 'good news' is for all humans. God 'made every nation of men from one source' (Acts 17: 26); Christ 'made [Jews and non-Jews] into one common humanity', as fellow-citizens (*sumpolitai*) (Eph. 2: 15–16, 19). The rejection of Judaism was a rejection of all racial barriers (Boyarin 1994).

Still more radically, St Paul broke the link between Yahwism and the Mosaic law. This was not now seen as the means to salvation; indeed, it had no spiritual significance whatsoever. Jesus himself did not go this far. Christians detribalized monotheism, but at the same time they carried over into their new cosmopolitanism the sense and praxis of belonging to a community with a destiny. This could (bizarrely) dovetail with the Roman-imperial project.

The social revolution outlined by Jesus, and to some degree practised in early Christian communities, extended to the family itself. In the Kingdom of Heaven family relationships are unimportant (Matt. 10: 37–8, 19: 29; Luke 14: 26); therefore one has the same obligations to everyone regardless of kinship. Marriage itself, though accepted as legitimate, was not exactly encouraged. Some early Christians regarded all sexual acts as intrinsically bad.[6] Sexual acts outside a strictly monogamous relationship carried the stigma of ritual pollution. Early Christian culture produced fevered minds and restless bodies.

The long-term effect of all this was to reduce the moral status of clan and tribe, as well as of nation. This went against the ethics of every other civilization. It may have been decisive in shaping modern Western civilization. Revenge and physical violence of any kind were forbidden: 'if someone slaps you on your right cheek, turn and offer him your left...love your enemies' (Matt. 5: 39, 44). This too ran counter to the ethos of clan and tribe, indeed of the state itself. The first Christians refused to use physical force at all, including military service.[7]

The status of women was also changed. Women are more prominent in the gospels than in other writings of the period.[8] Children were cited as models of humanity (Matt. 18: 1–4; Mark 10: 13–16). In Christian communities women had special roles (Brown 1988: 145–50). Differences of race, status, and gender are all insgnificant: 'there is no such thing as Jew or Greek, no such thing as slave or free, no such thing as male and female, for you are all one in Christ Jesus' (Gal. 3: 28).

More than any other moral code, Jesus' teaching, especially in the Sermon on the Mount (Matt. 5–7), focused on forgiveness and reconciliation. This was presented as a central factor both in the relationship between god and humans, and in relationships between human beings. Jesus insisted that these were complementary: god will only forgive you, if you forgive other people.[9] This may have helped to promote social peace in human societies not based on kinship, and also to generate the degree of social consensus necessary for stable democracy. Islam, by contrast, which was and is clan-friendly and tribe-friendly (Vatikiotis 1987), came to depend more on monarchy or dictatorship in order to outlaw sectional strife.

Jesus' teaching attached special importance to the individual, however socially marginal, hopeless, or just ordinary: every human person is equal in the sight of god. The crucifixion narrative put the individual definitively above the crowd: one individual may be right and everyone else wrong. Christian theory made a single individual, the god-man Jesus Christ, the linchpin of the cosmic story.

Christianity therefore discouraged sacrifice of an individual for the sake of the group. This was a momentous development in political thought. In most cultures and ethical systems—for example, China and Utilitarianism—the needs of the majority may legitimately override the very existence of a given individual. Christianity has been the driving-force behind the emphasis on the individual, which in turn lies behind much talk of human rights. (It should not be assumed that this has always been beneficial.)

'Liberty' was emphasized by Paul as a mark of the true Christian (2 Cor. 3: 17; Gal. 4: 25 and 5: 1). This meant not social or political liberty, but liberty of 'the Spirit': that is, a spontaneous desire to do what is right. (This was the view of liberty developed by Hegel.) But, alongside this teaching about love and forgiveness, there were elements in early Christianity less pleasing to the modern ear. Some of these are in the teachings of Jesus himself. As well as making moving pleas for gentleness and generosity, Jesus made savage verbal attacks on those who refused to believe his teaching, in particular the Pharisees. One side of the portrait is peaceful, the other promises divine violence. Early Christians were similarly bitter in their condemnation of anyone who refused to believe, who abandoned belief, or who just adopted a different interpretation from that of the writer. Paul was particularly vindictive on god's behalf. In this way Christianity created a new form of hatred, discrimination, and conflict.

AFTER JESUS

The moral revolution advocated by Jesus was carried over into the early Christian groups, but gradually it became muted, and to a large extent marginalized. The early Christian communities provided for those in need (Dodds 1965: 137); Christians' unrestrained generosity to one another was noticed by opponents (EB 453). At first, the church in Jerusalem practised communism: everyone had to sell their belongings, 'and they distributed [the proceeds] to everyone according to each person's need' (Acts 2: 45, 4: 32–5). This practice was soon abandoned; but it was revived later in monasticism, in medieval millenarian movements (Cohn 1957), and later in modern Communism and Anarchism. Marxism also reproduced the psychological thrill of a promised new world order. On a more moderate note, St Paul thought the Christian ethic required economic equality (*isotēs*) among believers: people should give according to their means to meet the needs of other members, who will later reciprocate (2 Cor. 8: 14).

Early Christians rejected all social distinctions within their communities: you should treat the poor, lower-class person with the same respect as you treat the wealthy, upper-class person (James 2: 1–13). Each believer, however humble, had his or her special function in the complex society that constituted the body of Christ on earth. Paul used the comparison between the Christian society and the human body (see below) to explain how a diversity of functions (healing, teaching, and so on), which was necessary for the body to function, gave added strength: 'For just as the body is one and has many limbs, and all the body's limbs, though many, constitute one body, so too is Christ'. Paul wanted to demonstrate that each kind of ability is useful in its own way. And in the process he made the characteristically Christian point that not only is each type of worker of equal importance, but the 'less honourable' parts of the body and of society have 'special honour'.[10]

There are, however, differences in tone and emphasis between the teachings of Jesus (insofar as it is possible to reconstruct these) and what is found in the earliest surviving Christian writings, St Paul's Epistles (from the mid-first century onwards). Whether this involved a mutation in basic principles has been the subject of intense dispute. The Epistles reek of confined urban spaces. They still speak of 'the kingdom of god', but one senses a shift in meaning. The talk is now of salvation from 'sin' by means of 'faith' in Jesus' expiatory death and resurrection:[11] this metaphysical concept is the origin of 'are you saved?' The 'love' of god is now conditional on 'faith in Christ'. This meant not only a complete change of life, as Jesus certainly taught, but also accepting as true certain beliefs, including the historical 'fact' that Jesus rose from the grave.

HOW DO WE KNOW?

What distinguished Christianity from Stoicism, Platonism, and other well-intentioned schools of philosophy was not so much ethics as the view of how we know the truth (Dodds 1965: 120–1). Christianity claimed much more precise and certain knowledge about god, about the life, death, and resurrection of Jesus, and about human destiny. Christianity was unique in the importance it attached to 'believing' the right things ('orthodoxy') as a precondition for salvation. It was for this reason that Christians were so earnest in telling everyone what they 'knew' and persuading others to believe it too; and, later, in persecuting those of different beliefs.

The 'facts', on acceptance of which salvation was said to depend, were supposed to be 'known' through a revelation from god, first in the Hebrew scriptures, and then in the teachings and actions of Jesus Christ and the first apostles. This second set of 'facts' was recorded both in the writings which became the New Testament, and in the day-to-day teaching of the church, which generally came to mean the church leaders, notably bishops, and, in cases of disagreement, councils of bishops. One basis for confidence in the truth of such statements is if you trust those who teach them.

Jesus himself may have indicated something of this kind, when he said that his message was 'hidden from the learned and wise' but 'revealed to the simple' (Luke 9: 21). Human beings ought to be open to new ideas ('seek and you shall find'; Matt. 7: 7), so that—but only so that—they can discover these particular new truths. There *was* dialogue in the gospels, but not open-ended discussion, rather demonstration (sometimes quite tendentious) of the superiority of one point of view (compare the behaviour of Socrates in Plato's dialogues). Paul too made an issue of his simple preaching, not relying (as he put it) on 'subtle arguments', for faith depends not on human wisdom but on 'the power of god' (1 Cor. 2: 4–5). Paul spoke of what 'god has revealed to us through the Spirit', which can *only* 'be judged in the light of the Spirit' (1 Cor. 2: 10–15).

This seems to imply that one seeks to persuade people by the feelings produced in them by the message whose truth is in question. This is obviously intuitive knowledge. The thought-processes involved may be seen as a form of rhetoric (in which St Augustine later excelled). Some Islamic thinkers later also took this approach. Christianity posited a unique category of religious knowledge, which they called 'faith', and they considered this both certain, *and* beyond the ordinary processes of the human mind. It meant accepting cosmic and historical facts as true without further question. To question them was thought sinful. The New Testament and other early Christian writings repeatedly suggested that what determines whether or not someone 'believed' was their inner (one might call it 'moral') disposition. It is terrifying to have salvation depend on such belief: those who do not believe go to hell.

One consequence of this approach was that religious knowledge, and therefore conversion, did not depend on education or intellectual training, as Stoic philosophy did. It was, therefore, open to all ranks of society on equal terms (Dodds 1965: 120). From the second century onwards, nonetheless, a few Christians began to see 'Greek philosophy' as a legitimate pathway to Christian faith, a 'schoolmaster' which brought 'Hellenism to Christ', just as the Judaic law brought the Jews.[12] The problems and implications of this approach were to form a significant part of Western philosophy.

Self-centred yet a great personality, St Paul made his own mystical experience the touchstone for salvation. He wrote as someone who has just discovered the elixir of life and wants to share it with everyone. He invoked his personal encounter with 'the risen Jesus Christ' (pointing the way towards the 'evangelical' tradition). For Paul, mystical experience is the new norm. His writings are packed with mental anguish; he suffered physical pain and several accidents. Jesus himself is, frankly, transformed into a creature of the imagination (as occurred with Muhammad in Islam).

This had a profound effect on ethical teaching, and indeed on the very notion of ethics. Paul put all ethics into the same category as the Jewish law, and dismissed both as secondary to what really mattered to him: a correct idea of god and his ways. Sometimes ethics is spoken of almost as an interim measure, something to fill in your time while waiting for the Second Coming. From reading Paul, you would hardly guess the content of the Sermon on the Mount, nor the personality of Jesus in the synoptic gospels.

Through this tortuous, often forced, reasoning (especially in the Epistle to the Romans, which inspired Martin Luther), sunshine occasionally breaks through. There is an exultant sense of community. Paul shows genuine concern for the practicalities of living in a community. There are pleas for mutual respect, courtesy, modesty, gentleness among Christians.[13] Despite his principled opposition to the belief that salvation depends on legal observance, Paul urged church members to respect each other's views on dietary law.[14] Christianity could lead to both tolerance and intolerance.

Christianity taught many of the same ethical principles as Stoicism. It combined a programme for the ascetic ascent of the soul in the Platonic manner, with beneficence towards the poor, such as we find in ancient Egypt (above, p. 27). It contained elements of humanism. Jesus insisted that the human person (*anthrōpos*) is more important than rules and regulations, even when these are thought to come from god (Matt. 12: 12; Mark 2: 27). You have to make it up with other people before you can have legitimate dealings with god (Matt. 5: 23–6). The fact that, according to most Christian teaching, god had become human in the person of Jesus Christ, could be seen as elevating all of humanity (*ECF* 81, 102).[15]

RITUAL

What differentiated Christianity was that its ethical teaching was integrated into a communal and ritual system. Perhaps the principal change between the teaching of Jesus and the functioning of the early church was that the promise of the kingdom of god was transformed into the creation through baptism of what was believed to be a new species of human being: a being purged of past errors and intrinsically capable of living in a way no ordinary mortal could. This was manifested in extreme forms of self-sacrifice, such as giving all one's possessions to the poor, celibacy, and martyrdom, the supreme 'witness' to the truth of the Christian faith: 'the blood of the martyrs is the seed of faith'.[16] In the Eucharist, the heavenly banquet was both prefigured and realized in the 'love (*agapē*)' among participants. Forgiveness was ritualized in the sacrament of penance.

In these and other ways, the kingdom promised by Jesus was transformed into a system of social and ritual practices, a programme of spiritual development. This was a particular type of ritual system, in which symbols were supposed not only to signify something, but to accomplish what they signified. All this was no doubt one way of realizing what Jesus had promised, but everyone knew that it left a lot out. Christians transferred much of the reality of the kingdom to the end time when Jesus would come again.[17]

THE CHURCH

The Christian church (*ekklēsia*) was the other partial realization of the Kingdom following Jesus' death. Christianity had the further advantage over other well-meaning philosophies that it presented an alternative functioning community, and on an worldwide scale. *Ekklēsia* referred both to the biblical notion of 'those called out' by god from the world of sin, and to an 'assembly' as in self-governing cities. Christians used it both of local groups, small enough to meet together to celebrate the Eucharist, and of the whole community of believers throughout the world (Goguel 1964: 26, 156). They saw themselves as the true 'remnant' of ancient Israel, the select few chosen by god, Yahweh's new witnesses to humanity.

Everywhere they went, the first Christians formed parallel societies: 'they live in their own countries, but as aliens; they share all duties like citizens and suffer all disabilities like foreigners; every foreign land is their country, and every country is foreign to them'.[18] It could be claimed that, despite differences in language, Christians in Germany, Spain, and Egypt all believed and practised the same traditions (Irenaeus, in *ECF* 92). Early Christianity was most unusual in combining ritual, ethics, and a belief system with a sense of membership in a new kind of social group, separate from the mainstream political and legal order, and with its own method of self-management. Their association paralleled, and even extended beyond, the Roman empire. Unlike Judaism, the Christian church could not be fitted into the Roman political order as a distinct 'people' with their own customs. The church had no territorial confines; its claims were universalist and exclusive.

For Christians, their church was more than a means of organization and association. It was said to have been founded by the risen Christ himself as the essential instrument for spreading his message. It had a cosmic and eschatological role as 'a prophetic but imperfect prototype' (Campenhausen 1969: 70) of the communion of saints in heaven. If one were to be saved, one had to be a member of the church. Excommunication did not involve physical coercion but was still a terrible punishment for a true believer. This created a new division in human society, this time between believers and unbelievers, supposedly prefiguring the ultimate division between saved and damned.

The church's cosmic status was most vividly expressed by saying that it was 'the body of Christ', the form taken in the present era by Christ himself. This analogy between society and the human body was to play an important part in European political thought (Kantorowicz 1957). Thus, for Christians, the *church* had at least as close a relationship to divinity as the sacred monarchical *state*—whether in Egypt, Mesopotamia, or China—had for its subjects.

In view of the ideal order which it was supposed to represent and prefigure, the church had to have certain visible qualities. First of these was unity (Cyprian, *Epistolae* 1076): on this the very credibility of the Christian message was held to depend (Campenhausen 1969: 99). The church was to be a community (*koinōnia*) of hearts and minds (Dodds 1965: 136–7). The repeated pleas for unanimity (*homonoia*: unity of mind) and the fierce condemnations of strife and schisms,[19] must be seen in the context of relatively unstructured, fragile groupings of believers. Unity meant above all an interior mindset: people must 'think the same thing, having the same love, together in their souls (*sumpsuchoi*)' (Phil. 2: 2). For early Christians, it was crucial that, in their attitude and conduct towards one another, members practise the supreme social virtue of their faith—love (*agapē, caritas*).

From earliest times, however, the Christian church suffered crippling divisions among members. These became most entrenched, and proved impossible to resolve, when they were about the content of the Christian faith. It was considered of the utmost importance that Christians throughout the world hold the same beliefs; this was part of the evidence that what they believed had been revealed by god. And yet the very nature of Christian epistemology—based, as we have seen, on intuition—made this impossible.

It was partly for this reason that, as early as the late first century, exponents of what would become the Catholic version of Christianity identified the church as a kind of public sphere, requiring order, discipline, and good governance, like any other organized society. Just two generations after Jesus' death, Clement (bishop of Rome, writing *c.* 96) was also applying the language and norms of Roman political discourse to the church: power (*potestas*), dignity (*honor*), status (*dignitas*), authority (*maiestas*), *fas* (divine right), *ius* (law/ justice).[20] Opposition to the established church leaders was 'tyranny' and 'sedition'.

Overall authority was, from the early second century, assigned to bishops (*episkopoi*: lit. overseers).[21] This proto-Catholic trend was contested by a significant number of early Christian individuals and groups, including the Montanists who believed in a 'new prophecy' which would maintain the charismatic spirit of the early church. The proto-Catholic view was that bishops were the successors of Christ's apostles, so that they, and they alone, had uncontaminated access to what Christ had really taught, and inherited Christ's own authority to forgive sin and to adjudicate. But the values of the gospel must also be upheld in the Christian community: those in authority have to behave like servants (sing. *diakonos*) (Matt. 20: 25–7; Luke 22: 24–7).

THE STATE

The first Christians saw the state as quite separate from their concerns. Jesus had apparently made the position clear when he authorized payment of (unpopular) taxes to the occupying Roman power with the words 'return to Caesar what is Caesar's and to God what is God's' (Mark 12: 16–17; Luke 20: 25). This established the separation of church from state as once and for all a canonical Christian doctrine. St Paul insisted on the divine origin and divinely ordained purpose of the state as god's servant (*diakonos* again), established by him to punish wrongdoing (Rom. 13: 1–6; 1 Pet. 2: 13–15). Some early Christians saw the Roman empire as a useful prop to social and even moral order, and thanked it for providing a peace which facilitated their own peaceful mission.[22] Others saw it as the agent of the devil.

The church presented itself as an institution with its own leaders and procedures, quite separate from the state. We are so familiar with this idea that we forget what a novelty it was. The church made no territorial claims, but it made moral and legal ones.

As time went by, Christianity showed a remarkable ability to soak up social and political ideas from its environment. In the fourth century it contracted an alliance with the Roman empire. But the absence of any specific political theory from early Christian discourse meant that later generations of Christians did not feel bound to any one model of the state. As the Western Roman empire crumbled, church leaders strove to make the best of whatever social and political conditions confronted them.

NOTES

1. This is presumably why most histories of political thought make little mention of early Christianity, and when they do, resort to clichés. One exception is Henry Chadwick (*CHMPT* 11–20).
2. According to one recent scholar: 'This strange marginal Jew, this eschatological prophet and miracle-worker, *is* the historical Jesus retrievable by modern historical methods applied soberly to the data' (Meier 1994: 1045). We are concerned here with the New Testament as a vehicle of ideas, not as a historical record.
3. Matt. 19: 22–4; Luke 6: 24–6; 1 Tim. 3: 8, 6: 9–10. See also Mark 12: 44, Matt. 6: 26–34, 8: 20–2.
4. Matt. 25: 35–45; *ECW* 54–5; NE 57.
5. See especially 1 Thess. 4: 15–17; 2 Thess. 1: 8–10, 2: 1–12.
6. Brown 1988. Christianity in both East and West has since advocated celibacy as an ideal to which one should aspire.
7. NE 226; *ECF* 156; EB 456–7; *CHMPT* 17.
8. Women are mentioned separately in greetings and moral advice in the Epistles and other early Christian documents; there was a special duty to look after widows.
9. Matt. 6: 12, 14–15; 18: 21–35; similarly the Didache (*c.*100 CE): 'if any man has a quarrel with his friend, let him not join your assembly until they are reconciled' (*ECF* 52).

10. 1 Cor. 12: 4–30; Rom. 13: 1–6; Eph. 4: 11–13. He means that the anus is as important as the hand, the garbage-collector as important as the architect. Clement of Rome used the analogy of army ranks to make the same point (*ECW* 42–3).

11. Paul uses several neologisms as he struggles to express his new idea.

12. Notably Justin Martyr (d. *c.*169) and Clement of Alexandria (fl. *c.* 200). John 1: 9 calls Jesus 'the light which enlightens every man'. See also Irenaeus, in *ECF* 101; Origen, in *ECF* 199; and *ECF* 58–60, 168–9. Gilson thought 'Christian philosophy' began with Justin Martyr (Étienne Gilson, *History of Christian Philosophy in the Middle Ages* (London: Sheed and Ward, 1955), 11–13).

13. Rom. 14: 4–6, 10, 13–16; Ignatius of Antioch (d. *c.*115): 'be patient and gentle with one another as god is with you' (*ECW* 129).

14. We should 'accept as our own burden the tender scruples of weaker men ... Each of us must consider his neighbour and think what is for his good'; Rom. 14: 23–15: 2.

15. Origen (*c.*185–254) said: 'Jesus began a weaving together of the divine and human nature in order that human nature ... might become more divine, not only in Jesus, but also in all who believe in Jesus and try to live as he taught' (*ECW* 226). See also Acts 13: 46–8; 15: 7–9; Irenaeus (bishop of Lyons, late second century), in *ECF* 92.

16. *ECF* 166; Dodds 1965: 132–3.

17. As the late Adrian Hastings put it, 'we were promised the kingdom; what we got was the church' (personal communication).

18. Epistle to Diognetus (*c.*124 CE), in Dodds 1965: 20; see also *ECF* 176, 184, n. 4.

19. See, among many examples, Clement of Rome (*ECW* 24–6); Ignatius (*ECW* 127).

20. Campenhausen 1969: 274 n.; Brown 1988: 192. St Cyprian (bishop of Carthage 248–58) commended *gravitas* and *moderatio*.

21. See e.g. Ignatius (*ECW* 76).

22. Clement of Rome prayed for rulers, especially in their role as providers of peace (*ECF* 35).

12

Themes: Similarities and Differences Between Cultures

We may now ask what ideas were held in common by several cultures, and what the most significant variations between them were.

SACRED MONARCHY

The most widespread idea was undoubtedly sacred monarchy. We have already discussed reasons why sacred monarchy appeared in practically all early civilizations (above, pp. 15–19). It was not quite universal: the Greeks and Romans practised and believed in government by the people.[1] The Graeco-Roman world adopted sacred monarchy when the Roman empire made Christianity its official creed. The earlier mutation of sacred monarchy in Israel, when royalty was ascribed to god, now mutated back again, to make the emperor the new god's representative on earth. This Christian version of sacred monarchy, inherited by Russia, lasted a surprisingly long time. Indeed in China, Russia, the Ottoman empire, Iran, and Japan, sacred monarchy persisted into the early twentieth century. Its abolition was accompanied by cataclysm. In some cases, the successor regimes still face problems of legitimacy.

Kingship seems everywhere to have been tied into religious belief and ritual, kings having a cosmic status. In virtually every case, sacred monarchy was a part of people's view of the world, nature, and the social order. (Yet religion pre-dated monarchy, and several religions had a life of their own under (and after) monarchy.)

There were major differences in the way the king was perceived. In Egypt, Assyria, Israel, and India he was a warrior; in Egypt he was also chief priest; in China he was chief priest and also sage. In Egypt and Mesopotamia he was a shepherd. The king was most closely identified with gods in Egypt. The most elaborate theory of sacred monarchy, and the most long-lived, was the Chinese. There the supreme divine being (Heaven) was an impersonal and impartial force; its 'Mandate' was conditional. The king was seen as a sage who, being in harmony with cosmic and natural forces, ruled by inaction through ministers, and by the performance of essential rituals.

One reason for the prevalence of monarchy in the ancient world, and of democracy in the modern world, may be that in pre-industrial civilizations it was far more difficult to channel public opinion to the centre. Pre-modern republics were small.

THE STATE

In Egypt, Sumer, India, and China an idea of the state came out of sacred monarchy: divinity willed a king; when one king died, the gods would provide another. The state was a religious construct, and existed in heaven independently of its earthly office-bearers (see, for example, above, p. 38). The early European notion of the state also had a religious basis (Kantorowicz 1957). Few ancient peoples distinguished between the sacred and the secular. The Greeks detached the state from religion more than any. In Chinese culture, the state—conceived as the Son of Heaven holding the Mandate of Heaven—was more central to religion and philosophy than it was in any other culture.

Kautilya, by contrast, defined the state in more down-to-earth and secular terms; in fact his definition was remarkably similar to that of Cicero and Sallust (above, pp. 75, 176, 199 n. 4). For the Greeks, the state was the polis (the political community); for the Romans, the res publica (public sphere).

In the discourse of the Near and Middle East, the political was framed in religious language. Political institutions and norms were seen as part of the all-embracing domain of the gods. In India, on the other hand, *artha* (politics and economics) was regarded, at least by Kautilya, as an independent discipline with its own norms and method of enquiry. In China, the political was seen not as a separate sphere but, like the rest of the cosmos and nature, it functioned in ways partly comprehensible to humans. The fact that there was not the same emphasis on the transcendent as in the Middle East perhaps meant that the cosmos, nature, and society were more accessible to human understanding and manipulation.

The most striking feature of sacred monarchy was, in all instances—indeed, in the very nature of the case—the unlimited power of the ruler. However, in every ancient society kings were bound by the religious and moral code of their society. The satisfactory functioning of the forces of nature, and the social order itself, were thought to depend upon the monarch's due performance of his moral and ritual duties.

The sacred monarchies of Egypt, Mesopotamia, Iran, India, and China were all believed to be world states; the deities which these monarchies represented were held to be universal powers. Sacred monarchy tended to sanction global imperialism.

The Jewish Messiah was also programmed to be a world ruler. The republican city-states of Athens, Carthage, and Rome, on the other hand, though they acquired empires, did not aspire to be universal rulers.[2] In practice, Alexander of Macedon (r. 336–323 BCE) (not himself regarded as a sacred monarch by his own people) was the first successful globalizer, paving the way for the Muslim Caliphate.[3]

JUSTICE

The purpose of royal government was, first, to be pleasing to god or heaven, and second, to ensure the well-being of society. These generally entailed are another. Both depended upon the maintenance of justice. Benevolence was universally seen as the essential quality of a ruler. Kautilya gave a uniquely down-to-earth and detailed account of the social and economic responsibilities of a king, arising out of his view that a king's power depends on his tax-base, and that this in turn depends on the socio-economic infrastructure (above, pp. 82–3). In every civilization justice was seen as the central social and political value. But the meaning given to justice varied so greatly across cultures that it can only be treated as a common factor at a high level of abstraction.

In all the cultures we have examined, including Greece, justice referred to a right order of things in both the human and natural domains. It was seen as part of the objective order of reality, inherent in the way things are, championed by the gods. In all cultures, the moral system and its obligations were thought to exist independently of human beings. Disregard of justice would imperil both monarch and realm. Individuals who infringed justice would suffer dire consequences, in either this world or the afterlife, or both. The penalties for infringing justice were most emphatically incurred by whoever was in power or had great wealth (their capacity for injustice being the greatest).

Some Greek thinkers came to the conclusion that the moral law was inscribed in human nature, from which the Stoics developed the idea of a natural moral law. This differed from other views in making justice independent of regime or culture, something common to all peoples and states.

In Egypt, Mesopotamia, and China, monarch and morality were believed to depend upon each other: without monarchy, there would be disorder and justice would disappear. This was as powerful a statement of the dependence of morality upon the presence of coercive sanctions as has ever been made. In the political theories of India and Israel, on the other hand, the moral code was independent of the king.

THE ORIGINS OF KINGSHIP

These considerations were related to theories of the origins of kingship, or of the state, which were put forward in Mesopotamia, India, China, and Greece. These set out to explain how people became socially organized, why government was introduced, and what its purposes were. In China equal importance was attached to ranks and norms as remedies for anarchy. In Greece theories of society and the state were based on the need for collaboration and education.

Part of the king's duty, arising out of the virtues of justice and benevolence, was to help the poor, weak, disadvantaged—the underdog. This is found very early in both Egypt and Mesopotamia and also in India and China. It was emphasized by Confucius. It subsequently appeared in Judaic messianism ('he shall rescue the needy from their rich oppressors'; Ps. 72: 12–14); and finally, in its best-known version, in the mouth of Jesus. Only there the list of good works has become the set of criteria on which the Son of Man will judge every individual (Matt. 25: 34–40).

Ancient conceptions of justice included the rule of law and procedural justice. The ideas of the rule of law, and of equality before the law, were most fully articulated in Greece. The king was supposed to implement justice through fair trials and effective sanctions. This, as well as sacred monarchy itself, may have been part of the dynamic of passing from tribal to political society. Once tribes mingled, so that disputes could no longer be settled by tribal custom alone, there had to be a new way of agreeing rules and new methods of enforcement.

Tribes are rarely mentioned except in Israelite thought. Rather, it was equal treatment of the powerful and the weak, the rich and the poor, which was stipulated. Egyptians thought it important that a king and his vizier 'administer equal justice to all', regardless of wealth, status, or kinship (Engnell 1967: 12). 'I judged two trial partners so as to content them. I saved the weak from one stronger than he', said a funerary autobiography of the late third millenium, perhaps the earliest statement of the rule of law.[4] A Sumero-Akkadian hymn said the just king should be like god, who punishes the unrighteous judge and rewards those who refuse bribes (*ANE* 388). The prophet Jeremiah proclaimed equal treatment under the law for rich and poor, redress of grievance for the weak against the strong, as part of Israel's Covenant with her god (Jer. 22: 3–9).

In Israel and India, but not in Egypt, Mesopotamia, or Iran, it was said that the law had been revealed by god. In China the code of norms was revered as of immemorial antiquity. The Romans held ancestral custom and the code of laws in great respect, but did not give them religious or metaphysical status.

In all sacred monarchies, kings were urged to appoint ministers on merit rather than ancestry. 'Do not prefer the wellborn to the commoner, choose a man on account of his skills' (Egypt, *c.* 2000 BCE: above, p. 27). In China meritocracy was advocated on all sides. In all these cases moral qualities tended to be emphasized as much as, or more than, intellectual or technical ability.

Peace and reconciliation were a common undercurrent in political thought. This may be seen as a third ideal, alongside sacred monarchy and the rule of law, for societies becoming organized in states rather than tribes. Homer's *Iliad* and *Odyssey*, and also the *Mahabharata*, all of which celebrated the military hero (West 2007), concluded on a note of reconciliation.

In no ancient civilization, with the exceptions of Greece and Rome, was liberty seen as a political value. This is perhaps the greatest difference between ancient and modern political thought. What was valued was not freedom of choice but making the right choice,[5] which usually meant living according to traditional and religious norms. In Greece, especially at Athens, on the other hand, liberty was a fundamental political value. For Greeks, liberty meant freedom from slavery, from foreign rule, and from domestic tyranny. It also meant being able to vindicate wrongs in a fair trial—the rule of law again. It referred both to political autonomy for the state, and to freedom of speech within the state.

THE PEOPLE

The common people were an important factor in the political thought of all ancient societies. In the sacred monarchies they were the objects of benevolence from king and gods. The people's well-being was everywhere conceived as the main purpose of the state. It was particularly emphasized in China, where the Mandate of Heaven depended upon its being achieved. Both Confucius and, in India, Kautilya saw the interests of people and ruler as interdependent. Chinese realists saw the satisfaction of people's wants as the ultimate aim of political violence. In Egypt, Mesopotamia, and China the ruler was supposed to ensure the spiritual as well as material welfare of the people.

There was no suggestion in any sacred monarchy that the people should have a say as to what constituted their happiness, or what should be done to achieve it. Their happiness had been defined long in advance, by sages or gods. In Greece, Israel, and Rome, on the other hand, the people *were* seen as political actors on their own behalf. In the Greek poleis and in Rome various powers were given to some or all of the people, with elections, consultation, and assemblies. In the Christian church, too, decisions were taken by elders and congregations. In Israel the political community was based on a quasi-contractual agreement between the people and god. This gave all the (male) people the same basic political obligations and rights. At the same time it gave Yahweh unlimited scope and authority. Such were the alternatives to sacred monarchy.

In no ancient political culture or theory do we find a place given to women in politics or public affairs (see Reade 2002). In every single case, women were confined to the private sphere of the household. This applied at all levels of society. The one exception was Plato's Republic (above, p. 153).[6]

SOCIAL CATEGORIES

Only the Greeks and the Romans thought seriously about *humanity* at large. This led to the idea of a worldwide community, consisting of all rational and social beings, actually existing here and now, but (only) in the realm of the mind (cosmopolis). This was not a world state. Again, only the Greeks and Romans envisaged a single universal law of nature, giving the same duties and rights to all human beings. In some post-Exilic Jewish texts Yahweh was said to care for all peoples.

What of the *nation*? In Egypt and China outsiders were viewed as inferior (above, pp. 24, 104). In India it was the lower castes who were inferior. Achaemenid Iran respected subject nations, and allowed them to keep their own laws and religion. The Greeks had a strong sense of linguistic and cultural nationhood; they thought those who spoke Greek and lived in city-states were superior to others. But Greek thinkers saw this as an accidental difference due to climate. For Romans, the fundamental difference was between those who were prepared to be ruled by Rome—whatever their race—and those who were not. The extension of Roman citizenship to all of Italy (91 BCE) had the effect of creating a sense of Italian identity.

The only people who identified the state with the nation were the Israelites. Here, race was the basis of social, political, religious, and legal identity. The Jews saw themselves as a nation fundamentally different from all the others; the nation, rather than the monarch, was sacred.

A distinction between upper and lower *classes* was recognized everywhere, but it was conceived in different ways. Class distinctions were taken most seriously in India; except in Buddhism, castes were central to social, moral, and political thought, at least as important as sacred monarchy itself. The Chinese regarded status differences as necessary for social order. The *Guanzi* divided society into four categories: scholar-gentry (*shih*), farmers, artisans, merchants—in that order. These were somewhat similar to the four classes later found in Irano-Islamic literature (Black 2008: 73). Less importance was attached to class in Egypt, Mesopotamia, Israel, Greece, and Rome. In all of these (and in China), it was argued that a talented person should be able to rise from the bottom to the top. Israel was unique in being inimical to class as such (within the chosen people). The principal distinction in Israel was between Jews and non-Jews; in Greece and Rome it was between citizens and non-citizens.

In Israel and Rome a distinction was made between elders (or patriciate) and the people at large, but it had no existential meaning. In Greece and Rome tensions between patriciate and plebs generated constitutional conflicts. It was only in Greece and Rome that such conflicts came to be recognized as a normal feature of political life. The special path taken by Athens began with the attempt by Solon to reconcile the conflicting interests of rich and poor.

GENRES

There were significant differences between the genres and kinds of argument used. In India and Israel political ideas were expressed in religious texts which had the authority of divine revelation. What they said was incontrovertible though subject to interpretation. Outsiders were excluded from the benefits of the god-given polity. Thus, revealed theology had social as well as epistemological consequences.

During the middle and later parts of the first millenium BCE, individual thinkers and reformers in China, Greece, and Israel initiated new ways of thinking, attracted clusters of followers, and circulated their ideas throughout society. They relied on subtle speech and persuasion by argument; rhetoric replaced ritual.[7]

Political philosophy, using logic and dialectic, was born independently in Greece and China. Here there was public debate with open disagreement. In both cases it died out, following the conquests of Alexander on the one hand, and the unification of China on the other. (Perhaps philosophy flourished only when power was contested.) China produced a greater number of authors and schools, but no political thinker as systematic as Plato or Aristotle.

Only in Greece were the advantages and disadvantages of different constitutions discussed; only in Greece was there a variety of constitutions to discuss. Aristotle examined in particular oligarchy and demokratia, using a mass of empirical data, to which he applied nuanced value-judgements in a remarkably consistent way. Both he and (later) Polybius proposed a 'mixed' constitution as the most practicable and enduring option.

Aristotle and Kautilya, independently of each other, developed political science: the systematic recording, classifying, and comparing of data, based on observation. Aristotle focused on different types of constitution, Kautilya on different types of strategy. But no one else followed up what either of these had done.

THEORY AND PRACTICE; ETHICS AND EXPEDIENCY

The new ethical ideals of the 'axial' period (from *c.* 600 BCE onwards) gave rise to new tensions between theory and practice, between what could be done and what should be done, between might and right. Before the religious and philosophical developments of the mid-first millenium, the problem of theory versus practice did not exist in the way it did ever after. Before that, once one understood what the actual state was, one would see that it was the ideal state. This was how the Egyptians seem to have thought. So too did the Chinese, with an acute awareness of historical decline from the ideal, and of the need to restore what had been and should be.

This problem was tackled in different ways. In China there was a head-on collision between Confucian idealists, who taught that the methods one uses directly affect the end-result, and Legalist realists, who justified the use of violence in order to achieve what the people really want. Legalists saw the *methods* of political enforcement as transcending ethics. 'Correlative cosmology' was one way round this: different types of behaviour are appropriate—for a Son of Heaven, at least—at different points in the cosmic and natural cycle. In fact, the Chinese empire, having being unified by ruthless force, adopted Confucian ideals.

The conflict between ethics and expediency was the subject of the remarkable debate between Krishna and Arjuna in the *Bhagavad Gita*. The answer presented there was that, so long as you follow the obligations of your calling and status group—in Arjuna's case, those of a warrior—karma (the law of moral cause and effect) will sort everything out. Since souls are reborn, the act of killing is not what it seems. Here the solution of the moral problem was wholly dependent on the religio-philosophical context. Kautilya, on the other hand, permitted a wide range of political action, purely and simply on grounds of expediency (above, pp. 81–2). But he did not go as far as Machiavelli: his goal was always an ethically desirable state.

Within Judaism and Christianity (and, later, Shi'ite Islam), some found a solution in apocalyptic messianism.[8] You should behave morally without concern for the overall result because god will bring about true justice in his own good time. Right will triumph by divine intervention, preceded by an apocalyptic struggle at the end of time (which recurred quite frequently). This view led to non-resistance: you fulfil god's ethical demands by accepting whatever horrors unbelievers choose to impose on you, without striking back, in the knowledge that you will be vindicated one day. Stoicism counselled similar behaviour but without the pay-off.

Perhaps the most extreme form of the dichotomy between theory and practice was Plato's *Republic*, which was also, as it happened, the founding document of social and political philosophy. Both Plato and, still more, Aristotle went to great lengths to reconcile the ideal constitution with what was politically possible.

Cicero, in the final book of *On Duties*—the last major work of Graeco-Roman political philosophy—took a consistently Kantian line. This was his last will and testament. There was, for Cicero, no ultimate conflict between ethics and expediency. One must adhere to ethical principles through and through, in politics as in everything else. It is never right (*honestum*) to abandon moral standards in order to achieve political goals. And it is never expedient (*utile*) either, because what you achieve by immoral means will never be the good that you aim for. Both Stoics and Christians took the view that, if you cannot adhere to your moral principles, then you should abandon politics. Many Confucians, notably Mengzi, said the same.

On Duties was to inform the Western tradition on this issue until Machiavelli, who, reflecting on the very republic which Cicero had been powerless to save, went to the other extreme, insisting that there are many occasions in politics when one has to operate independently of moral principles altogether.

NOTES

1. I avoid 'republic' because it is too laden with modern meanings.
2. The later Roman empire occasionally did.
3. Several Muslim monarchs explicitly modelled themselves on him: *EI* s.v. Iskandar.
4. The same was said on behalf of Ashoka, Buddhist king of India: above, pp. 87–8.
5. Hegel's view of liberty looks like an attempt to synthesize pre-modern and modern thought.
6. Women played a role in Greek and Jewish mythology.
7. Hence the misleading notion of 'the axial period': Jaspers 1947. See Antony Black, 'The "Axial Period": What Was It and What Does It Signify?', *Review of Politics*, 70 (2008), 23–39.
8. John Gray, *Black Mass: Apocalyptic Religion and the Death of Utopia* (London: Allen Lane, 2007).

13

General Conclusion

Let us now return to the questions with which we began. This study underlines the differences between ancient ways of thinking and our own. This alerts us to the possibility that our own assumptions and ways of thinking may one day appear as strange, as arbitrary and unwarranted, to our successors, as those of our predecessors appear to us.

We have also found a clear distinction between political ideology (public justifications of policies and of institutions) and political philosophy, or systematic reflection. We have found political ideology in all literate cultures, but philosophy only in China, Greece, and (to a much lesser degree) India. Political ideology seems to have been necessary in all ordered societies and states (as many would say it is today). But people could survive without philosophy, whatever its long-term benefits. Political philosophy arose out of contemporary conditions, but it did not necessarily reflect them.

What (if anything) can be learned from ancient political thought as a whole? It has become clear that there is no political ideal or value system in the world today that was not first invented in the ancient world. Even nationalism (the idea of the state as an exclusive racial or cultural unit), often thought to be peculiarly modern, had roots in the ancient world (above, pp. 24, 57). Indeed, at the other end of the spectrum, we have failed to recognize something which ancient thought has to offer: the possibility of a cosmopolitan political society, based on the very characteristics which make us human in the first place (above, p. 208).

There have, of course, been many new applications and extensions of ancient political ideas. For example, in the ancient world there were notions of social contract, but these were not made into a systematic philosophy as they were by Hobbes or Rawls. There were theories of communism, but not of class war. It was not thought necessary to secure the liberty of the individual *from* a democratic state (de Tocqueville was the first to argue this), nor to keep the economy free from political intervention.

Again, Confucian ethics and Graeco-Roman humanism are examples of value systems which were primarily secular, and did not depend on religious belief. Secular political values are not uncommon in the modern world (for example, the Rawlsian theory of justice), but it is not generally recognized that they have an ancient pedigree.

The comparative study of political thought does indeed throw light on the factors which have shaped European and Western political thought (above, p. 3). These were a combination of, on the one hand, Christianity, which already contained some Israelite ideas, and on the other hand, Greek philosophy together with Roman political culture.[1] (Greece and Rome were the only ancient traditions anywhere without sacred texts, and they survived partly by being carried by cultures with a text.) Thus the influences of Greece and Rome worked side by side with those of Christianity and Israel. For example, Europeans drew their notions of monarchy from both Rome and Israel, the idea of kingship which became prevalent in Europe being modelled on the sovereignty of the emperor in Roman law, and on the Old Testament king as 'the Lord's anointed'.[2] They drew their ideas of liberty from both Greece and Rome. There was thus interaction between two originally distinct sets of ancient ideas, which already themselves contained a fusion of different elements. This combination, with its inherent tensions, has been a dynamic force driving the development of political thought (and much else) in the West.

Philosophical enquiry was to start up again when, in twelfth-century Europe, for the second time in human history, significant numbers of people were experiencing self-government. From then on, European thinkers adopted an increasingly critical approach to their predecessors (Bolgar 1957).

Time and again, ancient language was used to legitimize new practices. This could sometimes obscure the extent to which these differed from the ancient models. For example, Polybius' view that the best form of government is a 'mixed' constitution, containing elements of rule by one, the best, and the many, was used to describe and justify the roles of kings, grandees, and parliaments in medieval states.[3]

Greek demokratia had been all but forgotten by the beginning of the first millenium CE. The independence of Greek poleis had come to an abrupt end while the Greeks were still at the height of their intellectual creativity. Rome had switched from republic to principate at the moment of her Hellenic enlightenment. But it was the ideals of Greek demokratia, Graeco-Roman liberty, Israelite nationalism, and messianic justice which, in the long term, inspired European political thought and popular ideology.

Chinese Legalism and, in our own day, Marxism focused on power structures but had little (if anything) to say about ethics. They achieved cataclysmic changes in the way people were ruled, but each seems to have proved largely ineffective as a basis for political legitimacy. For this, ideas which focused on the wider concerns of humanity—such as Confucianism, Stoicism, or Christianity—seem to have been required.

Whatever our disagreements with ancient political ideas, there have been few thinkers in the entire history of political thought, Western or non-Western, to compare in originality and depth with—in their different ways—Confucius, Plato, Shang Yang, Aristotle, or Kautilya.

NOTES

1. Lintott 1999: 233–55; Annabel Brett et al. (eds.), *Rethinking the Foundations of Modern Political Thought* (Cambridge: Cambridge University Press, 2006).
2. Joachim Ehlers, 'Grundlagen der europäischen Monarchie in Spätantike und Mittelalter', *Majestas*, 8–9 (2000–1), 49-80.
3. J. M. Blythe, *Ideal Government and the Mixed Constitution in the Middle Ages* (Princeton: Princeton University Press, 1992).

Bibliography

PRIMARY SOURCES

For Greek and Roman texts the editions in the Loeb Classical Library (Cambridge, Mass.: Harvard University Press) have generally been used. I have made my own translations unless otherwise stated.

ARISTOTLE, *Nicomachaean Ethics*, trans. T. Irwin (Indianapolis: Hackett, 1999); *Politics*, trans. Stephen Everson (Cambridge: Cambridge University Press, 1988).

BARKER, ERNEST, *From Alexander to Constantine: Passages and Documents Illustrating the History of Social and Political Ideas 336 BC–AD 337* (Oxford: Oxford University Press, 1956) = EB.

The Bhagavad Gita, trans. J. Mascaro (Harmondsworth: Penguin, 1962).

CONFUCIUS, *The Analects*, trans. D. C. Lau (Harmondsworth: Penguin, 1979); *The Original Analects: Sayings of Confucius and his Successors*, trans. E. Bruce Brooks and A. Taeko Brooks (New York: Columbia University Press, 1998) = B&B.

CYPRIAN, St, *Epistolae*, ed. W. Hartel, *Corpus Scriptorum Ecclesiasticorum Latinorum*, vol. III/2 (Vienna: Boehlau, 1871).

Daodejing (Classic of the Power of the Way: Tao Te Ching), ascribed to Laozi (Lao Tzu), trans. D. C. Lau (Harmondsworth: Penguin, 1963); trans. Stephen Addiss and Stanley Lombardo (Indianapolis: Hackett, 1993).

DIELS, HERMANN and KRANZ, WALTHER, *Die Fragmente der Vorsokratiker* (Berlin: Wiedmannsche, 1956).

The Early Christian Fathers, ed. and trans. H. Bettenson (Oxford: Oxford University Press, 1956) = ECF.

Early Christian Writings: The Apostolic Fathers, trans. M. Staniforth (Harmondsworth: Penguin, 1968) = ECW.

Early Greek Political Thought from Homer to the Sophists, trans. and ed. Michael Gagarin and Paul Woodruff (Cambridge: Cambridge University Press, 1995) = EG.

FOSTER, BENJAMIN R., *From Distant Days: Myths, Tales and Poetry of Ancient Mesopotamia* (Bethesda, Md.: CDL Press, 1995).

Guanzi: Political, Economic and Philosophical Essays from Early China, trans. W. Allyn Rickett, 2 vols., Princeton Library of Asian Translations (Princeton: Princeton University Press, 1985–9).

HAN FEIZI/HAN FEI TZU, *Basic Writings*, trans. Burton Watson (New York: Columbia University Press, 1967).

The Kautiliya Arthashastra, ed. and trans. R. P. Kangle, 2nd edn. (Bombay: University of Bombay, 1969), part 2 = KA.

LICHTHEIM, MIRIAM, *Ancient Egyptian Literature: A Book of Readings*, vol. 1: *The Old and Middle Kingdoms*; vol. 2: *The New Kingdom* (Berkeley: University of California Press, 1973–6).

—— *Moral Values in Ancient Egypt* (Göttingen: Vandenhoeck & Rupprecht, 1997).

MARCUS AURELIUS, *Meditations*, trans. Martin Hammond (London: Penguin, 2006).

MENCIUS (MENGZI), trans. D. C. Lau (Harmondsworth: Penguin, 1970).

MOZI/MO TZU, *Basic Writings*, trans. Burton Watson (New York: Columbia University Press, 1967).

The New English Bible (Oxford: Oxford University Press 1970).

PARKINSON, R. B., *Voices from Ancient Egypt: An Anthology of Middle Kingdom Writings* (London: British Museum Press, 1991) = *VAE*.

PLATO, *The Republic*, trans. F. M. Cornford (Oxford: Oxford University Press, 1941); ed. and trans. G. Ferrari and Tom Griffith (Cambridge: Cambridge University Press, 2000).

—— *The Laws*, trans. A. E. Taylor (London: Dent, 1969).

PRITCHARD, JAMES B. (ed.), *Ancient Near Eastern Texts Relating to the Old Testament* (Princeton: Princeton University Press, 1955) = *ANE*.

The Book of Lord Shang (Shang Yang) (Shang jun shu), trans. J. J. L. Duyvendak (London: Probsthain, 1928).

Sources of Chinese Tradition, vol. 1: *From Earliest Times to 1600*, compiled by Wm. Theodore de Bary and Irene Bloom (New York: Columbia University Press, 1999) = *ST*.

STEVENSON, J. (ed.), *A New Eusebius* (London: SPCK, 1960) = *NE*.

XUNZI/HSUN TZU, *Basic Writings*, trans. Burton Watson (New York: Columbia University Press, 1967).

SECONDARY SOURCES

AALDERS, G. J. D. (1975), *Political Thought in Hellenistic times* (Amsterdam: Hakkert).

AHN, GREGOR (1992), *Religiöse Herrschaftslegitimation im Achaemenidischen Iran*, Acta Iranica, 31 (Leiden: Brill & Peeters).

AIELLO, L. C. and DUNBAR, R. I. M. (1993), 'Neocortex Size, Group Size and the Evolution of Language', *Current Anthropology*, 34: 184–93.

AL-AZMEH, AZIZ (1997), *Muslim Kingship: Power and the Sacred in Muslim, Christian, and Pagan Politics* (London: I. B. Tauris).

AMES, ROGER T. (1983), 'Is Political Taoism Anarchism?', *Journal of Chinese Philosophy*, 10: 36–52.

—— (1994), *The Art of Rulership: A Study of Ancient Chinese Political Thought* (Albany, NY: State University of New York Press).

ANDO, CLIFFORD (2003), *Roman Religion* (Edinburgh: Edinburgh University Press).

ANNAS, JULIA (1981), *An Introduction to Plato's 'Republic'* (Oxford: Oxford University Press).

ASSMANN, JAN (2001), *The Search for God in Ancient Egypt*, trans. D. Lorton (Ithaca, NY: Cornell University Press).

—— (1995), *Politische Theologie zwischen Aegypten und Israel*, 2nd edn. (Munich: Carl Friedrich von Siemens Stiftung).

AXELROD, ROBERT (1981), 'The Emergence of Co-operation Among Egoists', *American Political Science Review*, 75: 306–18.

BAECHLER, JEAN (1985), *Démocraties* (Paris: Calmann-Levy).

BALDRY, H. C. (1965), *The Unity of Mankind in Greek Thought* (Cambridge: Cambridge University Press).

BARNES, JONATHAN (1982), *The Presocratic Philosophers*, rev. edn. (London: Routledge and Kegan Paul).

BARON, HANS (1966), *The Crisis of the Early Italian Renaissance* (Princeton: Princeton University Press).

BARON, SALO W. (1952), *A Social and Religious History of the Jews*, 2nd edn., vol. 2 (New York: Columbia University Press).

BARRELET, M.-TH. (1974), 'La "figure du roi" dans l'iconographie et dans les textes depuis Ur-Nanse jusqu'au la fin de la 1er dynastie de Babylon', in Garelli, ed. (1974), 20–42.

BARRETT, LOUISE, DUNBAR, ROBIN, and LYCETT, JOHN (2002), *Human Evolutionary Psychology* (London: Palgrave).

de BARY, WM. THEODORE (1991), *The Trouble with Confucianism* (Cambridge, Mass.: Harvard University Press).

BASHAM, A. L., ed. (1975), *A Cultural History of India* (Oxford: Oxford University Press).

—— (1980), 'The Background to the Rise of Buddhism', in A. K. Narain (ed.), *Studies in the History of Buddhism* (Delhi: B. R. Publishing, 1980).

BLACK, ANTONY (1970), *Monarchy and Community* (Cambridge: Cambridge University Press).

—— (1992), *Political Thought in Europe 1250–1450* (Cambridge: Cambridge University Press).

—— (2001), *The History of Islamic Political Thought from the Prophet to the Present* (Edinburgh: Edinburgh University Press).

—— (2003), *Guild and State: European Political Thought from the Twelfth Century to the Present* (London: Transaction).

—— (2008), *The West and Islam: Religion and Political Thought in World History* (Oxford: Oxford University Press).

BODDE, DERK (1981), *Essays on Chinese Civilization* (Princeton: Princeton University Press).

—— (1991), *Chinese Thought, Society and Science: The Intellectual and Social Background of Science and Technology in Pre-modern China* (Honolulu: University of Hawai'i Press).

BOLGAR, R. R. (1958), *The Classical Heritage and its Beneficiaries* (Cambridge: Cambridge University Press).

BOORN, G. P. F. van den (1988), *The Duties of the Vizier: Civil Administration in the New Kingdom* (London: Routledge and Kegan Paul).

BOYARIN, DANIEL (1994), *A Radical Jew: Paul and the Politics of Identity* (Berkeley: University of California Press).

BOYCE, MARY (1984), 'Persian Religion in the Achaemenid Age', in W. D. Davies and Louis Finkelstein eds., *The Cambridge History of Judaism*, vol. I (Cambridge: Cambridge University Press), 279–300.

BRAITHWAITE, MARY (1984), 'Ritual and Prestige in the Prehistory of Wessex c. 2200–1400 BC', in David Miller and Chris Tilley eds., *Ideology, Power and Prehistory* (Cambridge: Cambridge University Press), 172–91.

BRIANT, PIERRE (1982), *Rois, tributs et paysans: études sur les formations tributaires du môyen-orient ancien* (Paris: Les Belles Lettres).

—— (1996), *Histoire de l'empire Perse* (Paris: Fayard).

BRINKMAN, J. A. (1974a), 'Monarchy in the Time of the Kassite Dynasty', in Garelli, ed., 392–408.

—— (1974b), 'The Early Neo-Babylonian Monarchy', in Garelli, ed., 410–15.

—— (1984), *Prelude to Empire: Babylonian Society and Politics 747–626 BC* (Philadephia: Babylonian Fund).

BROWN, DONALD E. (1991), *Human Universals* (Philadelphia: Temple University Press).

BROWN, PETER (1988), *The Body and Society: Men, Women and Sexual Renunciation in Early Christianity* (London: Faber & Faber).

BRUNT, P. A. (1975), 'Stoicism amd the Principate', *Papers of the British School at Rome*, 43: 7–36.

—— (1989), 'Philosophy and Religion in the Late Republic', in Griffin and Barnes, eds., 174–98.

BRYANT, JOSEPH M. (1996), *Moral Codes and Social Structure in Ancient Greece* (Albany, NY: State University of New York Press).

Cambridge Ancient History (= *CAH*), 3rd edn., vol. I, part 2 (1971), ed. I. E. S. Edwards et al.

    vol. II, part 1 (1973), ed. I. E. S. Edwards et al.

    vol. II, part 2 (1971), ed. I. E. S. Edwards et al.

    vol. VII, part 1, 2nd edn. (1984), ed. R. Ling.

    vol. VIII, part 2, 2nd edn. (1989), ed. A. E. Astin et al.

    vol. X (1934), ed. S. A. Cook et al.

    vol. XI, 2nd edn. (2000), ed. Alan Bowman et al.

Cambridge Companion to the Roman Republic, ed. Harriet I. Flowers (Cambridge: Cambridge University Press, 2004) = *CCRR*.

Cambridge History of Ancient China from the Origins of Civilization to 221 BC, ed. Michael Loewe and Edward L. Shaughnessy (Cambridge: Cambridge University Press, 1999) = *CHAC*.

Cambridge History of China, vol. I: *The Ch'in and Han Empires, 221 BC–AD 220*, ed. Denis Twitchett and Michael Loewe (Cambridge: Cambridge University Press, 1986) = *CHC*.

Cambridge History of Greek and Roman Political Thought, ed. Christopher Rowe and Malcolm Schofield (Cambridge: Cambridge University Press, 2000) = *CGR.*

Cambridge History of Hellenistic Philosophy, ed. K. Algra et al. (Cambridge: Cambridge University Press, 1999) = *CHP.*

Cambridge History of Iran, vol. II, ed. Ilya Gershevitch (Cambridge: Cambridge University Press, 1985) = *CHI.*

Cambridge History of Medieval Political Thought c. 350–c.1450, ed. J. H. Burns (Cambridge: Cambridge University Press, 1988) = *CHMPT.*

CAMPENHAUSEN, HANS VON (1969), *Ecclesiastical Authority and Spiritual Power in the Church of the First Three Centuries*, trans. J. Barker (Stanford: Stanford University Press).

CARTLEDGE, PAUL (1997), '"Deep Plays": Theatre as Process in Greek Civic Life', in P. E. Easterling ed., *The Cambridge Companion to Greek Tragedy* (Cambridge: Cambridge University Press), 3–35.

CAUVIN, JACQUES (2000), *The Birth of the Gods and the Origin of Agriculture*, trans. T. Watkins (Cambridge: Cambridge University Press).

CHAGNON, NAPOLEON A. (1982), 'Sociodemographic Attributes of Nepotism in Tribal Populations: Man the Rule-breaker', in *Current Problems in Sociobiology* (Cambridge: Cambridge University Press), 291–317.

CHAKRAVARTI, UMA (1987), *The Social Dimensions of Early Buddhism* (Delhi: Oxford University Press).

CHAN, JOSEPH (2007), 'Democracy and Meritocracy: Towards a Confucian Perspective', *Journal of Chinese Philosophy*, 34: 179–93.

CHOMSKY, NOAM (1957), *Syntactic Structures* (The Hague: Mouton).

CLAESSEN, HENRI J. M. (1978), 'The Early State: A Structural Approach' in Claessen and Skalnik, eds., 558–75.

—— and SKALNIK, PETER eds. (1978), *The Early State* (The Hague: Mouton).

CLARK, J. DESMOND (1970), *The Prehistory of Africa* (London: Thames and Hudson).

COGAN, MORTON (1974), *Imperialism and Religion: Assyria, Judah and Israel in the 8th and 7th centuries BC* (Missoula, Mont.: Scholars Press).

COHEN, RONALD (1978), 'State Origins: A Reappraisal' in Claessen and Skalnik, eds., 39–73.

COHN, NORMAN (1957), *The Pursuit of the Millenium: Revolutionary Millenarians and Mystical Anarchists of the Middle Ages* (London: Secker & Warburg).

COLEMAN, JANET (2000), *A History of Political Thought from Ancient Greece to Early Christianity* (Oxford: Blackwell).

COOPER, JERROLD (1993), 'Paradigm and Propaganda', in Liverani ed., 11–23.

CREEL, HERRLEE G. (1970), *The Origins of Statecraft in China: The Western Chou Empire* (Chicago: University of Chicago Press).

—— (1974), *Shen Pu-Hai: A Chinese Political Philosopher of the Fourth Century BC* (Chicago: Chicago University Press).

CRONE, PATRICIA (1986), 'The Tribe and the State', in John A. Hall ed., *States in History* (Oxford: Blackwell), 48–77.

Cruden's Concordance, 3rd edn. (London: Epworth Press, 1948).

DANDAMAEV, MUHAMMAD A. (1988), 'The Neo-Babylonian Popular Assembly', in Petr Vavrousek ed., *Sulmu: Papers on the Ancient Near East* (Prague: Charles University), 63–71.

—— and LUKONIN, VLADIMIR, G. (1989), *The Culture and Social Institutions of Ancient Iran*, trans. P. Kohl and D. Dadson (Cambridge: Cambridge University Press).

DAWKINS, RICHARD (1976), *The Selfish Gene* (Oxford: Oxford University Press).

DERRETT, J. and DUNCAN M. (1975), 'Social and Political Thought and Institutions', in Basham ed., 124–40.

DODDS, E. R. (1951), *The Greeks and the Irrational* (Berkeley: University of California Press).

—— (1965), *Pagan and Christian in an Age of Anxiety: Some Aspects of Religious Experience from Marcus Aurelius to Constantine* (Cambridge: Cambridge University Press).

DONLAN, WALTER (1998), 'Political Reciprocity in Dark Age Greece: Odysseus and his Hetairoi', in Christopher Gill et al. eds., *Reciprocity in Ancient Greece* (Oxford: Oxford University Press), 51–71.

DUMONT, LOUIS (1970), *Homo Hierarchicus: The Caste System and its Implications*, rev. edn. (Chicago: University of Chicago Press).

—— (1974), 'On the Comparative Understanding of Non-modern Civilizations', *Daedalus*, 104: 158–72.

DVORNIK, FRANCIS (1966), *Christian and Byzantine Political Philosophy*, 2 vols. (Washington, DC: Dumbarton Oaks Centre for Byzantine Studies).

EHRENBERG, VICTOR (1969), *The Greek State*, 2nd edn. (London: Methuen).

ELVIN, MARK (1973), *The Pattern of the Chinese Past* (London: Eyre Methuen).

Encyclopaedia of Islam, 2nd edn., ed. H. A. R. Gibb et al. (Leiden: Brill, 1960–96) = *EI.*

ENGNELL, IVAN (1967), *Studies in Divine Kingship in the Ancient Near East* (Oxford: Blackwell).

FINER, E. S. (1997), *The History of Government*, 3 vols. (Oxford: Oxford University Press).

FINLEY, M. I. (1963), *The Ancient Greeks* (London: Chatto and Windus).

—— (1983), *Politics in the Ancient World* (Cambridge: Cambridge University Press).

FLANNERY, KENT V. (1972), 'The Cultural Evolution of Civilizations', *Annual Review of Ecology and Systematics*, 3: 399–426.

FORTES, M. and EVANS-PRITCHARD, E. E. (1940), *African Political Systems* (Oxford: Oxford University Press).

FOWDEN, GARTH (1993), *Empire to Commonwealth: Consequences of Monotheism in Late Antiquity* (Princeton: Princeton University Press, 1993).

FRANKFORT, HENRI (1948), *Kingship and the Gods* (Chicago: Chicago University Press, 1948).

—— et al. (1946), *The Intellectual Adventure of Ancient Man* (Chicago: Chicago University Press).

GARELLI, PAUL (1979), 'L'État et la légitimité royale sous l'empire assyrien', in Larsen, ed., 319–28.

—— ed. (1974), *Le Palais et la royauté* (Paris: Paul Geuthner).

GEORGE, A. R. (1997), ' "Bond of the Lands": Babylon, the Cosmic Capital', in G. Wilhelm ed., *Die orientalische Stadt: Kontinuität, Wandel, Bruch* (Saarbrucken: SDV), 125–37.

GEERTZ, CLIFFORD (1973), *The Interpretation of Cultures* (New York: Basic Books).

GHOSHAL, U. N. (1959), *A History of Indian Political Ideas: The Ancient Period and the Period of Transition to the Middle Ages* (Oxford: Oxford University Press).

GLEDHILL, JOHN, et al., eds. (1988), *State and Society: The Emergence and Development of Social Hierarchy and Political Centralization* (London: Unwin Hyman).

GLUCKMAN, MAX (1965), *Politics, Law and Ritual in Tribal Society* (Oxford: Blackwell).

GNOLI, GHERARDO (1974), 'Politique réligieuse sous les Achémenides', *Acta Iranica*, 2: 117–90.

GOGUEL, M. (1964), *The Primitive Church*, trans. H. Snape (London: Allen and Unwin).

GOLDIN, PAUL R. (2007), 'Xunzi and Early Han Philosophy', *Harvard Journal of Asiatic Studies*, 67: 135–66.

GOMBRICH, RICHARD (1988), *Theravada Buddhism: A Social History from Ancient Benares to Modern Colombo* (London: Routledge and Kegan Paul).

GONDA, J. (1956–7), 'Ancient Indian Kingship from the Religious Point of View', *Numen*, 3–4: 36–71.

—— (1957), 'Ancient Indian Kingship from the Religious Point of View (continued)', *Numen*, 5: 24–58, 127–64.

GOODY, JACK and WATT, IAN (1968), 'The Consequences of Literacy', in Jack Goody ed., *Literacy in Traditional Societies* (Cambridge: Cambridge University Press), 35–55.

GOTTWALD, NORMAN K. (1979), *The Tribes of Yahweh: A Sociology of the Religion of Liberated Israel, 1250–1050 BCE* (Maryknoll, NY: Orbis Books; repr. Sheffield Academic Publishers, 1991).

—— (1985), *The Hebrew Bible—A Socio-literary Introduction* (Philadelphia: Fortress Press).

GRAHAM, A. C. (1989), *Disputers of the Tao: Philosophical Argument in Ancient China* (La Salle, Ill.: Open Court).

GREENHALGH, P. A. L. (1972), 'Aristocracy and its Advocates in Archaic Greece', *Greece and Rome*, 19: 190–207.

GRIFFIN, MIRIAM (1989), 'Philosophy, Politics and Politicians', in Griffin and Barnes, eds., 3–37.

—— and BARNES, JONATHAN, eds. (1989), *Philosophia Togata: Essays on Philosophy and Roman Society* (Oxford: Oxford University Press).

HALPERN, BARUCH (1981), *The Constitution of the Monarchy in Israel* (Chico, Calif.: Scholars Press).

HARE, R. M. (1982), *Plato* (Oxford: Oxford University Press).

HARRIS, W. V. (1979), *War and Imperialism in Republican Rome, 327–70 BC* (Oxford: Clarendon Press).

HAWKES, JACQUETTA and WOOLLEY, SIR LEONARD (1963), *Prehistory and the Beginnings of Civilization* (Geneva: UNESCO).

HAYEK, F. A. (1982), *Law, Legislation and Liberty: A New Statement of the Liberal Principles of Justice and Political Economy*, 3 vols. (London: Routledge and Kegan Paul).

HEESTERMANN, J. C. (1979), 'Power and Authority in Indian Tradition', in R. J. Moore ed., *Tradition and Politics in South Asia* (New Delhi: Vikas), 13–32.

——(1985), *The Inner Conflict of Tradition: Essays in Indian Ritual, Kingship and Society* (Chicago: University of Chicago Press).

——(1998), 'The Conundrum of the King's Authority', in J. F. Richards ed., *Kingship and Authority in South Asia* (Delhi: Oxford University Press), 13–37.

HODDER, I., ed. (1982), *Symbolic and Structural Archaeology* (Cambridge: Cambridge University Press).

HÖGEMANN, PETER (1992), *Das alte Vorderasien und die Achaemeniden* (Wiesbaden: Reichert).

HOPKINS, KEITH (1979), 'Divine Emperors or the Symbolic Unity of the Roman Empire', in *Conquerors and Slaves* (Cambridge: Cambridge University Press), 197–242.

HORNUNG, ERIK (1983), *Conceptions of God in Ancient Egypt: The One and the Many*, trans. J. Baines (London: Routledge).

HSIAO, KUNG-CHUAN, *A History of Chinese Political Thought*, vol. I: *From the Beginnings to the Sixth Century AD*, trans. F. W. Mote (Princeton: Princeton University Press, 1979) = *HPT*.

HSU, CHO-YUN (1965), *Ancient China in Transition: An Analysis of Social Mobility 722–222 BC* (Stanford: Stanford University Press).

HUMPHREYS, S. C. (1978), *Anthropology and the Greeks* (London: Routledge and Kegan Paul).

INGNALLS, DANIEL H. (1954), 'Authority and Law in Ancient India', *Journal of the American Oriental Society*, 17: 34–45.

JACOBSEN, THORKILD (1943), 'Primitive Democracy in Ancient Mesopotamia', *Journal of Near Eastern Studies*, 2: 159–72.

——(1957), 'Early Political Developments in Mesopotamia', *Zeitschrift für Assyriologie und Vorderasiatische Archäologie*, 52: 91–140.

JASPERS, KARL (1947), 'The Axial Period', in *The Origin and Goal of Human History* (New Haven: Yale University Press), 1–25.

JOHNSON, GARY R. (1987), 'In the Name of the Fatherland: An Analysis of Kin Term Usage in Patriotic Speech and Literature', *International Political Science Review*, 8: 165–74.

JOLOWICZ, H. F. and NICHOLAS BARRY (1972), *Historical Introduction to Roman Law*, 3rd edn. (Cambridge: Cambridge University Press).

JONES, A. H. M. (1966), *The Decline of the Ancient World* (Harlow: Longman).

KANTOROWICZ, E. H. (1957), *The King's Two Bodies: A Study in Medieval Political Theology* (Princeton: Princeton University Press).

KEEL, O. (1978), *The Symbolism of the Biblical World: Ancient Near-Eastern Iconography and the Book of Psalms*, trans. J. J. Hallett (London: SPCK).

KEIGHTLEY, DAVID N. (2000), *The Ancestral Landscape: Time, Space and Community in Late Shang China (c. 1200–1945 BC)* (Berkeley: Institute of East Asian Studies).
—— ed. (1983), *The Origins of Chinese Civilization* (Berkeley: University of California Press).

KELLENS, JEAN (1991), 'Questions préalables', in *La Réligion Iranienne à l'époque Achéménide* (Ghent: Iranica Antiqua).

KEMP, BARRY J. (1989), *Ancient Egypt: Anatomy of a Civilization* (London: Routledge).

KERFERD, G. B. (1981), *The Sophistic Movement* (Cambridge: Cambridge University Press).

KIRK, G. S., RAVEN, J. E., and SCHOFIELD, M. (1983), *The Presocratic Philosophers: A Critical History with a Selection of Texts*, 2nd edn. (Cambridge: Cambridge University Press) = KRS.

KITTO, H. D. F. (1951), *The Greeks* (Harmondsworth: Penguin).

KOCH, KLAUS (1984), 'Weltordnung und Reichsidee im alten Iran', in Peter Fries and Klaus Koch eds., *Reichsidee und Reichsorganisation im Perserreich Darius I* (Göttingen: Vandenhoeck & Rupprecht).

KRAEMER, JOEL L. (1992), *Humanism in the Renaissance of Islam*, 2nd edn. (Leiden: Brill).

KRAMER, SAMUEL NOAH (1963), *The Sumerians: Their History, Culture and Character* (Chicago: Chicago University Press).
—— (1974), 'Kingship in Sumer and Akkad', in Garelli, ed., 163–77.

KRAUS, F. R. (1974), 'Das Altbabylonische Königtum', in Garelli, ed., 235–59.
—— (1982), '"Karum", ein organ städtischer Selbstverwaltung der Altbabylonischen Zeit', in Institut des Hautes Études Belgique ed., *Les Pouvoirs locaux en Mésopotamie et dans les régions adjacentes* (Brussels).

KREBS, J. R. and DAVIES, N. B., eds. (1984), *Behavioural Ecology: An Evolutionary Approach*, 2nd edn. (Oxford: Blackwell).

KULKE, HERMANN and ROTHERMUND, DIETMAR (1998), *History of India*, 3rd edn. (London, Routledge) = KR.

LABAT, RENÉ (1939), *Le Caractère réligieuse de la royauté Assyro-Babylonienne* (Paris, Adrien Maisonneuve).

LAKS, ANDRÉ and SCHOFIELD, MALCOLM, eds. (1995), *Justice and Generosity: Studies in Hellenistic Social and Political Philosophy* (Cambridge: Cambridge University Press).

LAMBERG-KARLOVSKY, C. C. (1986), 'Third Millenium Structure and Process: From the Euphrates to the Indus and the Oxus to the Indian Ocean', *Oriens Antiquus*, 25: 189–214.

LALAND, KEVIN N. and BROWN, GILLIAN R. (2002), *Sense and Nonsense: Evolutionary Perspectives on Human Behaviour* (Oxford: Oxford University Press).

LAMOTTE, ÉTIENNE (1988), *History of Indian Buddhism from the Origins to the Saka Era*, trans. S. Webb-Boin (Louvain-la-Neuve: Institut Catholique de l'Universite Catholique de Louvain).

LARSEN, MOGENS TROLLE (1974), 'The City and its King: On the Old Assyrian Notion of Kingship', in Garelli, ed., 285–99.

——(1976), *The Old Assyrian City-state and its Colonies* (Copenhagen: Akademisk Forlag).

——(1979), 'The Tradition of Empire in Mesopotamia', in Larsen, ed., 75–106.

——ed. (1979), *Power and Propaganda: A Symposium on Ancient Empires* (Copenhagen: Akademisk Forlag).

Lévi-Strauss, Claude (1963), *Structural Anthropology*, trans. C. Jacobson and B. G. Schoepf (London: Allen Lane).

Lewis, David (1990), *Public Property in the City*, in Murray, ed., 245–63.

Lewis, Mark Edward (1990), *Sanctioned Violence in Ancient China* (Albany, NY: SUNY Press).

——(1999), *Writing and Authority in Early China* (Albany, NY: SUNY Press).

Lingat, R. (1989), *Royautés bouddhiques* (Paris: École Hauts Études en Sciences Sociales).

Lintott, Andrew (1987), 'Democracy in the Middle Republic', *Zeitschrift der Savigny-Stiftung für Rechtsgeschichte*, 104: 42–51.

——(1999), *The Constitution of the Roman Republic* (Oxford: Clarendon Press).

Liverani, Mario (1979), 'The Ideology of the Assyrian Empire', in Larsen, ed., 297–318.

——(1990), *Prestige and Interest: International Relations in the Near East c.1600–1100 bc* (Padua: Sargon).

——(1993), 'Model and Actualization', in Liverani, ed., 45–60.

——ed. (1993), *Akkad, the First World Empire* (Padua: Sargon).

Lloyd, G. E. R. (1968), *Aristotle: The Growth and Structure of his Thought* (Cambridge: Cambridge University Press)

——(1979), *Magic, Reason and Experience: Studies in the Origin and Development of Greek Science* (Cambridge: Cambridge University Press).

——(2002), *The Ambitions of Curiosity: Understanding the World in Ancient Greece and China* (Cambridge: Cambridge University Press).

——(2004), *Ancient Worlds, Modern Reflections: Philosophical Perspectives on Greek and Chinese Science and Culture* (Oxford: Oxford University Press).

Lloyd-Jones, Hugh (1971), *The Justice of Zeus* (Berkeley: University of California Press).

Loewe, Michael (1994), *Divination, Mythology and Monarchy in Han China* (Cambridge: Cambridge University Press).

Long, A. A. (1995), 'Cicero's Politics in *De Officiis*', in Laks and Schofield, eds., 213–40.

MacDonald, Nathan (2003), *Deuteronomy and the Meaning of 'Monotheism'* (Tübingen: Mohr).

Mair, Lucy (1962), *Primitive Government* (Harmondsworth: Penguin).

Mann, Michael (1986), *The Sources of Social Power*, vol. I (Cambridge: Cambridge University Press).

Mattern, Susan (1999), *Rome and the Enemy: Imperial Strategy in the Principate* (Berkeley: University of California Press).

McClelland, J. S. (1996), *A History of Western Political Thought* (London: Routledge).

McConville, J. G. (1998), 'King and Messiah in Deuteronomy', in John Day ed., *King and Messiah in Israel and the Ancient Near East* (Sheffield: Sheffield Academic Press), 271–95.

Meier, Christian (1990), *The Greek Discovery of Politics*, trans. David McLintock (Cambridge, Mass.: Harvard University Press).

Meier, J. P. (1994), *A Marginal Jew: Rethinking the Historical Jesus*, vol. II (New York: Doubleday).

Mettinger, Tryggve N. D. (1976), *King and Messiah: The Civil and Sacred Legitimation of the Israelite Kings* (Lund: C. W. K. Gleerup).

Michalowski, Piotr (1993), 'Memory and Deed: The Historiography of the Political Expansion of the Akkad State', in Liverani, ed., 69–90.

Mieroop, Marc van de (1997), *The Ancient Mesopotamian City* (Oxford: Oxford University Press).

Millar, Fergus (1984), 'The Political Character of the Classical Roman Republic', *Journal of Roman Studies*, 74: 1–19.

—— (1986), 'Politics, Persuasion and the People Before the Social War (150–90 BC)', *Journal of Roman Studies*, 76: 1–11.

Mithen, Steven (1996), *The Prehistory of the Mind: A Search for the Origins of Art, Religion and Science* (London: Thames and Hudson).

Momigliano, Arnoldo (1987), 'The Disadvantages of Monotheism for a Universal State', in *Ottavo contributo alla storia degli studi classici in mondo antico* (Rome: Edizione di storia e letteratura), 313–28.

Moody, Peter J. (1997), 'The Legalism of Han Fei-Tzu and its Affinities with Modern Political Thought', *International Philological Quarterly*, 19: 318–29.

Morstein-Marx, Robert (2004), *Mass Oratory and Political Power in the Late Roman Republic* (Cambridge: Cambridge University Press).

Mulgan, R. G. (1977), *Aristotle's Political Theory: An Introduction for Students of Political Theory* (Oxford: Oxford University Press).

Murray, Oswyn (1990), 'Cities of Reason', in Murray, ed., 1–25.

—— ed. (1990), *The Greek City from Homer to Alexander* (Oxford: Oxford University Press).

Nederman, Cary and Shogimen, Takashi, eds. (2009), *Western Political Thought in Dialogue with Asia* (Lexington, Ky.: Lexington Books).

North, J. A. (1990), 'Democratic Politics in Republican Rome', *Past and Present*, 126: 7–26.

Ober, Josiah (1989), *Mass and Elite in Democratic Athens: Rhetoric, Ideology, and the Power of the People* (Princeton: Princeton University Press).

Olson, Mancur (1982), *The Rise and Decline of Nations* (New Haven: Yale University Press).

Ostwald, Martin (1986), *From Popular Sovereignty to the Sovereignty of Law: Law, Society and Politics in Fifth-century Athens* (Berkeley: University of California Press).

Oxford Companion to Classical Literature, ed. Paul Harvey (Oxford: Clarendon Press, 1937) = *OCCL*.

Oxford History of Ancient Egypt, ed. Ian Shaw (Oxford: Oxford University Press, 2000) = *OHAE*.

Oxford History of Greece and the Hellenistic world, ed. John Boardman, Jasper Griffin, and Oswyn Murray (Oxford: Oxford University Press, 1986).

Oxford History of the Roman World, ed. John Boardman et al. (Oxford: Oxford University Press, 1991) = *OHR*.

PARKER, GEOFFREY, A. (1984), 'Evolutionarily Stable Strategies', in Krebs and Davies, eds., 30–61.

PAUL, SHALOM M. (1970), *Studies in the Book of the Covenant in the Light of Cuneiform and Biblical Law* (Leiden: Brill).

PEERENBOOM, R. P. (1993), *Law and Morality in Ancient China: The Silk Manuscripts of Huang-Lao* (Albany, NY: SUNY Press).

PINES, YURI (2000a), 'Disputers of the *Li*: Breakthroughs in the Concept of Ritual in Preimperial China', *Asia Major*, 3rd ser., 13/1: 1–41.

—— (2000b), ' "The One That Pervades the All" in Ancient Chinese Political Thought: The Origins of the "Great Unity" Paradigm', *T'oung Po*, 86: 280–324.

—— (2002), *Foundations of Confucian Thought: Intellectual Life in the Chunqiu Period, 722–453 BCE* (Honolulu: University of Hawai'i Press).

—— (2009), *Envisioning Eternal Empire: Chinese Political Thought of the Warring States Period* (Honolulu: University of Hawai'i Press).

—— and SHELACH, GIDEON (2004), ' "Using the Past to Serve the Present": Comparative Perspectives on Chinese and Western Theories of the Origins of States', in Shaul Shaked et al. eds., *Genesis and Regeneration* (Jerusalem: Israeli Academy of Arts and Sciences), 127–63.

PINKER, STEVEN (1994), *The Language Instinct* (Harmondsworth: Penguin).

—— (1997), *How the Mind Works* (Harmondsworth: Penguin).

POCOCK, J. G. A. (1975), *The Machiavellian Moment* (Princeton: Princeton University Press).

POLLOCK, SUSAN (1999), *Ancient Mesopotamia* (Cambridge: Cambridge University Press).

POSENER, G. (1956), *Littérature et politique dans l'Égypte de la XIIe dynastie* (Paris: Champion).

—— (1960), *De la divinité du Pharaon, Cahiers de la Societe Asiatique*, 15 (Paris: Imprimerie Nationale).

POSTGATE, J. N. (1992), *Early Mesopotamia: Society and Economy at the Dawn of History* (London: Routledge and Kegan Paul).

RAPPAPORT, ROY A. (1999), *Ritual and Religion in the Making of Humanity* (Cambridge: Cambridge University Press).

READE, JULIAN, 'Imperial Ideologies in the Ancient Near East', unpublished paper, Royal Asiatic Society lecture (1996).

READE, JULIAN (2002), 'Sexism and Homoethism in Ancient Iraq', in S. Parpola and D. Whiting eds., *Sex and Gender in the Ancient Near East* (Helsinki: Neo-Assyrian Text Corpus Project), 551–67.

REDFORD, DONALD B. (1992), *Egypt, Canaan and Israel in Ancient Times* (Princeton: Princeton University Press).

ROBINET, ISABELLE (1997), *Taoism: The Growth of a Religion*, trans. P. Brooks (Stanford: University of Stanford Press).

ROETZ, HEINER (1993), *Confucian Ethics of the Axial Age: A Reconstruction Under the Aspect of the Breakthrough Towards Postconventional Thinking* (Albany, NY: SUNY Press).

ROOT, MARGARET COOL (1979), *King and Kingship in Achaemenid Art: Essays on the Creation of an Iconography of Empire* (Leiden: Brill).

ROUSSEL, DENIS (1976), *Tribu et cité* (Paris: Les Belles Lettres).

ROY, KUMKUM (1994), *The Emergence of Monarchy in North India Eighth–Fourth Centuries B.C. as Reflected in Brahmanical Tradition* (Delhi: Oxford University Press).

RUEPKE, JOERG (2004), 'Roman Religion', in *CCRR* 179–95.

SABINE, GEORGE H. and THORSEN, THOMAS L. (1973), *A History of Political Theory*, 4th edn. (Fort Worth, Tex.: Harcourt Brace).

SATO, MASAYUKI (2003), *The Confucian Quest for Order: The Origins and Foundations of the Political Thought of Xun Zi* (Leyden: Brill).

SCHARFE, HARTMUT (1989), *The State in Indian Tradition* (Leiden: Brill).

SCHMITT-PANTEL, PAULINE (1990), 'Collective Activities and the Political', in Murray, ed., 193–213.

SCHOFIELD, MALCOLM (1991), *The Stoic Idea of the City* (Cambridge: Cambridge University Press).

——(1995), 'Cicero's Definition of *Res Publica*', in G. J. F. Powell, ed., *Cicero's Philosophy* (Oxford: Oxford University Press), 63–83.

——(2006), *Plato: Political Philosophy* (Oxford: Oxford University Press).

SCHWARTZ, BENJAMIN I. (1985), *The World of Thought in Ancient China* (Cambridge, Mass.: Harvard University Press).

SCULLARD, H. H. (1980), *A History of the Roman World, 753–146 BC*, 2nd edn. (London: Methuen).

SCULLY, STEPHEN (1990), *Homer and the Sacred City* (Ithaca, NY: Cornell University Press).

SELLMANN, JAMES D. (1999), 'The Origin and Role of the State According to the *Lüshi Chunqiu*', *Asian Philosophy*, 9: 193–218.

SHAH, K. J. (2003), 'Of Arthas and Arthashastra', in Anthony Parel et al. eds., *Comparative Political Philosophy* (Lexington, Ky.: Lexington Books).

SHAHAR, MEIR and WELLER, ROBERT P. (1996),'Introduction: Gods and Society in China', in Shahar and Weller eds., *Unruly Gods: Divinity and Society in China* (Honolulu: University of Hawai'i Press).

SHARMA, J. P. (1968), *Republics in Ancient India c.1500 BC–500 BC* (Leiden: Brill).

SHAW, B. D. (1985), 'The Divine Economy: Stoicism as Ideology', *Latomus*, 44: 16–54.

SHERWIN-WHITE, A. N. (1973), *The Roman Citizenship*, 2nd edn. (Oxford: Clarendon Press).

SINCLAIR, R. K. (1988), *Democracy and Participation in Athens* (Cambridge: Cambridge University Press).

SKALNIK, PETER (1978), 'The Early State as a Process', in Claessen and Skalnik, eds., 601–18.

SMITH, BRIAN K. (1994), *Classifying the Universe: The Ancient Indian Varna System and the Origins of Caste* (New York: Oxford University Press).

SMITH, JOHN MAYNARD (1975), *The Theory of Evolution*, 3rd edn. (Harmondsworth: Penguin).

SPELLMAN, JOHN W. (1964), *Political Theory of Ancient India: A Study in Kingship from the Earliest Times to AD 300* (Oxford: Oxford University Press).

SPRINGBORG, PATRICIA (1987), 'The Contractual State: Orientalism and Despotism', *HPT* 8: 195–433.

STALLEY, R. F. (1983), *An Introduction to Plato's 'Laws'* (Oxford: Basil Blackwell).

TAMBIAH, S. (1976), *World Conqueror and World Renouncer* (Cambridge: Cambridge University Press).

TARN, W. W. (1933), 'Alexander the Great and the Unity of Mankind', *Proceedings of the British Academy*, 19: 123–66.

——and GRIFFITH, G. T. (1930), *Hellenistic Civilisation*, 2nd edn. (London: Edward Arnold).

THAPAR, ROMILA (1966), *A History of India*, vol. I (Harmondsworth: Penguin).

——(1975*a*), 'Ethics, Religion and Social Protest in the First Millenium BC in Northern India', *Daedalus*, 104: 119–32.

——(1975*b*) 'Ashokan India and the Gupta Age', in Basham, ed., 38–50.

——(1984), *From Lineage to State: Social Formations in the Mid-First Millenium BC in the Ganga Valley* (Bombay: Oxford University Press).

——(2002), *Early India from the Origins to AD 1300* (London: Allen Lane).

TRAPP, MICHAEL (2007), *Philosophy in the Roman Empire: Ethics, Politics and Society* (Aldershot: Ashgate).

TRIGGER, BRUCE G. (2003), *Understanding Early Civilizations: A Comparative Study* (Cambridge: Cambridge University Press).

TRIVERS, ROBERT (1971), 'The Evolution of Reciprocal Altruism', *Quarterly Review of Biology*, 46: 35–57.

——(1985), *Social Evolution* (Menlo Park, Calif.: Benjamin/Cummings).

UNGERN-STERNBERG, JÜRGEN (2004), 'The Crisis of the Republic', in *CCRR* 89–110.

VATIKIOTIS, P. J. (1987), *Islam and the State* (London: Croom Helm).

VERBA, SIDNEY (1961), *Small Groups and Political Behavior: A Study of Leadership* (Princeton: Princeton University Press).

VERMES, GEZA (1973), *Jesus the Jew: A Historian's Reading of the Gospels* (London: Collins).

VERNANT, JEAN-PIERRE (1982), *The Origins of Greek Thought* (London: Methuen).

VERNUS, PASCAL (1995), 'La Grande Mutation idéologique du Nouvel Empire', *Bulletin de la Société d'Égyptologie de Genève*, 19: 69–95.

VEYNANSE, PAUL (1990), *Bread and Circuses: Historical Sociology and Political Pluralism*, trans.. B. Pearce (London: Allen Lane).

VLASTOS, GREGORY (1947), 'Equality and Justice in Early Greek Cosmologies', *Classical Philology*, 42: 156–78.

VOEGELIN, ERIC (1957), *Order and History*, vol I: *Israel and Revelation* (Baton Rouge: Louisiana State University Press).

WALEY, ARTHUR (n.d.), *Three Ways of Thought in Ancient China* (Garden City, NY: Doubleday).

WANG, AIHE (2000), *Cosmology and Political Culture in Ancient China* (Cambridge: Cambridge University Press).

WANG, HSIAO-PO and CHANG, LEO S. (1986), *The Philosophical Foundations of Han Fei's Political Theory* (Honolulu: University of Hawai'i Press).

WEBER, MAX (1968), *Wirtschaft und Gesellschaft*, 5th edn. (Tübingen: J. C. B. Mohr, 1921/1971); English trans., *Economy and Society*, ed. Guenther Roth and Claus Wittich, 2 vols. (Berkeley: University of California Press, 1968).

WEINFELD, MOSHE (1990), 'The Common Heritage of the Covenantal Tradition in the Ancient World', in L. Canfora et al. (eds.), *I Trattati nel mondo antico* (Rome: Bretschneider).

WEST, M. L. (2007), *Indo-European Poetry and Myth* (Oxford: Oxford University Press).

WESTENHOLZ, AAGE (1979), 'The Old Akkadian Empire in Contemporary Opinion', in Larsen, ed., 107–24.

——(1993), 'The World View of Sargonic Officials', in Liverani, ed., 157–69.

WHITELAM, KEITH W. (1979), *The Just King: Monarchical Judicial Authority in Ancient Israel* (Sheffield: JSOT Press).

WIESEHOEFER, JOSEF (2001), *Ancient Persia* (London: Tauris).

WILSON, EDWARD O. (1975), *Sociobiology* (Cambridge, Mass.: Harvard University Press).

WIRSZUBSKI, C. (1950), *Libertas as a Political Idea at Rome During the Late Republic and Early Principate* (Cambridge: Cambridge University Press).

WONG, KATE (2006), 'The Morning of the Modern Mind', *Scientific American*, 16/2: 74–83.

YANG, C. K. (1957), 'The Functional Relationship Between Confucian Thought and Chinese Religion', in John K. Fairbank ed., *Chinese Thought and Institutions* (Chicago: Chicago University Press), 279–90.

YATES, ROBIN (2001), 'Cosmos, Central Authority, and Communities in the Early Chinese Empire', in Susan E. Alcock ed., *Empire: Perspectives from Archaeology and History* (Cambridge: Cambridge University Press), 351–68.

ZAEHNER, R. C. (1962), *Hinduism* (Oxford: Oxford University Press).

ZHENGYUAN FU (1996), *China's Legalists: The Earliest Totalitarians and their Art of Ruling* (Armonk, NY: M. E. Sharpe).

Index

Achaemenids 47–9
Aelius Aristides 196, 206, 213 n.13
Aeschylus 107, 131, 143–4
Africa 10–11, 14–15, 17–18, 21 n.28, 170
agriculture 18, 82, 87, 111, 115, 120,
    197, 205
Akbar 31 n.12
Akkad 34
Alexander 158, 204–5, 213 n.11
Amarna 25
America *see* U.S.A.
anthropology 6
Antony, Mark 186, 188
archaeology 6
aristocracy 94, 185
Aristophanes 137
Aristotle 133–4, 136, 156, *158–68*, 179,
    194, 203–4, 234, 238
    Politics 67, 159, 161–7
arthashastra 70–1, 80, 84
Ashoka 75, 87–8
assemblies 36, 42–4, 59, 67 n.31, 87, 130,
    133, 137, 177; *see also* Roman
Assmann, Jan 31 n.22
Assyria 34, 37, 39
Athens 133–4, 137–45, 147–8, 159, 194,
    206, 233
Augustine, St. 18, 86, 109, 220
Augustus 184–5, 191, 195–6, 213 n.13

Babylon 34, 41–2, 44, 47, 63
    New Babylonia 35, 44
Bagehot, Walter 154
balance of power 139
benevolence (beneficence) 18, 24, 26–7,
    47, 65, 77, 126 n.21, 195–6, 210,
    229–30
Bentham, Jeremy 114, 161

Bhagavad Gita 80, 235
bin Laden 21 n.22
brahmins 69, 72, 77–8. 89 n.37
Buddha 85–6, 152
Buddhism 69, 84–8, 96, 124
bureaucracy 93, 119, 123
Burke 179

Caesar, Julius 185, 189
Calvinism 62
Carthage 182–3
caste 72–3, 77–8, 86
Celsus 192
China 2, chapter 7 *passim*, 156, 170,
    197–9, 228–9, 233–4, 237
Christianity 2, 193, 195, 197–9, 227, 235
    early 192, chapter 11 *passim*
Christians 63, 193–4, 210
Chrysippus 294
Cicero 156, 175–7, 179–84, *186–91*,
    207–9
    On Duties 190, 208–9. 235
cities 44–5
city-states 15, 33, 36, 182 ; *see also* polis
civil society 15, 192
class 13, 28, 123, 139, 150–1, 219,
    233; *see also* caste, rich and poor,
    status
Cleanthes 210
Clement of Rome 224
coercion 110–12, 122
commerce 15, 205, 213 n.15, 237
communism 153, 219
Communism, Chinese 115
comparison 1, 5 n.10, chapter 12
    passim, 237 ; *see also* Europe
Confucianism 122–5, 198–9; *see also*
    Han Confucianism

Confucians 99–102, 196–7
Confucius 2, 92, 94–5, 99–104, 125, 133,
    140, 153, 169, 180, 231, 239
conquest 14–15, 23–4, 53, 62, 84, 111,
    182–3
consensus 179 ; *see also* persuasion
Constant, Benjamin 141
constitution 58, 137, 154–5, 162, 173
    n.79, 191; *see also* mixed, Roman
corporations 56, 192
correlative cosmology 122–3
cosmopolitanism 189, chapter 10
    passim, 217, 232, 237
covenant 53–7, 61–2, 64
Crates 204
Cyprian, St. 201–2 n.63
Cyrus 48, 52

Dao *see* Way
Daodejing 111, 115 ; *see also* Laozi
Daoism 96, 118, 122, 124
Darius I 47, 49 n.6
David, King 54
democracy 2, 11, 43, 56, 58, 60, 64, 99,
    104, 134, 141, 178–9, 185–7, 189,
    228, 237 ; *see also dēmokratia*
Democritus 142, 146, 170 n.8
dēmokratia 14, 131–3, 138, *140–5*, 154,
    162, 165–7, 239
dharma 69, 79–80, 84
dialectic 147
dialogue 2, 133, 144, 177 n.13, 220
Diodorus Siculus 205
Diogenes 204
Dumont, Louis 5 n.10
duty *see* public service

economy 70, 80–3, 106, 113, 127 n.50,
    168, 229 ; *see also* agriculture
Egypt 13, 15, 19, chapter 2 *passim*, 40,
    45, 60, 62, 65, 78, 182, 228
elders 42–4, 55, 59, 67 n.32
    and the people 57–8, 233
Empedocles 134, 136

empire 182 ; *see also* Roman
Ennius 206–7
Epictetus 189, 192, 197, 205, 209
equality 28, 51, 54, 134, 139
    under the law 64, 134, 138, 140, 168,
        187 ; *see also* justice, procedural; law,
        rule of
ethics 148, 159–60, 221
    and expediency 71, 79–80, 82, 115,
        190, *234–5* ; *see also Realpolitik*
    see also morality
Europe comparisons with 88 n.3, 89
    n.38, 99, 117, 121, 127 n.60, 172
    n.51, 211
    continuity with 142, 162, 201 n.50
    influences on 156, 167, 187–8, 193,
        200 n.7, 237–8; *see also* West
Euripides 133, 142, 146
evolution 37, 136
expediency *see* ethics

family 18, 108, 110–11, 131, 153, 208–9;
    see also kinship
al-Farabi 156–7
federalism 105, 141, 206
First Emperor 115, 120–1
foreign policy 83–4, 183
Franklin, Benjamin 158
freedom 2, 42, 138, 141–3, 155, 168, 178,
    187–8, 191–2, 231, 237
French Revolution 59

Geertz, Clifford 4 n.6
gentleman *see* junzi
Gibbon 199
Gilgamesh epic 42
globalization 2, 205
glory 176, 183
Gracchus, Tiberius 184
Greece 1, 13, 37, 206, 230, 237
Greeks 19, 94, chapter 8 *passim*, 203–4,
    232–4, 238
    influence 175, 179–80
group size 8, 11, 20 n.7

Guanzi, the 99, 111, 233
guilds 42

Hammurabi 34, 37, 41–2
Han dynasty 92, 98, 122
Han Confucianism 122, 198
Han Feizi 111, 114, 118–20
Heaven 95–9, 107
  and Earth 117–18, 123
  Mandate of 93, 95–8, 123–4, 228, 231
  Son of 93, 98–9, 106, 116, 119
  see also All-under-Heaven
Hebrew scriptures 50–1, 53, 56, 60–1
Hegel 103, 157
Heraclitus 2, 133–4, 136, 171 n.14
hereditary succession 99
Herodotus 142
Hesiod 130–1, 135, 137
hierarchy 12–14, 34, 73, 100
Hittites 55
Hobbes, Thomas 18–19, 76–7, 81–2,
  109, 212
Homer 17, 130, 135–7
Horace 175
human (as category) 203–4, 212
  nature 7–8, 149, 212, 229; *see also*
    natural law
humaneness (ren) 99–100, 102–4,
  106–7, 127 n.38
humanity 232
humans 6–10, 20 n.8, 145–6,203–4,
  208–11

Ibn Khaldun 21 n.27, 35, 167
ideology 4, 29–30, 34, 51, 73, 185,
  199, 237
India 2, 13, chapter 6 *passim*, 233
individuals 29, 31 n.18, 56, 131, 218, 237
individualism 64
Indo-European 69, 72, 88 n.11
Indo-Iranian 49 n.9
intolerance 57, 193, 199
Iran chapter 4 *passim*, 84, 232
Irano-Islamic 233

Isaiah 62
Islam 2, 56, 84, 156–8, 182, 199, 220–1
  Shi-ite 63, 235
Isocrates 165–6, 194
Israel chapter 5 *passim*, 232–3
Italy 195, 206

Jacobsen 42–3
Jeremiah 58, 68 n.41, 231
Jerusalem 52, 58–9, 213 n.19
Jesus 27, 65, 74, *215–20*
Jewish law 51, 54, 56, 61, 63
Jews 48, 192, 215, 233 ; *see also* Hebrew
  scriptures, promised land
Joshua 56
Judaism 2, 215, 223, 235
Julian, emperor 198, 213
junzi (gentleman, noble person) 95, 104
jurists 192–3, 211
justice 9, 18, 24, 26–7, 36, 78, 149–51,
  166, 192–3, *229*
  procedural 27–8, 40–1, 104, 135, 142,
    230–1; *see also* equality; law, rule of;
    natural law
  see also war, just

Kant 148, 190, 211, 235
karma 74, 86, 235
Kautilya 70–1, 74–5, 79–84, 228, 231, 234
king as saviour 24, 62
  as shepherd 23, 40
  as warrior 24, 35
  religious functions 23, 39, 93
kingship 17–19, 35–6, 38–9, 49, 60–2,
  69, 71, 74–5, 77–8, 137, *227–8*, 238
  origin of 76–7, 89 n.26, 230; *see also*
    monarchy
kinship 7–8, 18, 20 n.8, 107, 113, 132 ;
  see also family

Lactantius 214 n.34
language 7, 10
Laozi 102, 111, 116–18 ; *see also*
  Daodejing

law 9, 41, 112, 117–18, 134, 141–2, 154–5
  rule of 139–40, 141–2, 193 ; *see also*
    equality; justice
  sovereignty of 166, 188, 230
  see also Jewish law; Manu; natural law
Legalists, Chinese 92, 101, 110–12,
    114–15, 117, 121–2, 125, 198,
    234, 238
liberty, *see* freedom
li (rites) 100, 103–5
Livy 187, 206
Locke, John 76, 144, 172 n.53, 188, 212
logos (reason) 133, 148, 197, 205
Lucretius 176, 181
Lüshi Chunqiu 96 116, 119, 121, 123
Luther, Martin 221

Macedon 158
  Philip of 136
Machiavelli 80, 82, 114–15, 119, 131,
    190, 235
Mahabharata 71, 76, 231 ; *see also*
    Bhagavad Gita
Mandate, *see* Heaven
Manu, laws of 69, 75, 77
Mao 115
Marcus Aurelius 191–2, 196, 198, 210
Marius 176, 181, 184, 187, 208
Marsilius 157
Marx 153, 169
Marxism 104, 219, 238
Mengzi 92, 94, 97, 101–6, 116, 153, 235
mercy 193 ; *see also* benevolence
merit as criterion for appointment 28,
    100–2, 107, 113, 180, 195, 231, 233
Mesopotamia 15, chapter 3 *passim*, 60,
    65, 78
Messiah 63, 68 n.42, 235
Mexico 15, 19
might and right *see* ethics and expediency
Mill, J. S. 158, 169, 192
mixed constitution 155, 166, 178–9, 238
Monarchy 50, 52, 58, 60, 115–18, 164–5,
    191, 193–5

absolute 22, 30, 35, 117, 125 n.8, 185
British 119
sacred 15–19, 22–5, 30, 47–9, 74, 181,
    195, *227–8* ; *see also* religion and
    state
see also kingship
monotheism 14, 51, 57, 66 n.6
morality 9, 136, 229 ; *see also* ethics
Moses 53–4
Mozi 92, 94, 99, 101, *107–9*, 116, 146
multiculturalism 2, 48, 195

nation 55–7, 232–3
nationalism 14, 24, 56–7, 122, 233, 237
natural law *136*, 211, 232
nature *see* human; science

Oakeshott, Michael 103, 146, 179
oligarchy 132, 153, 162, 165–6
Origen 226 n.15
'other', the 14, 57, 104

participation 45, 58, 100, 141–2, 178, 197
patriotism 131, 148, 176, 191, 206,
    209–10, 237–8
Paul, St. 144, 211, 217, 219–20
people, the 48, 53, 55–6, 59–60, 67 n.32,
    96–8, 100, 130, 188–9, *231–2* ; *see
    also* assembly, elders, Roman
Pericles 142–3
Persia *see* Iran
persuasion 105–6, 114, 144–5
philosophy 94, 132–3, 180 ; *see also*
    political
Pindar 148
Pines, Yuri 124
Plato 133, 145, *147–58*, 169–70, 189,
    194, 208, 238–9
  Laws 152–5, 157–8
  Republic 21 n.23, 148–56, 193, 204
Platonism 220
Pliny, the Younger 193, 195, 205
Plutarch 204–5, 209, 213 n.11
polis 19, *103–5*, 142, 159–62, 170 n.1

political philosophy 1–2, 94, 132–4, 156, 170, 196–7, 234
    science 2, 70, 81, 136, 159, 162–4, 167–8, 174 n.83, 234
    skill 136, 145–6
    thought *4*, 6, 22, 29–80; *see also* ideology
Polybius 141, 156, 177–80, 213 n.12, 238
Pompey 185–6
poor, *see* rich
pragmatism 79–80
priests 22, 31 n.11, 33, 39, 45, 61, 75, 96
Principate, *see* Roman
promised land 53, 64
property 13, 65
Protagoras 145–6, 212 n.2
public service 95, 102, 176, 196–7

Qin 92, 111, 120–1

race 23, 53–4, 56, 72, 203, 218
racism 24
Rawls, John 154, 237
Realpolitik 110–15 ; *see also* ethics and expediency
reason *see* logos
rebellion 23, 44, 99
reciprocity 8–9, 108
religion 10, 16, 22, 33, 35, 98, 135
    and the state 130, 181, 195; *see also* monarchy, sacred
    see also priests
representation 141, 155
republic 74, 175, 191; *see also* Roman
rich and poor 13, 40, 65, 138–9, 142
Roman Assemblies 177–8, 184
    constitution 177–8
    empire 124, 192, 182–3, 197–8, 205, 209, 223
    influence 224
    law 157, 192–3
    people 177–8, 187–8
    Principate 175, *191–6*
    Republic *175–89*, 191

Senate 177, 182, 191
    see also jurists
Romans 19, 232
Rome chapter 9 *passim*, 238
Rousseau 158, 189, 212
Ruskin 153
Russia 227

Sallust 187, 208, 219 n.4
sangha 85–6
Sargon 34–5
Sasanian 49, 84
science, natural 133–4, 136, 141, 159
Seneca 194, 207, 210–11
Shang dynasty 92–3
Shang Yang 92, *110–15*, 117–18, 121, 239
Shen Bu-Hai 119–20, 126 n.32
shi 93–4, 99
Skinner, Q. 2
slavery 54, 168, 188–9. 193, 204
Smith, Adam 142
social biology 7, 9
    contract 148, 173 n.53
sociology 1, 150, 166–7
Socrates 133, *147–8*, 204
Solon *138–40*, 145, 169, 233
Son of Heaven *see* Heaven
sophists 143
Sophocles 133, 136
Sparta 138, 153, 180, 206
state, the 12, 15, 18–19, 21 n.35, 31 n.2, 36, 187
    views of 22, 35–6, 38, 75, 93, 144, 175–6, 189, 224–5, *228*
    church and 224–5
    theories of the origin of 19, 22–3, 31, 108–10, 113, 145–6, 150, 162, 189 ; *see also* kingship, origin of
    views of the purposes of 18, 23, 38–40, 81–4, 97, 111, 113–14, 160–1
    see also polis, religion
status 12–13, 73, 100, 104, 108, 113, 218; *see also* caste, class, hierarchy, rich and poor

Strauss, Leo 181
Stoicism 175, 189, 192–3, 195–7,
    207, 214
Sulla 184, 186
Sumer 33, 35, 37

Tacitus 192, 206, 210
Thales 134, 141
de Tocqueville 237
toleration 37, 48, 88, 198–9,
    202 n.71, 232
totalitarianism 115
Trajan 193, 205
tribes 7, 10, 12, 17–18, 50–1,
    56, 74, 230
trust 182, 187

U.S.A. 74, 158, 181, 189
unanimity 223
universalism 195, 203–4
Upanishads 69
Utilitarianism 25, 218
utility 112, 161, 196

Vergil 205
virtue 131, 151, 162, 180, 196, 204

war 23–4, 143, 183–4 ; just 114, 183–4
Way, the (Dao/ Tao) 98, 118–19
Weber, Max 3, 119, 167
West, influence on 169, 192, 217; *see also*
    Europe
women 56, 204, 212 n.4, 217–18, 232,
    236 n.6
world dominion 23–4, 37, 46 n.7, 48, 62,
    65–6, 84, 89, *229*; *see also* All-under-
    Heaven, empire

Xenophon 164–5, 194
Xunzi 92, 98, 101, 105, 109–11, 118–19,
    123

Zeno 204, 209, 213 n.11
Zhuangzi 117
Zhou dynasty 92–3, 96–7
    tradition 96, 101, 116, 122
Zoroaster 47–8